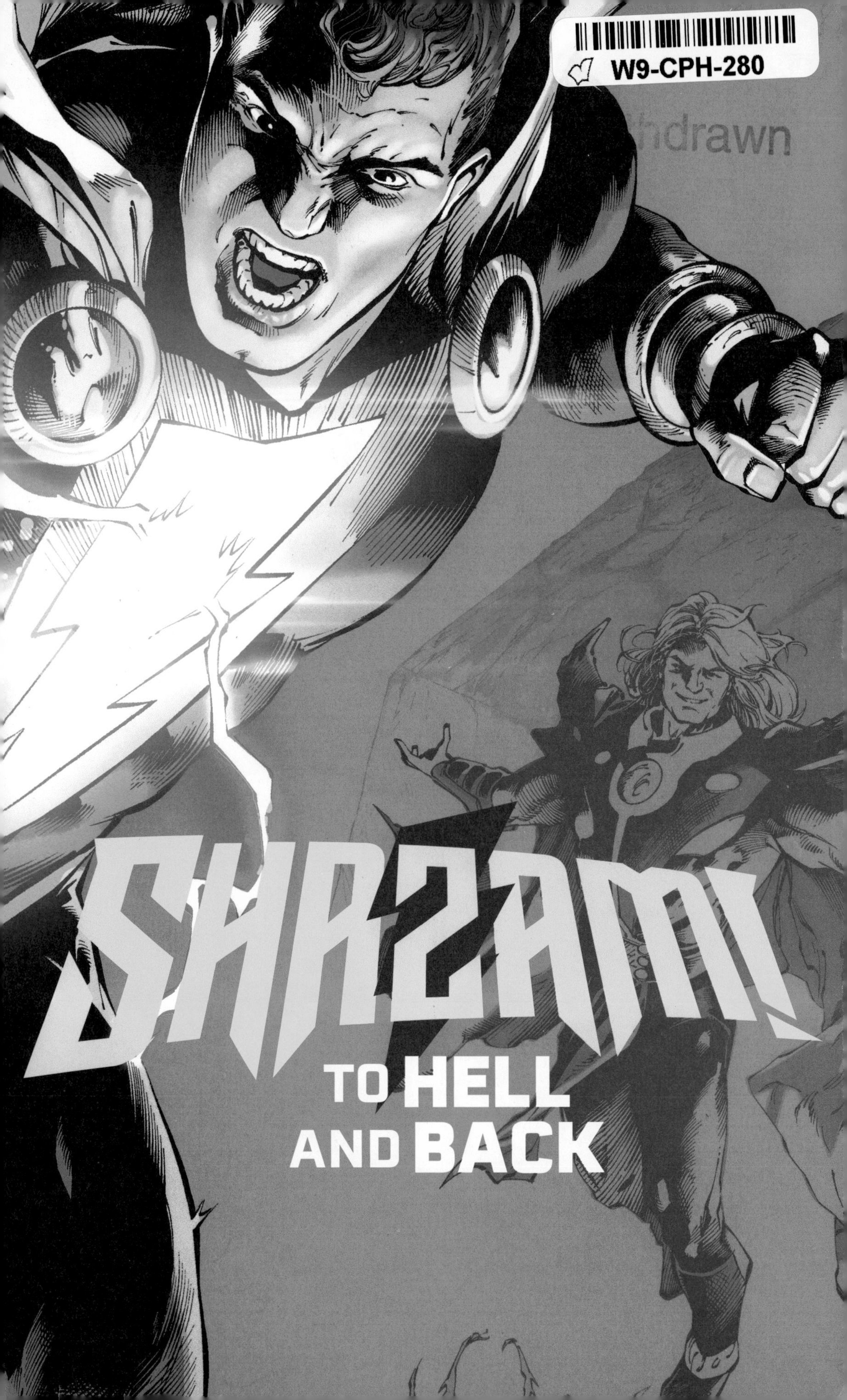
SHAZAM!
TO HELL
AND BACK

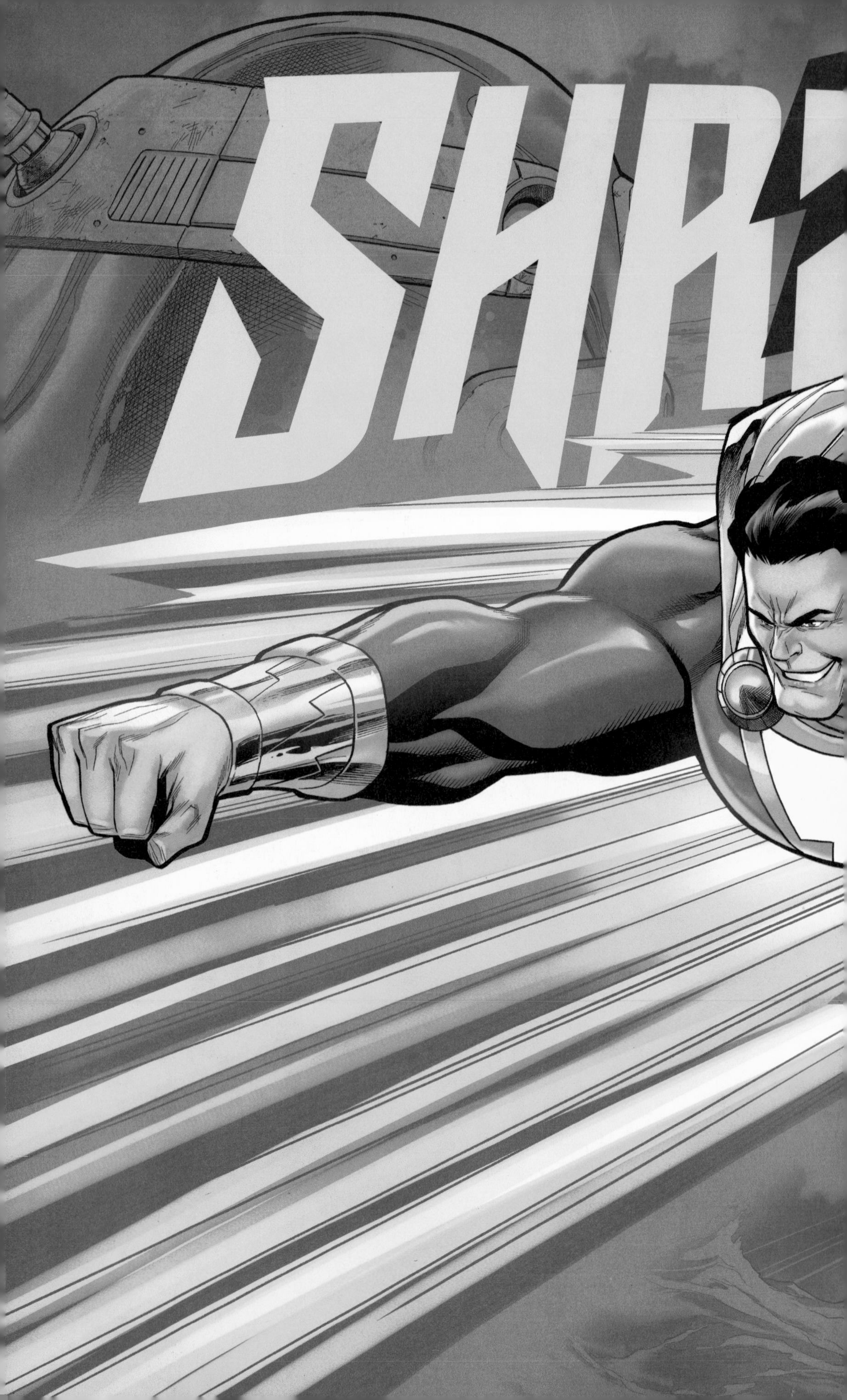
SHA

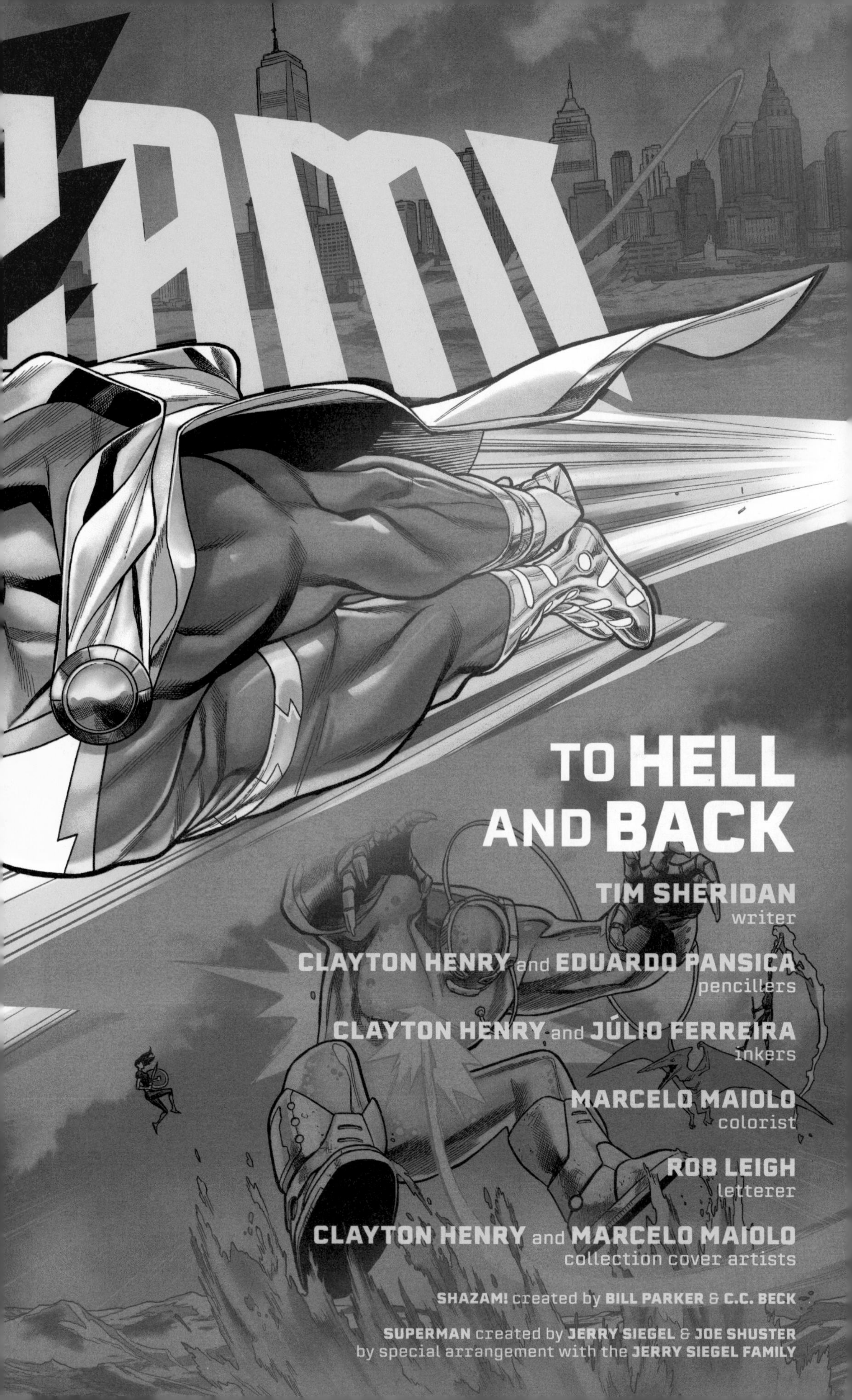

TO HELL AND BACK

TIM SHERIDAN
writer

CLAYTON HENRY and **EDUARDO PANSICA**
pencillers

CLAYTON HENRY and **JÚLIO FERREIRA**
inkers

MARCELO MAIOLO
colorist

ROB LEIGH
letterer

CLAYTON HENRY and **MARCELO MAIOLO**
collection cover artists

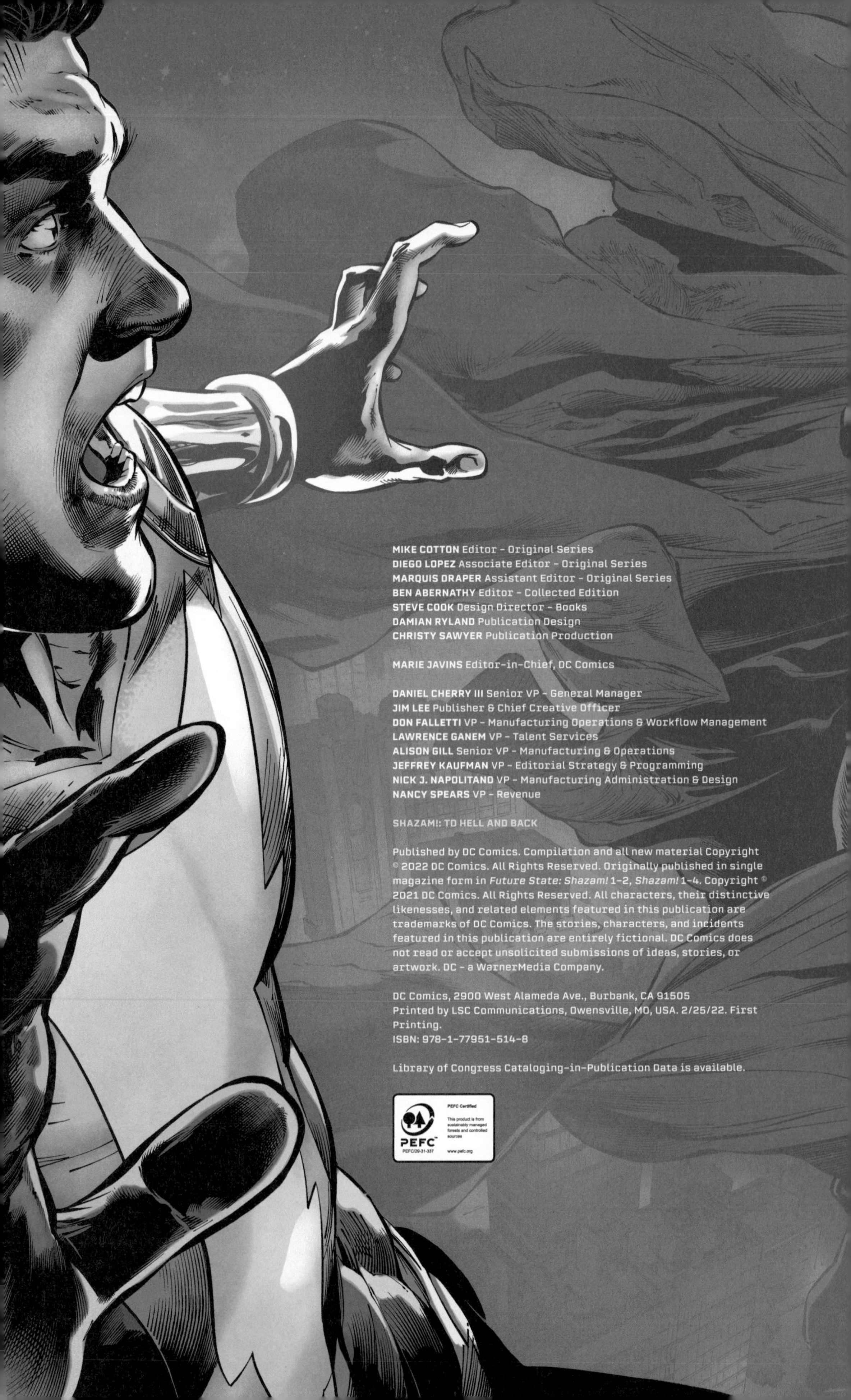

MIKE COTTON Editor – Original Series
DIEGO LOPEZ Associate Editor – Original Series
MARQUIS DRAPER Assistant Editor – Original Series
BEN ABERNATHY Editor – Collected Edition
STEVE COOK Design Director – Books
DAMIAN RYLAND Publication Design
CHRISTY SAWYER Publication Production

MARIE JAVINS Editor-in-Chief, DC Comics

DANIEL CHERRY III Senior VP – General Manager
JIM LEE Publisher & Chief Creative Officer
DON FALLETTI VP – Manufacturing Operations & Workflow Management
LAWRENCE GANEM VP – Talent Services
ALISON GILL Senior VP – Manufacturing & Operations
JEFFREY KAUFMAN VP – Editorial Strategy & Programming
NICK J. NAPOLITANO VP – Manufacturing Administration & Design
NANCY SPEARS VP – Revenue

SHAZAM!: TO HELL AND BACK

DC Comics, 2900 West Alameda Ave., Burbank, CA 91505
Printed by LSC Communications, Owensville, MO, USA. 2/25/22. First Printing.
ISBN: 978-1-77951-514-8

Library of Congress Cataloging-in-Publication Data is available.

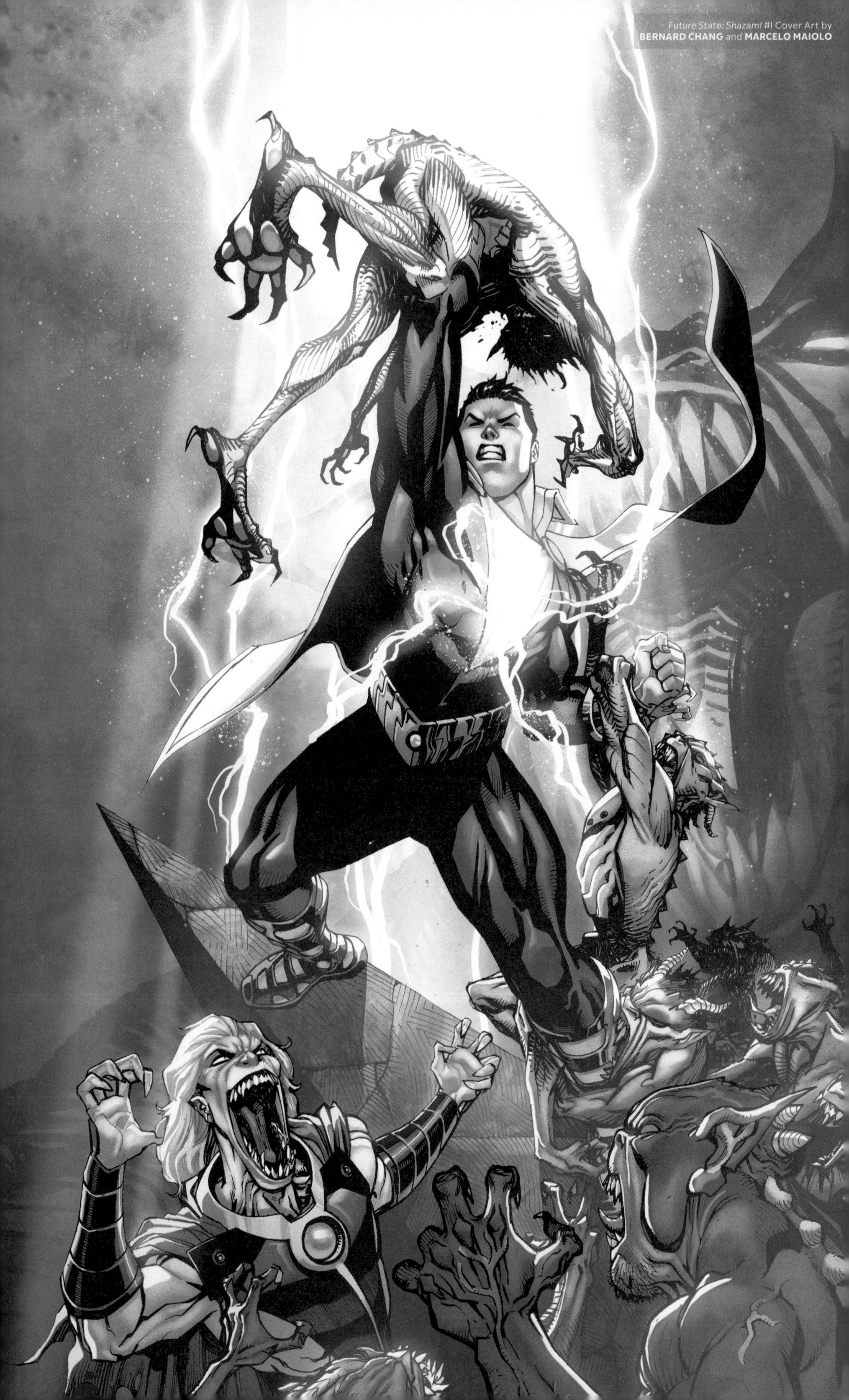

Future State: Shazam! #1 Cover Art by
BERNARD CHANG and **MARCELO MAIOLO**

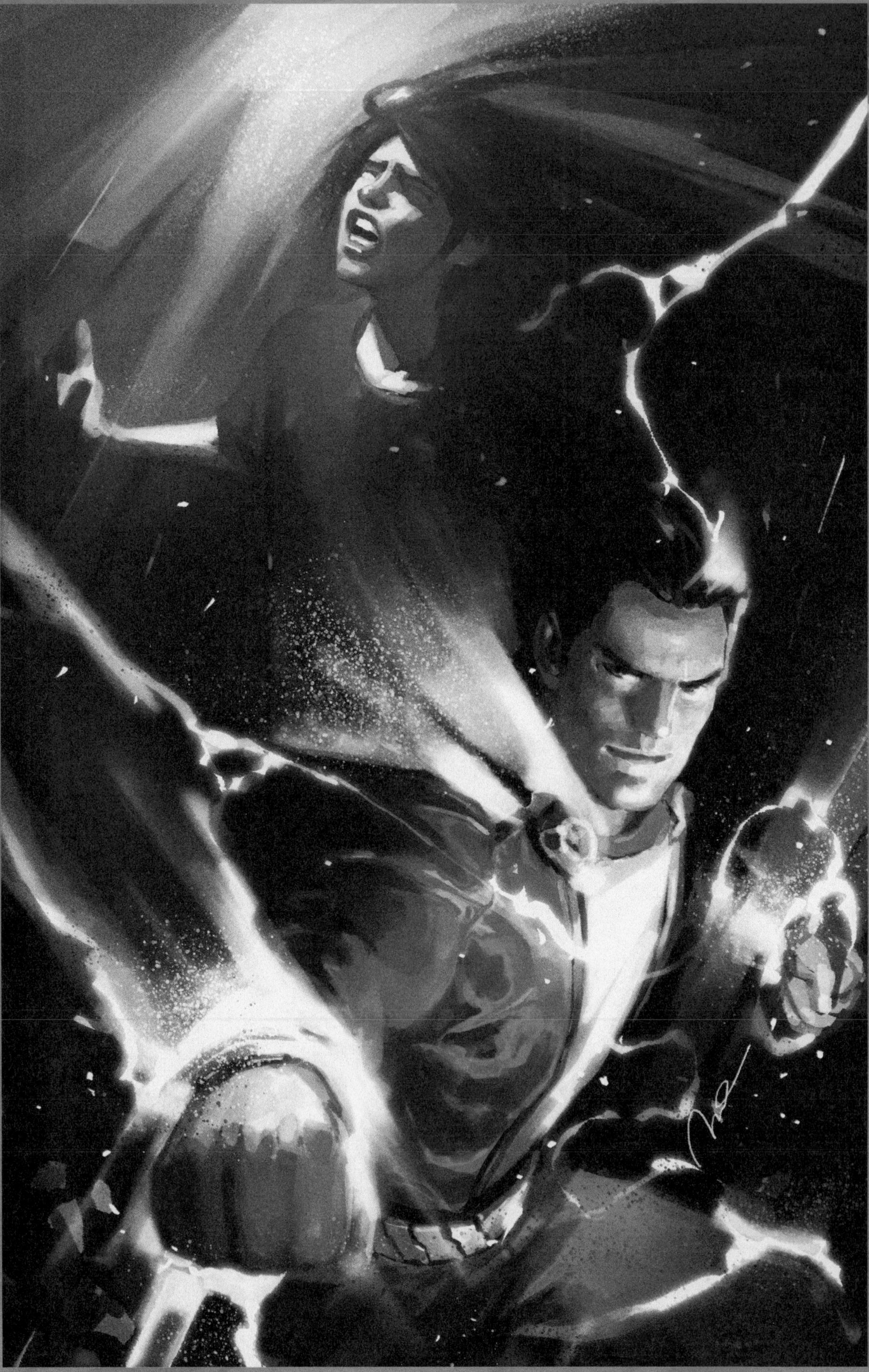

Future State: Shazam! #1 Variant Cover Art by **GERALD PAREL**

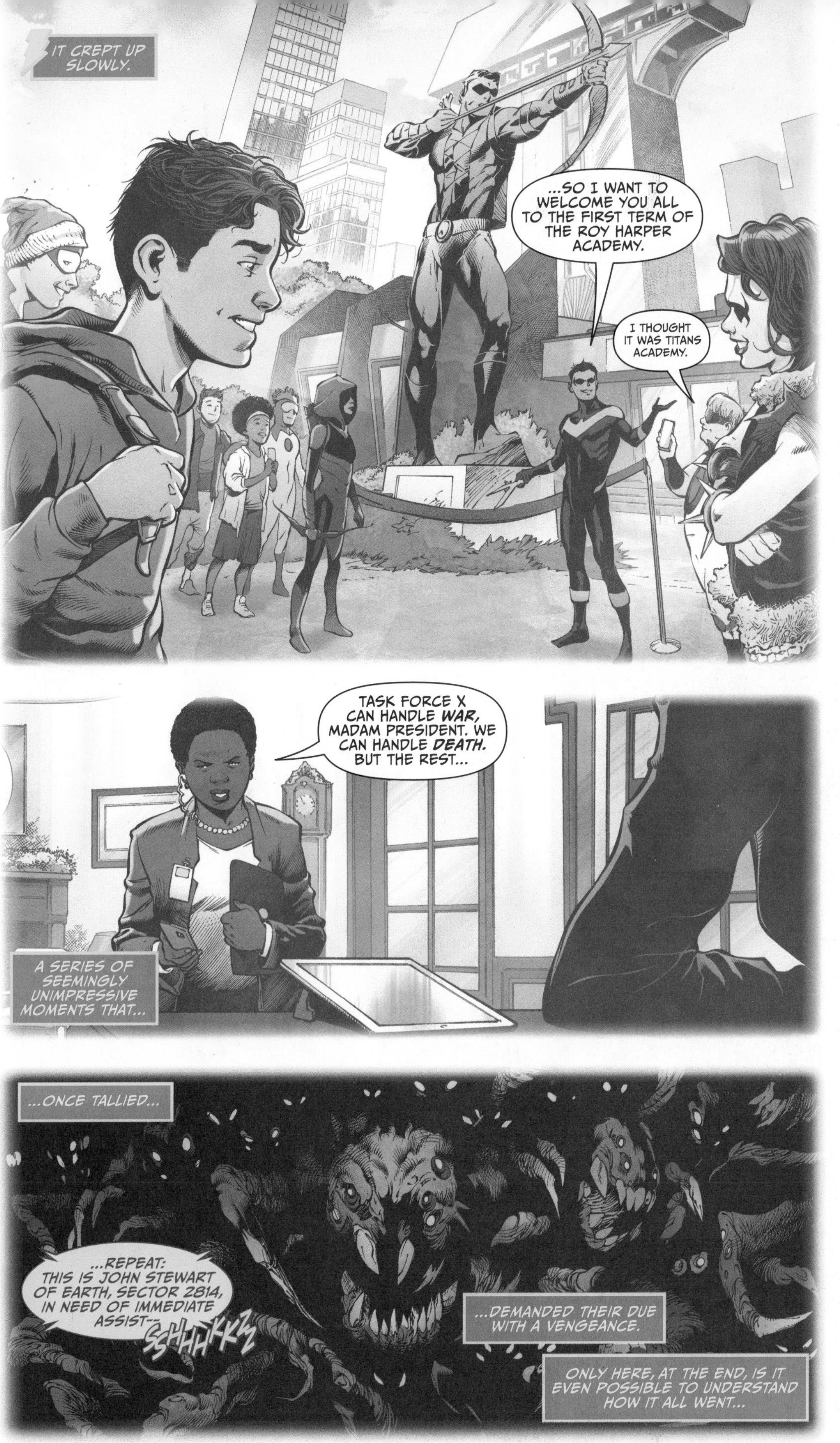
IT CREPT UP SLOWLY.
...SO I WANT TO WELCOME YOU ALL TO THE FIRST TERM OF THE ROY HARPER ACADEMY.
I THOUGHT IT WAS TITANS ACADEMY.
TASK FORCE X CAN HANDLE WAR, MADAM PRESIDENT. WE CAN HANDLE DEATH. BUT THE REST...
A SERIES OF SEEMINGLY UNIMPRESSIVE MOMENTS THAT...
...ONCE TALLIED...
...REPEAT: THIS IS JOHN STEWART OF EARTH, SECTOR 2814, IN NEED OF IMMEDIATE ASSIST--
SSHHHKKZZ
...DEMANDED THEIR DUE WITH A VENGEANCE.
ONLY HERE, AT THE END, IS IT EVEN POSSIBLE TO UNDERSTAND HOW IT ALL WENT...

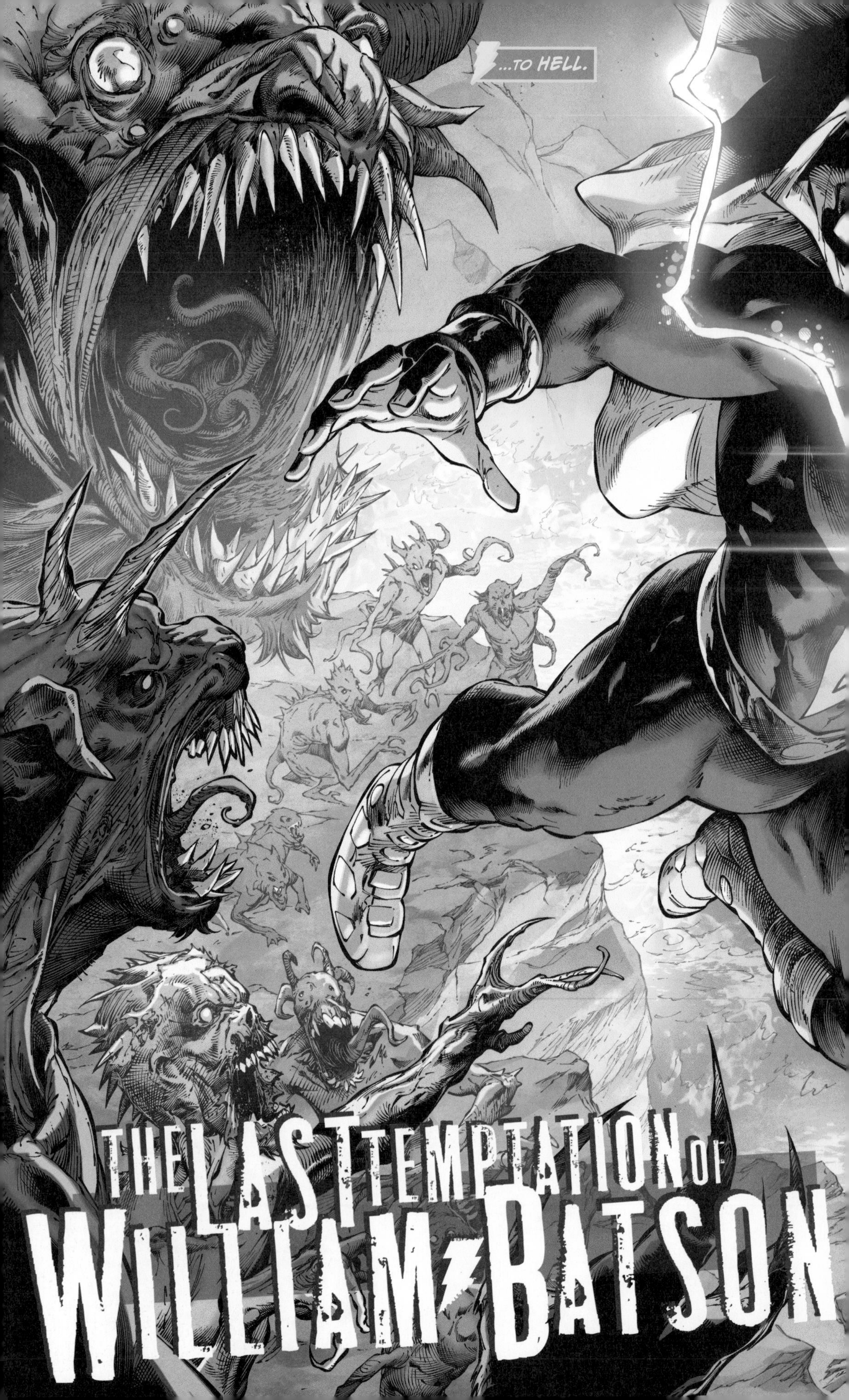
...TO HELL.
THE LAST TEMPTATION OF
WILLIAM BATSON

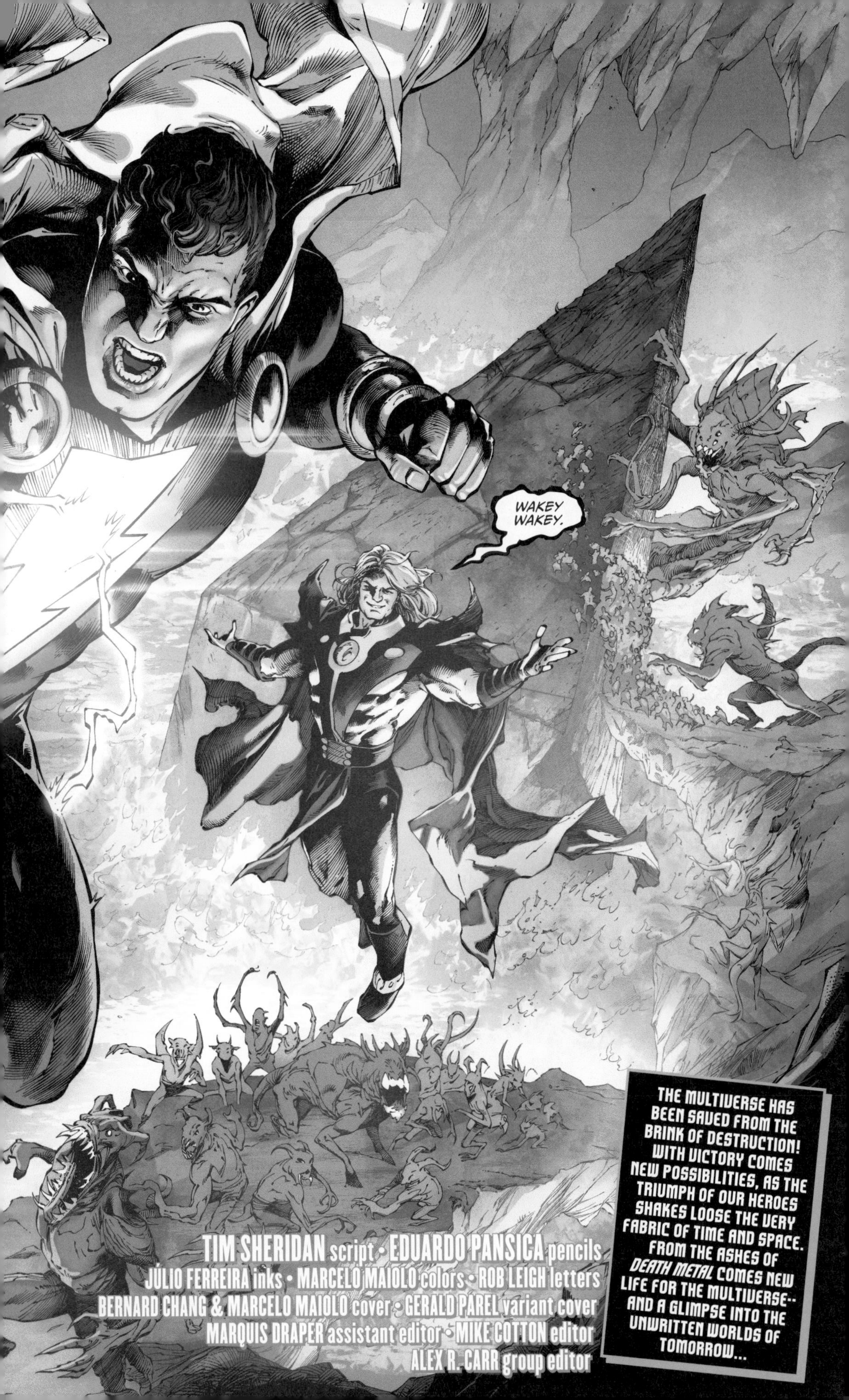
WAKEY WAKEY.
THE MULTIVERSE HAS BEEN SAVED FROM THE BRINK OF DESTRUCTION! WITH VICTORY COMES NEW POSSIBILITIES, AS THE TRIUMPH OF OUR HEROES SHAKES LOOSE THE VERY FABRIC OF TIME AND SPACE. FROM THE ASHES OF DEATH METAL COMES NEW LIFE FOR THE MULTIVERSE-- AND A GLIMPSE INTO THE UNWRITTEN WORLDS OF TOMORROW...
TIM SHERIDAN script • EDUARDO PANSICA pencils
JÚLIO FERREIRA inks • MARCELO MAIOLO colors • ROB LEIGH letters
BERNARD CHANG & MARCELO MAIOLO cover • GERALD PAREL variant cover
MARQUIS DRAPER assistant editor • MIKE COTTON editor
ALEX R. CARR group editor

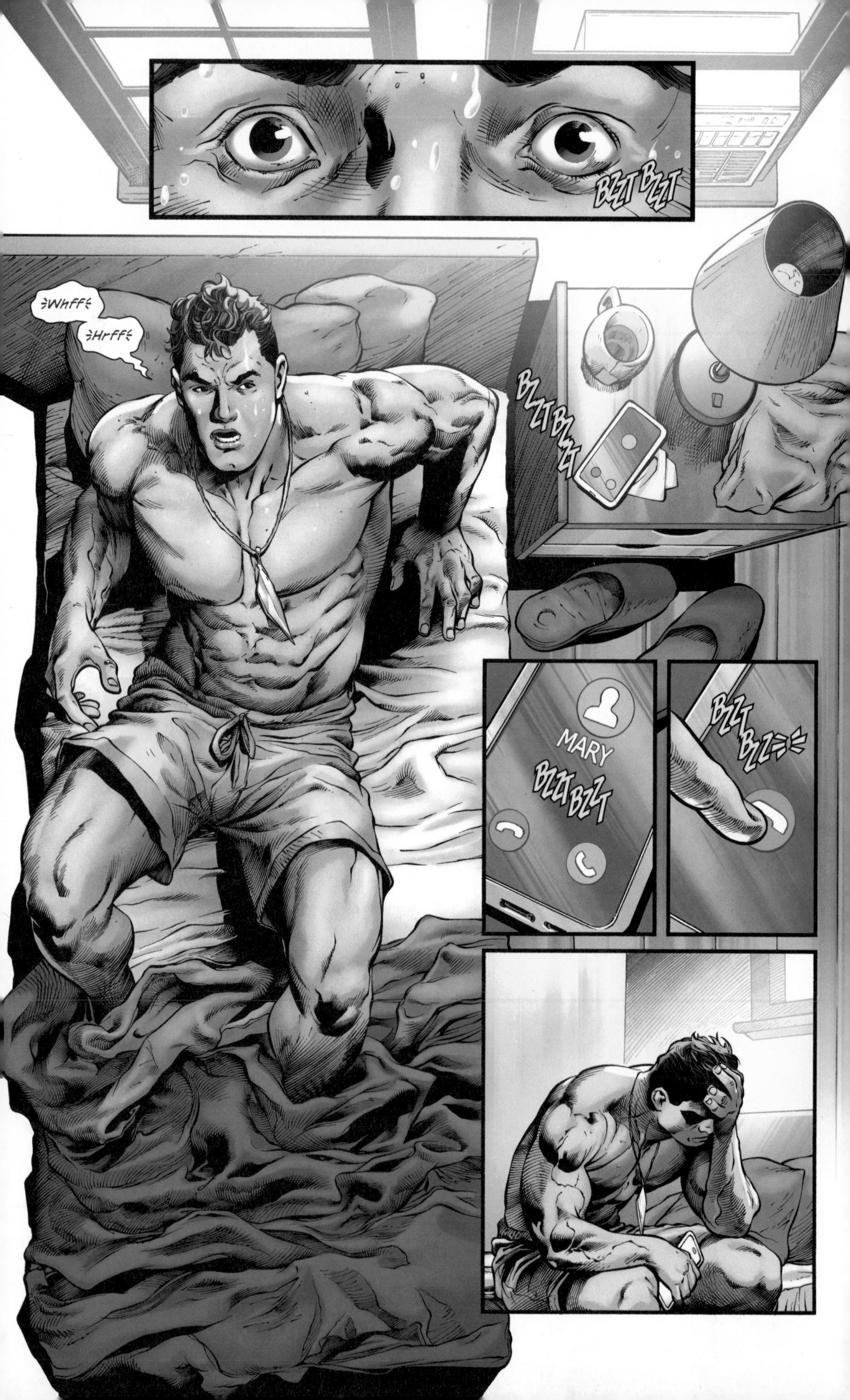
BZZT BZZT
≶Whff≶
≶Hrff≶
BZZT BZZT
MARY
BZZT BZZT
BZZT BZZ

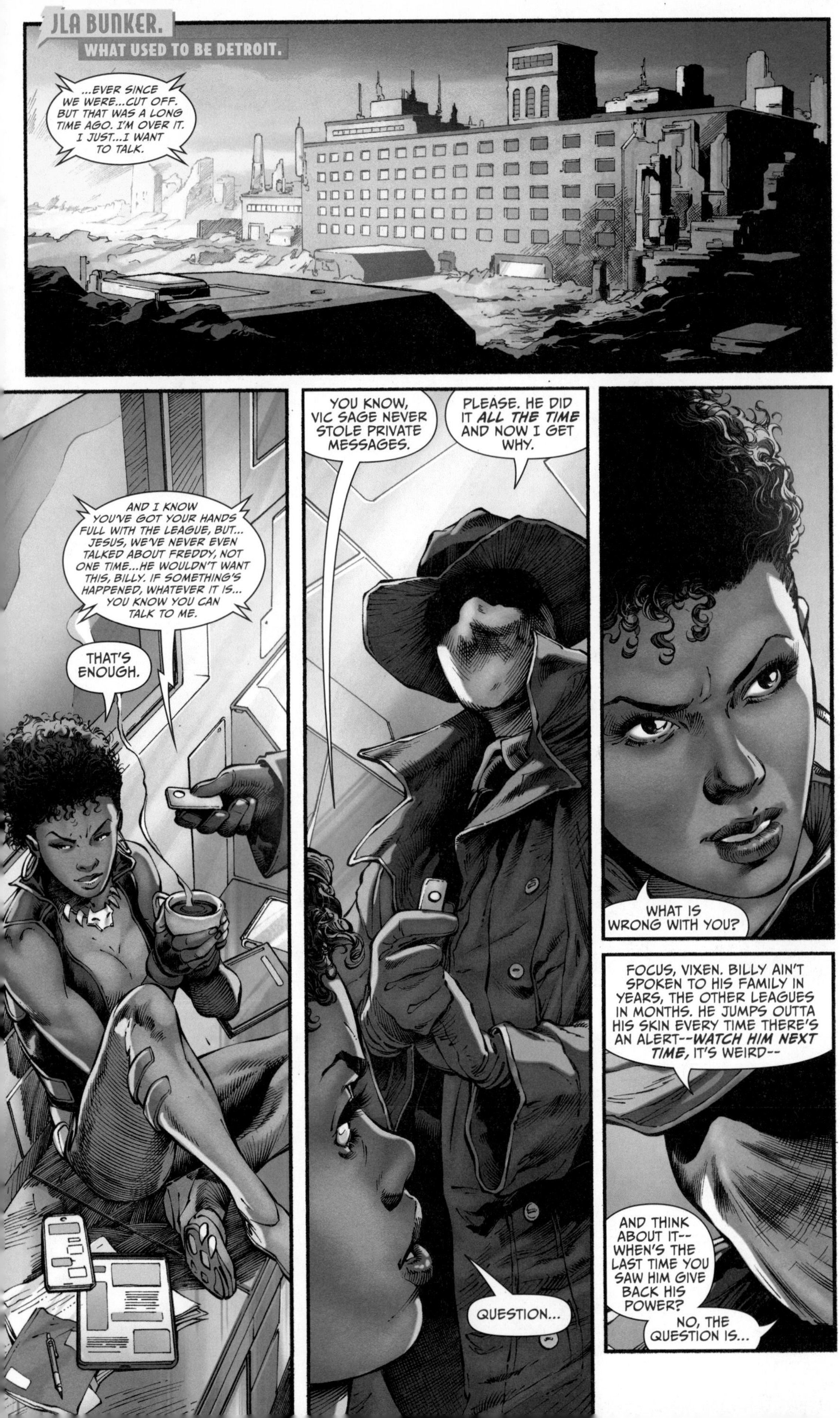
JLA BUNKER.
WHAT USED TO BE DETROIT.
...EVER SINCE WE WERE...CUT OFF. BUT THAT WAS A LONG TIME AGO. I'M OVER IT. I JUST...I WANT TO TALK.
AND I KNOW YOU'VE GOT YOUR HANDS FULL WITH THE LEAGUE, BUT... JESUS, WE'VE NEVER EVEN TALKED ABOUT FREDDY, NOT ONE TIME...HE WOULDN'T WANT THIS, BILLY. IF SOMETHING'S HAPPENED, WHATEVER IT IS... YOU KNOW YOU CAN TALK TO ME.
THAT'S ENOUGH.
YOU KNOW, VIC SAGE NEVER STOLE PRIVATE MESSAGES.
PLEASE. HE DID IT ALL THE TIME AND NOW I GET WHY.
QUESTION...
WHAT IS WRONG WITH YOU?
FOCUS, VIXEN. BILLY AIN'T SPOKEN TO HIS FAMILY IN YEARS, THE OTHER LEAGUES IN MONTHS. HE JUMPS OUTTA HIS SKIN EVERY TIME THERE'S AN ALERT--WATCH HIM NEXT TIME, IT'S WEIRD--
AND THINK ABOUT IT-- WHEN'S THE LAST TIME YOU SAW HIM GIVE BACK HIS POWER?
NO, THE QUESTION IS...

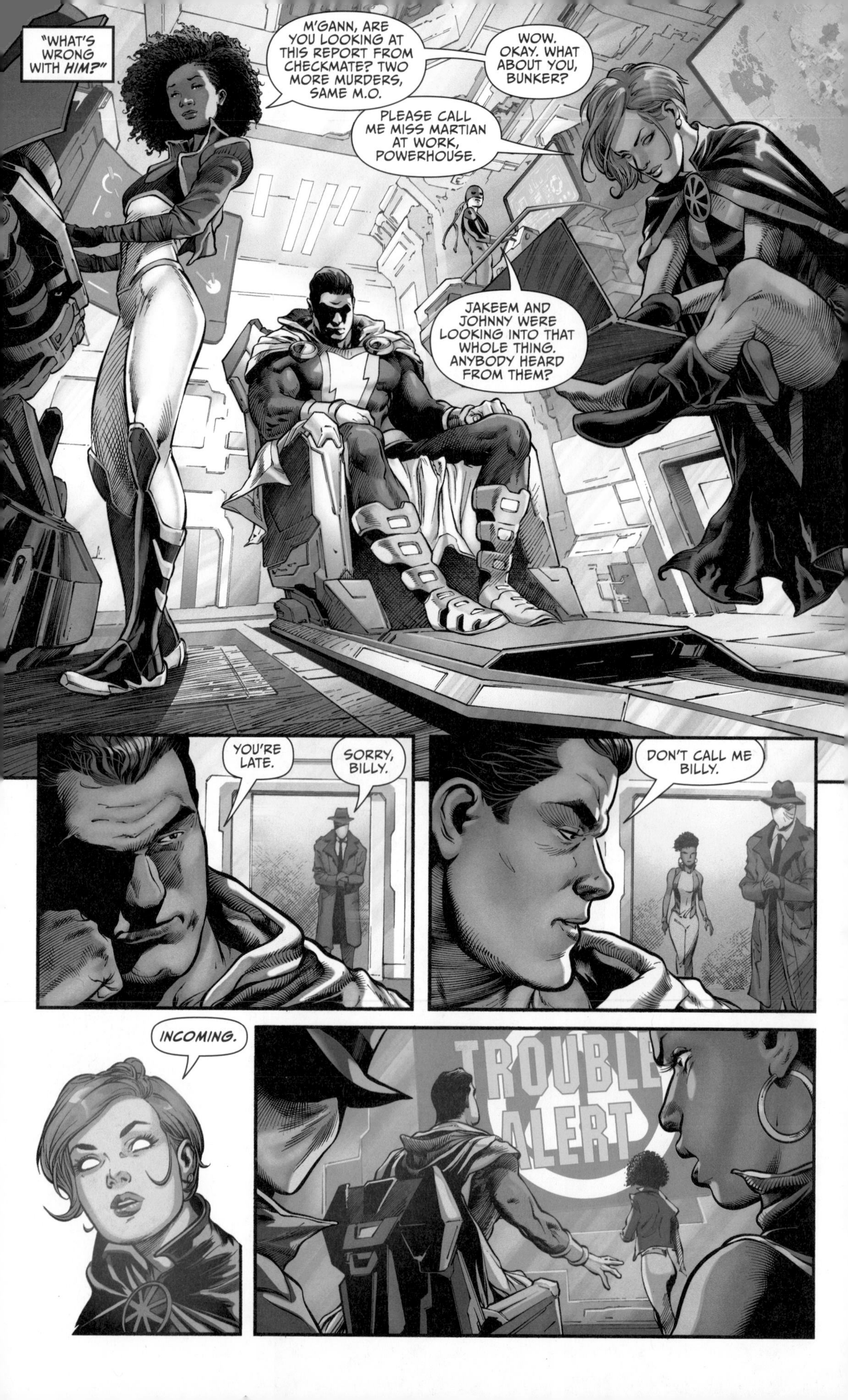
"WHAT'S WRONG WITH *HIM?*"
M'GANN, ARE YOU LOOKING AT THIS REPORT FROM CHECKMATE? TWO MORE MURDERS, SAME M.O.
PLEASE CALL ME MISS MARTIAN AT WORK, POWERHOUSE.
WOW. OKAY. WHAT ABOUT YOU, BUNKER?
JAKEEM AND JOHNNY WERE LOOKING INTO THAT WHOLE THING. ANYBODY HEARD FROM THEM?
YOU'RE LATE.
SORRY, BILLY.
DON'T CALL ME BILLY.
INCOMING.
TROUBLE ALERT

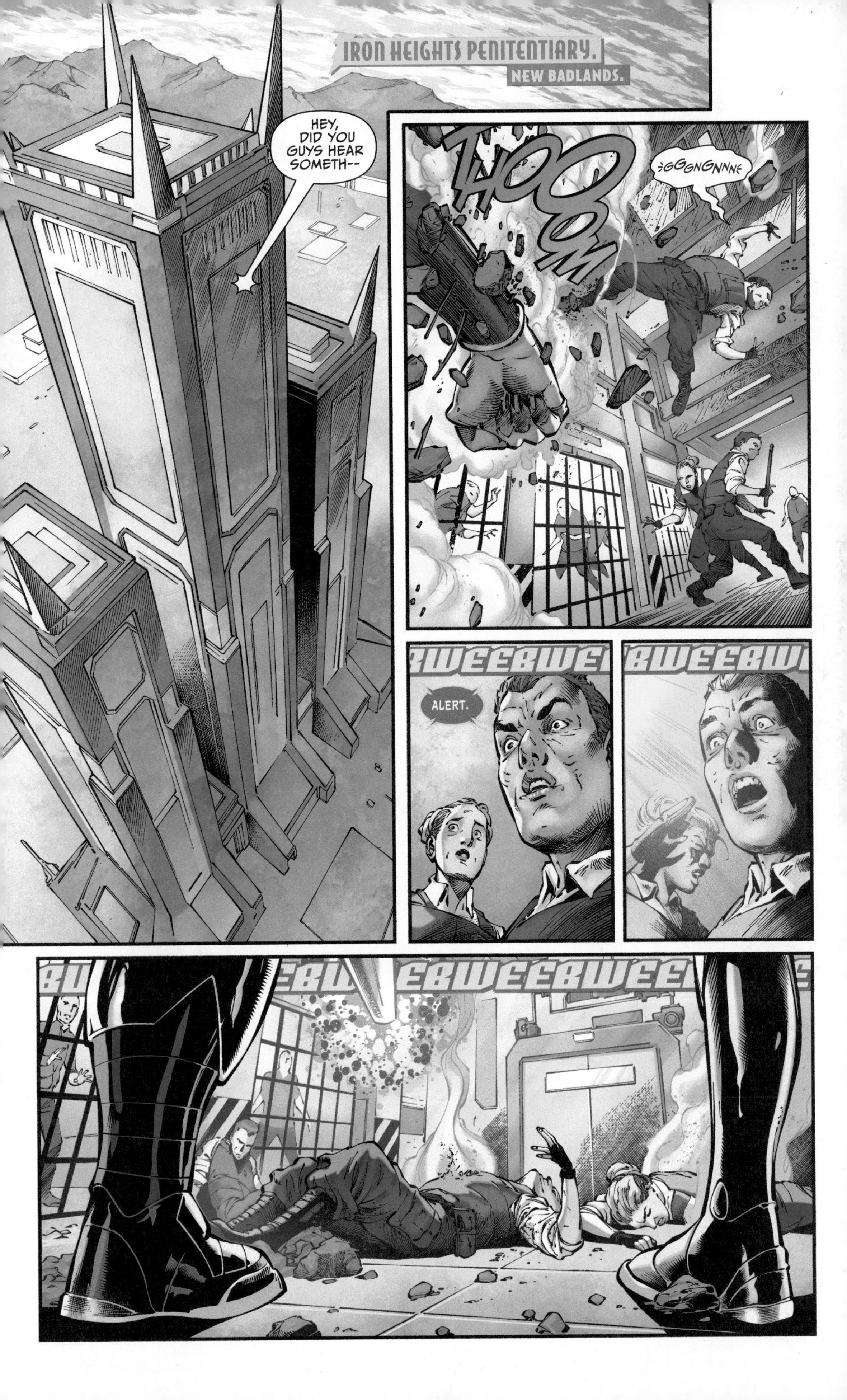
IRON HEIGHTS PENITENTIARY.
NEW BADLANDS.
HEY, DID YOU GUYS HEAR SOMETH--
THOOOM
GGGNGNNN
BWEEBWE
ALERT.
BWEEBWI
BWEEBWEEBWEE

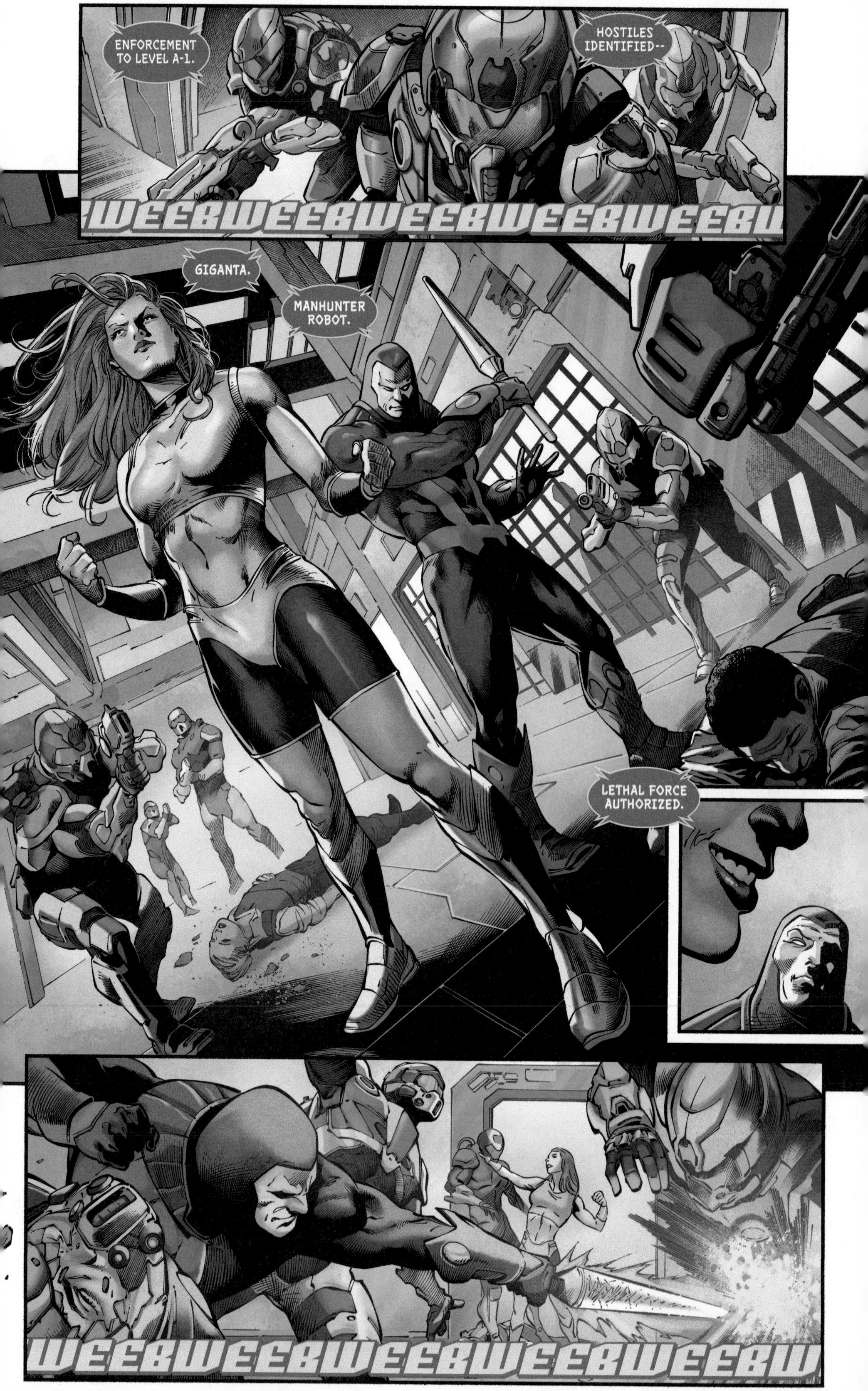
ENFORCEMENT TO LEVEL A-1.
HOSTILES IDENTIFIED--
WEEBWEEBWEEBWEEBWEEBU
GIGANTA.
MANHUNTER ROBOT.
LETHAL FORCE AUTHORIZED.
WEEBWEEBWEEBWEEBWEEBW

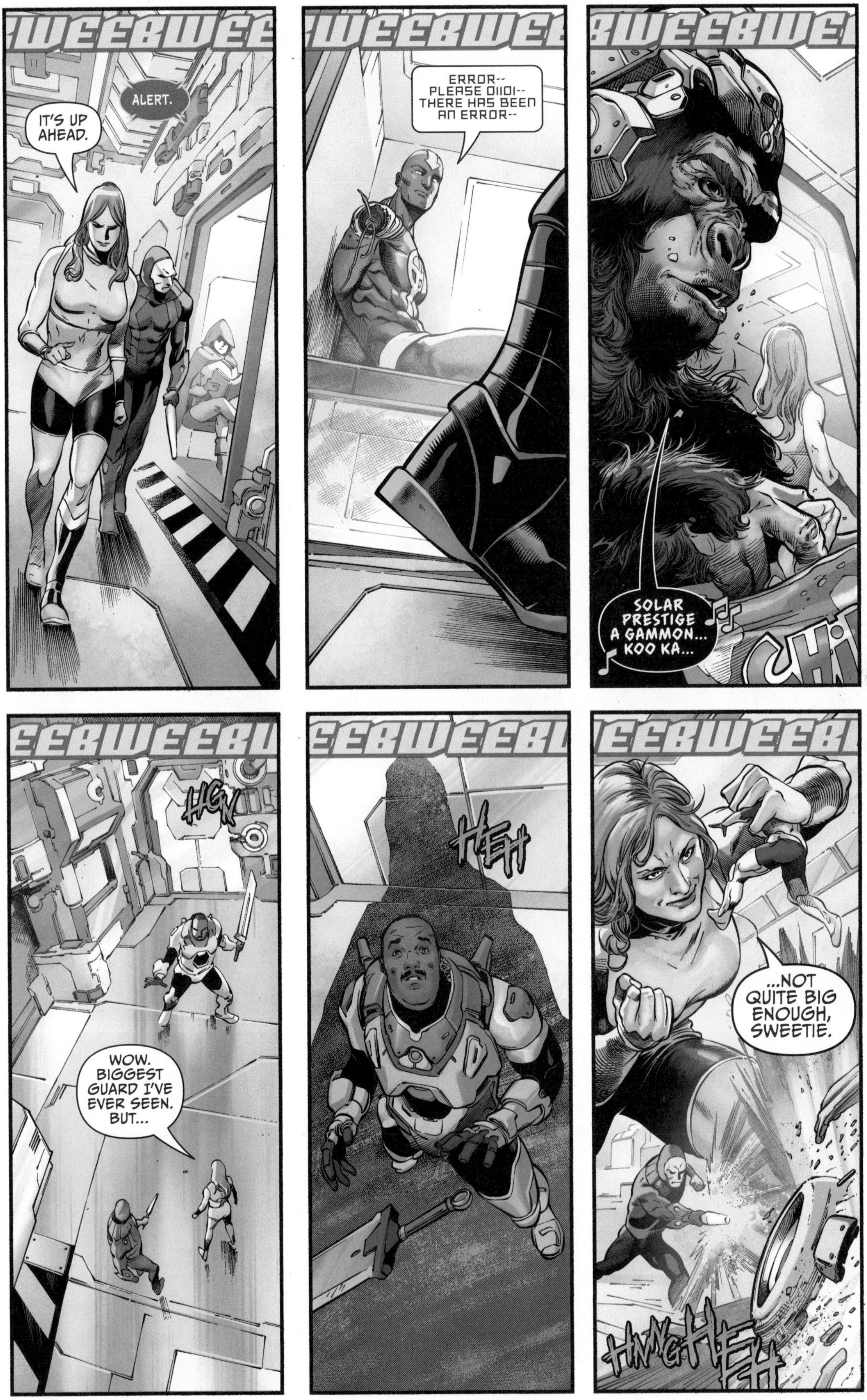
IT'S UP AHEAD.
ALERT.
ERROR-- PLEASE 01101-- THERE HAS BEEN AN ERROR--
SOLAR PRESTIGE A GAMMON... KOO KA...
HGN
WOW. BIGGEST GUARD I'VE EVER SEEN. BUT...
HEH
...NOT QUITE BIG ENOUGH, SWEETIE.
HNNG HEH

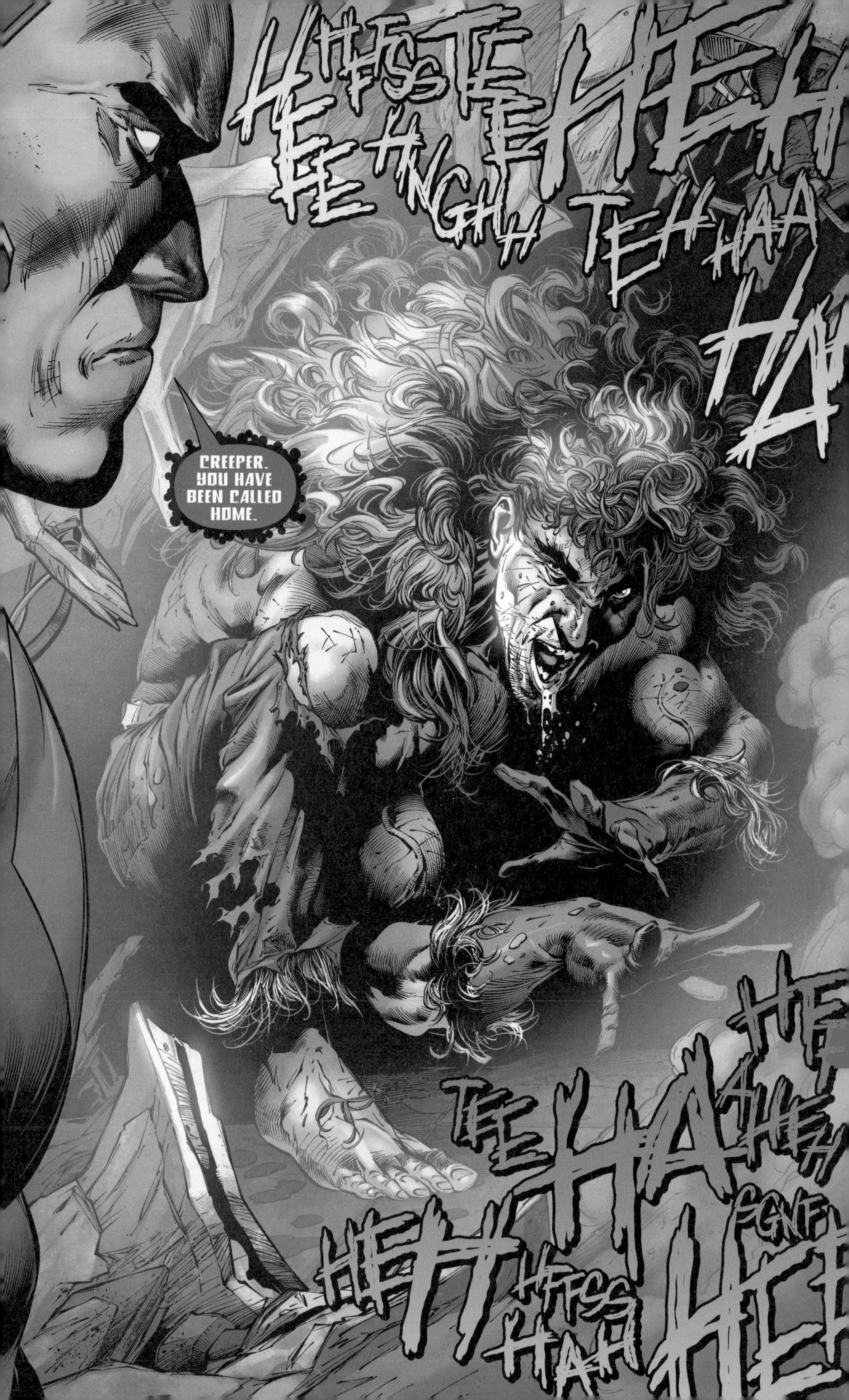
TEH HAA
HA
CREEPER. YOU HAVE BEEN CALLED HOME.
TEE HA
HAH

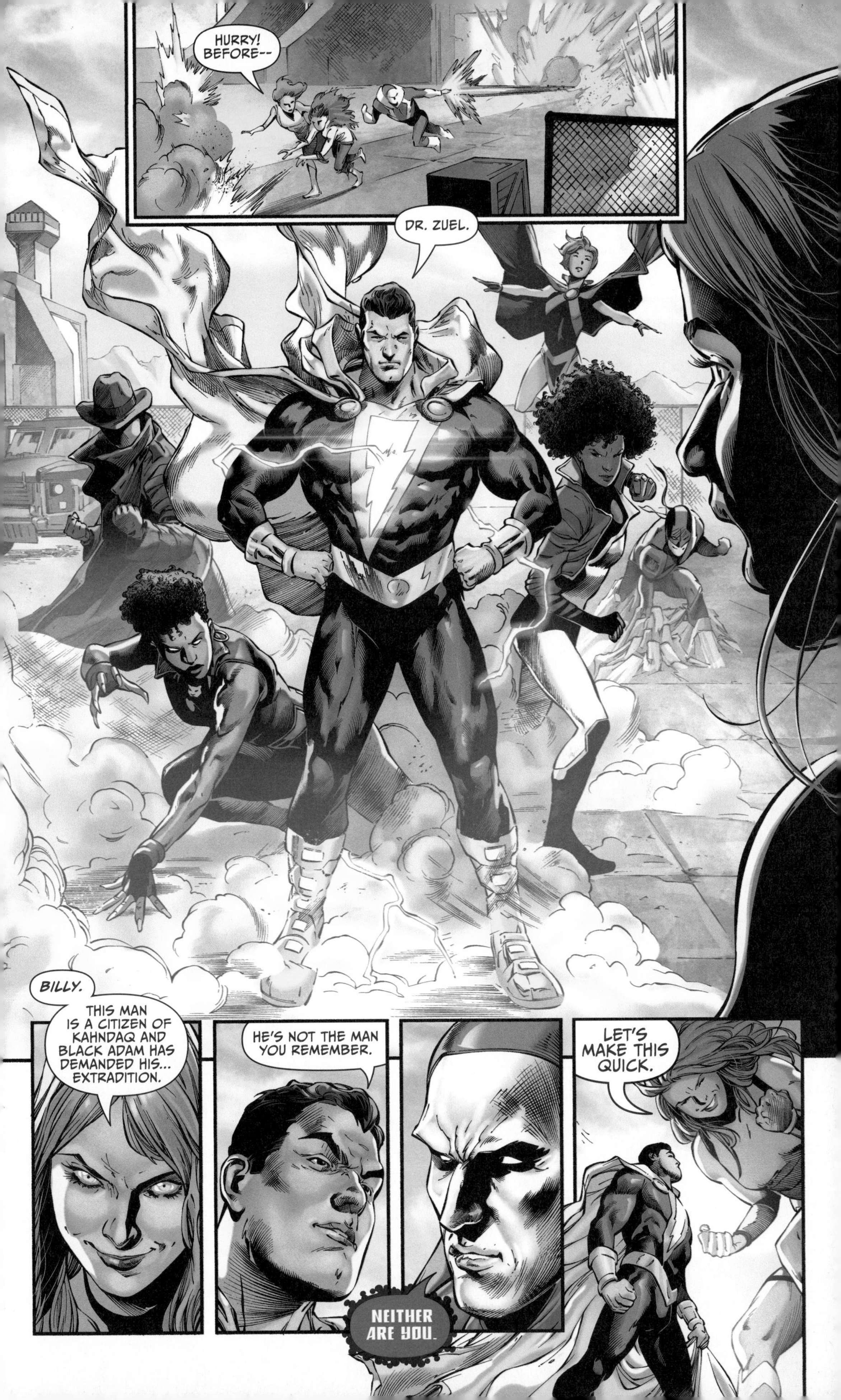
HURRY! BEFORE--
DR. ZUEL.
BILLY.
THIS MAN IS A CITIZEN OF KAHNDAQ AND BLACK ADAM HAS DEMANDED HIS... EXTRADITION.
HE'S NOT THE MAN YOU REMEMBER.
NEITHER ARE YOU.
LET'S MAKE THIS QUICK.

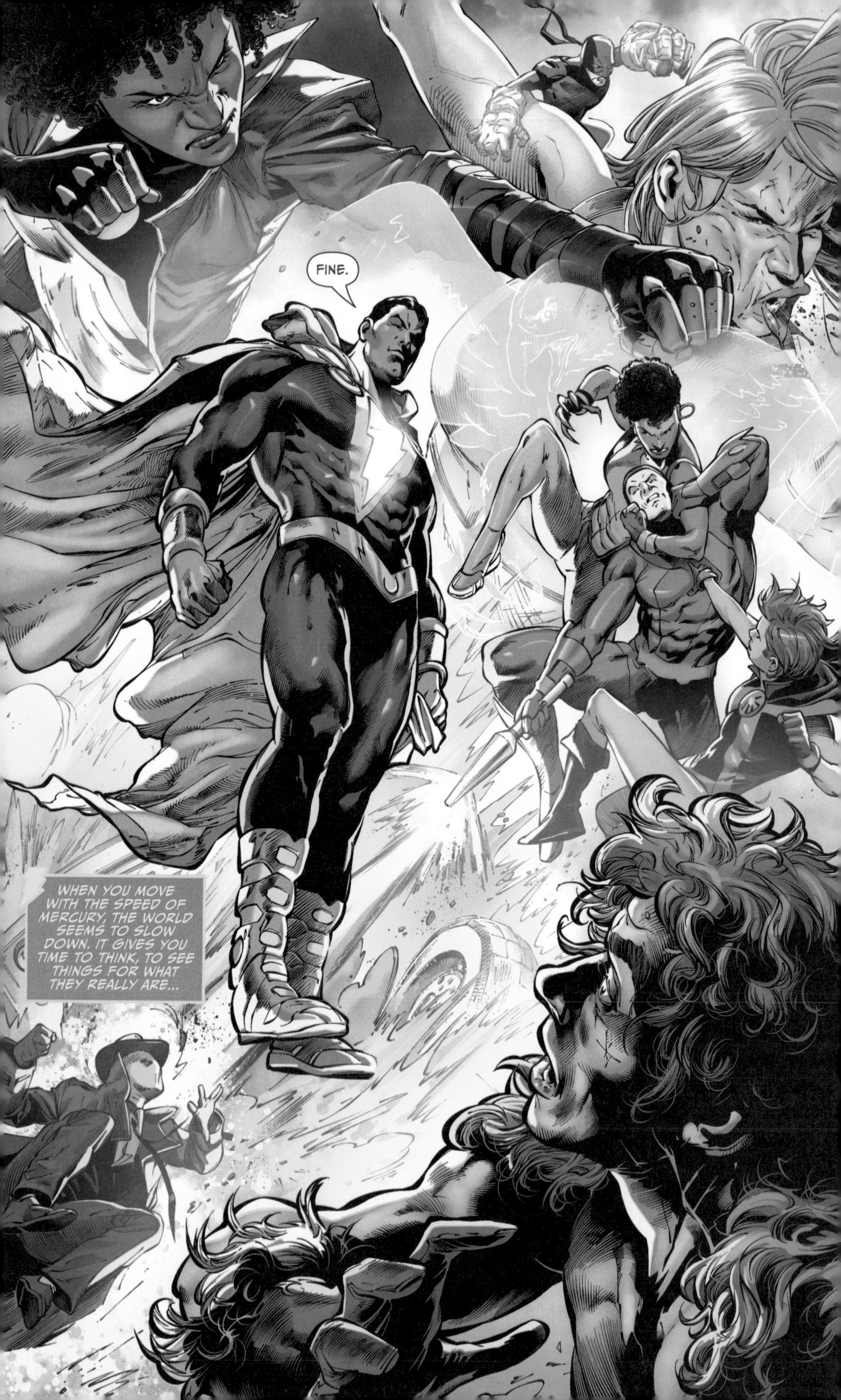
FINE.
WHEN YOU MOVE WITH THE SPEED OF MERCURY, THE WORLD SEEMS TO SLOW DOWN. IT GIVES YOU TIME TO THINK, TO SEE THINGS FOR WHAT THEY REALLY ARE...

...AND TO DEAL WITH THEM QUICKLY...

GOOD WORK. WAIT, WHERE'S--

CREEPER? I DON'T--

I DO.

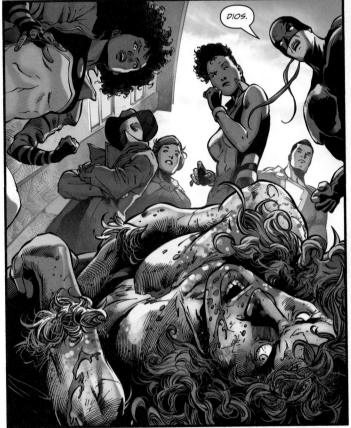

DIOS.

...AND ACCORDINGLY.

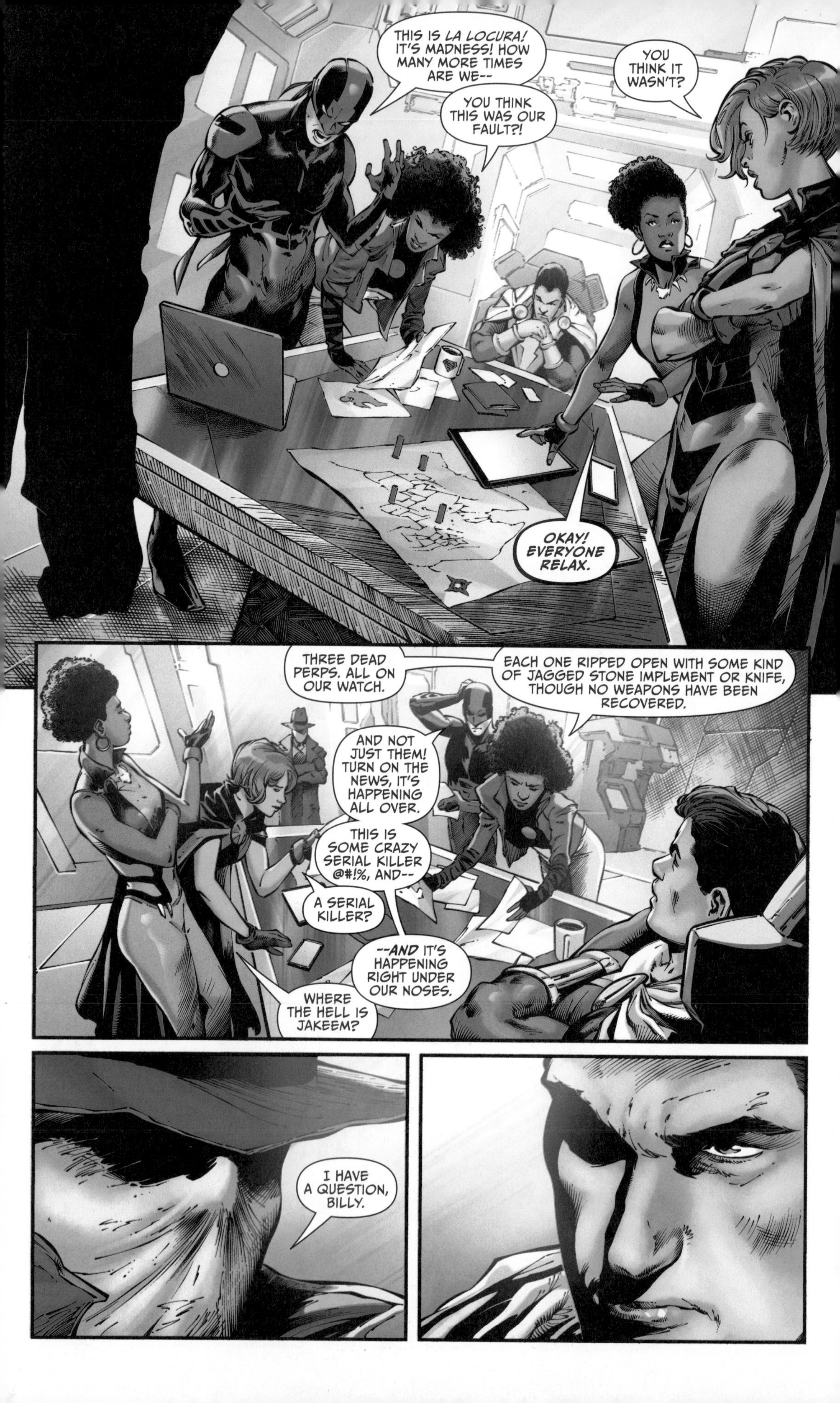

THIS IS *LA LOCURA!* IT'S MADNESS! HOW MANY MORE TIMES ARE WE--
YOU THINK THIS WAS OUR FAULT?!
YOU THINK IT WASN'T?
OKAY! EVERYONE RELAX.
THREE DEAD PERPS. ALL ON OUR WATCH.
EACH ONE RIPPED OPEN WITH SOME KIND OF JAGGED STONE IMPLEMENT OR KNIFE, THOUGH NO WEAPONS HAVE BEEN RECOVERED.
AND NOT JUST THEM! TURN ON THE NEWS, IT'S HAPPENING ALL OVER.
THIS IS SOME CRAZY SERIAL KILLER @#!%, AND--
A SERIAL KILLER?
--AND IT'S HAPPENING RIGHT UNDER OUR NOSES.
WHERE THE HELL IS JAKEEM?
I HAVE A QUESTION, BILLY.

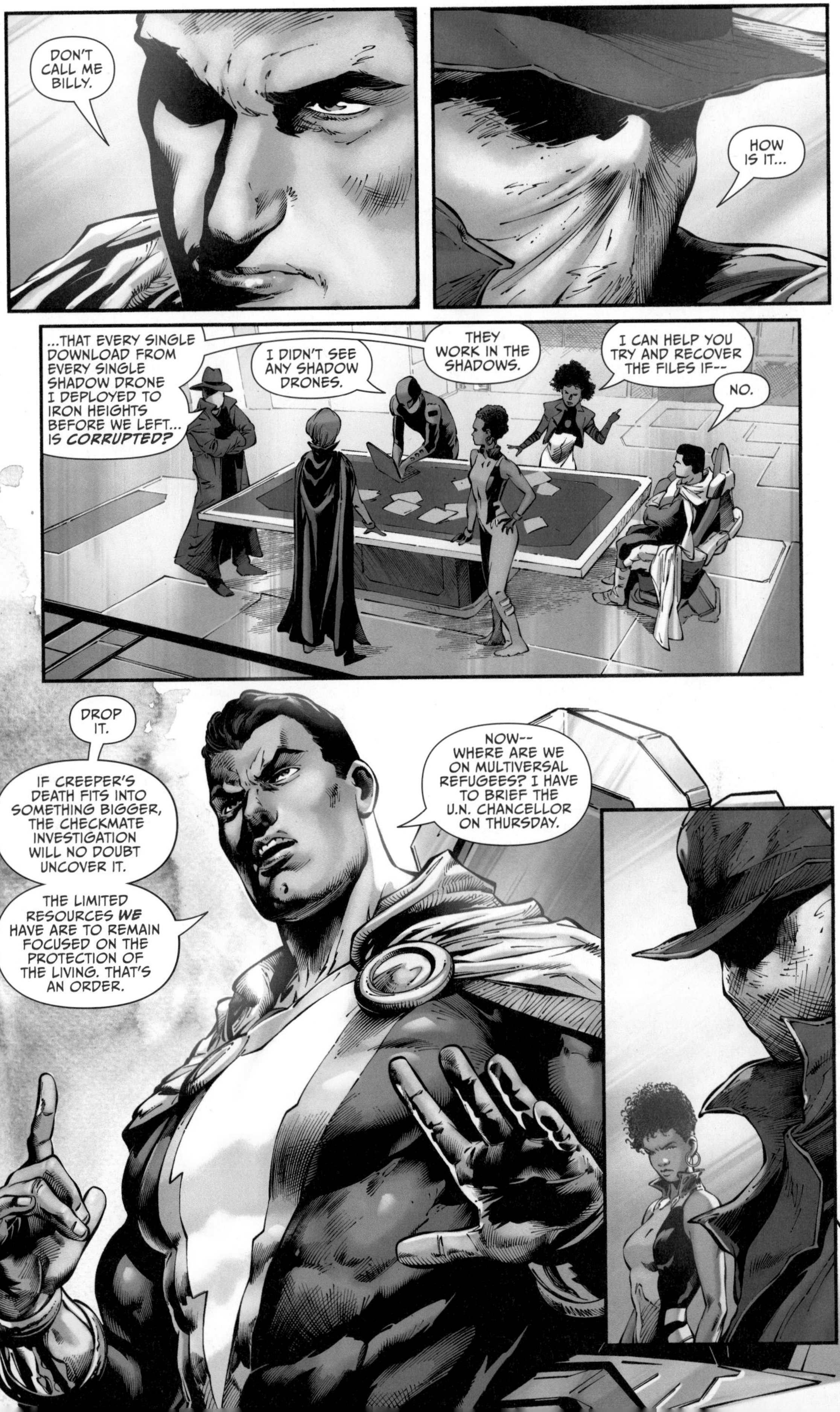
DON'T CALL ME BILLY.
HOW IS IT...
...THAT EVERY SINGLE DOWNLOAD FROM EVERY SINGLE SHADOW DRONE I DEPLOYED TO IRON HEIGHTS BEFORE WE LEFT... IS CORRUPTED?
I DIDN'T SEE ANY SHADOW DRONES.
THEY WORK IN THE SHADOWS.
I CAN HELP YOU TRY AND RECOVER THE FILES IF--
NO.
DROP IT.
IF CREEPER'S DEATH FITS INTO SOMETHING BIGGER, THE CHECKMATE INVESTIGATION WILL NO DOUBT UNCOVER IT.
THE LIMITED RESOURCES WE HAVE ARE TO REMAIN FOCUSED ON THE PROTECTION OF THE LIVING. THAT'S AN ORDER.
NOW-- WHERE ARE WE ON MULTIVERSAL REFUGEES? I HAVE TO BRIEF THE U.N. CHANCELLOR ON THURSDAY.

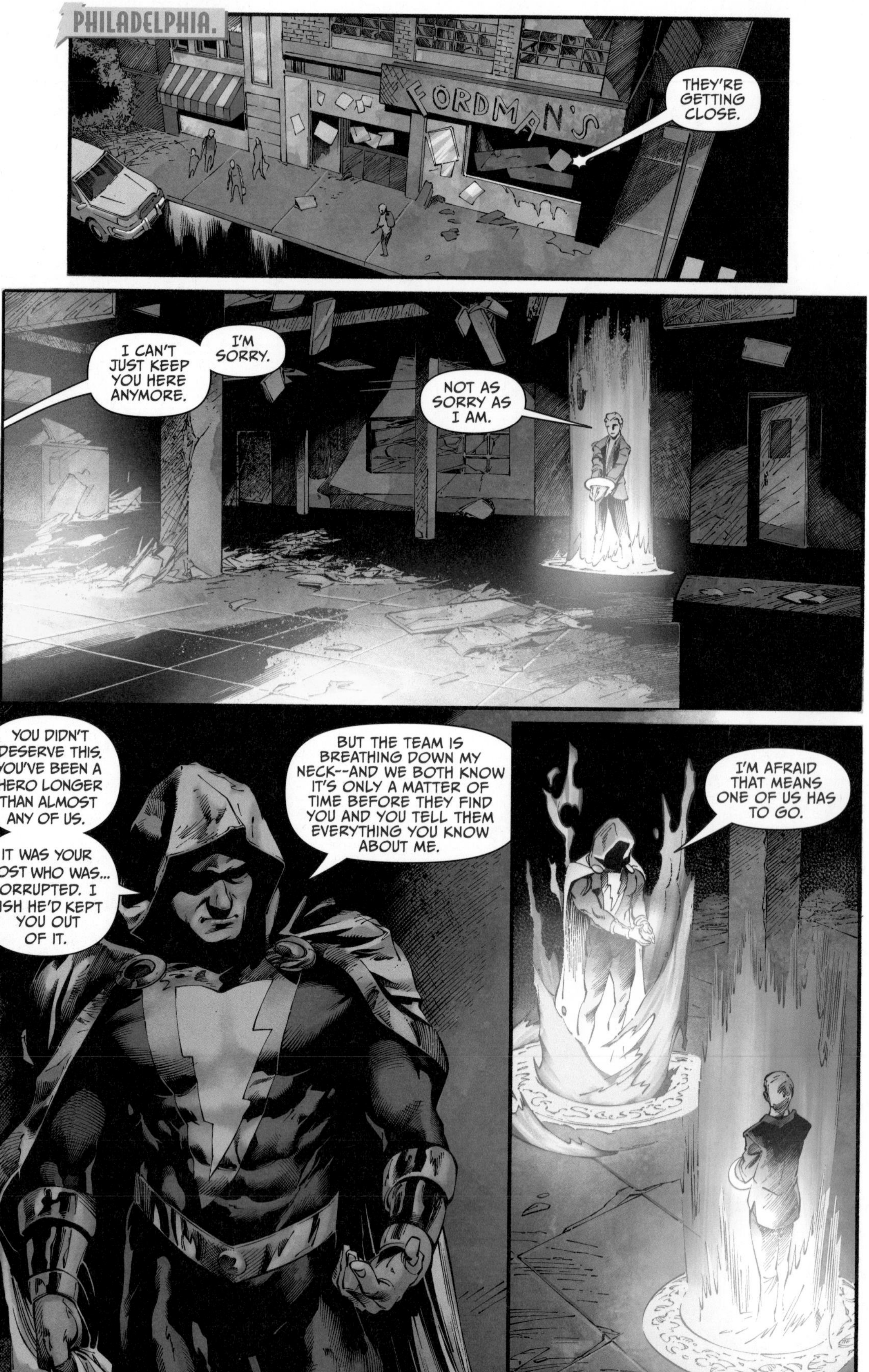

PHILADELPHIA.
FORDMAN'S
THEY'RE GETTING CLOSE.
I CAN'T JUST KEEP YOU HERE ANYMORE.
I'M SORRY.
NOT AS SORRY AS I AM.
YOU DIDN'T DESERVE THIS. YOU'VE BEEN A HERO LONGER THAN ALMOST ANY OF US.
IT WAS YOUR HOST WHO WAS... CORRUPTED. I WISH HE'D KEPT YOU OUT OF IT.
BUT THE TEAM IS BREATHING DOWN MY NECK--AND WE BOTH KNOW IT'S ONLY A MATTER OF TIME BEFORE THEY FIND YOU AND YOU TELL THEM EVERYTHING YOU KNOW ABOUT ME.
I'M AFRAID THAT MEANS ONE OF US HAS TO GO.

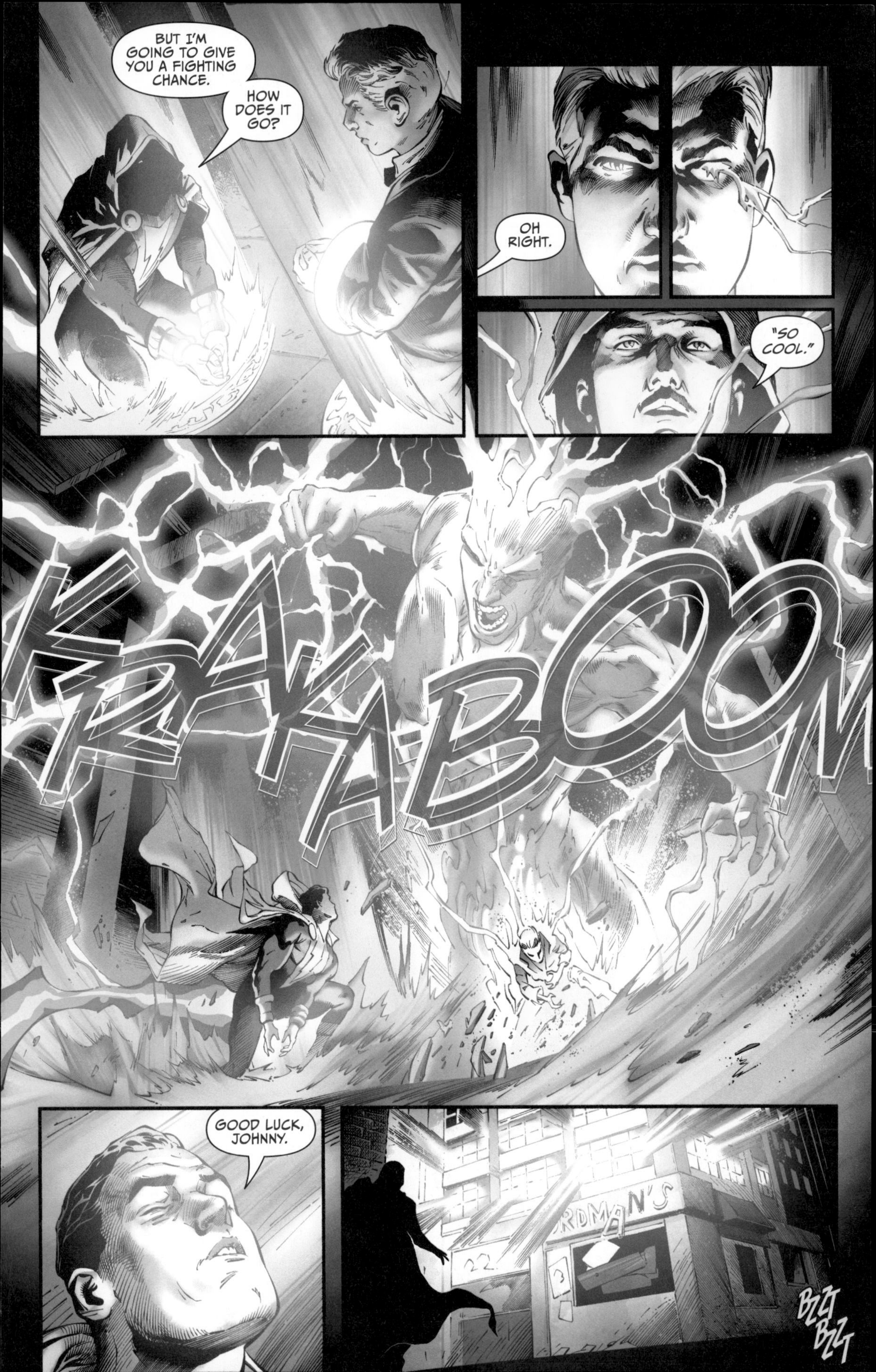
BUT I'M GOING TO GIVE YOU A FIGHTING CHANCE.
HOW DOES IT GO?
OH RIGHT.
"SO COOL."
KRAKA-BOOM
GOOD LUCK, JOHNNY.
RDMAN'S
BZZT BZZT

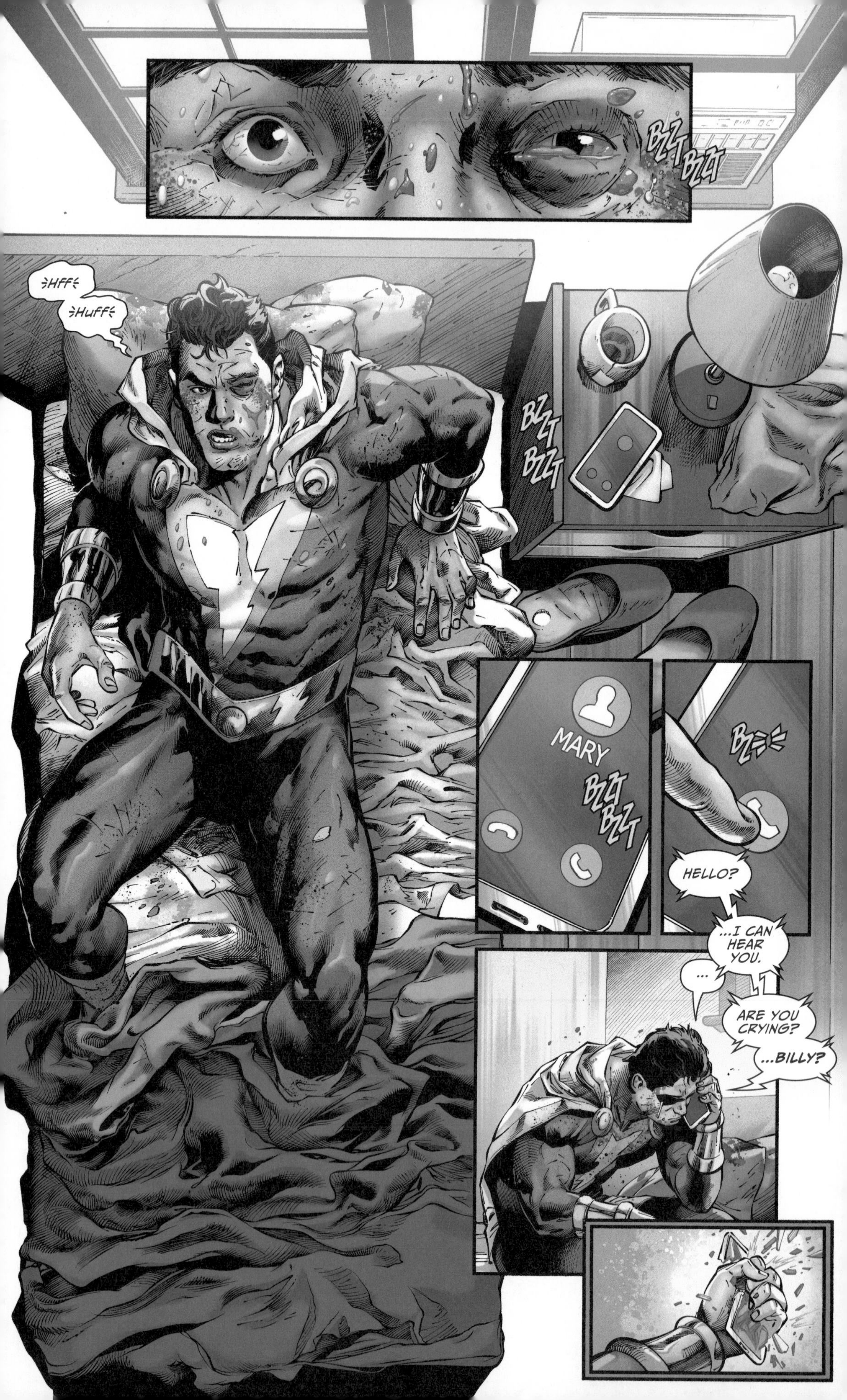
BZZT BZZT
HFF
HUFF
BZZT BZZT
MARY
BZZT BZZT
BZZ
HELLO?
...I CAN HEAR YOU.
...
ARE YOU CRYING?
...BILLY?

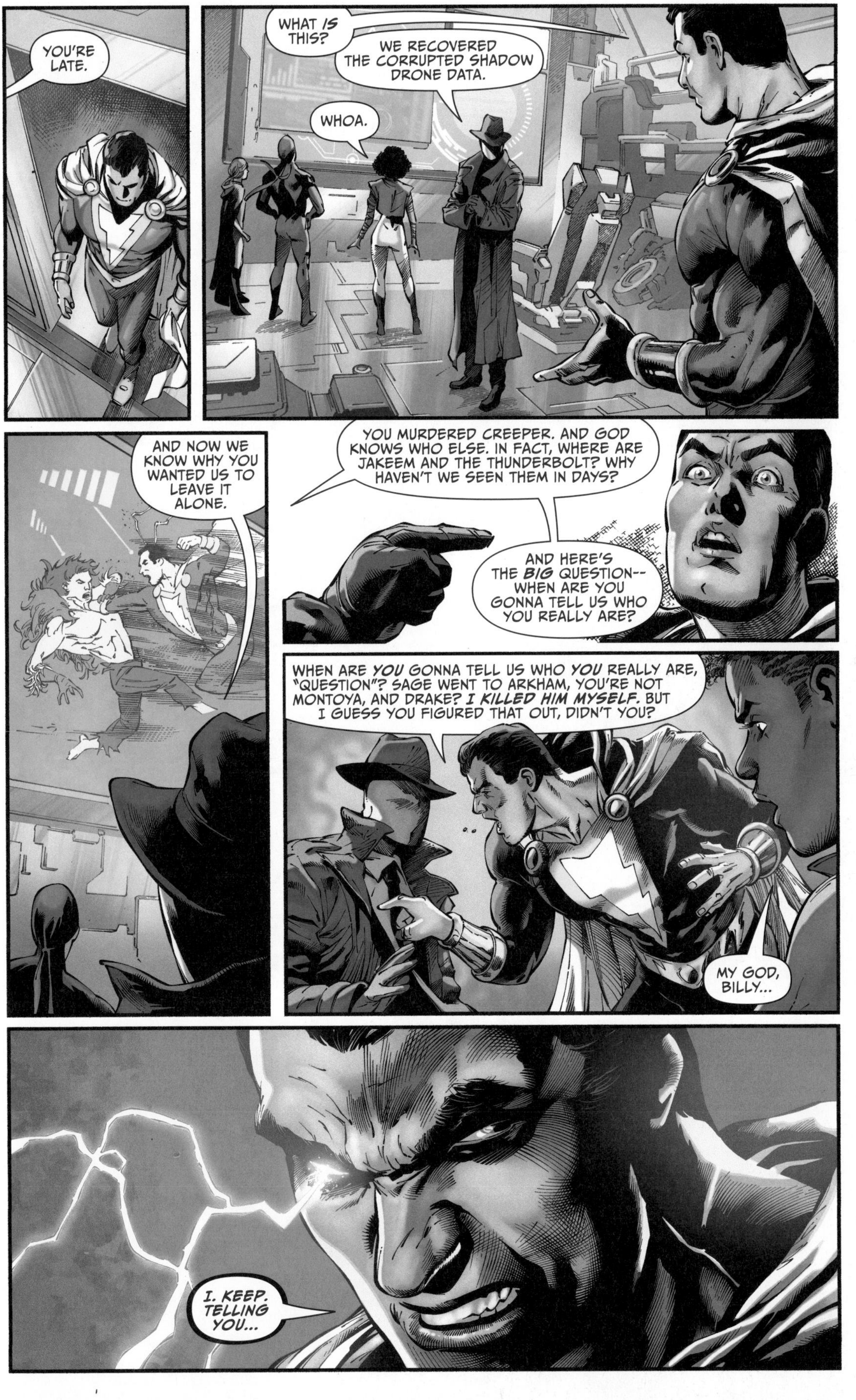
YOU'RE LATE.
WHAT *IS* THIS?
WE RECOVERED THE CORRUPTED SHADOW DRONE DATA.
WHOA.
AND NOW WE KNOW WHY YOU WANTED US TO LEAVE IT ALONE.
YOU MURDERED CREEPER. AND GOD KNOWS WHO ELSE. IN FACT, WHERE ARE JAKEEM AND THE THUNDERBOLT? WHY HAVEN'T WE SEEN THEM IN DAYS?
AND HERE'S THE *BIG* QUESTION-- WHEN ARE YOU GONNA TELL US WHO YOU REALLY ARE?
WHEN ARE *YOU* GONNA TELL US WHO *YOU* REALLY ARE, "QUESTION"? SAGE WENT TO ARKHAM, YOU'RE NOT MONTOYA, AND DRAKE? *I KILLED HIM MYSELF.* BUT I GUESS YOU FIGURED THAT OUT, DIDN'T YOU?
MY GOD, BILLY...
I. KEEP. TELLING YOU...

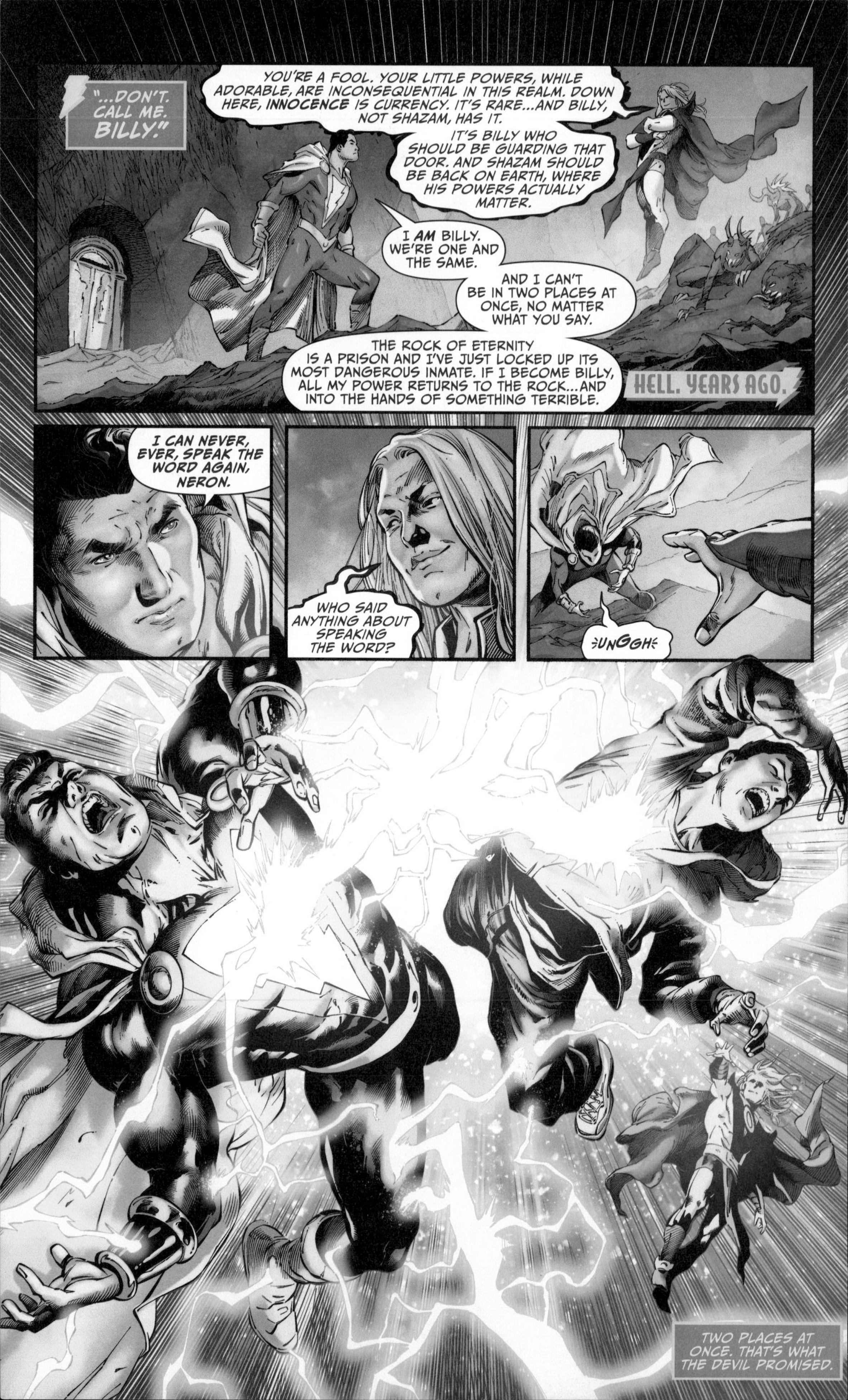
"...DON'T. CALL ME. BILLY!"
YOU'RE A FOOL. YOUR LITTLE POWERS, WHILE ADORABLE, ARE INCONSEQUENTIAL IN THIS REALM. DOWN HERE, INNOCENCE IS CURRENCY. IT'S RARE...AND BILLY, NOT SHAZAM, HAS IT.
IT'S BILLY WHO SHOULD BE GUARDING THAT DOOR. AND SHAZAM SHOULD BE BACK ON EARTH, WHERE HIS POWERS ACTUALLY MATTER.
I AM BILLY. WE'RE ONE AND THE SAME.
AND I CAN'T BE IN TWO PLACES AT ONCE, NO MATTER WHAT YOU SAY.
THE ROCK OF ETERNITY IS A PRISON AND I'VE JUST LOCKED UP ITS MOST DANGEROUS INMATE. IF I BECOME BILLY, ALL MY POWER RETURNS TO THE ROCK...AND INTO THE HANDS OF SOMETHING TERRIBLE.
HELL. YEARS AGO.
I CAN NEVER, EVER, SPEAK THE WORD AGAIN, NERON.
WHO SAID ANYTHING ABOUT SPEAKING THE WORD?
UNGGH
TWO PLACES AT ONCE. THAT'S WHAT THE DEVIL PROMISED.

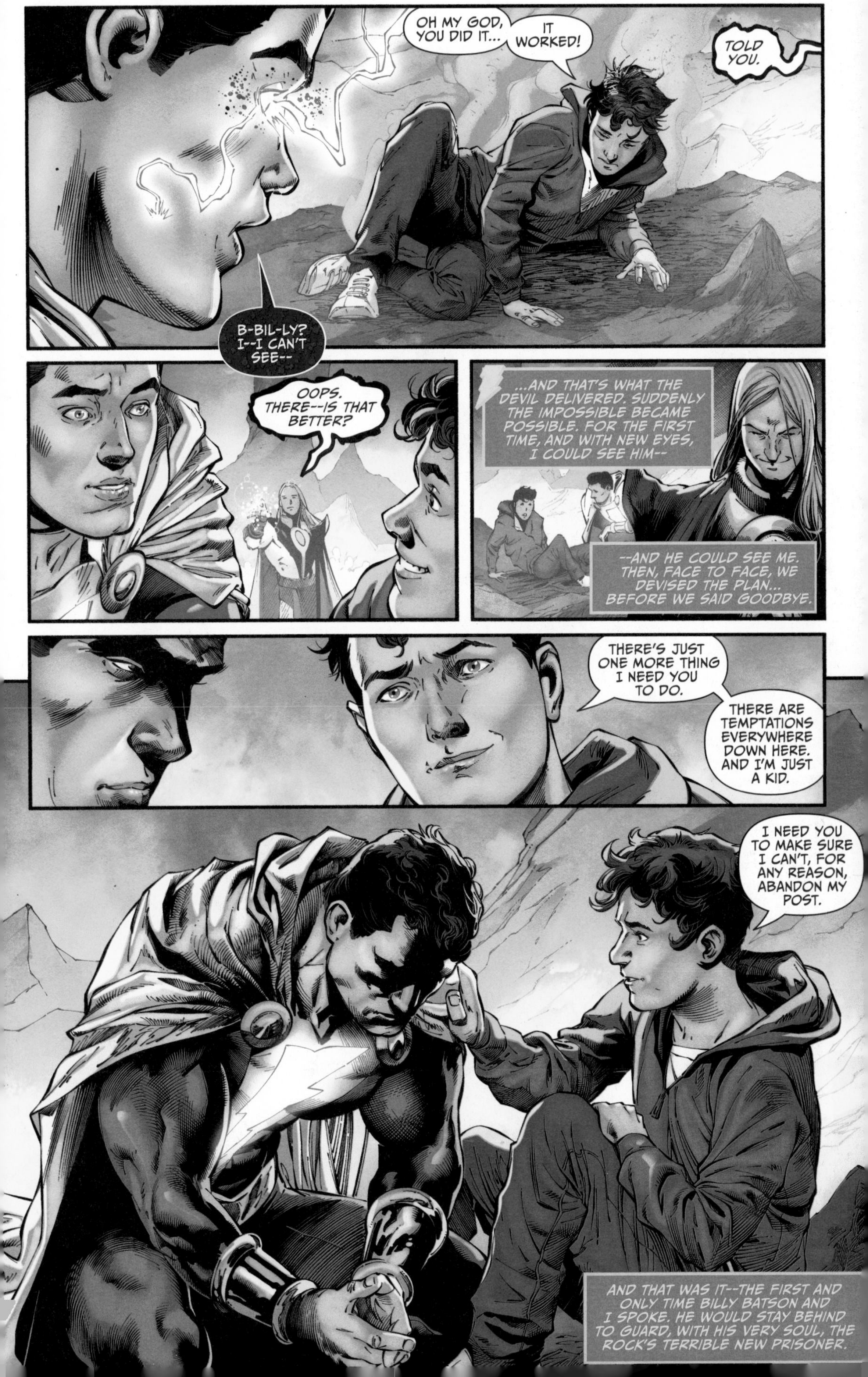
OH MY GOD, YOU DID IT...
IT WORKED!
TOLD YOU.
B-BIL-LY? I--I CAN'T SEE--
OOPS. THERE--IS THAT BETTER?
...AND THAT'S WHAT THE DEVIL DELIVERED. SUDDENLY THE IMPOSSIBLE BECAME POSSIBLE. FOR THE FIRST TIME, AND WITH NEW EYES, I COULD SEE HIM--
--AND HE COULD SEE ME. THEN, FACE TO FACE, WE DEVISED THE PLAN... BEFORE WE SAID GOODBYE.
THERE'S JUST ONE MORE THING I NEED YOU TO DO.
THERE ARE TEMPTATIONS EVERYWHERE DOWN HERE. AND I'M JUST A KID.
I NEED YOU TO MAKE SURE I CAN'T, FOR ANY REASON, ABANDON MY POST.
AND THAT WAS IT--THE FIRST AND ONLY TIME BILLY BATSON AND I SPOKE. HE WOULD STAY BEHIND TO GUARD, WITH HIS VERY SOUL, THE ROCK'S TERRIBLE NEW PRISONER.

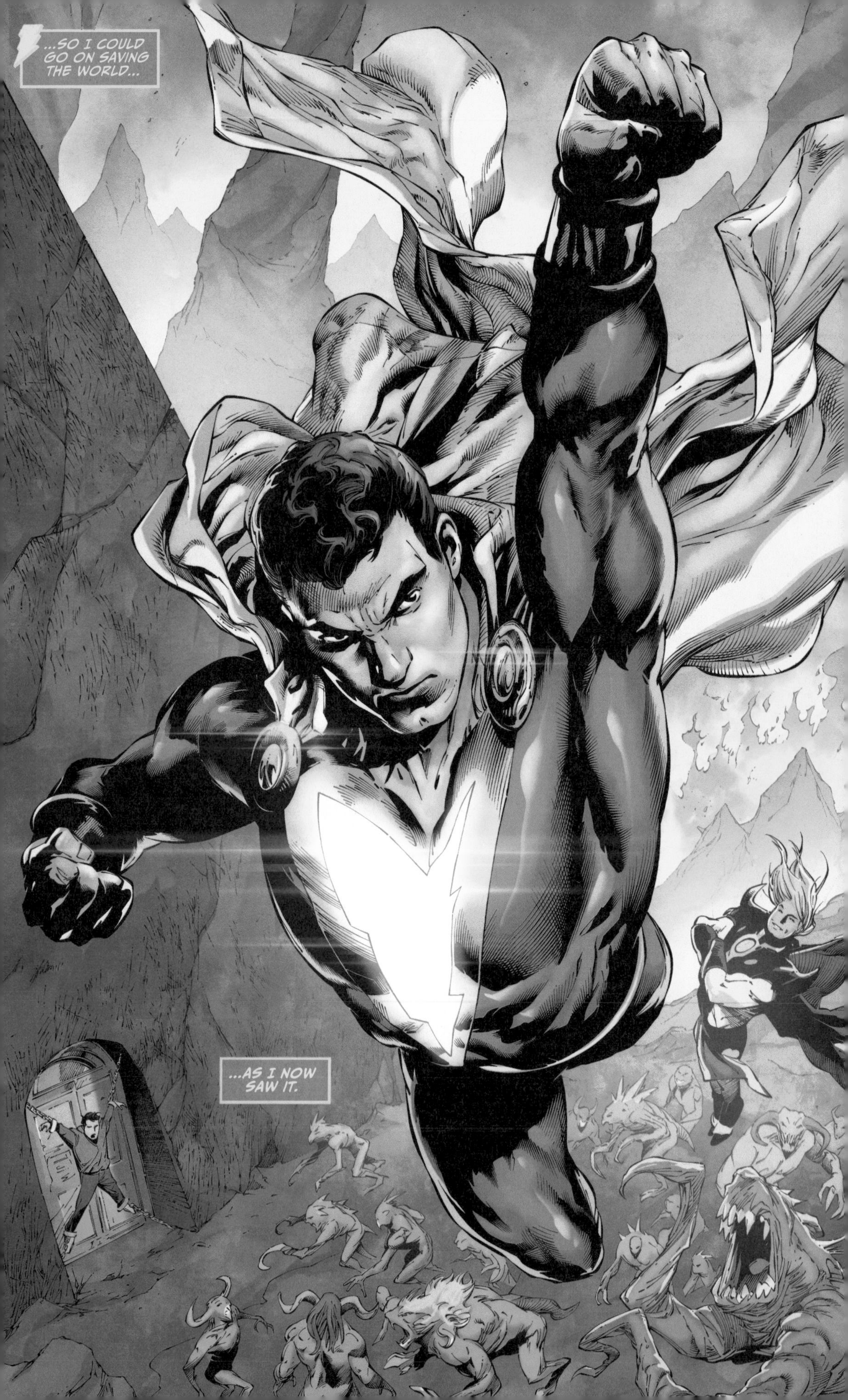
...SO I COULD GO ON SAVING THE WORLD...
...AS I NOW SAW IT.

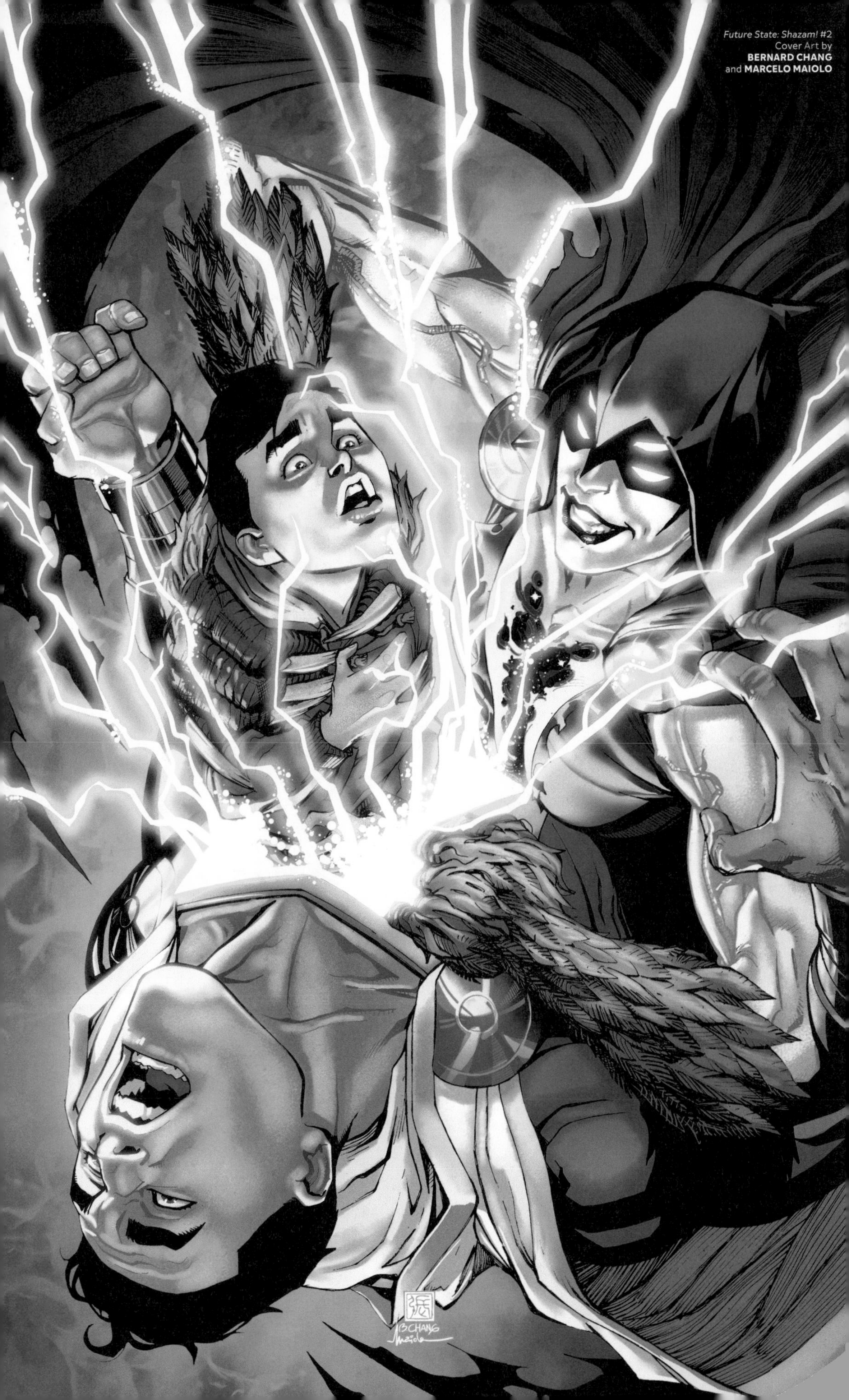
B CHANG

Future State: Shazam! #2
Cover Art by
BERNARD CHANG
and **MARCELO MAIOLO**

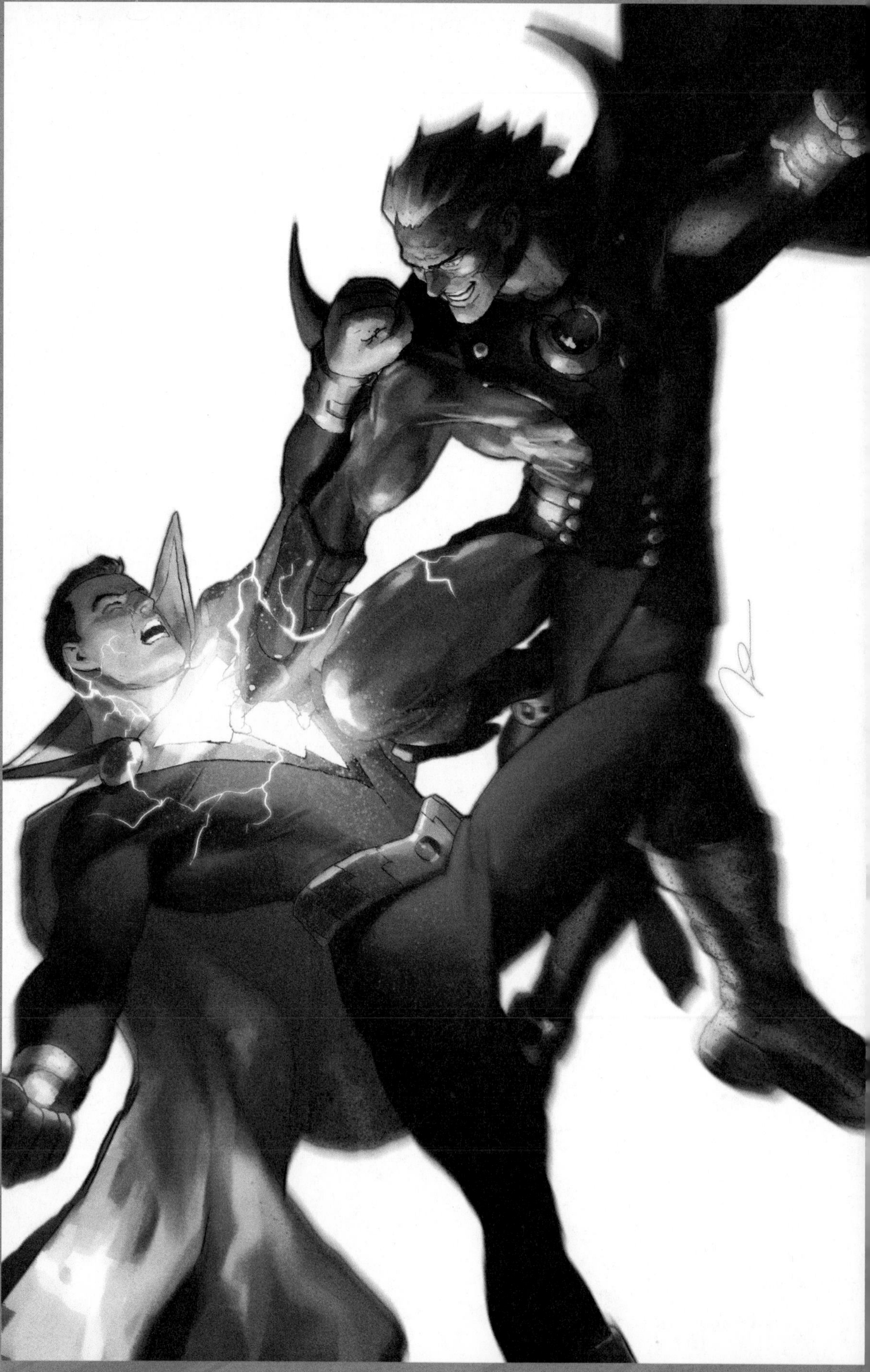

Future State: Shazam! #2 Variant Cover Art by **GERALD PAREL**

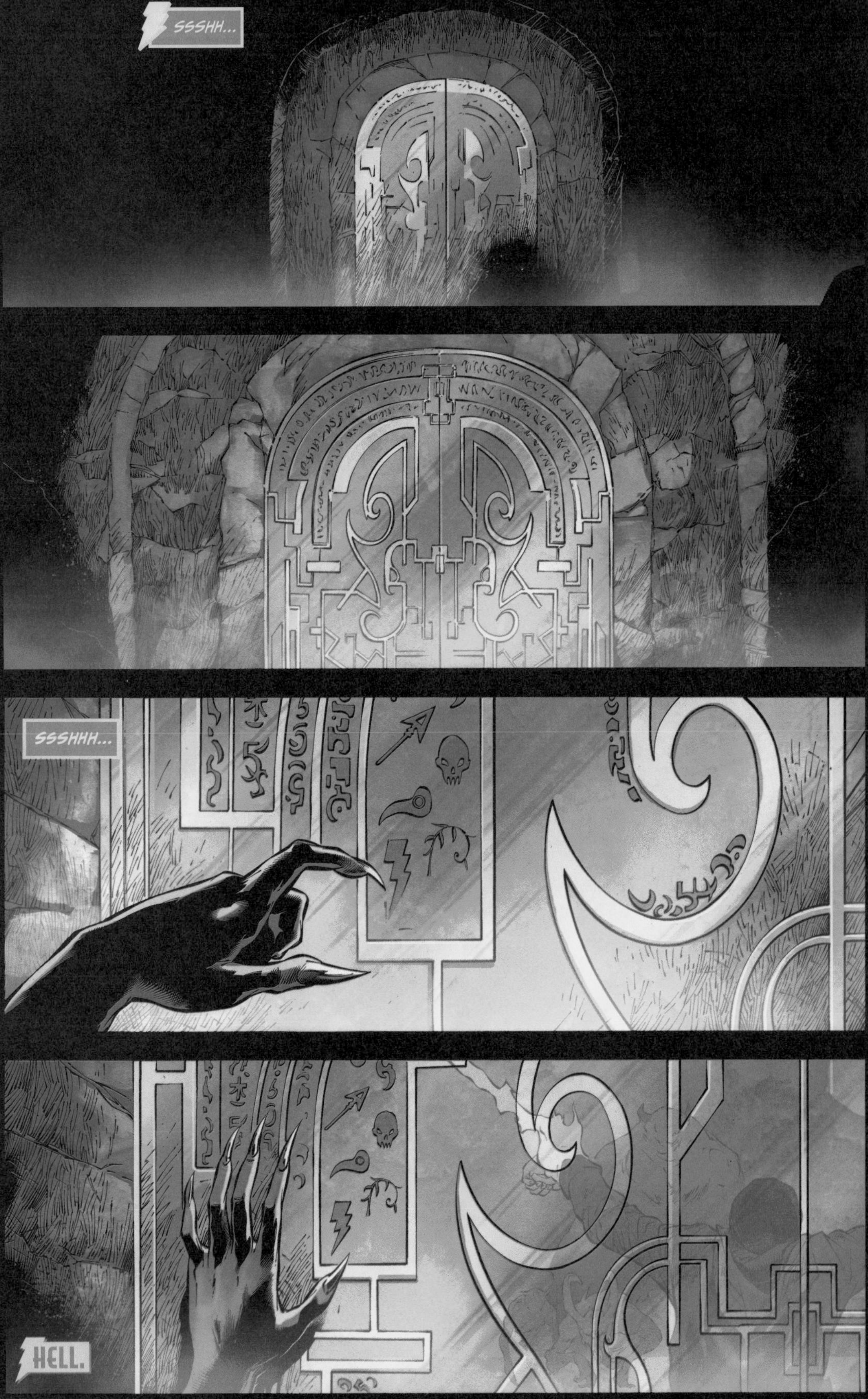
SSSHH...
SSSHHH...
HELL.

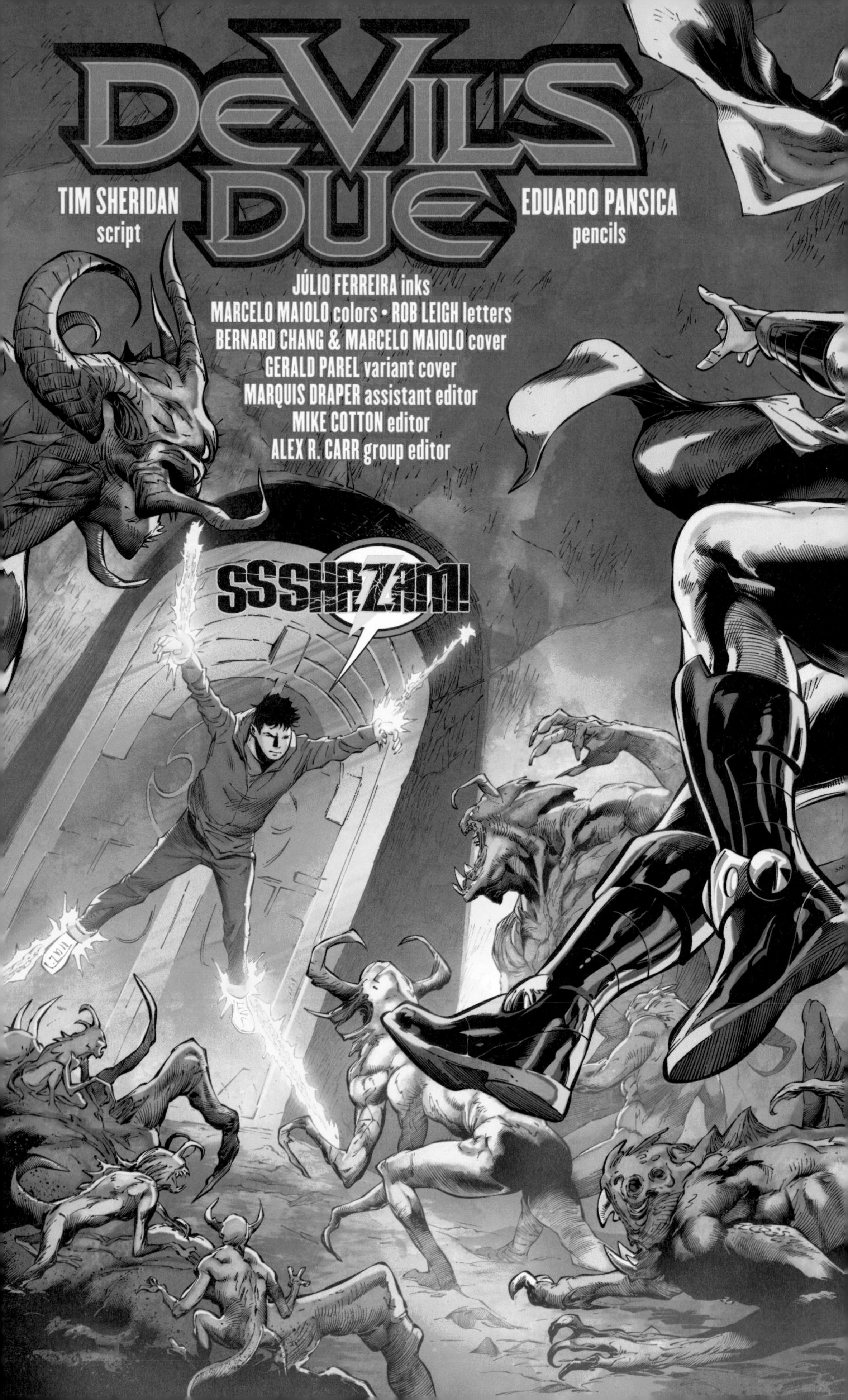
DEVIL'S DUE
TIM SHERIDAN script
EDUARDO PANSICA pencils
JÚLIO FERREIRA inks
MARCELO MAIOLO colors • ROB LEIGH letters
BERNARD CHANG & MARCELO MAIOLO cover
GERALD PAREL variant cover
MARQUIS DRAPER assistant editor
MIKE COTTON editor
ALEX R. CARR group editor
SSSHAZAM!

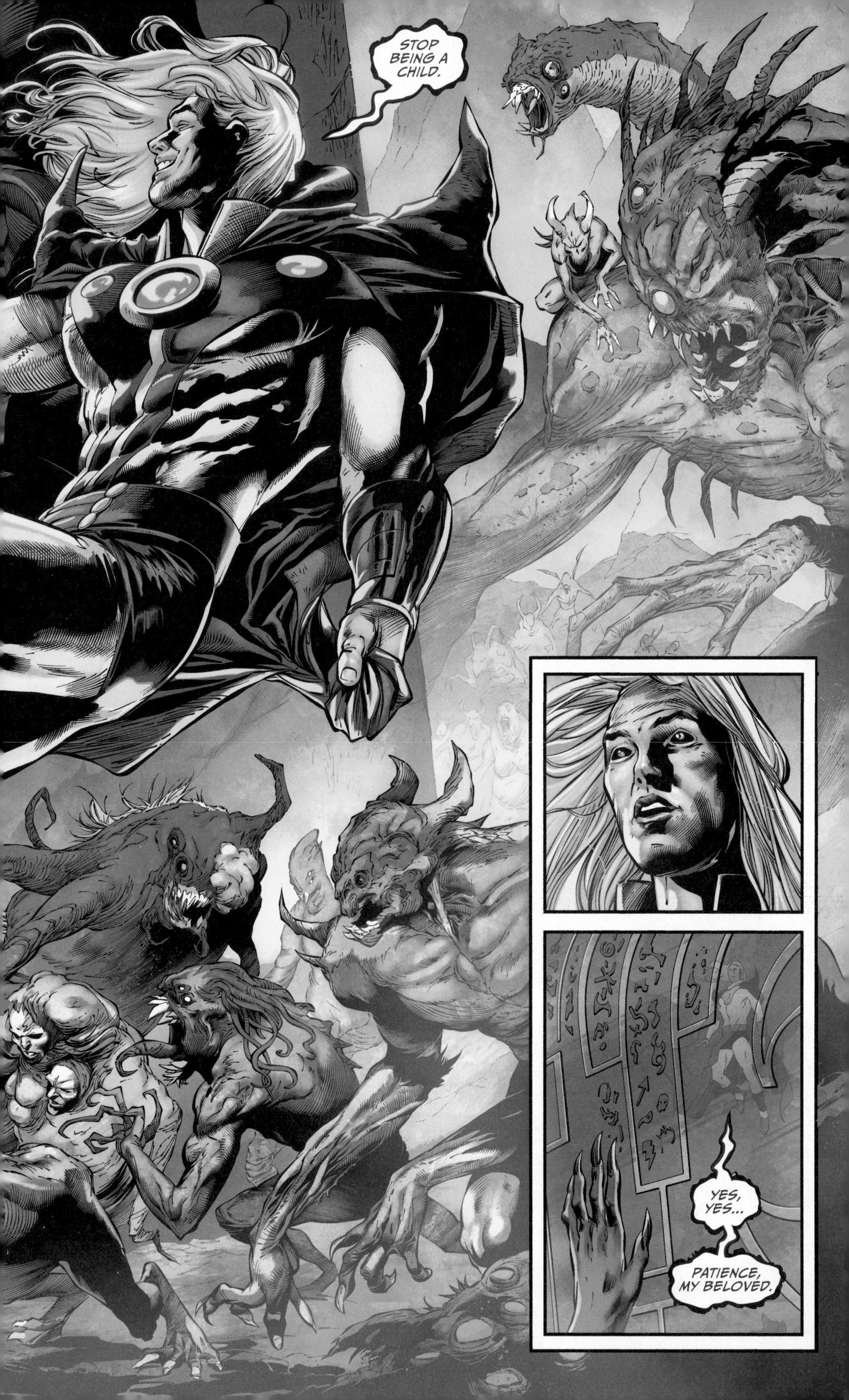
STOP BEING A CHILD.
YES, YES...
PATIENCE, MY BELOVED.

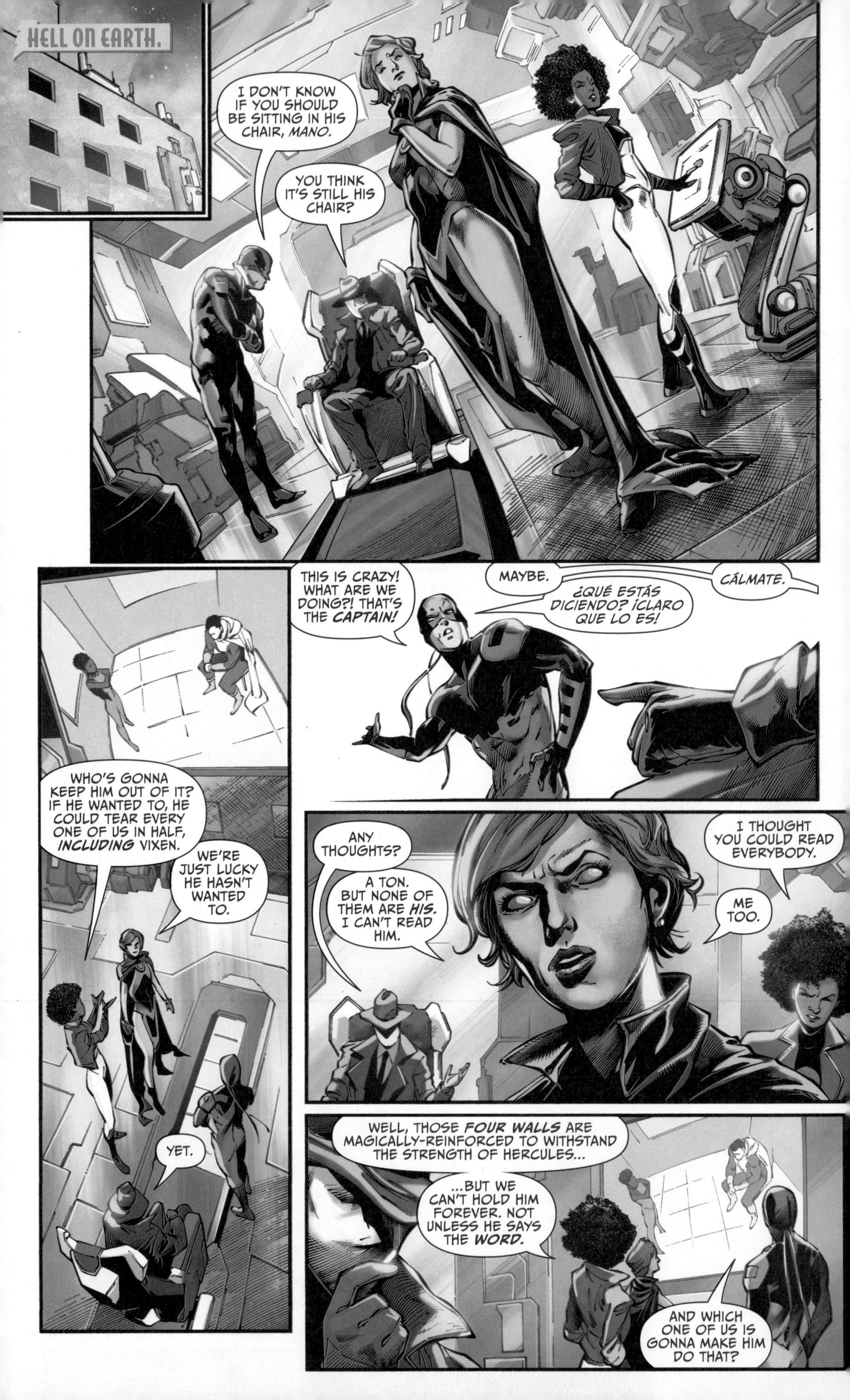
HELL ON EARTH.
I DON'T KNOW IF YOU SHOULD BE SITTING IN HIS CHAIR, *MANO.*
YOU THINK IT'S STILL HIS CHAIR?
THIS IS CRAZY! WHAT ARE WE DOING?! THAT'S THE *CAPTAIN!*
MAYBE.
¿QUÉ ESTÁS DICIENDO? ¡CLARO QUE LO ES!
CÁLMATE.
WHO'S GONNA KEEP HIM OUT OF IT? IF HE WANTED TO, HE COULD TEAR EVERY ONE OF US IN HALF, *INCLUDING* VIXEN.
WE'RE JUST LUCKY HE HASN'T WANTED TO.
YET.
ANY THOUGHTS?
A TON. BUT NONE OF THEM ARE *HIS.* I CAN'T READ HIM.
I THOUGHT YOU COULD READ EVERYBODY.
ME TOO.
WELL, THOSE *FOUR WALLS* ARE MAGICALLY-REINFORCED TO WITHSTAND THE STRENGTH OF HERCULES...
...BUT WE CAN'T HOLD HIM FOREVER. NOT UNLESS HE SAYS THE *WORD.*
AND WHICH ONE OF US IS GONNA MAKE HIM DO THAT?

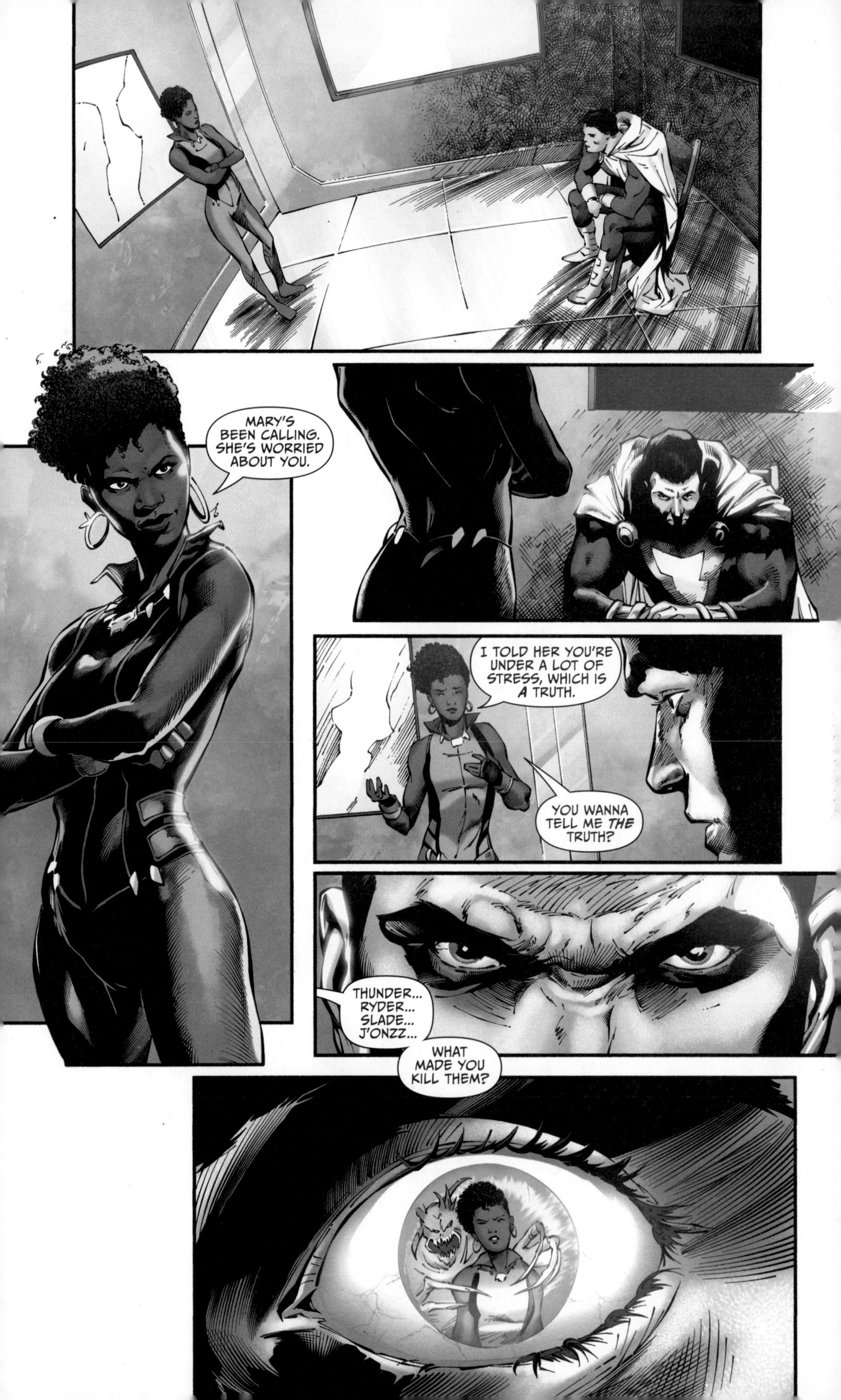
MARY'S BEEN CALLING. SHE'S WORRIED ABOUT YOU.
I TOLD HER YOU'RE UNDER A LOT OF STRESS, WHICH IS *A* TRUTH.
YOU WANNA TELL ME *THE* TRUTH?
THUNDER... RYDER... SLADE... J'ONZZ...
WHAT MADE YOU KILL THEM?

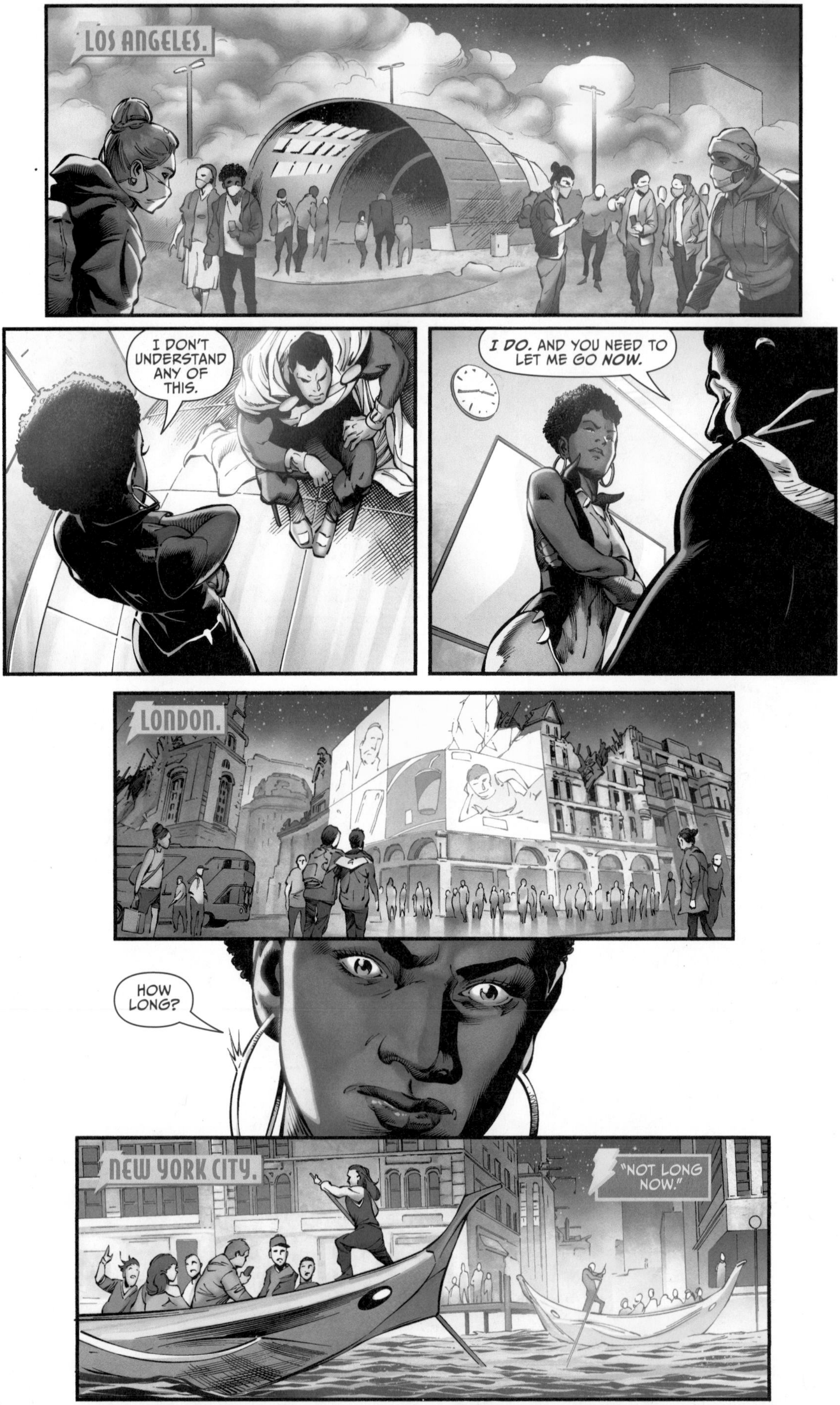
LOS ANGELES.
I DON'T UNDERSTAND ANY OF THIS.
I DO. AND YOU NEED TO LET ME GO NOW.
LONDON.
HOW LONG?
NEW YORK CITY.
"NOT LONG NOW."

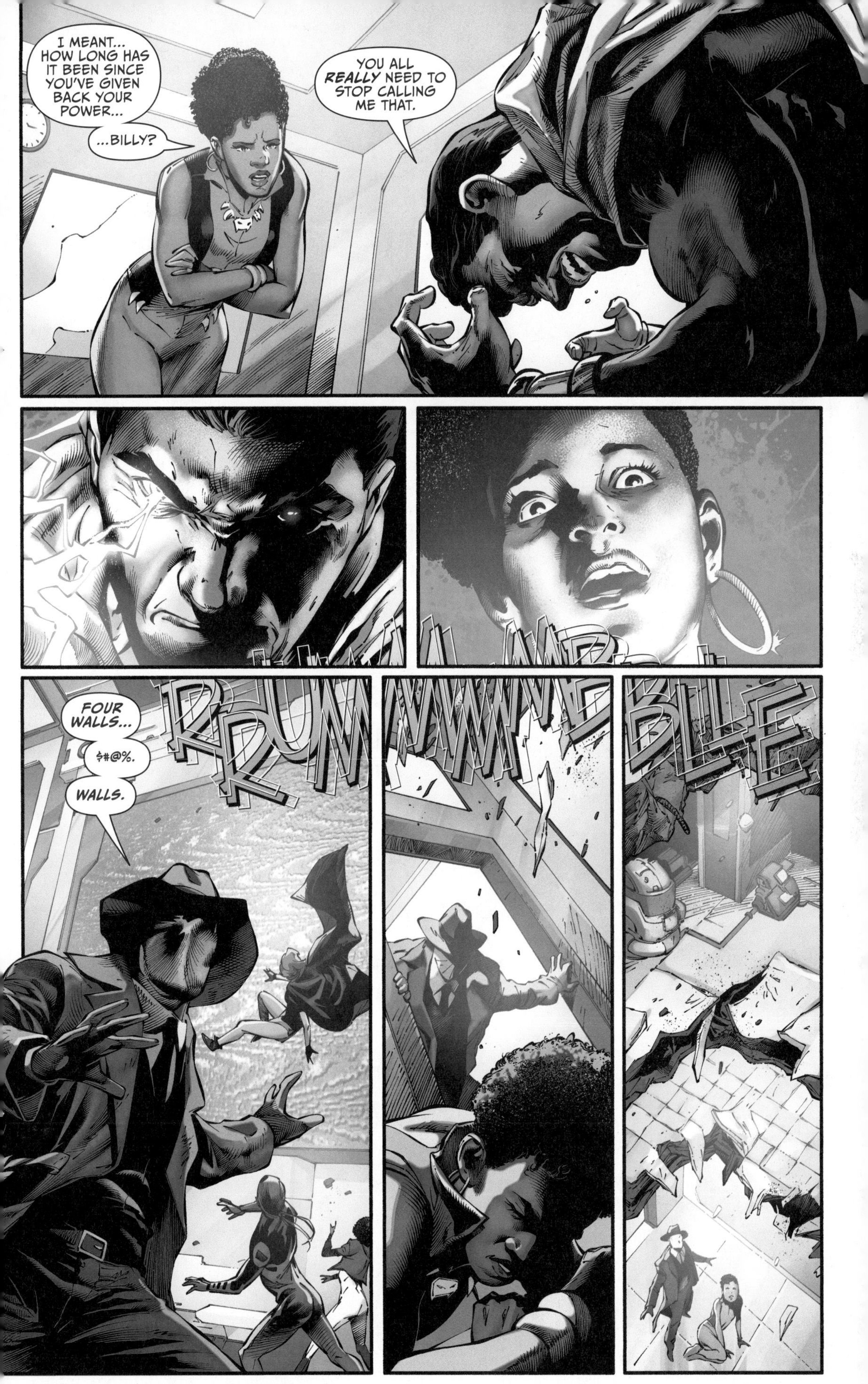
I MEANT... HOW LONG HAS IT BEEN SINCE YOU'VE GIVEN BACK YOUR POWER...
...BILLY?
YOU ALL REALLY NEED TO STOP CALLING ME THAT.
RRUMMMMMBLLE
FOUR WALLS...
$#@%.
WALLS.

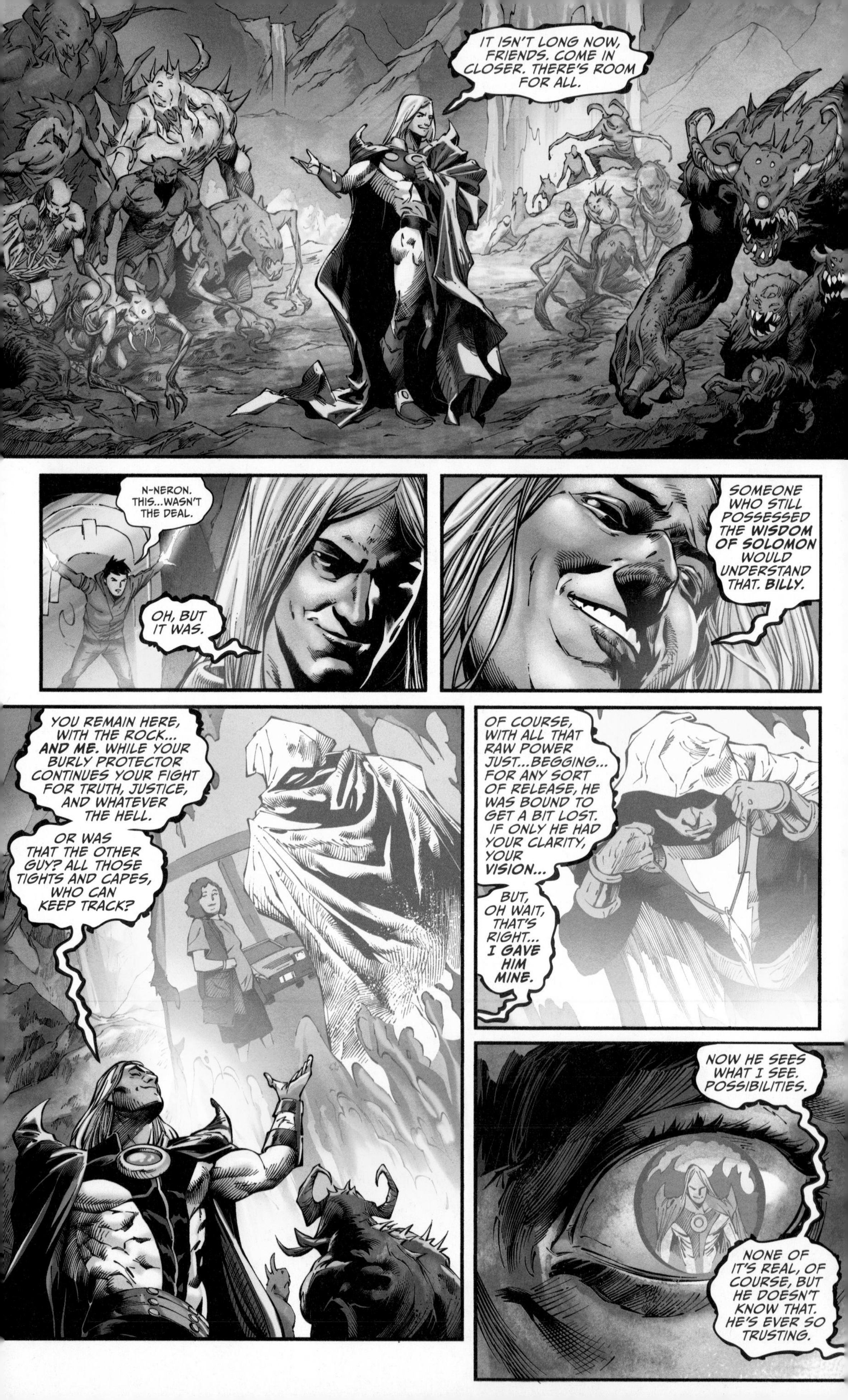
IT ISN'T LONG NOW, FRIENDS. COME IN CLOSER. THERE'S ROOM FOR ALL.
N-NERON. THIS...WASN'T THE DEAL.
OH, BUT IT WAS.
SOMEONE WHO STILL POSSESSED THE WISDOM OF SOLOMON WOULD UNDERSTAND THAT. BILLY.
YOU REMAIN HERE, WITH THE ROCK... AND ME. WHILE YOUR BURLY PROTECTOR CONTINUES YOUR FIGHT FOR TRUTH, JUSTICE, AND WHATEVER THE HELL.
OR WAS THAT THE OTHER GUY? ALL THOSE TIGHTS AND CAPES, WHO CAN KEEP TRACK?
OF COURSE, WITH ALL THAT RAW POWER JUST...BEGGING... FOR ANY SORT OF RELEASE, HE WAS BOUND TO GET A BIT LOST. IF ONLY HE HAD YOUR CLARITY, YOUR VISION...
BUT, OH WAIT, THAT'S RIGHT... I GAVE HIM MINE.
NOW HE SEES WHAT I SEE. POSSIBILITIES.
NONE OF IT'S REAL, OF COURSE, BUT HE DOESN'T KNOW THAT. HE'S EVER SO TRUSTING.

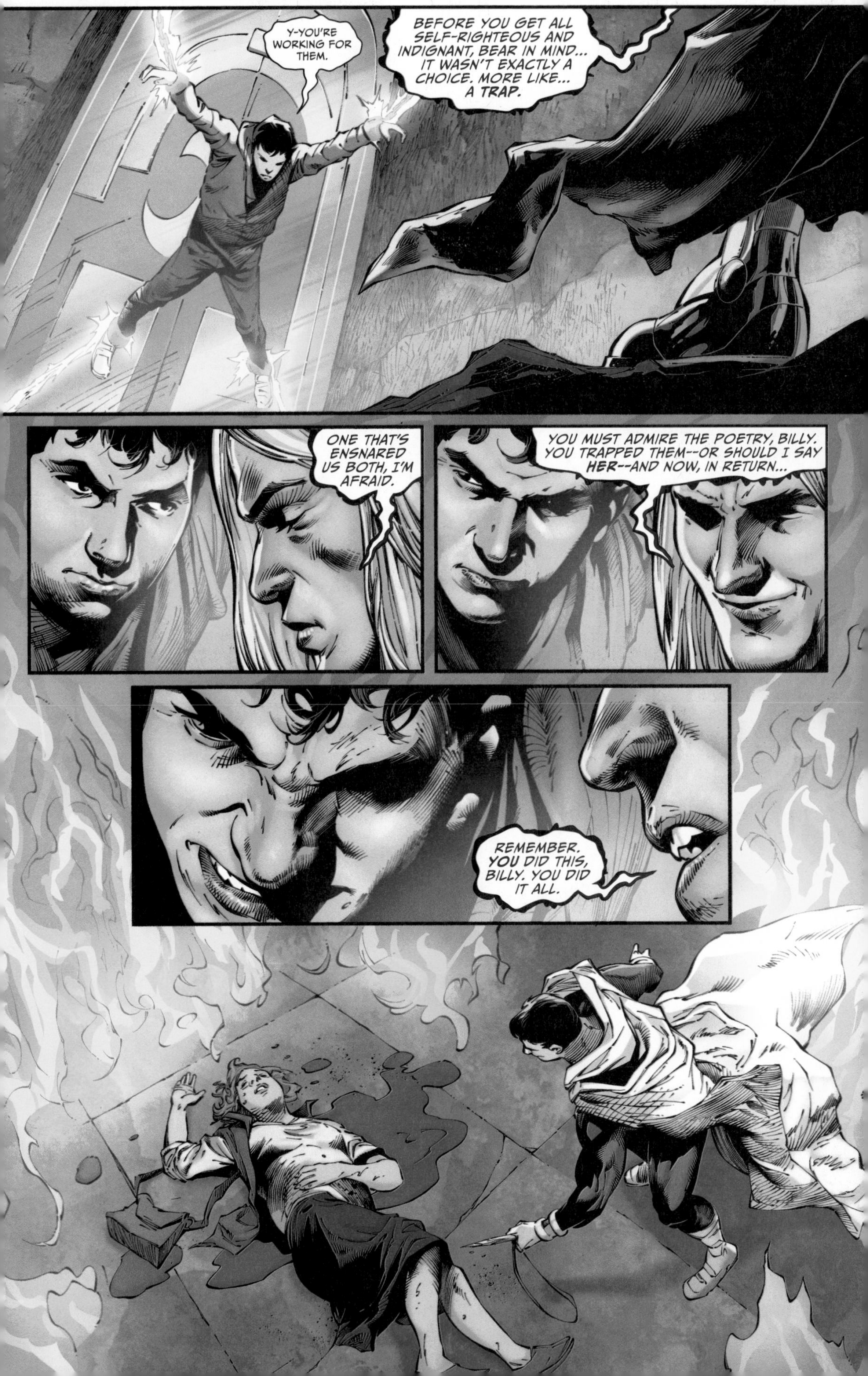
Y-YOU'RE WORKING FOR THEM.
BEFORE YOU GET ALL SELF-RIGHTEOUS AND INDIGNANT, BEAR IN MIND... IT WASN'T EXACTLY A CHOICE. MORE LIKE... A TRAP.
ONE THAT'S ENSNARED US BOTH, I'M AFRAID.
YOU MUST ADMIRE THE POETRY, BILLY. YOU TRAPPED THEM--OR SHOULD I SAY HER--AND NOW, IN RETURN...
REMEMBER. YOU DID THIS, BILLY. YOU DID IT ALL.

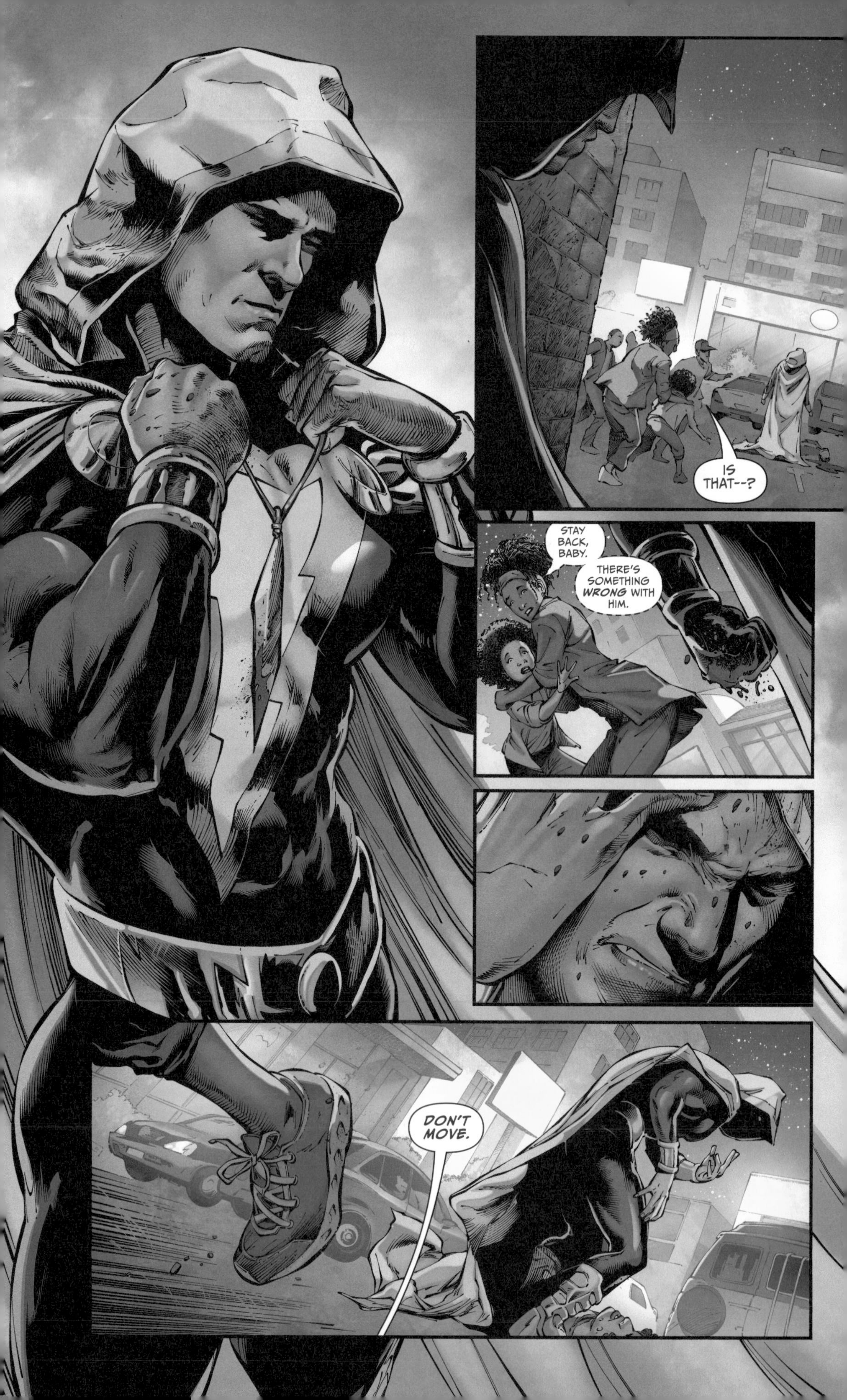
IS THAT--?
STAY BACK, BABY.
THERE'S SOMETHING *WRONG* WITH HIM.
DON'T MOVE.

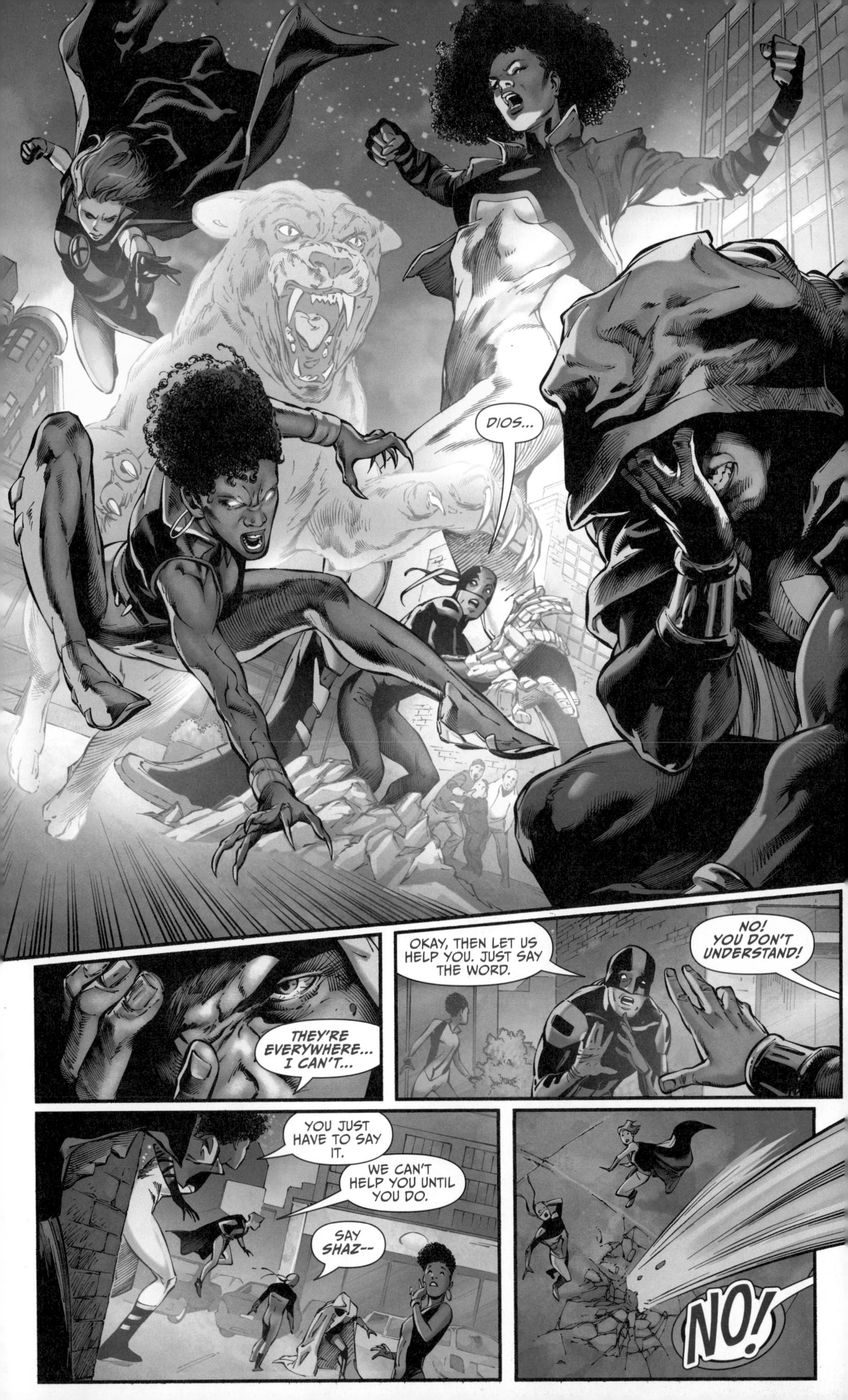
DIOS...
THEY'RE EVERYWHERE... I CAN'T...
OKAY, THEN LET US HELP YOU. JUST SAY THE WORD.
NO! YOU DON'T UNDERSTAND!
YOU JUST HAVE TO SAY IT.
WE CAN'T HELP YOU UNTIL YOU DO.
SAY SHAZ--
NO!

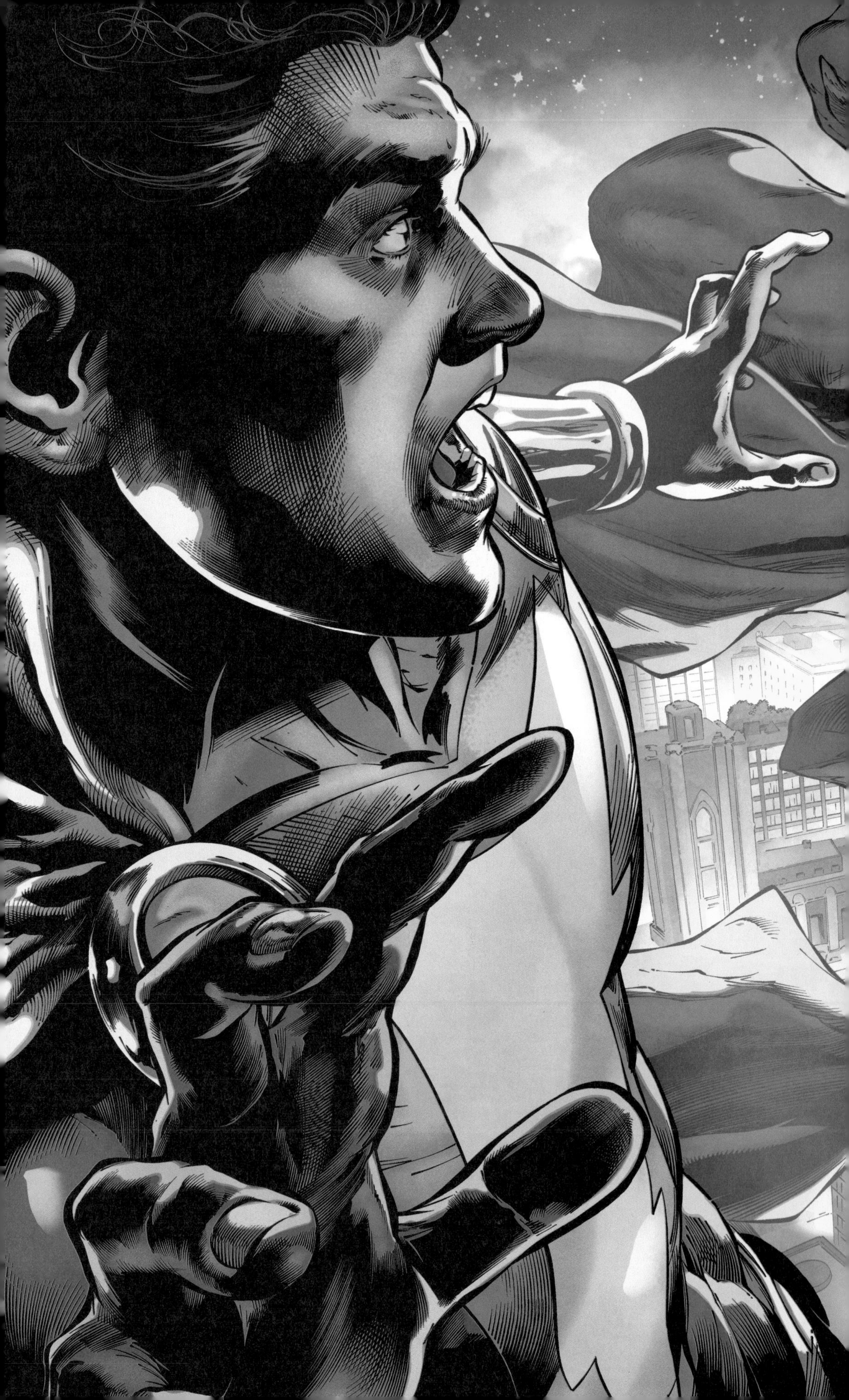

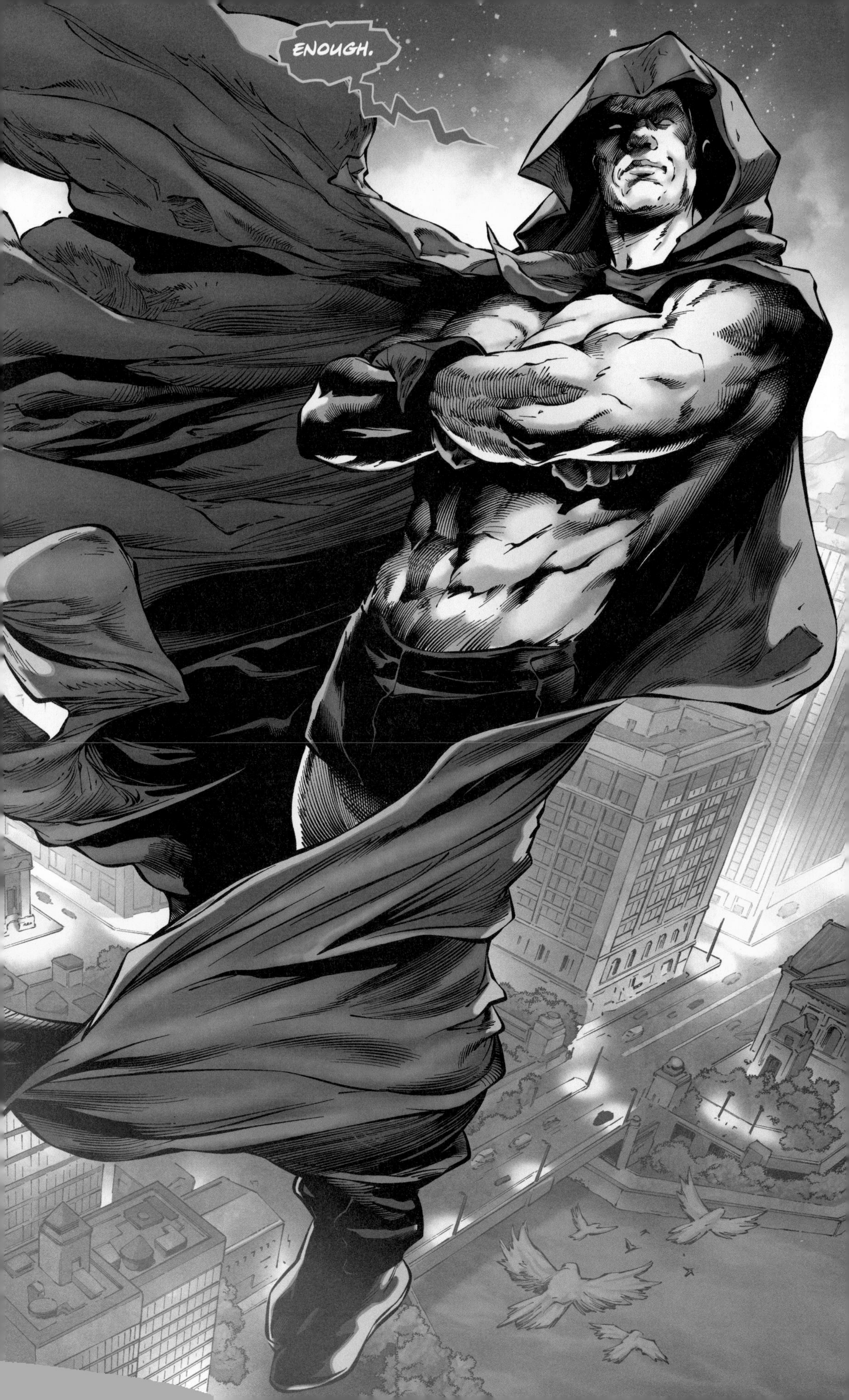
ENOUGH.

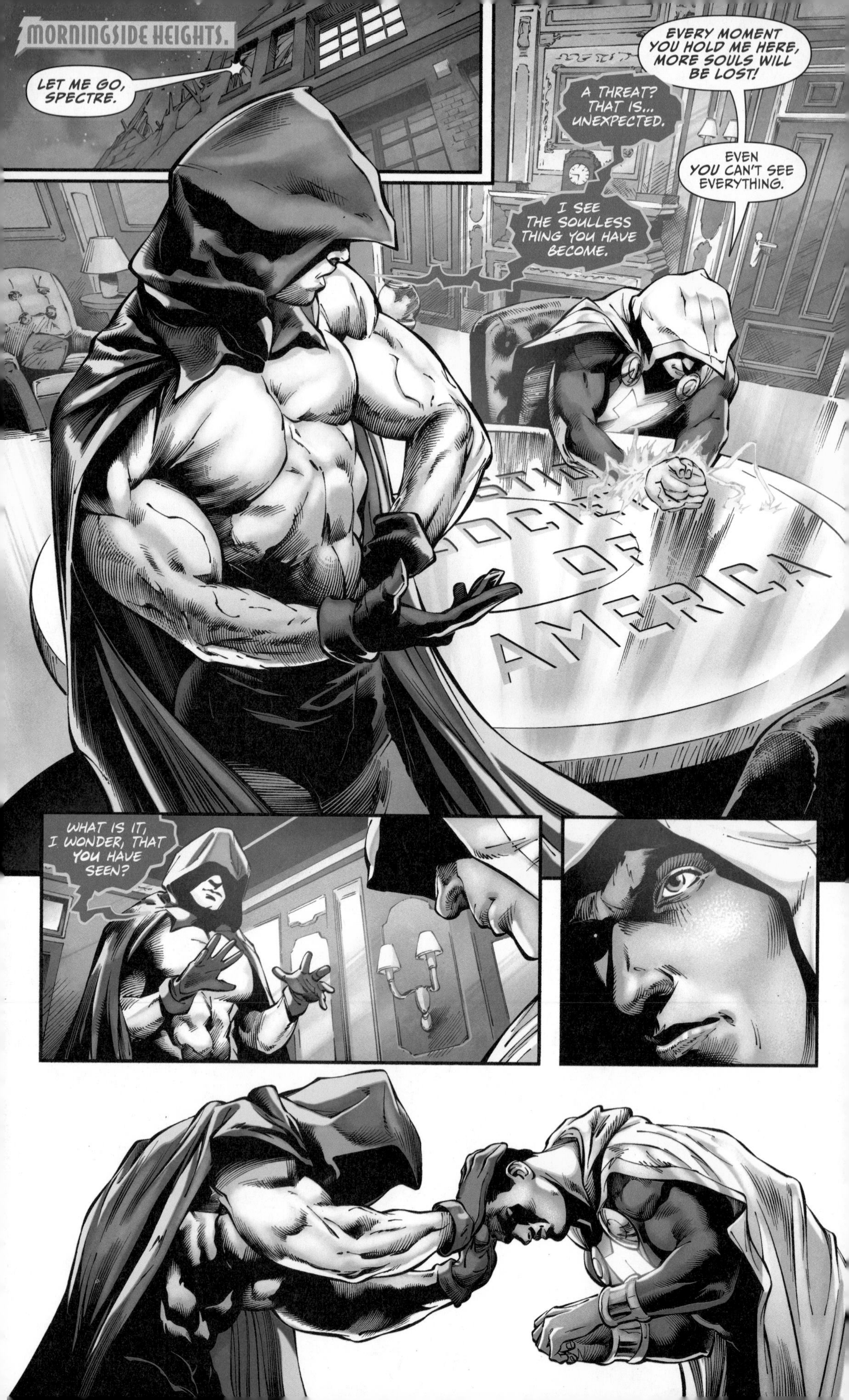
MORNINGSIDE HEIGHTS.
LET ME GO, SPECTRE.
EVERY MOMENT YOU HOLD ME HERE, MORE SOULS WILL BE LOST!
A THREAT? THAT IS... UNEXPECTED.
EVEN YOU CAN'T SEE EVERYTHING.
I SEE THE SOULLESS THING YOU HAVE BECOME.
AMERICA
WHAT IS IT, I WONDER, THAT YOU HAVE SEEN?

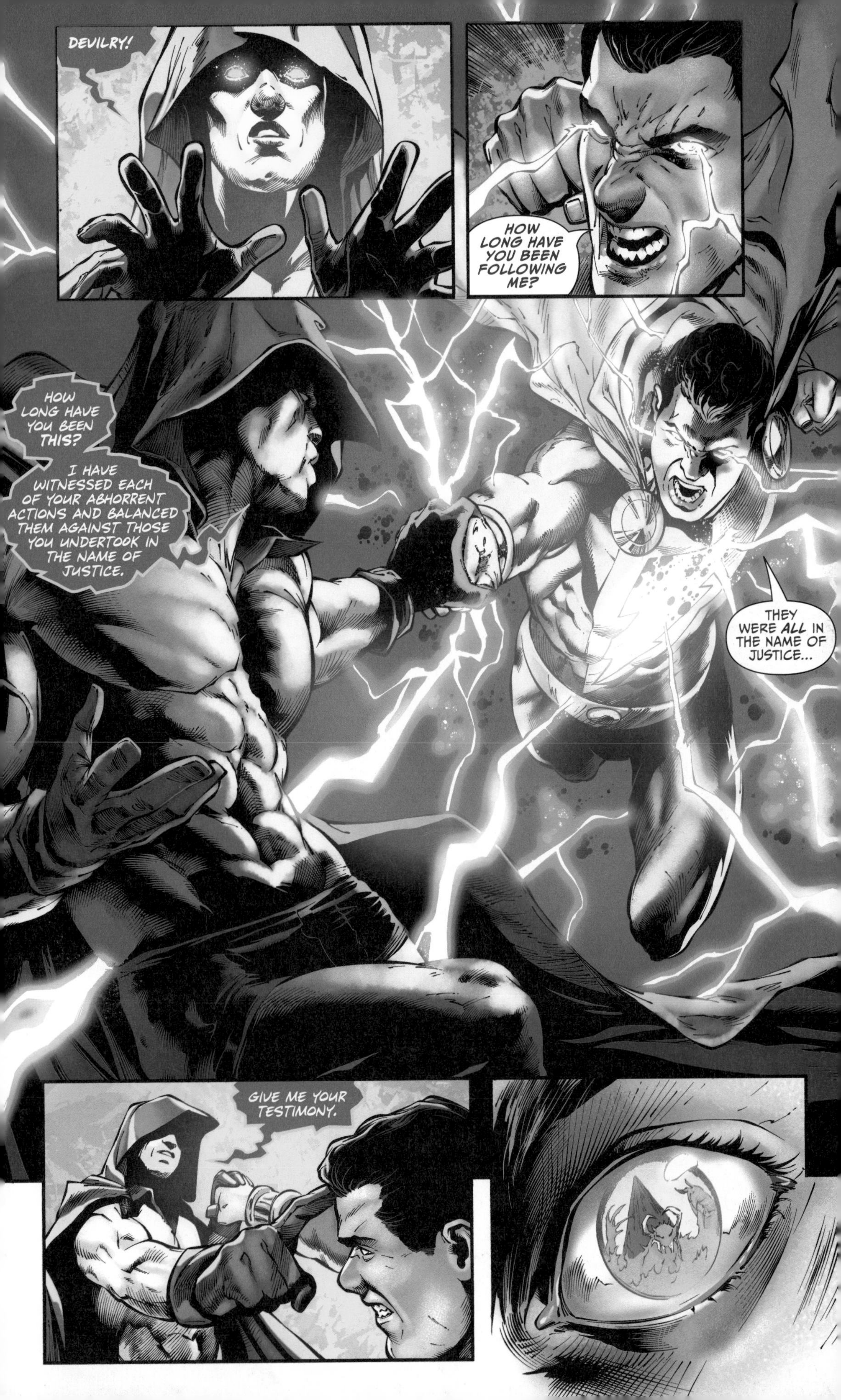

DEVILRY!
HOW LONG HAVE YOU BEEN FOLLOWING ME?
HOW LONG HAVE YOU BEEN THIS?
I HAVE WITNESSED EACH OF YOUR ABHORRENT ACTIONS AND BALANCED THEM AGAINST THOSE YOU UNDERTOOK IN THE NAME OF JUSTICE.
THEY WERE ALL IN THE NAME OF JUSTICE...
GIVE ME YOUR TESTIMONY.

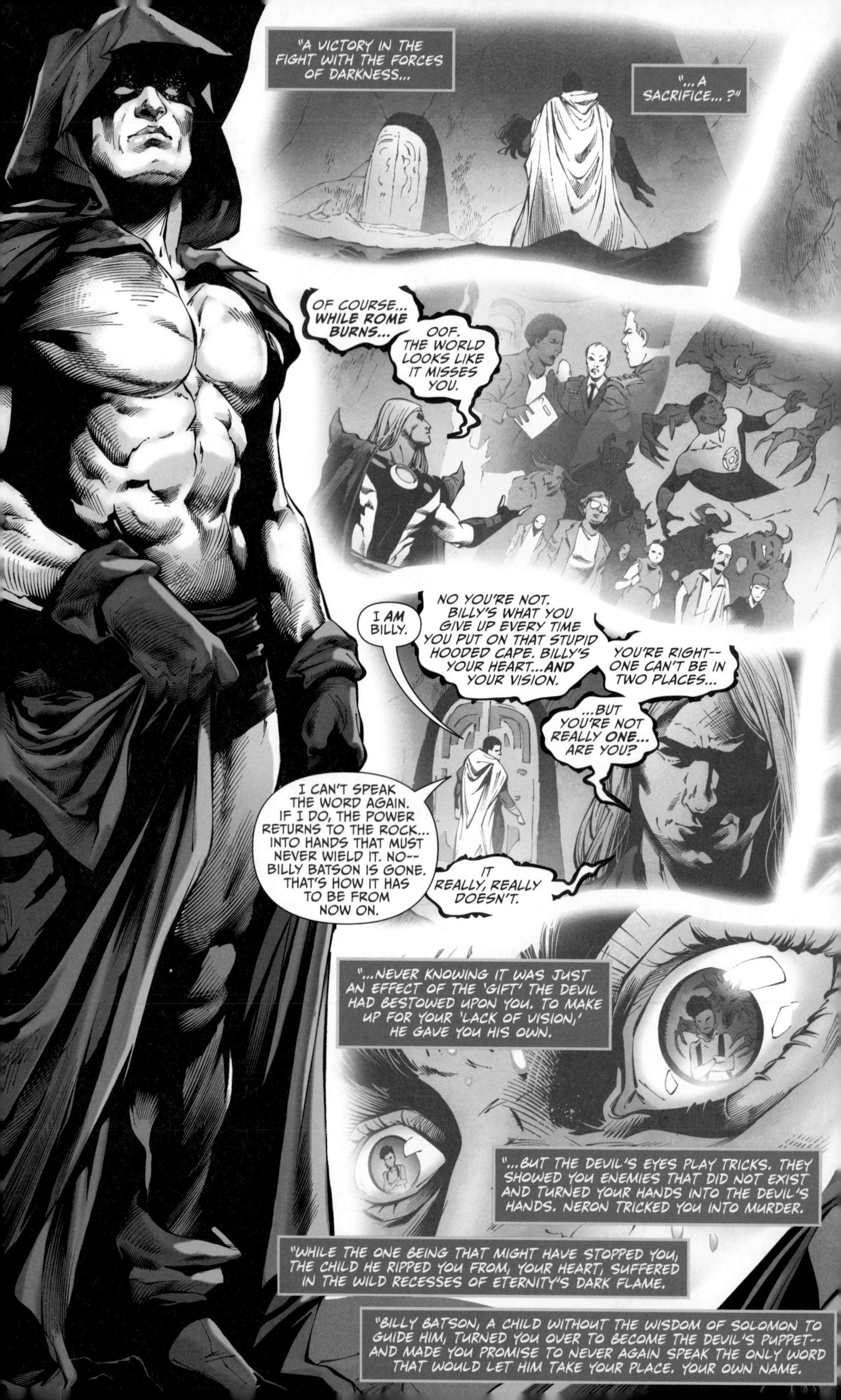
"A VICTORY IN THE FIGHT WITH THE FORCES OF DARKNESS...
"...A SACRIFICE...?"
OF COURSE... WHILE ROME BURNS...
OOF. THE WORLD LOOKS LIKE IT MISSES YOU.
I AM BILLY.
NO YOU'RE NOT. BILLY'S WHAT YOU GIVE UP EVERY TIME YOU PUT ON THAT STUPID HOODED CAPE. BILLY'S YOUR HEART...AND YOUR VISION.
YOU'RE RIGHT-- ONE CAN'T BE IN TWO PLACES...
...BUT YOU'RE NOT REALLY ONE... ARE YOU?
I CAN'T SPEAK THE WORD AGAIN. IF I DO, THE POWER RETURNS TO THE ROCK... INTO HANDS THAT MUST NEVER WIELD IT. NO-- BILLY BATSON IS GONE. THAT'S HOW IT HAS TO BE FROM NOW ON.
IT REALLY, REALLY DOESN'T.
"...NEVER KNOWING IT WAS JUST AN EFFECT OF THE 'GIFT' THE DEVIL HAD BESTOWED UPON YOU. TO MAKE UP FOR YOUR 'LACK OF VISION,' HE GAVE YOU HIS OWN.
"...BUT THE DEVIL'S EYES PLAY TRICKS. THEY SHOWED YOU ENEMIES THAT DID NOT EXIST AND TURNED YOUR HANDS INTO THE DEVIL'S HANDS. NERON TRICKED YOU INTO MURDER.
"WHILE THE ONE BEING THAT MIGHT HAVE STOPPED YOU, THE CHILD HE RIPPED YOU FROM, YOUR HEART, SUFFERED IN THE WILD RECESSES OF ETERNITY'S DARK FLAME.
"BILLY BATSON, A CHILD WITHOUT THE WISDOM OF SOLOMON TO GUIDE HIM, TURNED YOU OVER TO BECOME THE DEVIL'S PUPPET-- AND MADE YOU PROMISE TO NEVER AGAIN SPEAK THE ONLY WORD THAT WOULD LET HIM TAKE YOUR PLACE. YOUR OWN NAME.

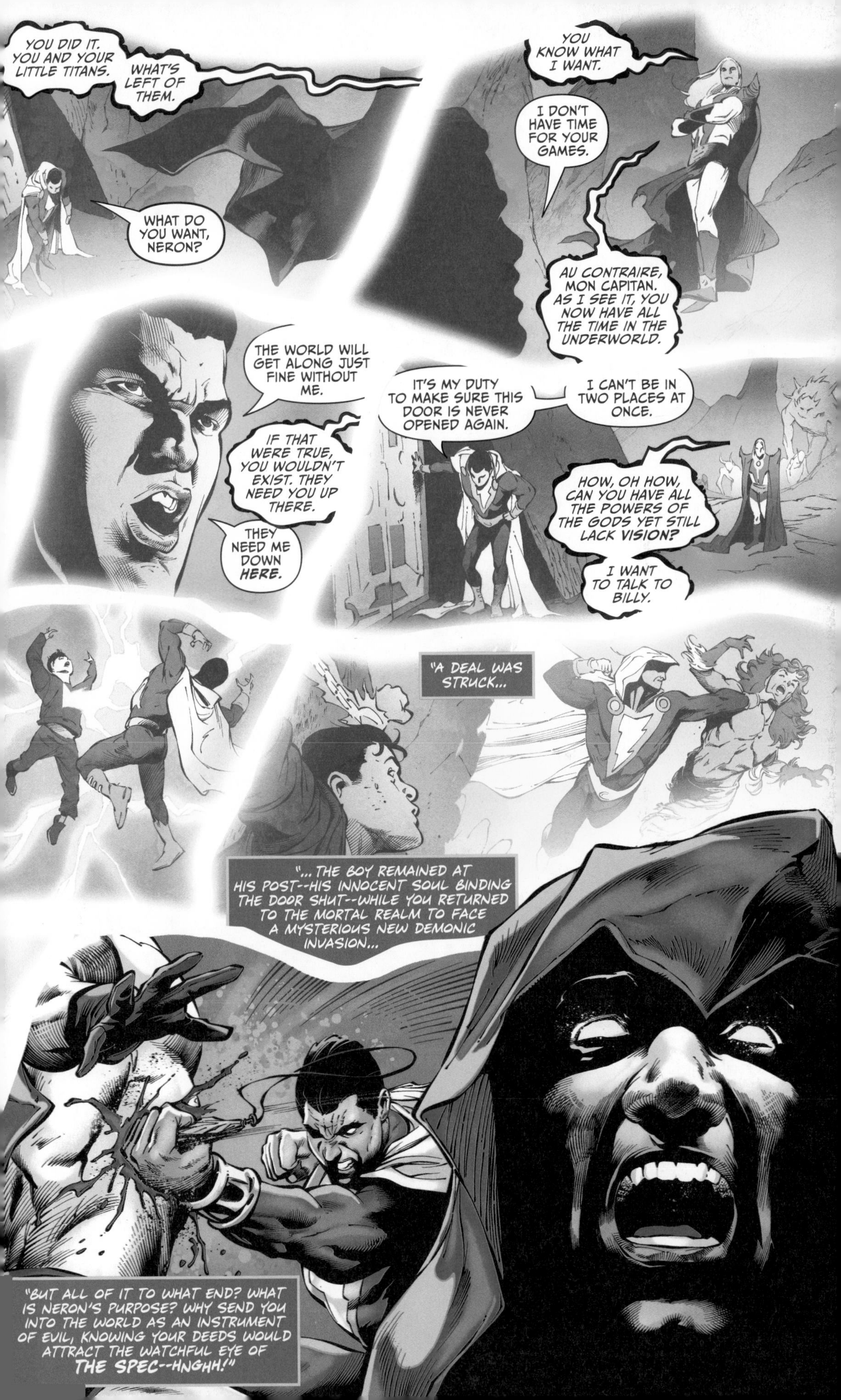
YOU DID IT. YOU AND YOUR LITTLE TITANS.
WHAT'S LEFT OF THEM.
WHAT DO YOU WANT, NERON?
YOU KNOW WHAT I WANT.
I DON'T HAVE TIME FOR YOUR GAMES.
AU CONTRAIRE, MON CAPITAN. AS I SEE IT, YOU NOW HAVE ALL THE TIME IN THE UNDERWORLD.
THE WORLD WILL GET ALONG JUST FINE WITHOUT ME.
IF THAT WERE TRUE, YOU WOULDN'T EXIST. THEY NEED YOU UP THERE.
THEY NEED ME DOWN HERE.
IT'S MY DUTY TO MAKE SURE THIS DOOR IS NEVER OPENED AGAIN.
I CAN'T BE IN TWO PLACES AT ONCE.
HOW, OH HOW, CAN YOU HAVE ALL THE POWERS OF THE GODS YET STILL LACK VISION?
I WANT TO TALK TO BILLY.
"A DEAL WAS STRUCK...
"...THE BOY REMAINED AT HIS POST--HIS INNOCENT SOUL BINDING THE DOOR SHUT--WHILE YOU RETURNED TO THE MORTAL REALM TO FACE A MYSTERIOUS NEW DEMONIC INVASION...
"BUT ALL OF IT TO WHAT END? WHAT IS NERON'S PURPOSE? WHY SEND YOU INTO THE WORLD AS AN INSTRUMENT OF EVIL, KNOWING YOUR DEEDS WOULD ATTRACT THE WATCHFUL EYE OF THE SPEC--HNGHH!"

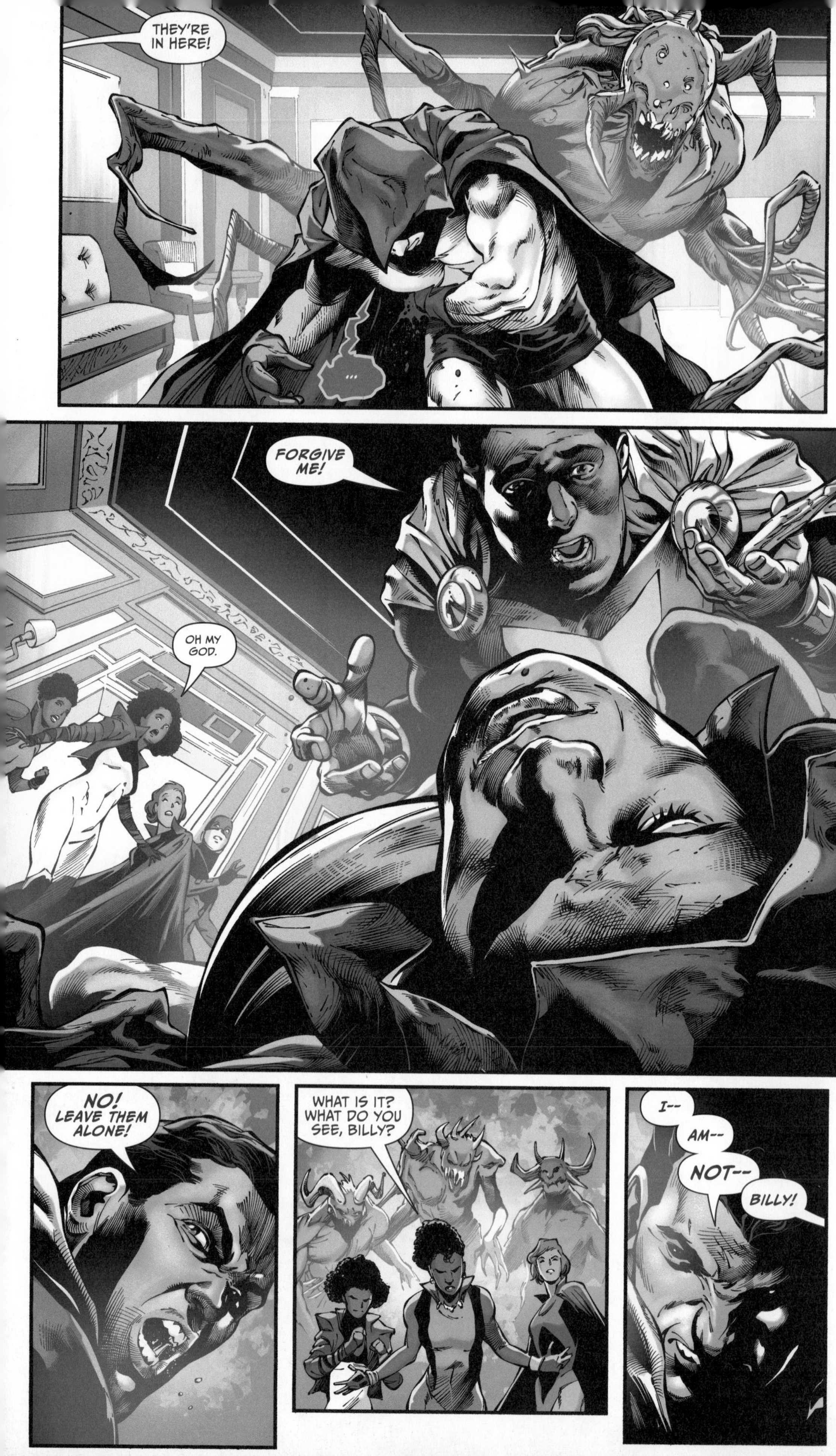

THEY'RE IN HERE!
...
FORGIVE ME!
OH MY GOD.
NO! LEAVE THEM ALONE!
WHAT IS IT? WHAT DO YOU SEE, BILLY?
I--
AM--
NOT--
BILLY!

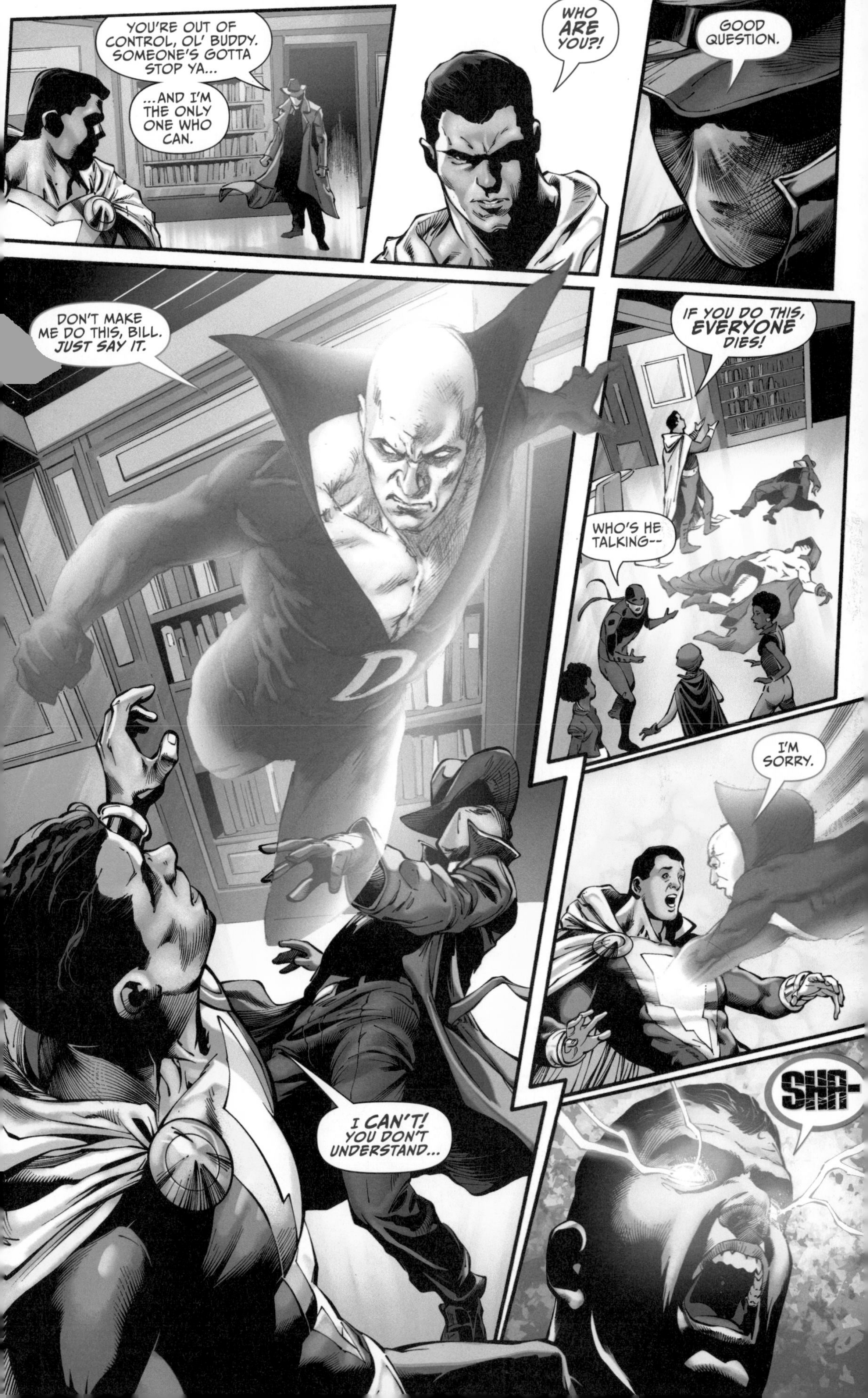
YOU'RE OUT OF CONTROL, OL' BUDDY. SOMEONE'S GOTTA STOP YA...
...AND I'M THE ONLY ONE WHO CAN.
WHO ARE YOU?!
GOOD QUESTION.
DON'T MAKE ME DO THIS, BILL. JUST SAY IT.
I CAN'T! YOU DON'T UNDERSTAND...
IF YOU DO THIS, EVERYONE DIES!
WHO'S HE TALKING--
I'M SORRY.
SHA-

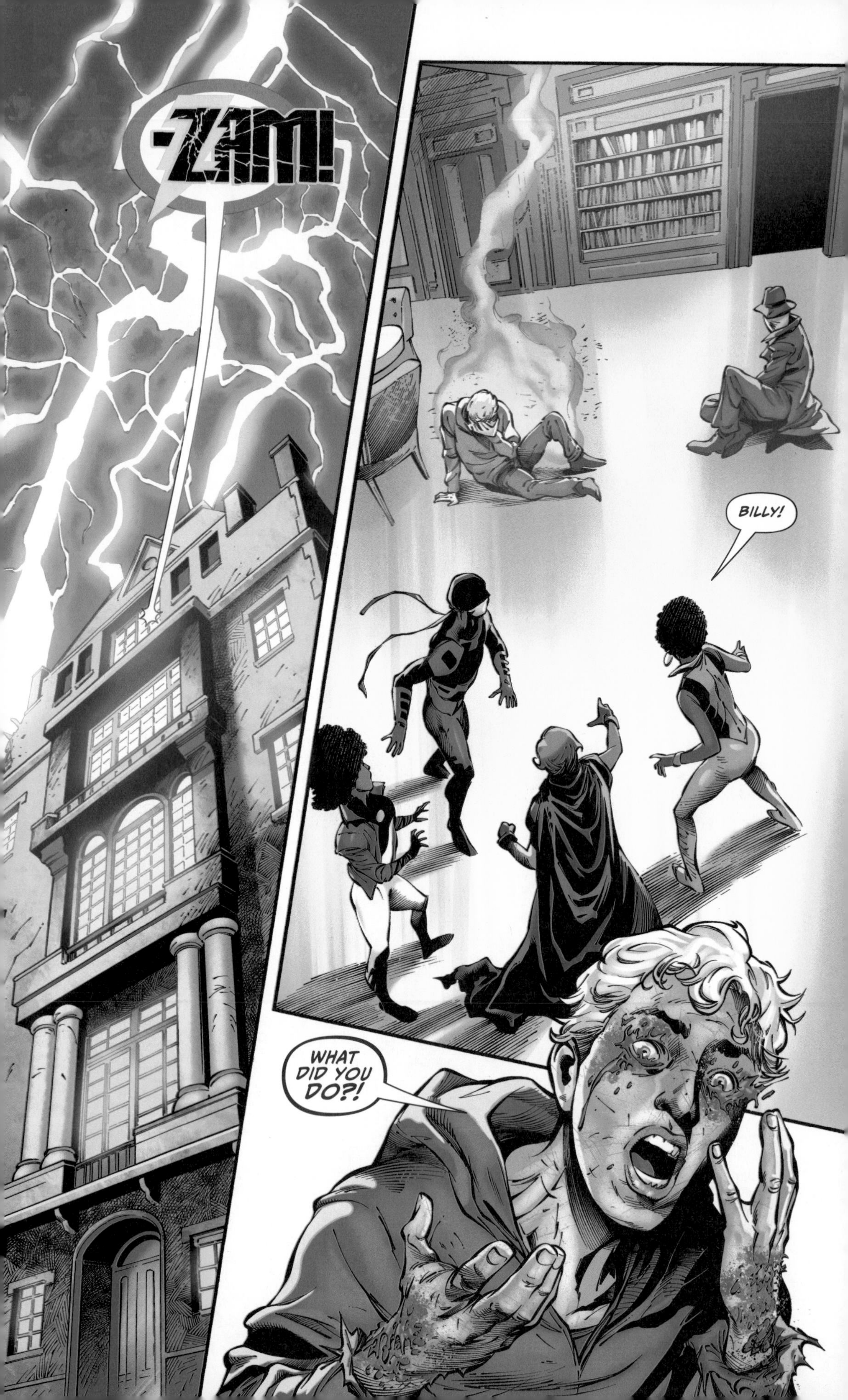
-ZAM!
BILLY!
WHAT DID YOU DO?!

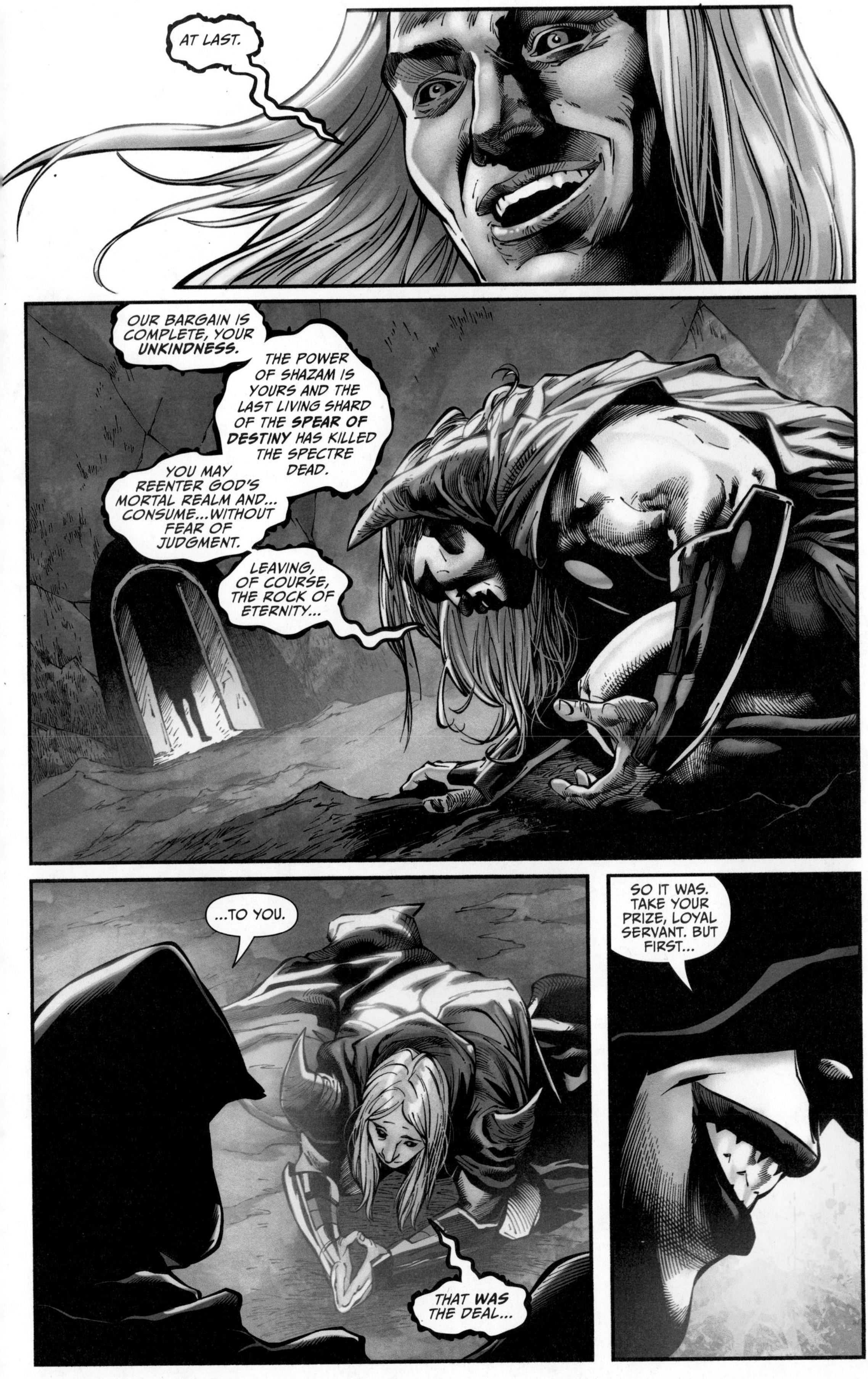
AT LAST.
OUR BARGAIN IS COMPLETE, YOUR UNKINDNESS.
THE POWER OF SHAZAM IS YOURS AND THE LAST LIVING SHARD OF THE SPEAR OF DESTINY HAS KILLED THE SPECTRE DEAD.
YOU MAY REENTER GOD'S MORTAL REALM AND... CONSUME...WITHOUT FEAR OF JUDGMENT.
LEAVING, OF COURSE, THE ROCK OF ETERNITY...
...TO YOU.
THAT WAS THE DEAL...
SO IT WAS. TAKE YOUR PRIZE, LOYAL SERVANT. BUT FIRST...

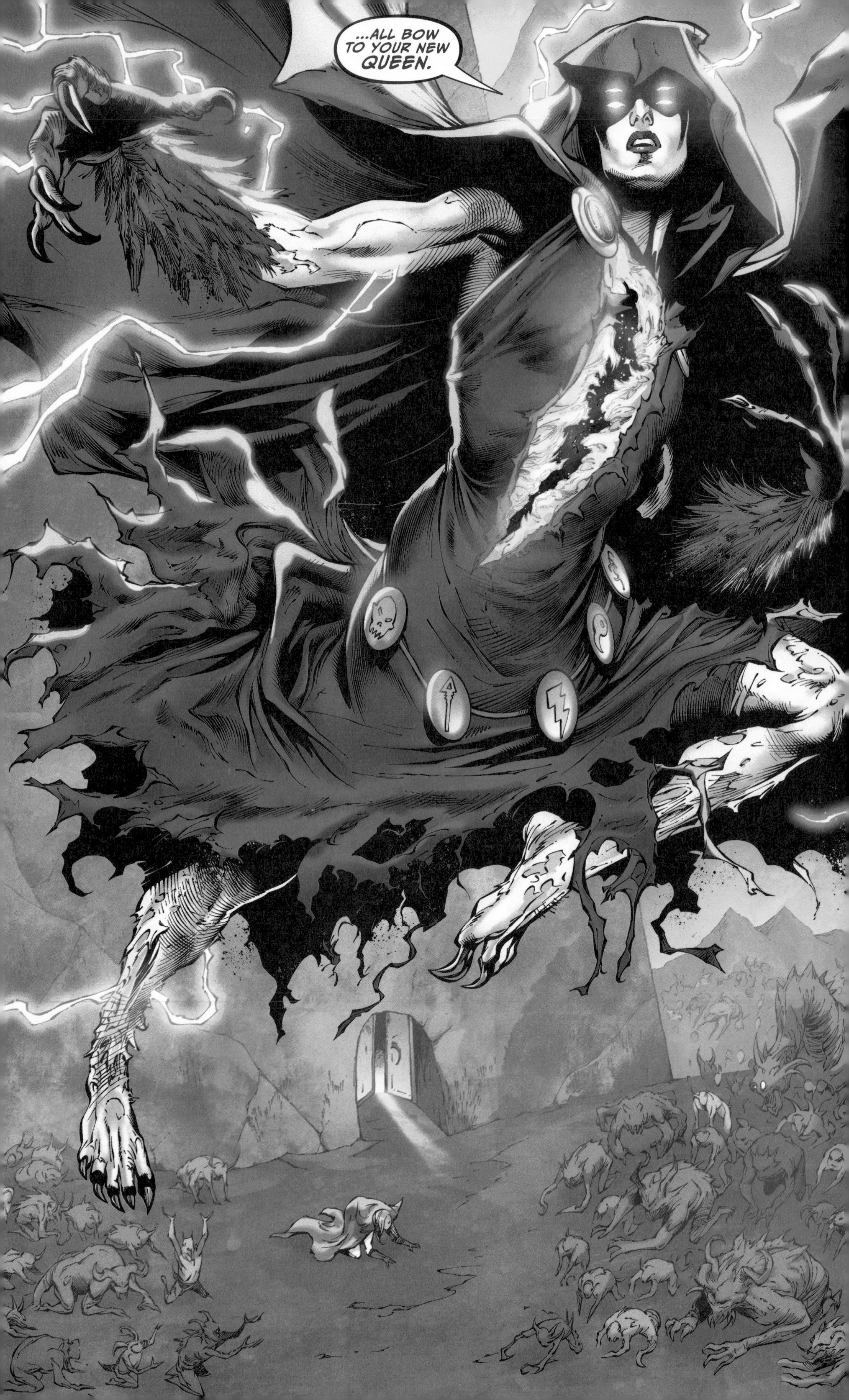
...ALL BOW TO YOUR NEW QUEEN.

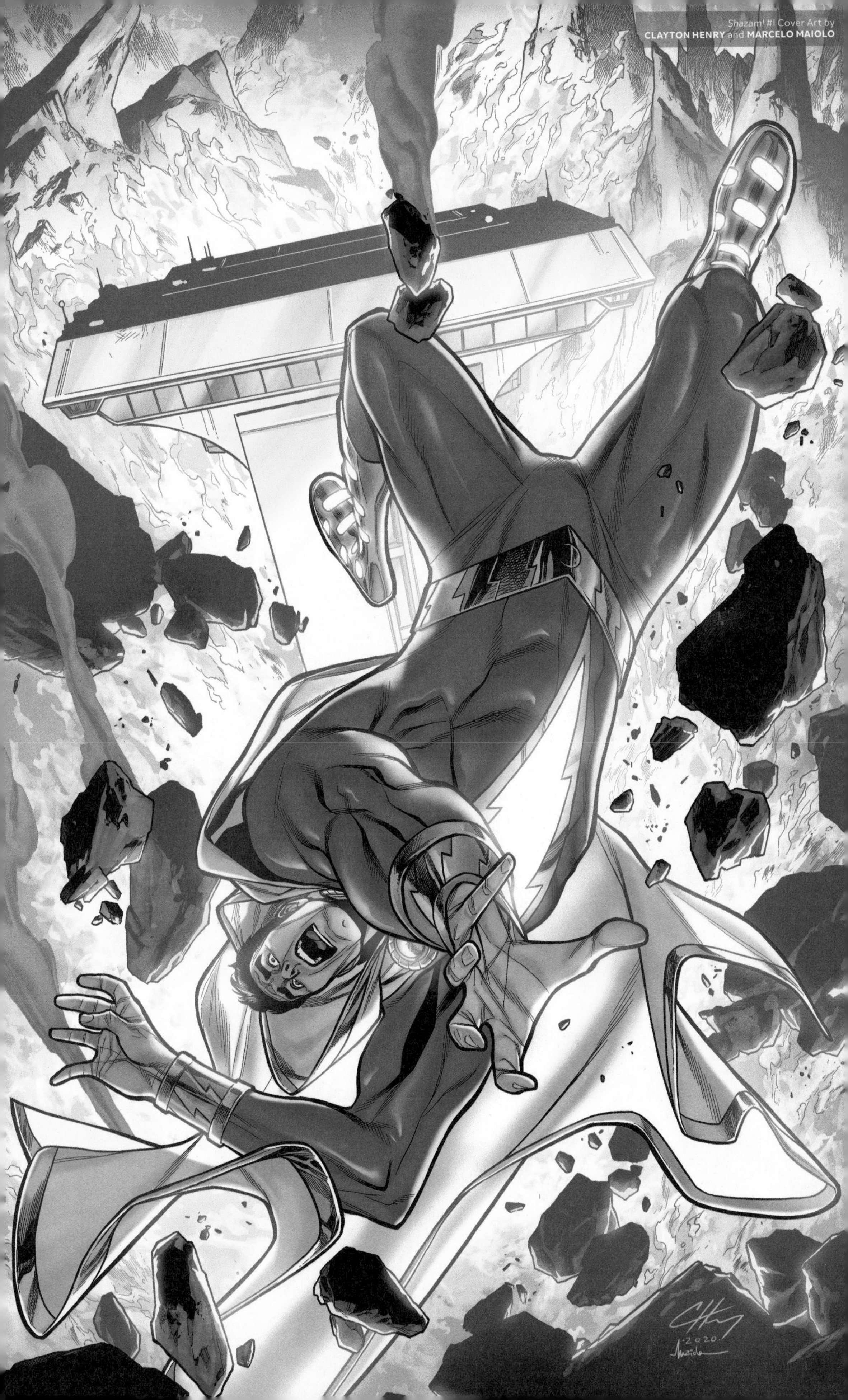

Shazam! #1 Cover Art by
CLAYTON HENRY and **MARCELO MAIOLO**

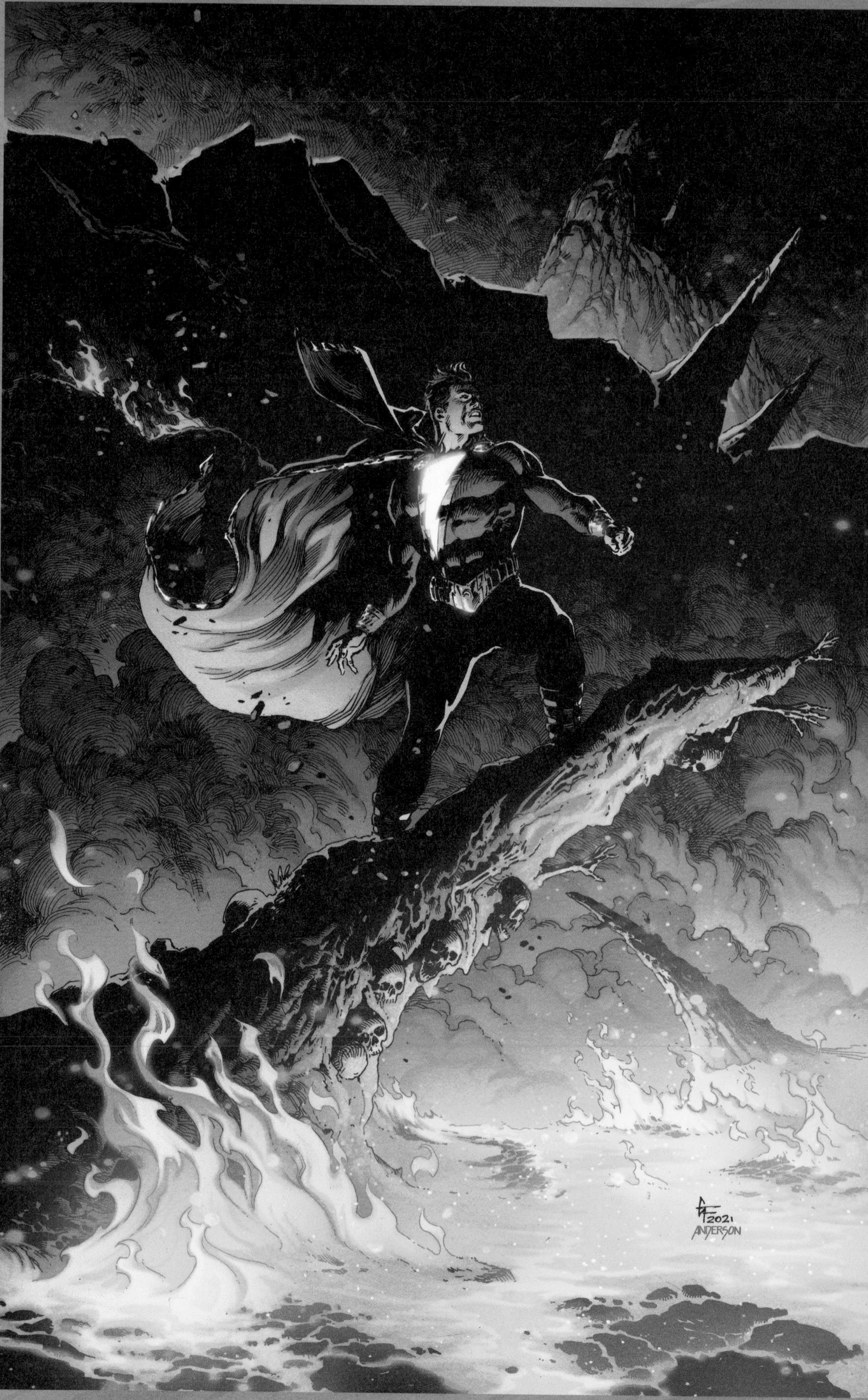
GF 2021
ANDERSON

Shazam! #1 Variant Cover Art by **GARY FRANK** and **BRAD ANDERSON**

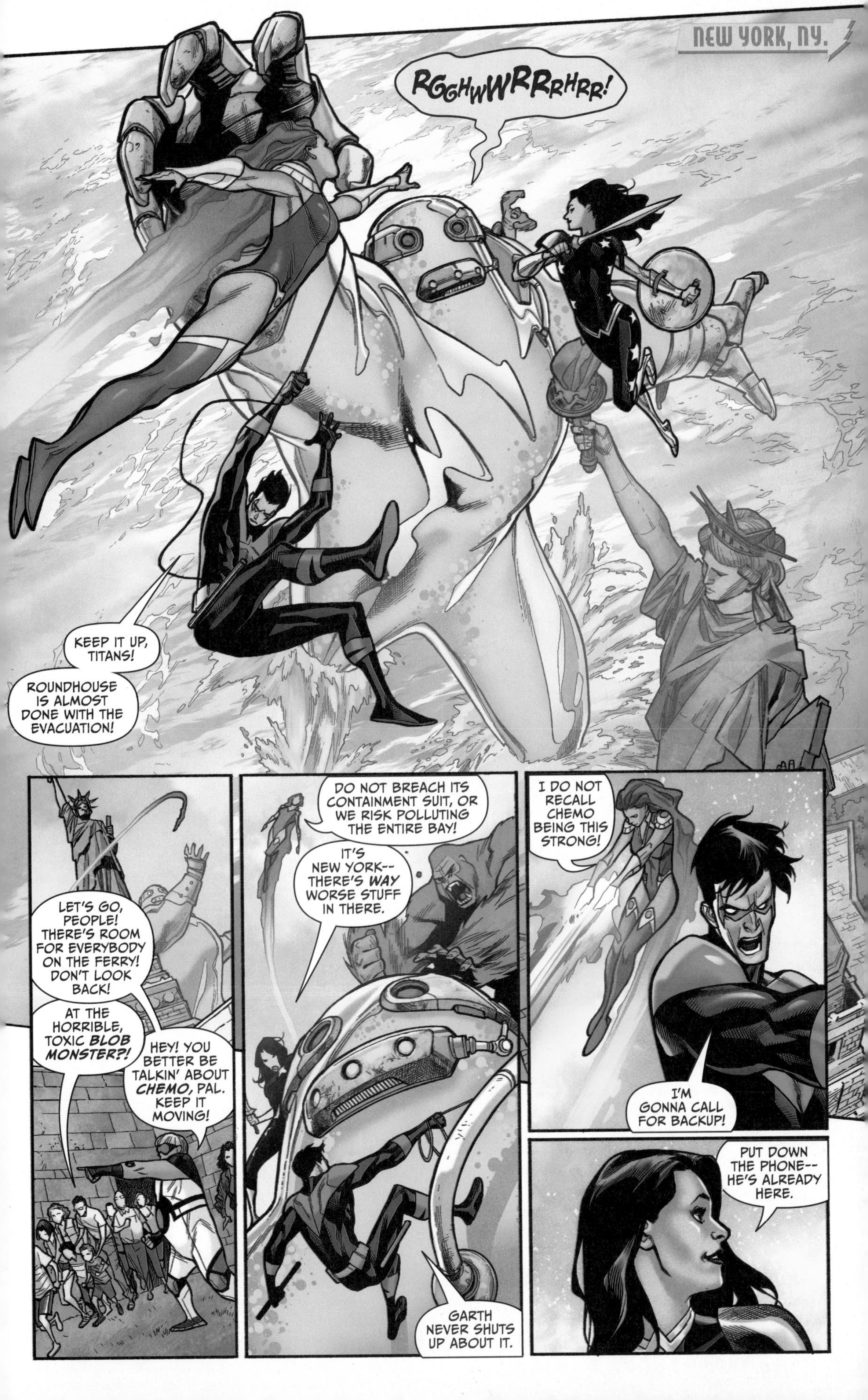
NEW YORK, NY.
RGGHWWRRRRHRR!
KEEP IT UP, TITANS!
ROUNDHOUSE IS ALMOST DONE WITH THE EVACUATION!
LET'S GO, PEOPLE! THERE'S ROOM FOR EVERYBODY ON THE FERRY! DON'T LOOK BACK!
AT THE HORRIBLE, TOXIC BLOB MONSTER?!
HEY! YOU BETTER BE TALKIN' ABOUT CHEMO, PAL. KEEP IT MOVING!
DO NOT BREACH ITS CONTAINMENT SUIT, OR WE RISK POLLUTING THE ENTIRE BAY!
IT'S NEW YORK-- THERE'S WAY WORSE STUFF IN THERE.
GARTH NEVER SHUTS UP ABOUT IT.
I DO NOT RECALL CHEMO BEING THIS STRONG!
I'M GONNA CALL FOR BACKUP!
PUT DOWN THE PHONE-- HE'S ALREADY HERE.

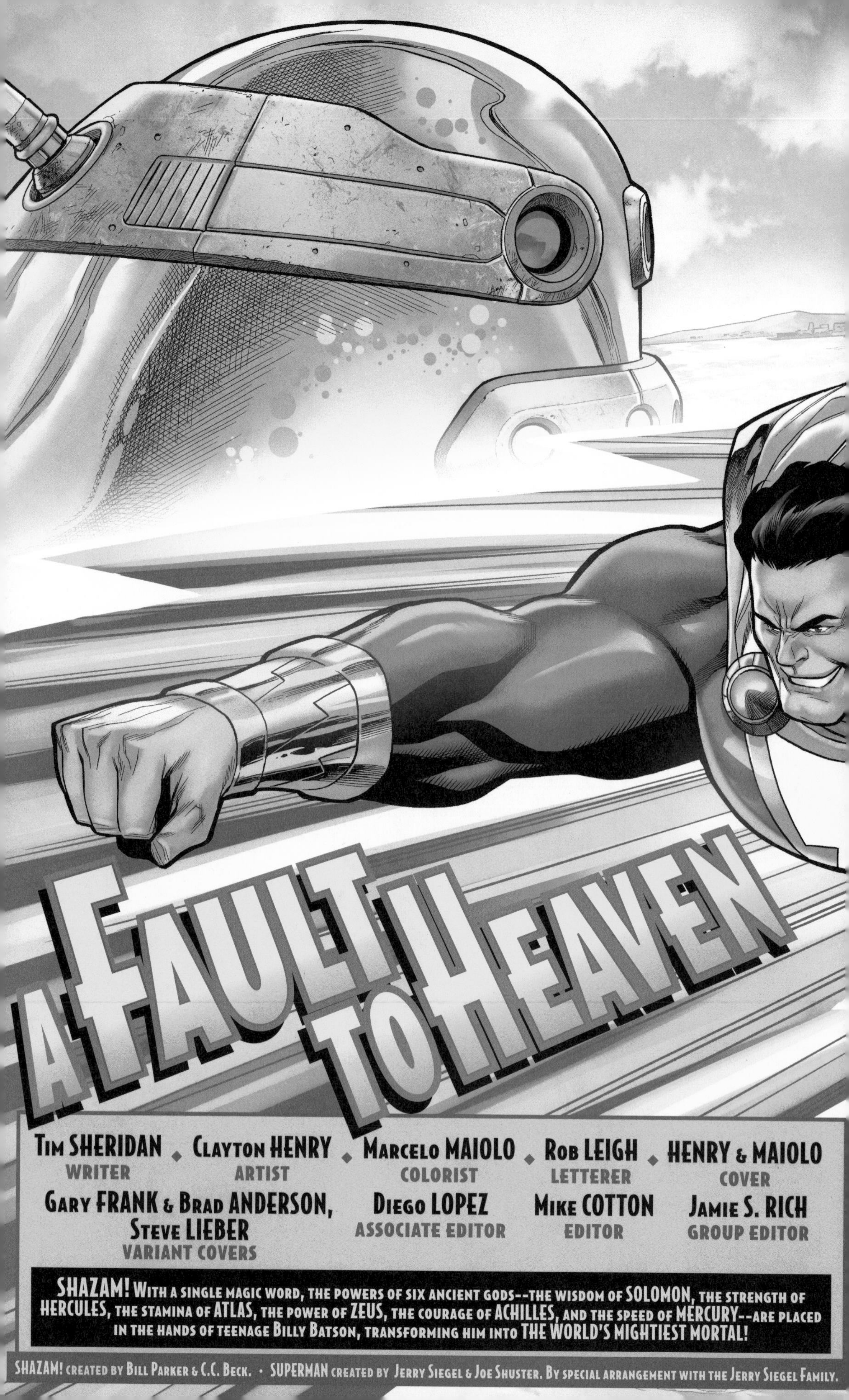
A FAULT TO HEAVEN

TIM SHERIDAN — WRITER
CLAYTON HENRY — ARTIST
MARCELO MAIOLO — COLORIST
ROB LEIGH — LETTERER
HENRY & MAIOLO — COVER

GARY FRANK & BRAD ANDERSON, STEVE LIEBER — VARIANT COVERS
DIEGO LOPEZ — ASSOCIATE EDITOR
MIKE COTTON — EDITOR
JAMIE S. RICH — GROUP EDITOR

SHAZAM! WITH A SINGLE MAGIC WORD, THE POWERS OF SIX ANCIENT GODS--THE WISDOM OF SOLOMON, THE STRENGTH OF HERCULES, THE STAMINA OF ATLAS, THE POWER OF ZEUS, THE COURAGE OF ACHILLES, AND THE SPEED OF MERCURY--ARE PLACED IN THE HANDS OF TEENAGE BILLY BATSON, TRANSFORMING HIM INTO THE WORLD'S MIGHTIEST MORTAL!

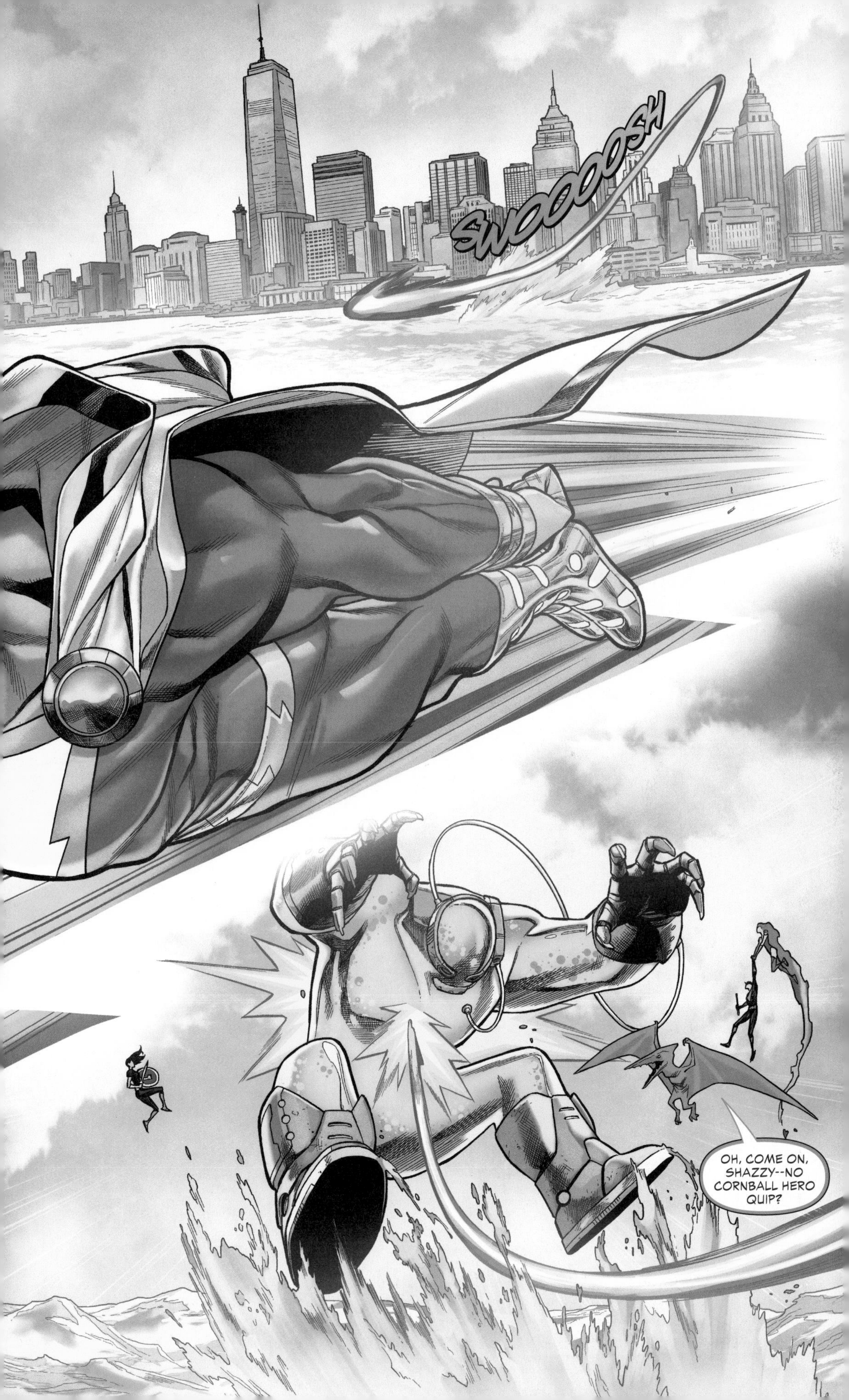
SWOOOOOSH
OH, COME ON, SHAZZY--NO CORNBALL HERO QUIP?

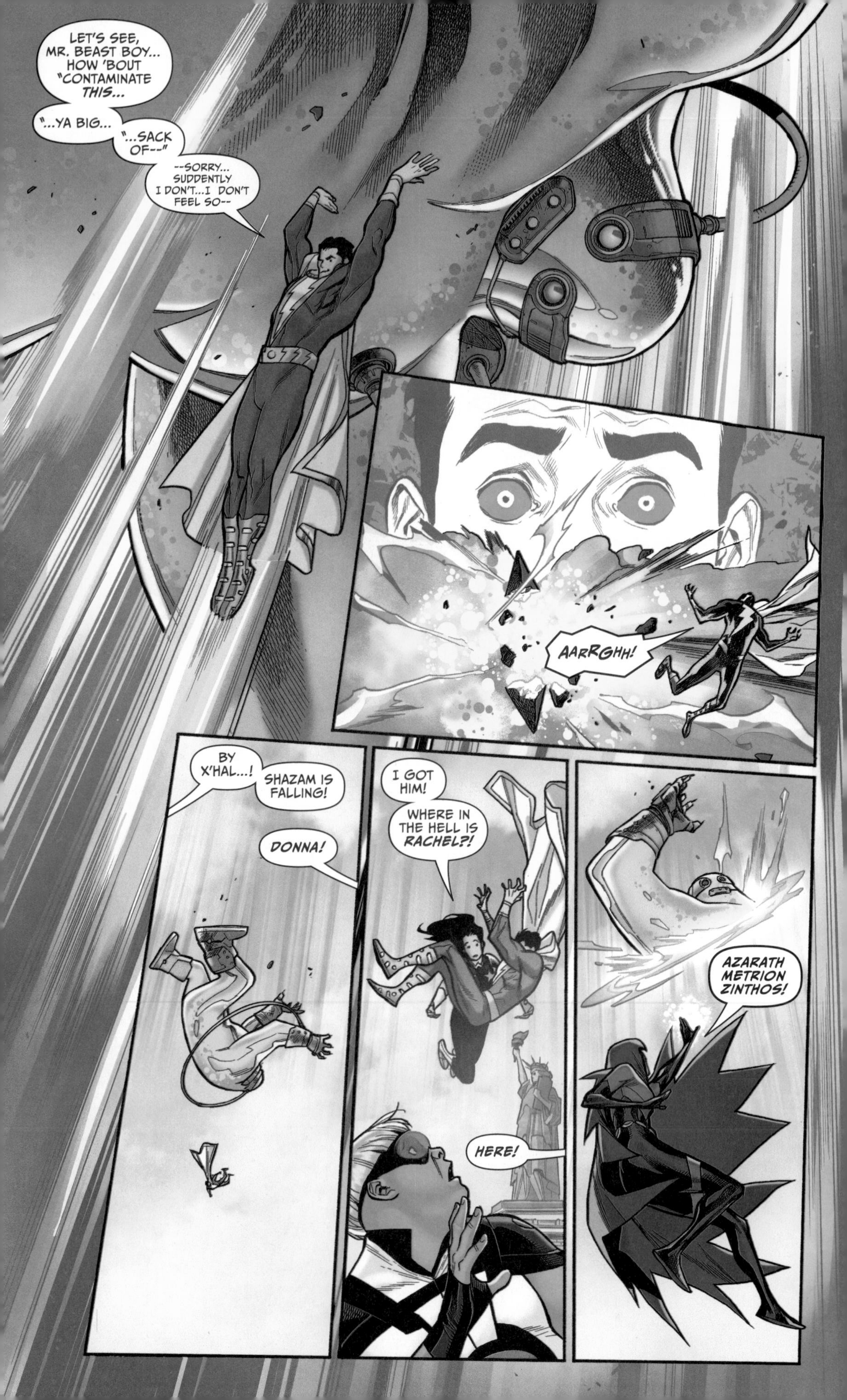
LET'S SEE, MR. BEAST BOY... HOW 'BOUT "CONTAMINATE THIS...
"...YA BIG...
"...SACK OF--"
--SORRY... SUDDENTLY I DON'T...I DON'T FEEL SO--
AARRGHH!
BY X'HAL...!
SHAZAM IS FALLING!
DONNA!
I GOT HIM!
WHERE IN THE HELL IS RACHEL?!
HERE!
AZARATH METRION ZINTHOS!

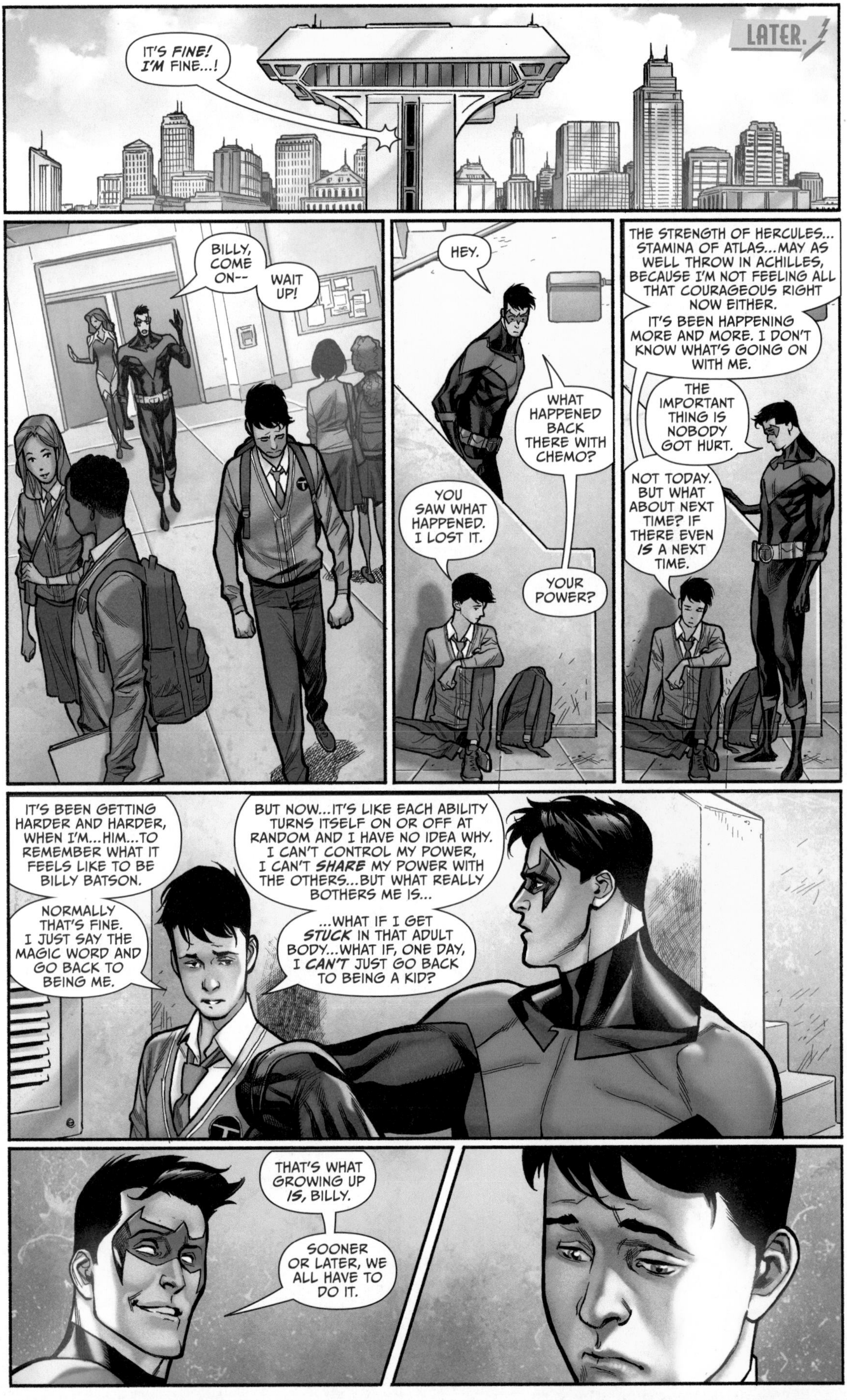
LATER.
IT'S FINE! I'M FINE...!
BILLY, COME ON--
WAIT UP!
HEY.
WHAT HAPPENED BACK THERE WITH CHEMO?
YOU SAW WHAT HAPPENED. I LOST IT.
YOUR POWER?
THE STRENGTH OF HERCULES... STAMINA OF ATLAS...MAY AS WELL THROW IN ACHILLES, BECAUSE I'M NOT FEELING ALL THAT COURAGEOUS RIGHT NOW EITHER.
IT'S BEEN HAPPENING MORE AND MORE. I DON'T KNOW WHAT'S GOING ON WITH ME.
THE IMPORTANT THING IS NOBODY GOT HURT.
NOT TODAY. BUT WHAT ABOUT NEXT TIME? IF THERE EVEN IS A NEXT TIME.
IT'S BEEN GETTING HARDER AND HARDER, WHEN I'M...HIM...TO REMEMBER WHAT IT FEELS LIKE TO BE BILLY BATSON.
NORMALLY THAT'S FINE. I JUST SAY THE MAGIC WORD AND GO BACK TO BEING ME.
BUT NOW...IT'S LIKE EACH ABILITY TURNS ITSELF ON OR OFF AT RANDOM AND I HAVE NO IDEA WHY. I CAN'T CONTROL MY POWER, I CAN'T SHARE MY POWER WITH THE OTHERS...BUT WHAT REALLY BOTHERS ME IS...
...WHAT IF I GET STUCK IN THAT ADULT BODY...WHAT IF, ONE DAY, I CAN'T JUST GO BACK TO BEING A KID?
THAT'S WHAT GROWING UP IS, BILLY.
SOONER OR LATER, WE ALL HAVE TO DO IT.

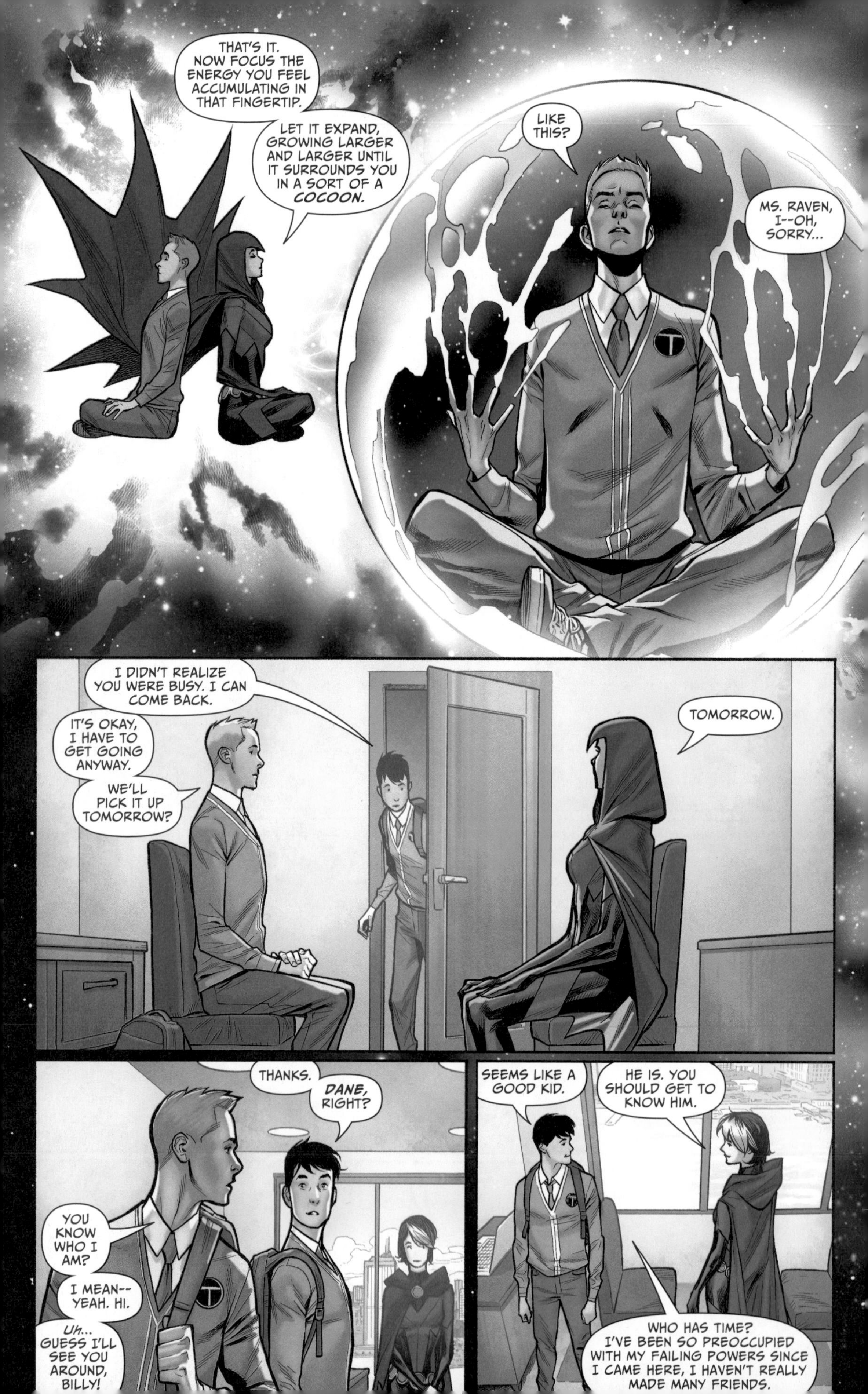
THAT'S IT. NOW FOCUS THE ENERGY YOU FEEL ACCUMULATING IN THAT FINGERTIP.
LET IT EXPAND, GROWING LARGER AND LARGER UNTIL IT SURROUNDS YOU IN A SORT OF A *COCOON.*
LIKE THIS?
MS. RAVEN, I--OH, SORRY...
I DIDN'T REALIZE YOU WERE BUSY. I CAN COME BACK.
IT'S OKAY, I HAVE TO GET GOING ANYWAY.
WE'LL PICK IT UP TOMORROW?
TOMORROW.
THANKS.
DANE, RIGHT?
YOU KNOW WHO I AM?
I MEAN-- YEAH. HI.
Uh... GUESS I'LL SEE YOU AROUND, BILLY!
SEEMS LIKE A GOOD KID.
HE IS. YOU SHOULD GET TO KNOW HIM.
WHO HAS TIME? I'VE BEEN SO PREOCCUPIED WITH MY FAILING POWERS SINCE I CAME HERE, I HAVEN'T REALLY MADE MANY FRIENDS.

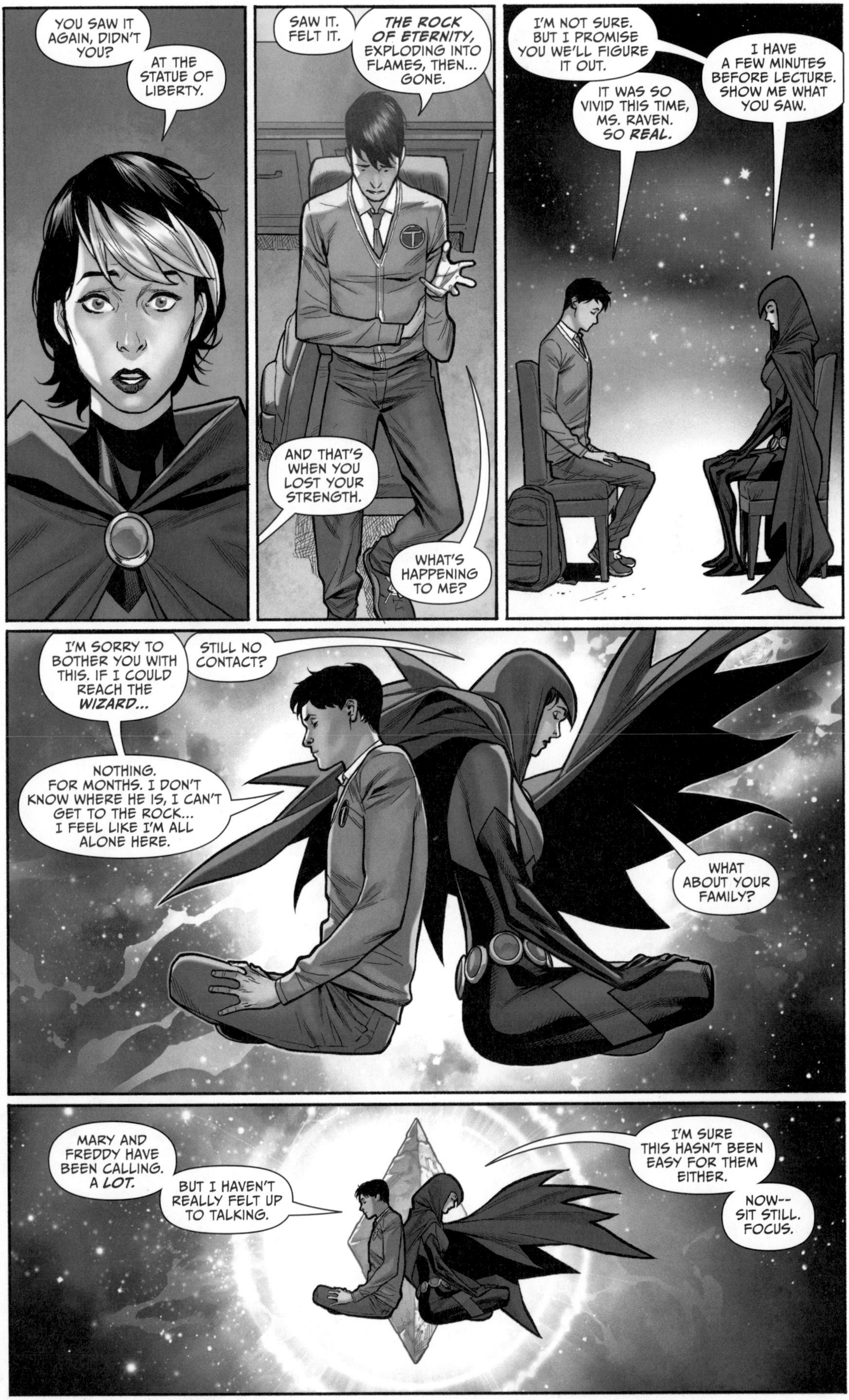
YOU SAW IT AGAIN, DIDN'T YOU?
AT THE STATUE OF LIBERTY.
SAW IT. FELT IT.
THE ROCK OF ETERNITY, EXPLODING INTO FLAMES, THEN... GONE.
AND THAT'S WHEN YOU LOST YOUR STRENGTH.
WHAT'S HAPPENING TO ME?
I'M NOT SURE. BUT I PROMISE YOU WE'LL FIGURE IT OUT.
IT WAS SO VIVID THIS TIME, MS. RAVEN. SO *REAL.*
I HAVE A FEW MINUTES BEFORE LECTURE. SHOW ME WHAT YOU SAW.
I'M SORRY TO BOTHER YOU WITH THIS. IF I COULD REACH THE *WIZARD...*
STILL NO CONTACT?
NOTHING. FOR MONTHS. I DON'T KNOW WHERE HE IS, I CAN'T GET TO THE ROCK... I FEEL LIKE I'M ALL ALONE HERE.
WHAT ABOUT YOUR FAMILY?
MARY AND FREDDY HAVE BEEN CALLING. A *LOT.*
BUT I HAVEN'T REALLY FELT UP TO TALKING.
I'M SURE THIS HASN'T BEEN EASY FOR THEM EITHER.
NOW-- SIT STILL. FOCUS.

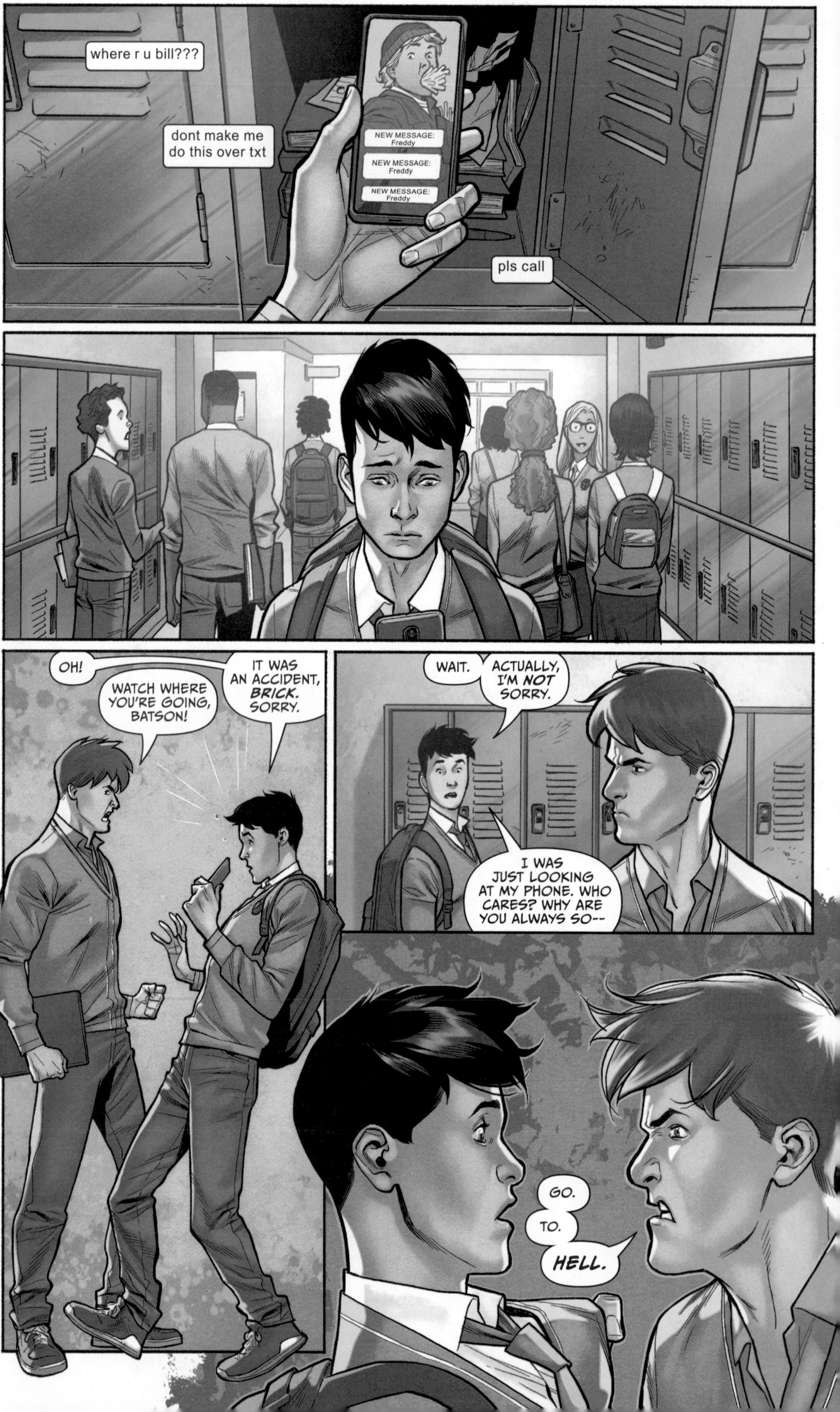
where r u bill???
dont make me do this over txt
NEW MESSAGE: Freddy
NEW MESSAGE: Freddy
NEW MESSAGE: Freddy
pls call
OH!
WATCH WHERE YOU'RE GOING, BATSON!
IT WAS AN ACCIDENT, BRICK. SORRY.
WAIT.
ACTUALLY, I'M NOT SORRY.
I WAS JUST LOOKING AT MY PHONE. WHO CARES? WHY ARE YOU ALWAYS SO--
GO.
TO.
HELL.

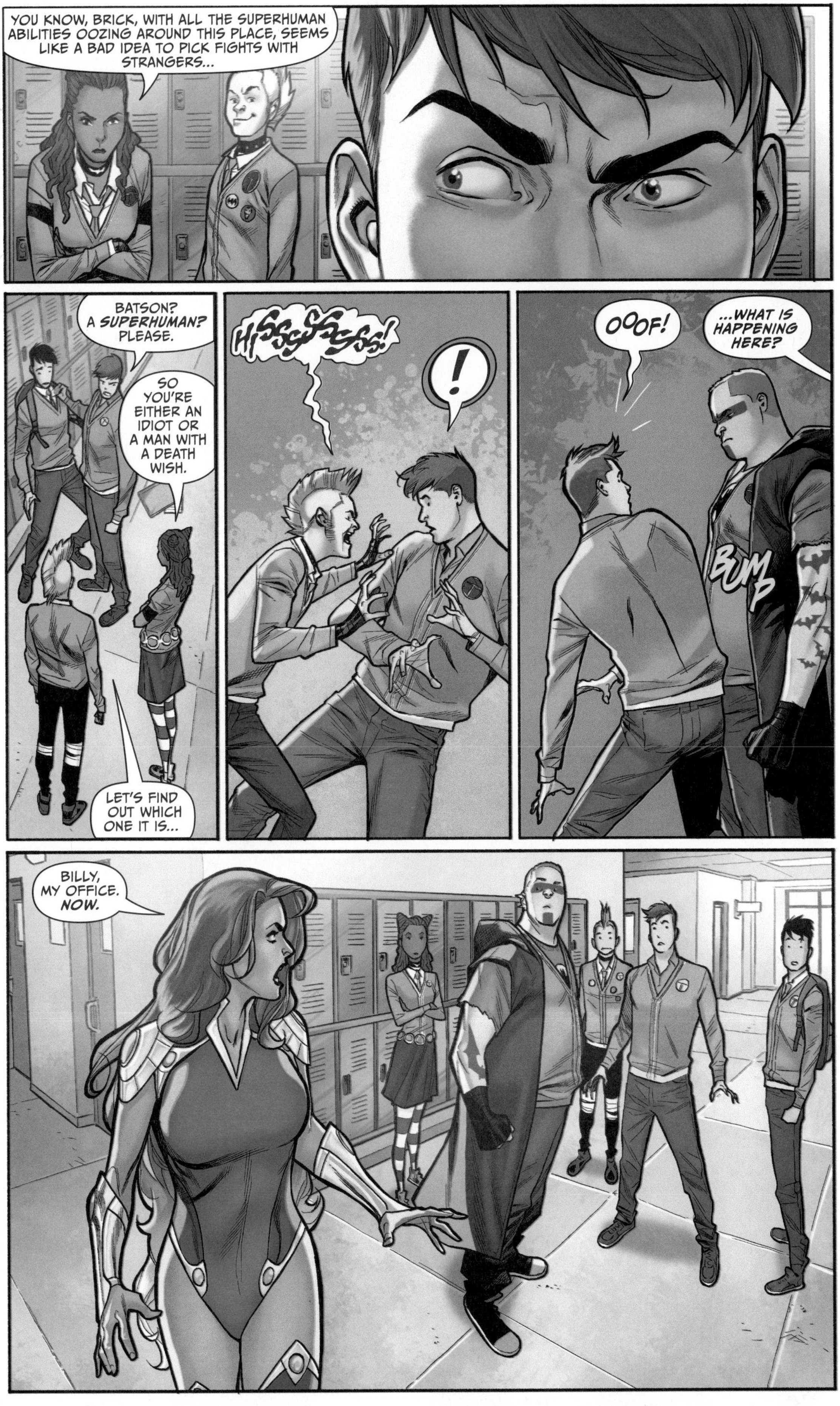
YOU KNOW, BRICK, WITH ALL THE SUPERHUMAN ABILITIES OOZING AROUND THIS PLACE, SEEMS LIKE A BAD IDEA TO PICK FIGHTS WITH STRANGERS...
BATSON? A *SUPERHUMAN?* PLEASE.
SO YOU'RE EITHER AN IDIOT OR A MAN WITH A DEATH WISH.
LET'S FIND OUT WHICH ONE IT IS...
HISSSSSSSSS!
!
OOOF!
...WHAT IS HAPPENING HERE?
BUMP
BILLY, MY OFFICE. **NOW.**

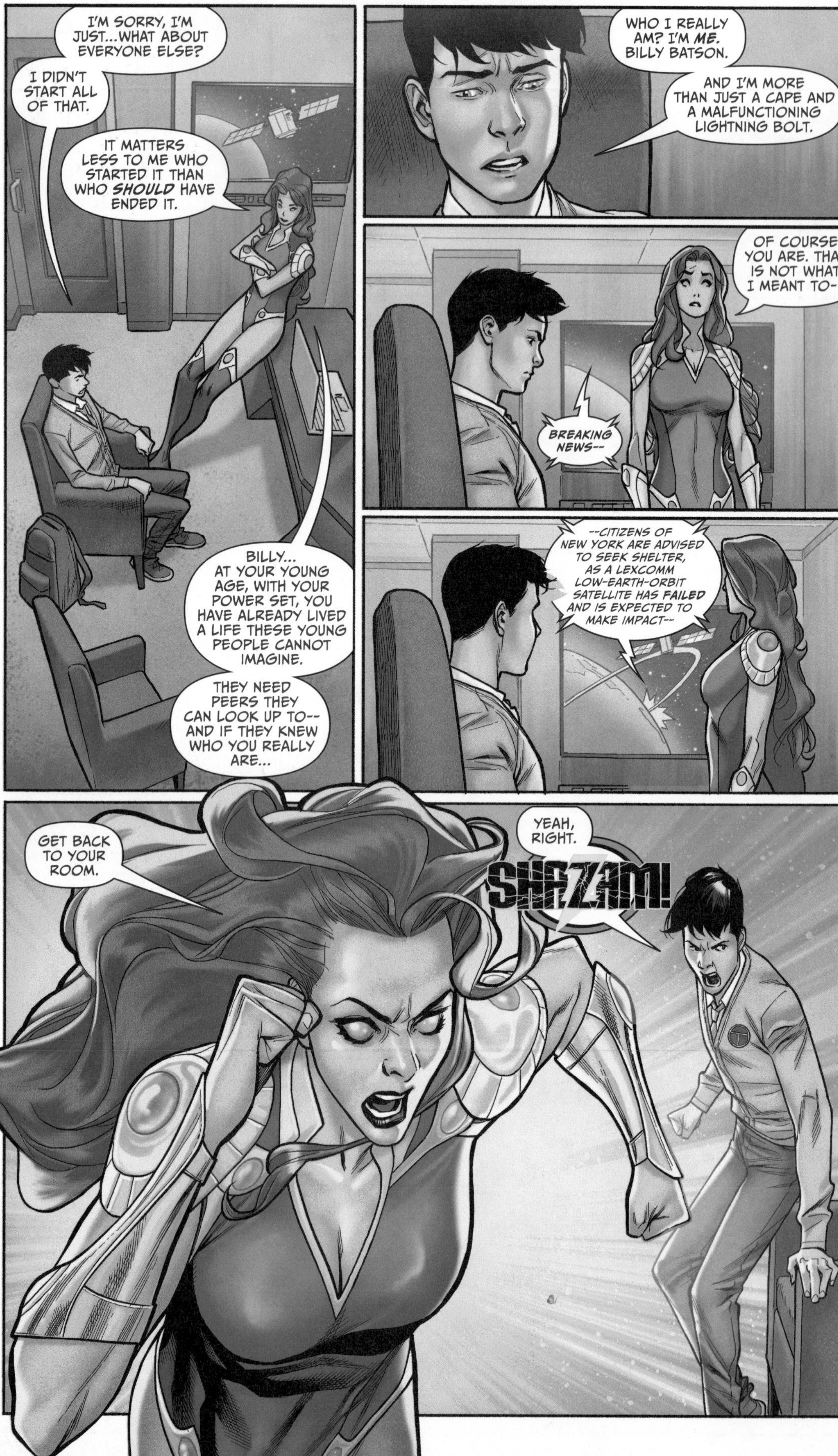
I'M SORRY, I'M JUST...WHAT ABOUT EVERYONE ELSE?
I DIDN'T START ALL OF THAT.
IT MATTERS LESS TO ME WHO STARTED IT THAN WHO SHOULD HAVE ENDED IT.
BILLY... AT YOUR YOUNG AGE, WITH YOUR POWER SET, YOU HAVE ALREADY LIVED A LIFE THESE YOUNG PEOPLE CANNOT IMAGINE.
THEY NEED PEERS THEY CAN LOOK UP TO-- AND IF THEY KNEW WHO YOU REALLY ARE...
WHO I REALLY AM? I'M ME. BILLY BATSON.
AND I'M MORE THAN JUST A CAPE AND A MALFUNCTIONING LIGHTNING BOLT.
OF COURSE YOU ARE. THAT IS NOT WHAT I MEANT TO--
BREAKING NEWS--
--CITIZENS OF NEW YORK ARE ADVISED TO SEEK SHELTER, AS A LEXCOMM LOW-EARTH-ORBIT SATELLITE HAS FAILED AND IS EXPECTED TO MAKE IMPACT--
GET BACK TO YOUR ROOM.
YEAH, RIGHT.
SHAZAM!

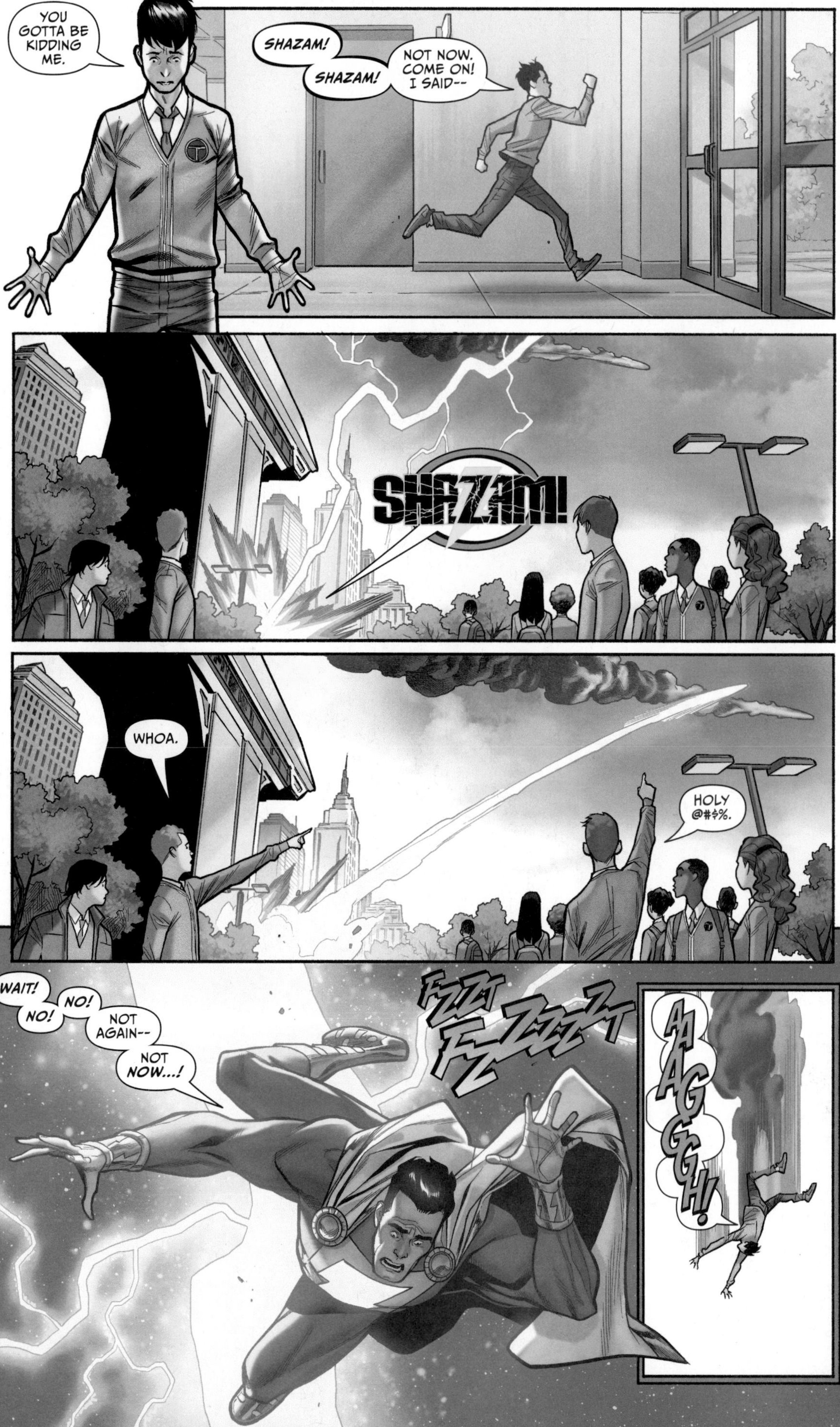

YOU GOTTA BE KIDDING ME.
SHAZAM!
SHAZAM!
NOT NOW. COME ON! I SAID--
SHAZAM!
WHOA.
HOLY @#$%.
WAIT!
NO!
NO!
NOT AGAIN--
NOT NOW...!
FZZZT FZZZZZZT
AAAGGGH!

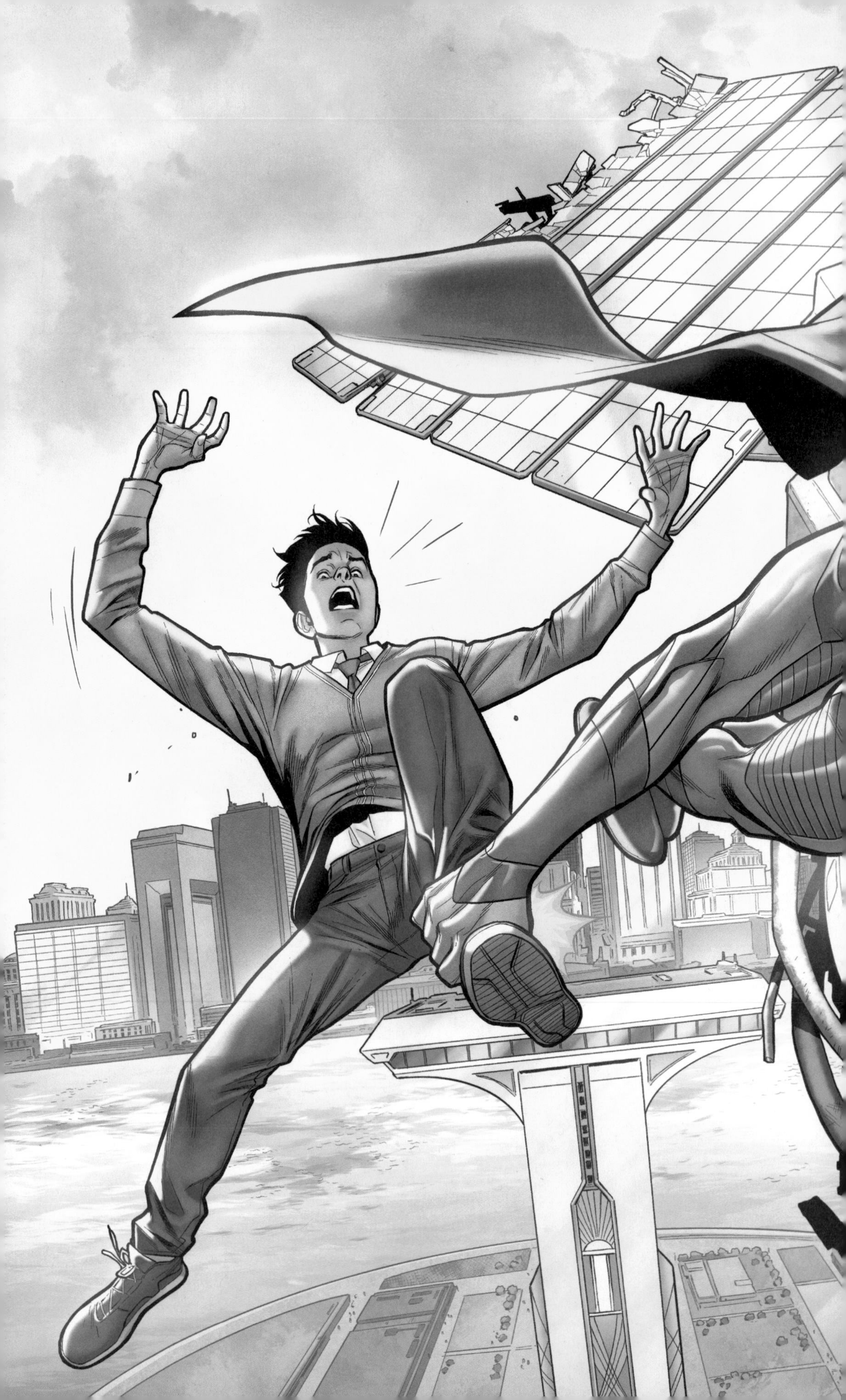

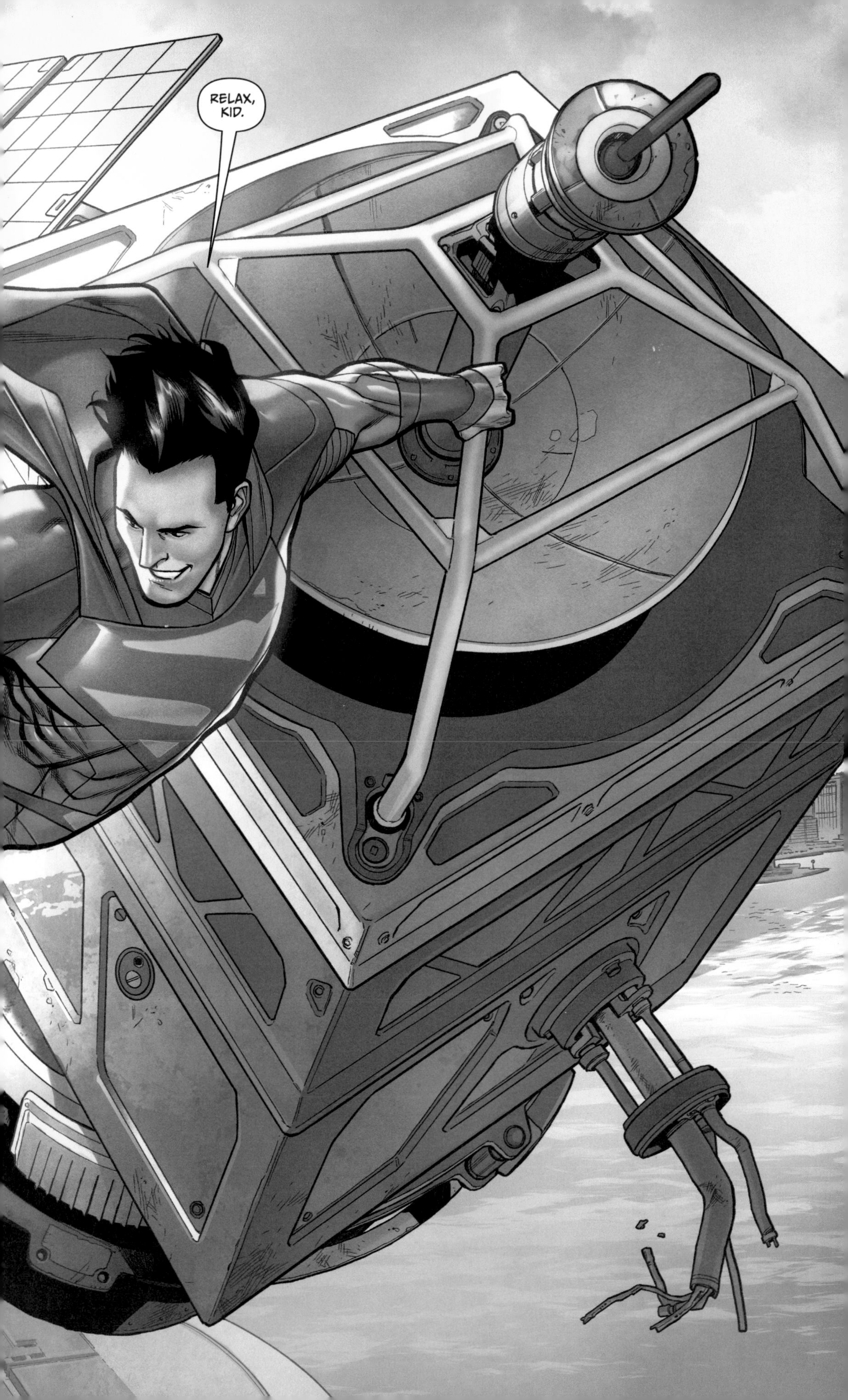
RELAX, KID.

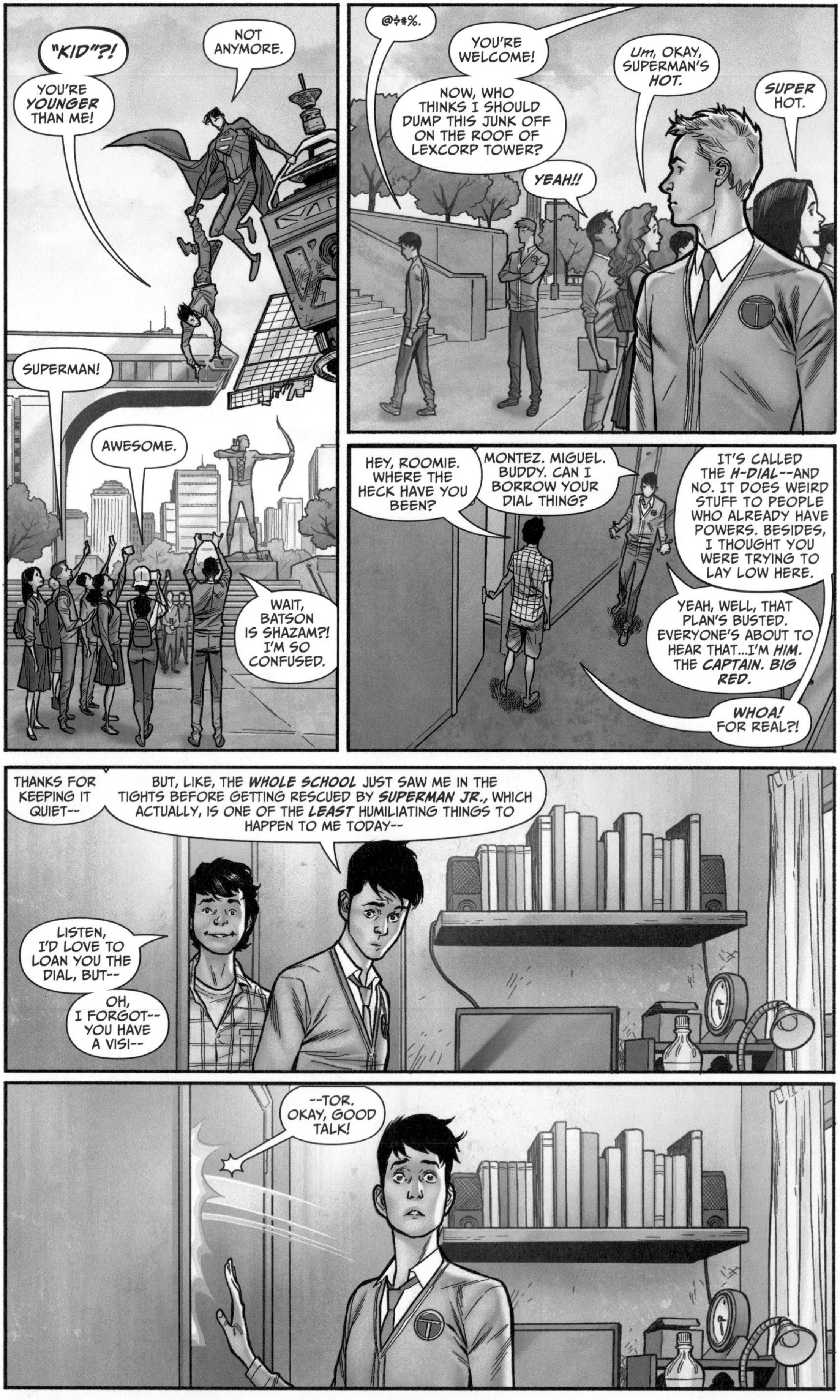
"KID"?!
YOU'RE YOUNGER THAN ME!
NOT ANYMORE.
SUPERMAN!
AWESOME.
WAIT, BATSON IS SHAZAM?! I'M SO CONFUSED.
@$#%.
YOU'RE WELCOME!
NOW, WHO THINKS I SHOULD DUMP THIS JUNK OFF ON THE ROOF OF LEXCORP TOWER?
YEAH!!
Um, OKAY, SUPERMAN'S HOT.
SUPER HOT.
HEY, ROOMIE. WHERE THE HECK HAVE YOU BEEN?
MONTEZ. MIGUEL. BUDDY. CAN I BORROW YOUR DIAL THING?
IT'S CALLED THE H-DIAL--AND NO. IT DOES WEIRD STUFF TO PEOPLE WHO ALREADY HAVE POWERS. BESIDES, I THOUGHT YOU WERE TRYING TO LAY LOW HERE.
YEAH, WELL, THAT PLAN'S BUSTED. EVERYONE'S ABOUT TO HEAR THAT...I'M HIM. THE CAPTAIN. BIG RED.
WHOA! FOR REAL?!
THANKS FOR KEEPING IT QUIET--
BUT, LIKE, THE WHOLE SCHOOL JUST SAW ME IN THE TIGHTS BEFORE GETTING RESCUED BY SUPERMAN JR., WHICH ACTUALLY, IS ONE OF THE LEAST HUMILIATING THINGS TO HAPPEN TO ME TODAY--
LISTEN, I'D LOVE TO LOAN YOU THE DIAL, BUT--
OH, I FORGOT-- YOU HAVE A VISI--
--TOR. OKAY, GOOD TALK!

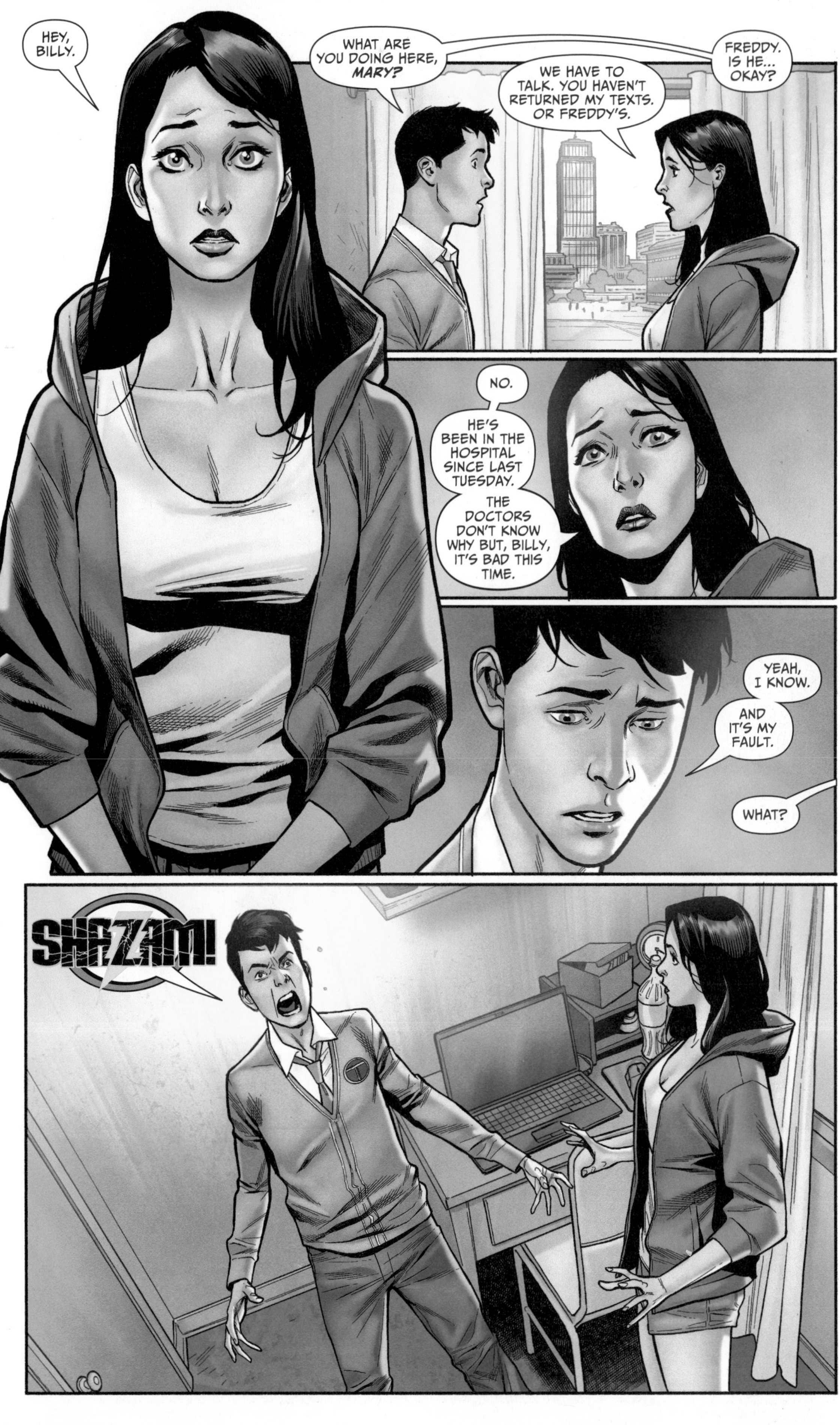
HEY, BILLY.
WHAT ARE YOU DOING HERE, *MARY?*
WE HAVE TO TALK. YOU HAVEN'T RETURNED MY TEXTS. OR FREDDY'S.
FREDDY. IS HE... OKAY?
NO.
HE'S BEEN IN THE HOSPITAL SINCE LAST TUESDAY.
THE DOCTORS DON'T KNOW WHY BUT, BILLY, IT'S BAD THIS TIME.
YEAH, I KNOW.
AND IT'S MY FAULT.
WHAT?
SHAZAM!

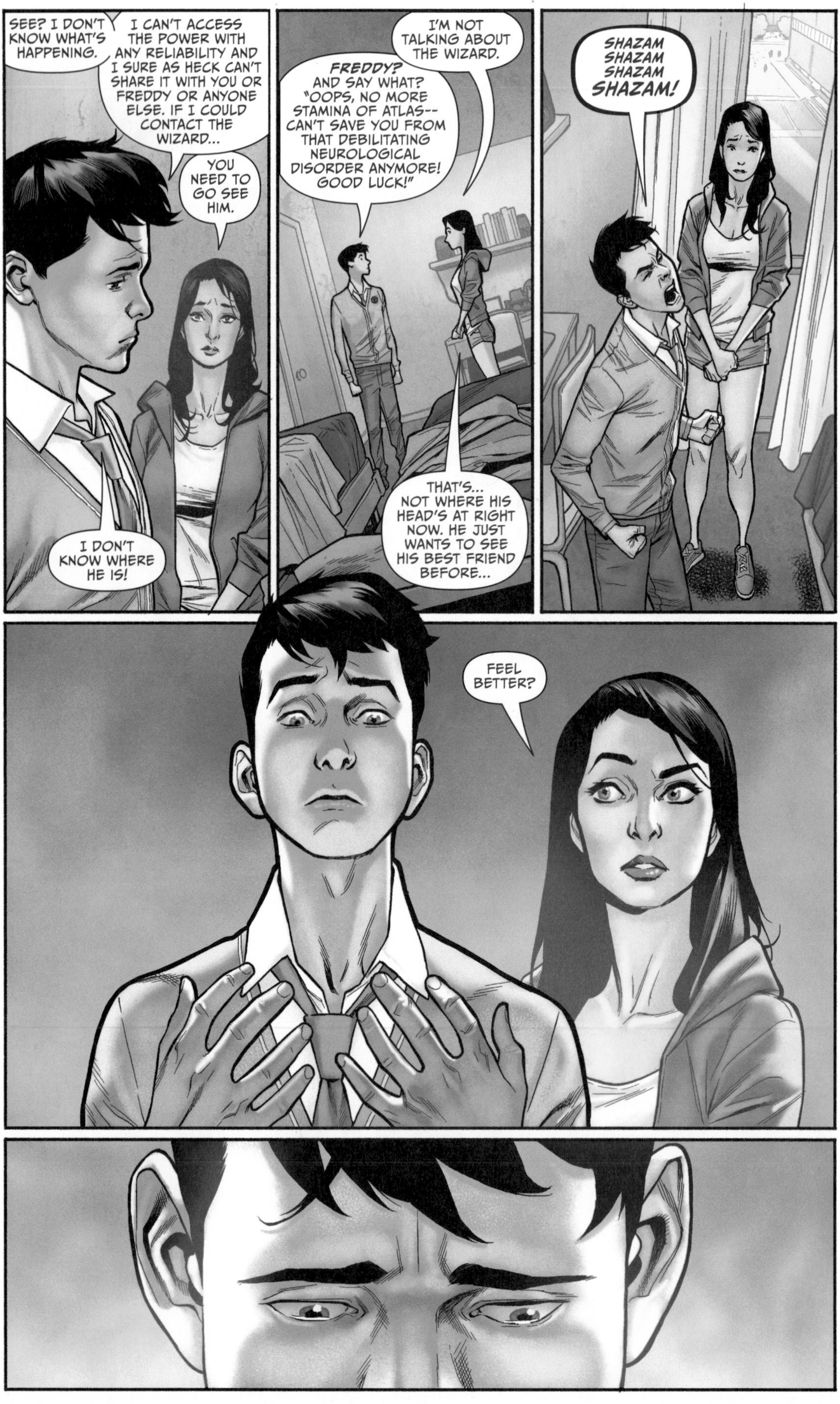
SEE? I DON'T KNOW WHAT'S HAPPENING.
I CAN'T ACCESS THE POWER WITH ANY RELIABILITY AND I SURE AS HECK CAN'T SHARE IT WITH YOU OR FREDDY OR ANYONE ELSE. IF I COULD CONTACT THE WIZARD...
YOU NEED TO GO SEE HIM.
I DON'T KNOW WHERE HE IS!
I'M NOT TALKING ABOUT THE WIZARD.
FREDDY? AND SAY WHAT? "OOPS, NO MORE STAMINA OF ATLAS-- CAN'T SAVE YOU FROM THAT DEBILITATING NEUROLOGICAL DISORDER ANYMORE! GOOD LUCK!"
THAT'S... NOT WHERE HIS HEAD'S AT RIGHT NOW. HE JUST WANTS TO SEE HIS BEST FRIEND BEFORE...
SHAZAM SHAZAM SHAZAM SHAZAM!
FEEL BETTER?

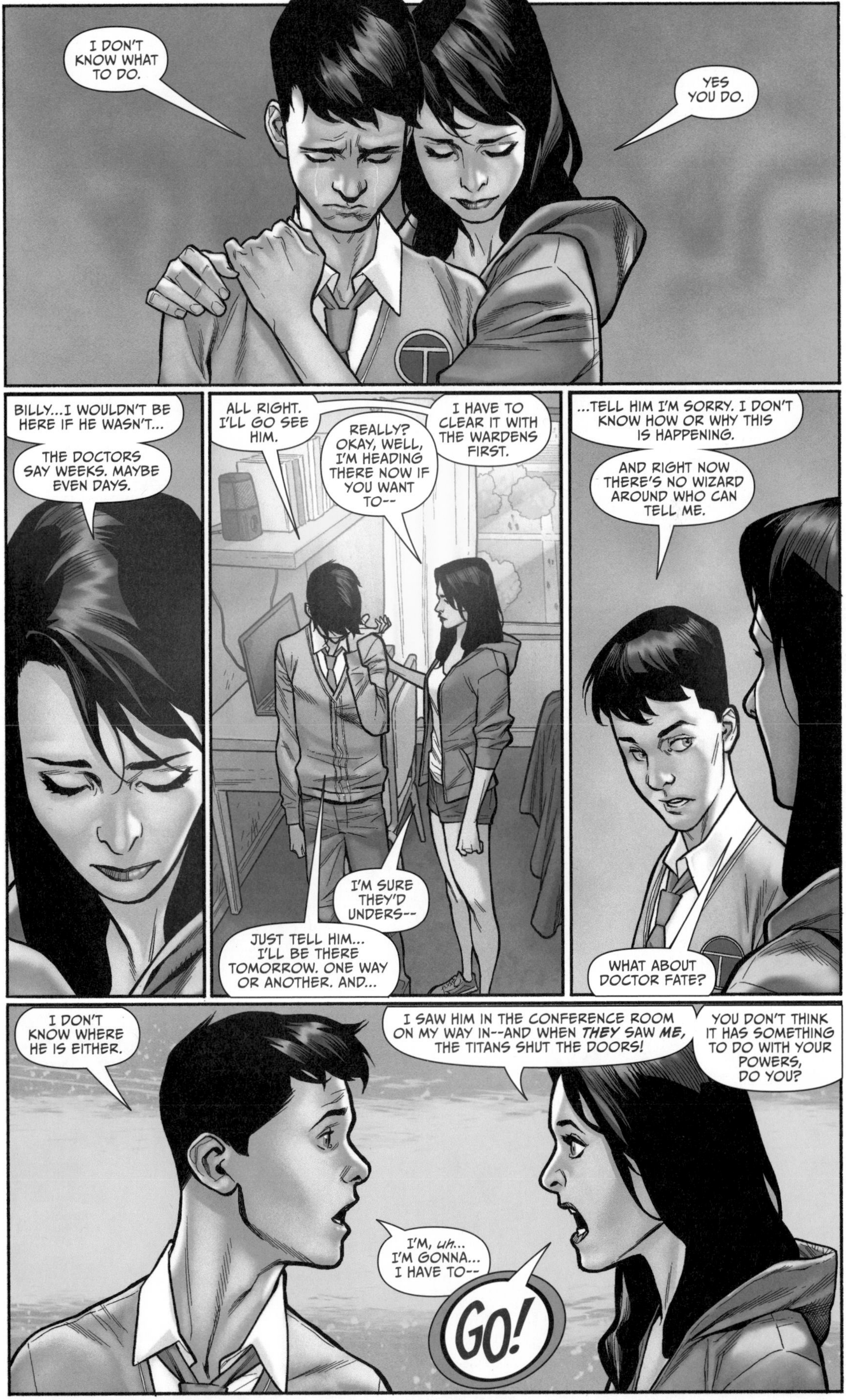

I DON'T KNOW WHAT TO DO.
YES YOU DO.
BILLY...I WOULDN'T BE HERE IF HE WASN'T...
THE DOCTORS SAY WEEKS. MAYBE EVEN DAYS.
ALL RIGHT. I'LL GO SEE HIM.
REALLY? OKAY, WELL, I'M HEADING THERE NOW IF YOU WANT TO--
I HAVE TO CLEAR IT WITH THE WARDENS FIRST.
I'M SURE THEY'D UNDERS--
JUST TELL HIM... I'LL BE THERE TOMORROW. ONE WAY OR ANOTHER. AND...
...TELL HIM I'M SORRY. I DON'T KNOW HOW OR WHY THIS IS HAPPENING.
AND RIGHT NOW THERE'S NO WIZARD AROUND WHO CAN TELL ME.
WHAT ABOUT DOCTOR FATE?
I DON'T KNOW WHERE HE IS EITHER.
I SAW HIM IN THE CONFERENCE ROOM ON MY WAY IN--AND WHEN *THEY* SAW *ME*, THE TITANS SHUT THE DOORS!
YOU DON'T THINK IT HAS SOMETHING TO DO WITH YOUR POWERS, DO YOU?
I'M, *uh*... I'M GONNA... I HAVE TO--
GO!

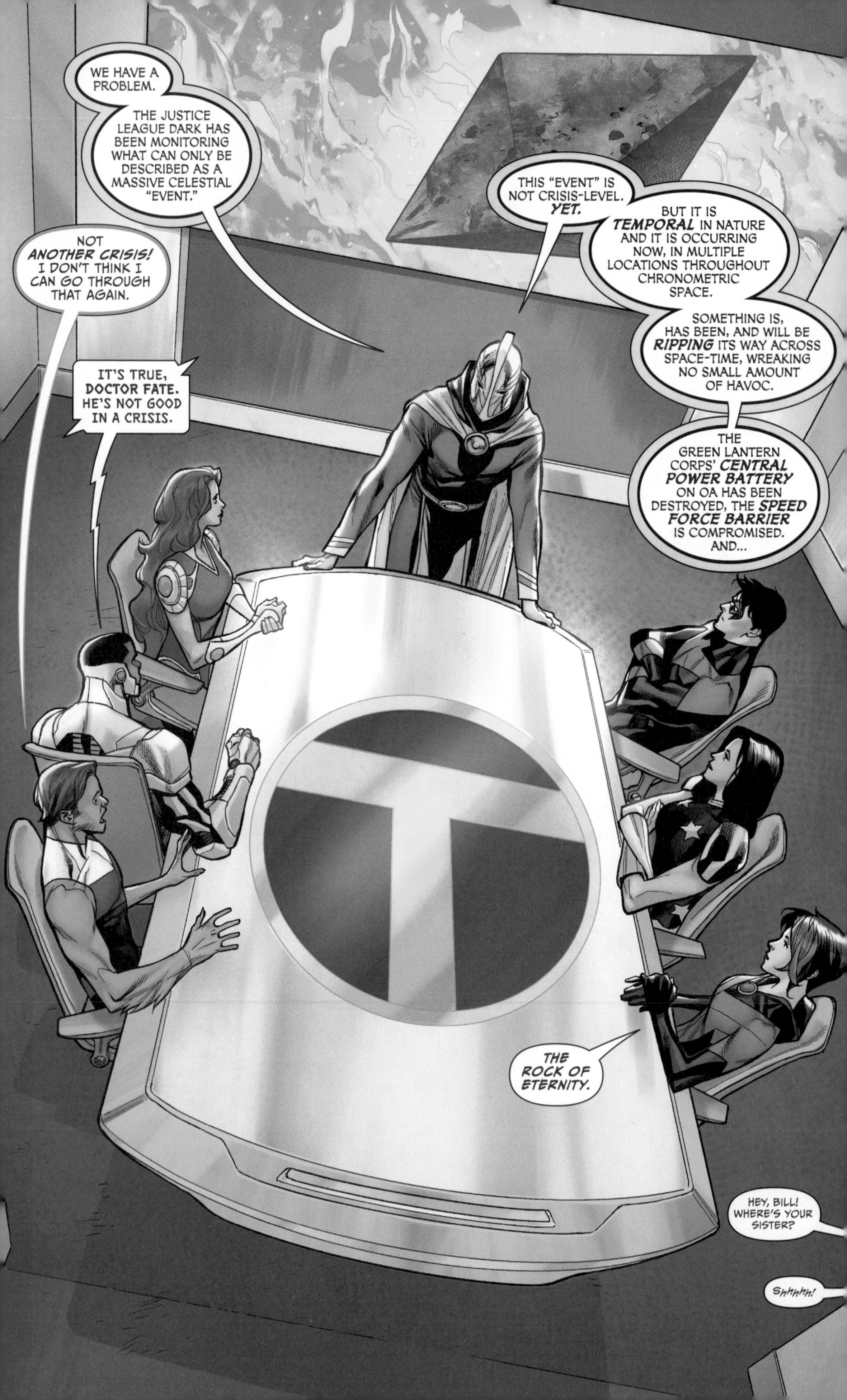
WE HAVE A PROBLEM.
THE JUSTICE LEAGUE DARK HAS BEEN MONITORING WHAT CAN ONLY BE DESCRIBED AS A MASSIVE CELESTIAL "EVENT."
NOT ANOTHER CRISIS! I DON'T THINK I CAN GO THROUGH THAT AGAIN.
IT'S TRUE, DOCTOR FATE. HE'S NOT GOOD IN A CRISIS.
THIS "EVENT" IS NOT CRISIS-LEVEL. YET.
BUT IT IS TEMPORAL IN NATURE AND IT IS OCCURRING NOW, IN MULTIPLE LOCATIONS THROUGHOUT CHRONOMETRIC SPACE.
SOMETHING IS, HAS BEEN, AND WILL BE RIPPING ITS WAY ACROSS SPACE-TIME, WREAKING NO SMALL AMOUNT OF HAVOC.
THE GREEN LANTERN CORPS' CENTRAL POWER BATTERY ON OA HAS BEEN DESTROYED, THE SPEED FORCE BARRIER IS COMPROMISED. AND...
THE ROCK OF ETERNITY.
HEY, BILL! WHERE'S YOUR SISTER?
Shhhhh!

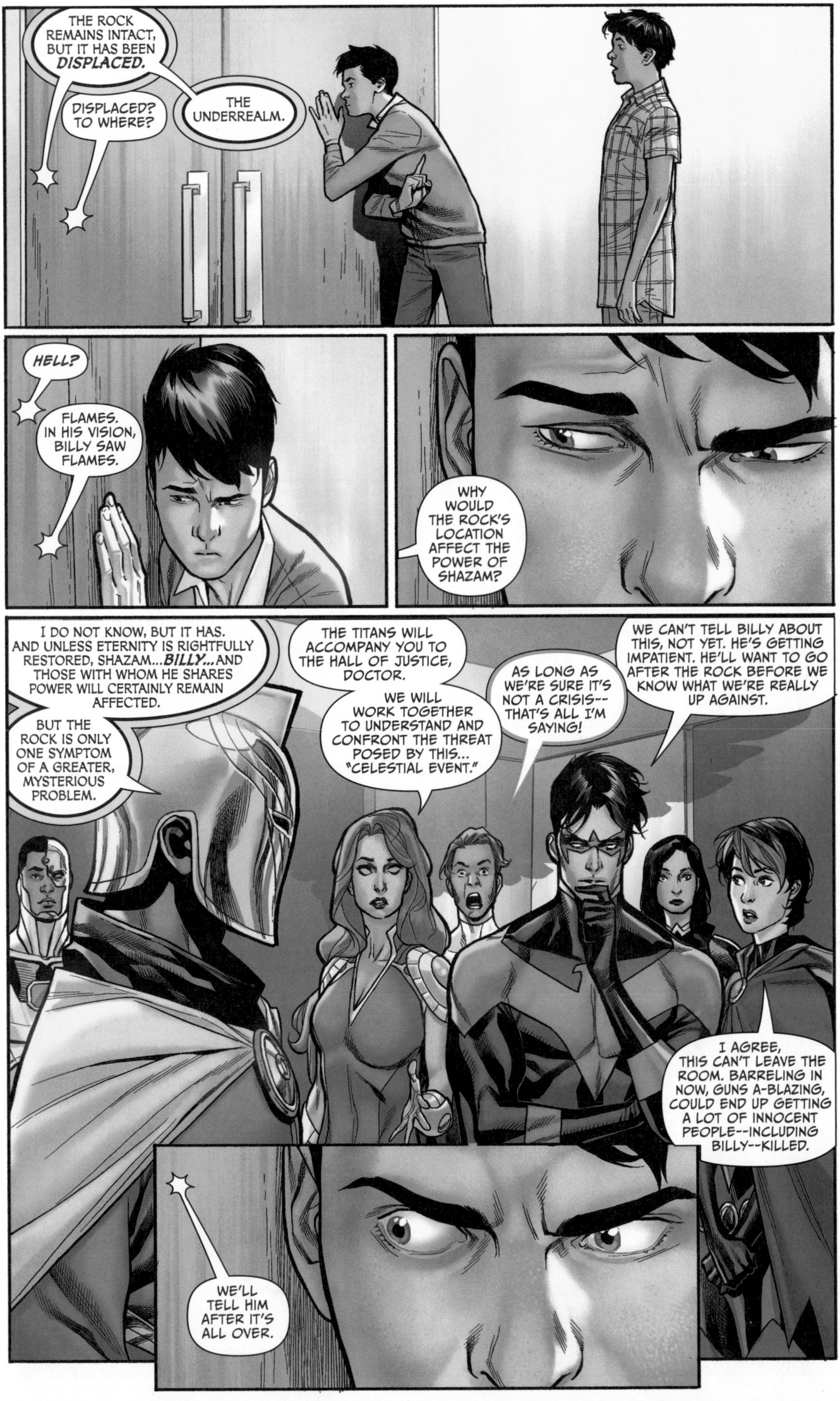
THE ROCK REMAINS INTACT, BUT IT HAS BEEN DISPLACED.
DISPLACED? TO WHERE?
THE UNDERREALM.
HELL?
FLAMES. IN HIS VISION, BILLY SAW FLAMES.
WHY WOULD THE ROCK'S LOCATION AFFECT THE POWER OF SHAZAM?
I DO NOT KNOW, BUT IT HAS. AND UNLESS ETERNITY IS RIGHTFULLY RESTORED, SHAZAM...BILLY...AND THOSE WITH WHOM HE SHARES POWER WILL CERTAINLY REMAIN AFFECTED.
BUT THE ROCK IS ONLY ONE SYMPTOM OF A GREATER, MYSTERIOUS PROBLEM.
THE TITANS WILL ACCOMPANY YOU TO THE HALL OF JUSTICE, DOCTOR.
WE WILL WORK TOGETHER TO UNDERSTAND AND CONFRONT THE THREAT POSED BY THIS... "CELESTIAL EVENT."
AS LONG AS WE'RE SURE IT'S NOT A CRISIS-- THAT'S ALL I'M SAYING!
WE CAN'T TELL BILLY ABOUT THIS, NOT YET. HE'S GETTING IMPATIENT. HE'LL WANT TO GO AFTER THE ROCK BEFORE WE KNOW WHAT WE'RE REALLY UP AGAINST.
I AGREE, THIS CAN'T LEAVE THE ROOM. BARRELING IN NOW, GUNS A-BLAZING, COULD END UP GETTING A LOT OF INNOCENT PEOPLE--INCLUDING BILLY--KILLED.
WE'LL TELL HIM AFTER IT'S ALL OVER.

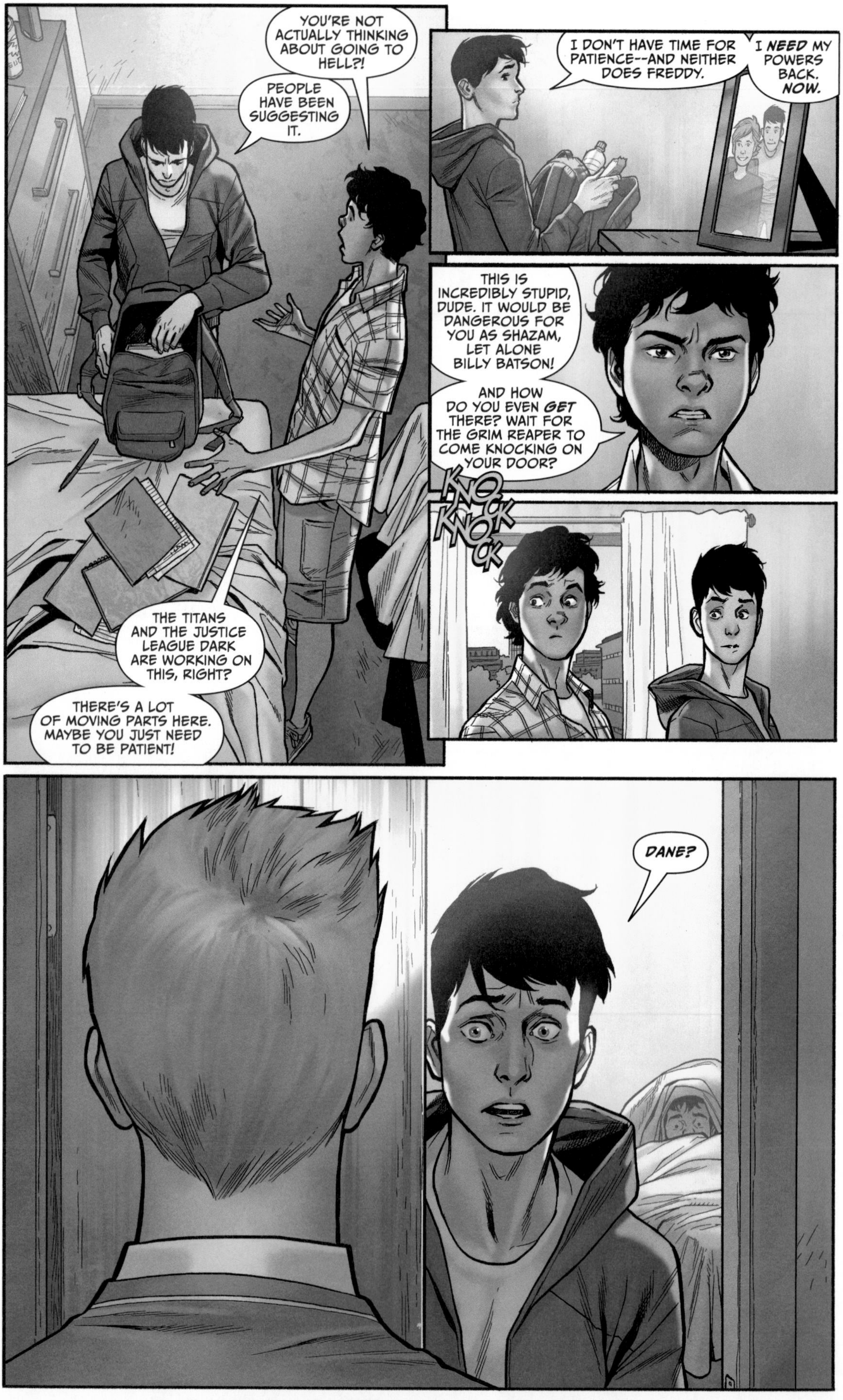
YOU'RE NOT ACTUALLY THINKING ABOUT GOING TO HELL?!
PEOPLE HAVE BEEN SUGGESTING IT.
THE TITANS AND THE JUSTICE LEAGUE DARK ARE WORKING ON THIS, RIGHT?
THERE'S A LOT OF MOVING PARTS HERE. MAYBE YOU JUST NEED TO BE PATIENT!
I DON'T HAVE TIME FOR PATIENCE--AND NEITHER DOES FREDDY.
I NEED MY POWERS BACK. NOW.
THIS IS INCREDIBLY STUPID, DUDE. IT WOULD BE DANGEROUS FOR YOU AS SHAZAM, LET ALONE BILLY BATSON!
AND HOW DO YOU EVEN GET THERE? WAIT FOR THE GRIM REAPER TO COME KNOCKING ON YOUR DOOR?
KNOCK KNOCK
DANE?

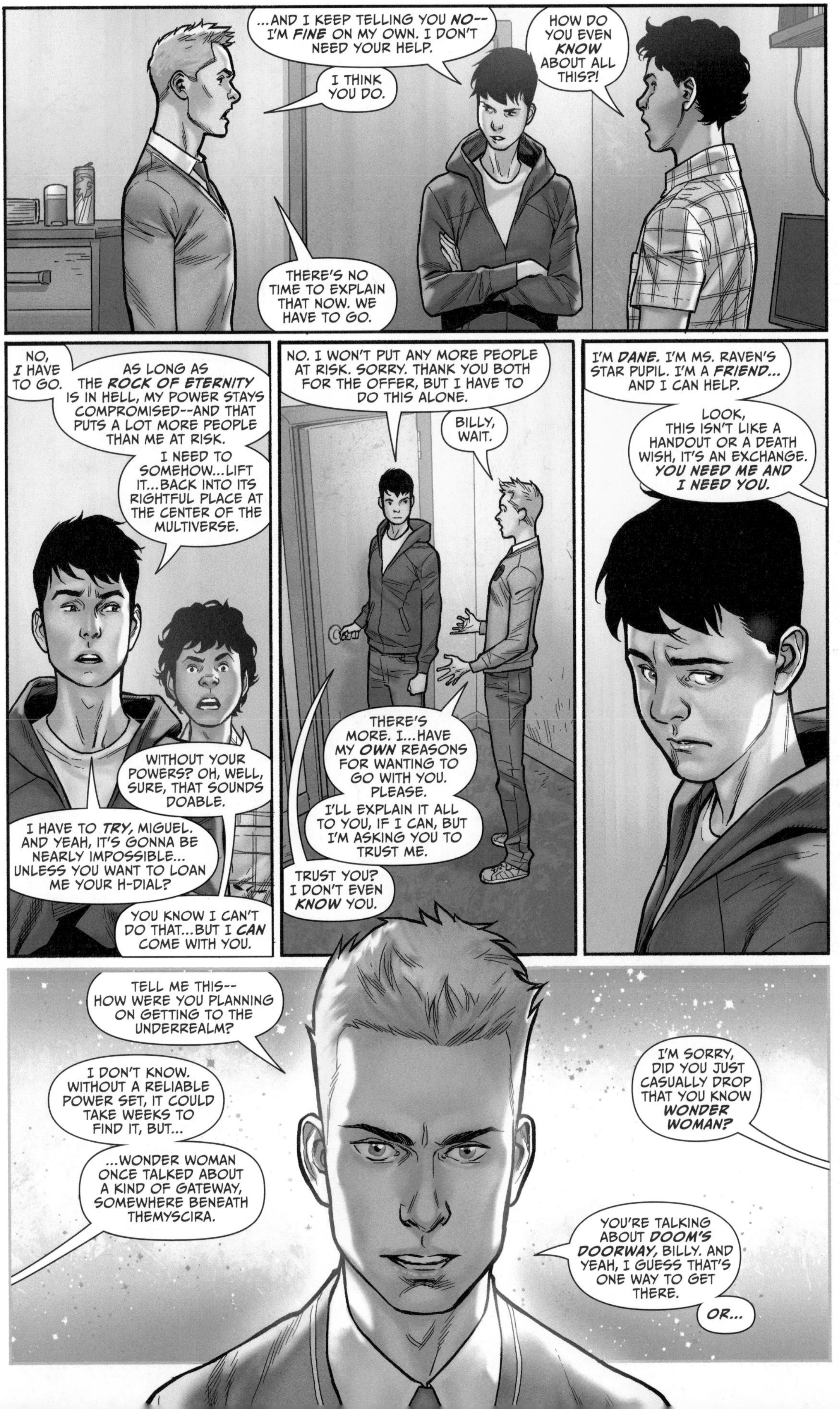
...AND I KEEP TELLING YOU NO--
I'M FINE ON MY OWN. I DON'T NEED YOUR HELP.
I THINK YOU DO.
HOW DO YOU EVEN KNOW ABOUT ALL THIS?!
THERE'S NO TIME TO EXPLAIN THAT NOW. WE HAVE TO GO.
NO, I HAVE TO GO.
AS LONG AS THE ROCK OF ETERNITY IS IN HELL, MY POWER STAYS COMPROMISED--AND THAT PUTS A LOT MORE PEOPLE THAN ME AT RISK.
I NEED TO SOMEHOW...LIFT IT...BACK INTO ITS RIGHTFUL PLACE AT THE CENTER OF THE MULTIVERSE.
WITHOUT YOUR POWERS? OH, WELL, SURE, THAT SOUNDS DOABLE.
I HAVE TO TRY, MIGUEL. AND YEAH, IT'S GONNA BE NEARLY IMPOSSIBLE... UNLESS YOU WANT TO LOAN ME YOUR H-DIAL?
YOU KNOW I CAN'T DO THAT...BUT I CAN COME WITH YOU.
NO. I WON'T PUT ANY MORE PEOPLE AT RISK. SORRY. THANK YOU BOTH FOR THE OFFER, BUT I HAVE TO DO THIS ALONE.
BILLY, WAIT.
THERE'S MORE. I...HAVE MY OWN REASONS FOR WANTING TO GO WITH YOU. PLEASE.
I'LL EXPLAIN IT ALL TO YOU, IF I CAN, BUT I'M ASKING YOU TO TRUST ME.
TRUST YOU? I DON'T EVEN KNOW YOU.
I'M DANE. I'M MS. RAVEN'S STAR PUPIL. I'M A FRIEND... AND I CAN HELP.
LOOK, THIS ISN'T LIKE A HANDOUT OR A DEATH WISH, IT'S AN EXCHANGE. YOU NEED ME AND I NEED YOU.
TELL ME THIS-- HOW WERE YOU PLANNING ON GETTING TO THE UNDERREALM?
I DON'T KNOW. WITHOUT A RELIABLE POWER SET, IT COULD TAKE WEEKS TO FIND IT, BUT...
...WONDER WOMAN ONCE TALKED ABOUT A KIND OF GATEWAY, SOMEWHERE BENEATH THEMYSCIRA.
I'M SORRY, DID YOU JUST CASUALLY DROP THAT YOU KNOW WONDER WOMAN?
YOU'RE TALKING ABOUT DOOM'S DOORWAY, BILLY. AND YEAH, I GUESS THAT'S ONE WAY TO GET THERE.
OR...

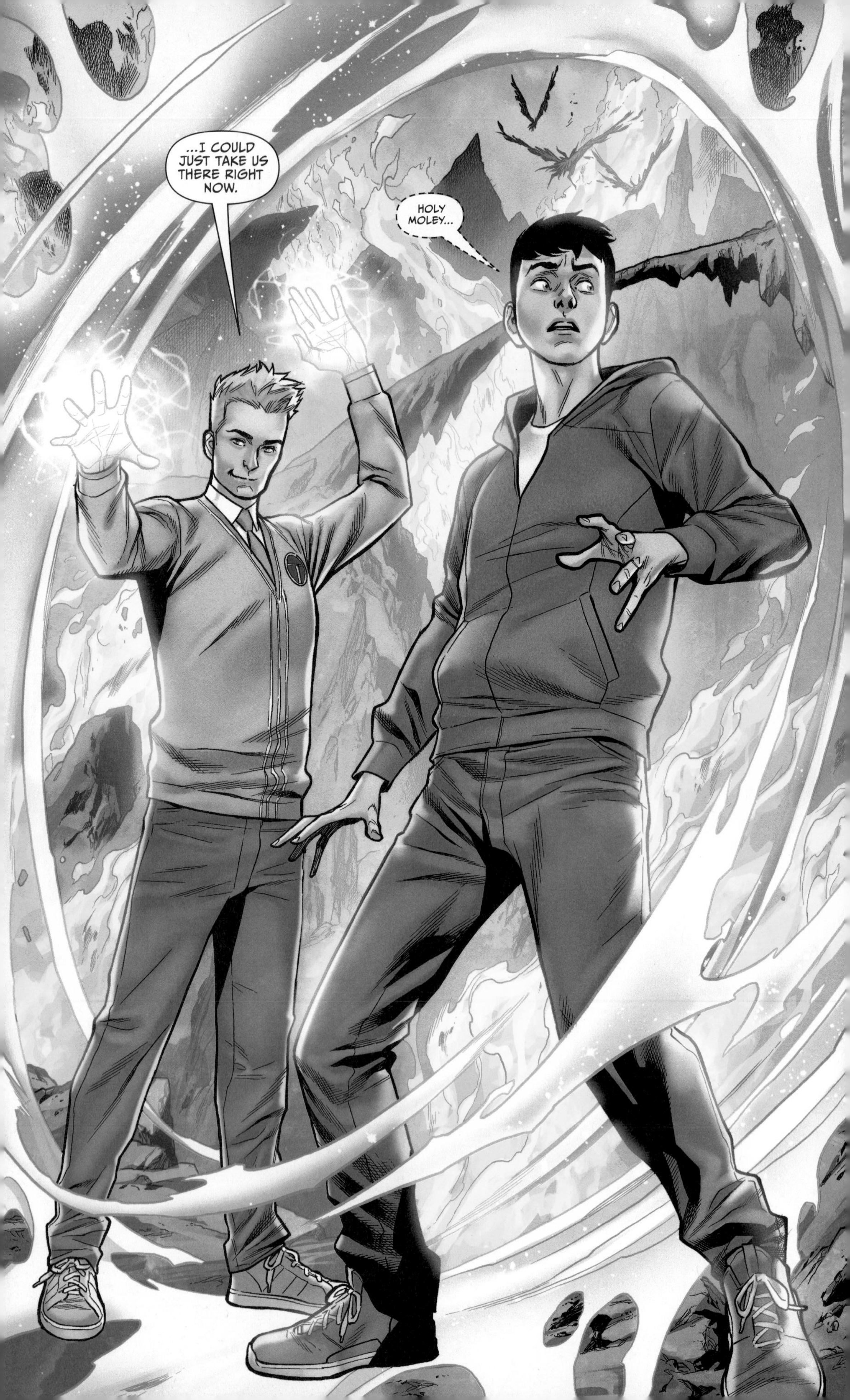
...I COULD JUST TAKE US THERE RIGHT NOW.
HOLY MOLEY...

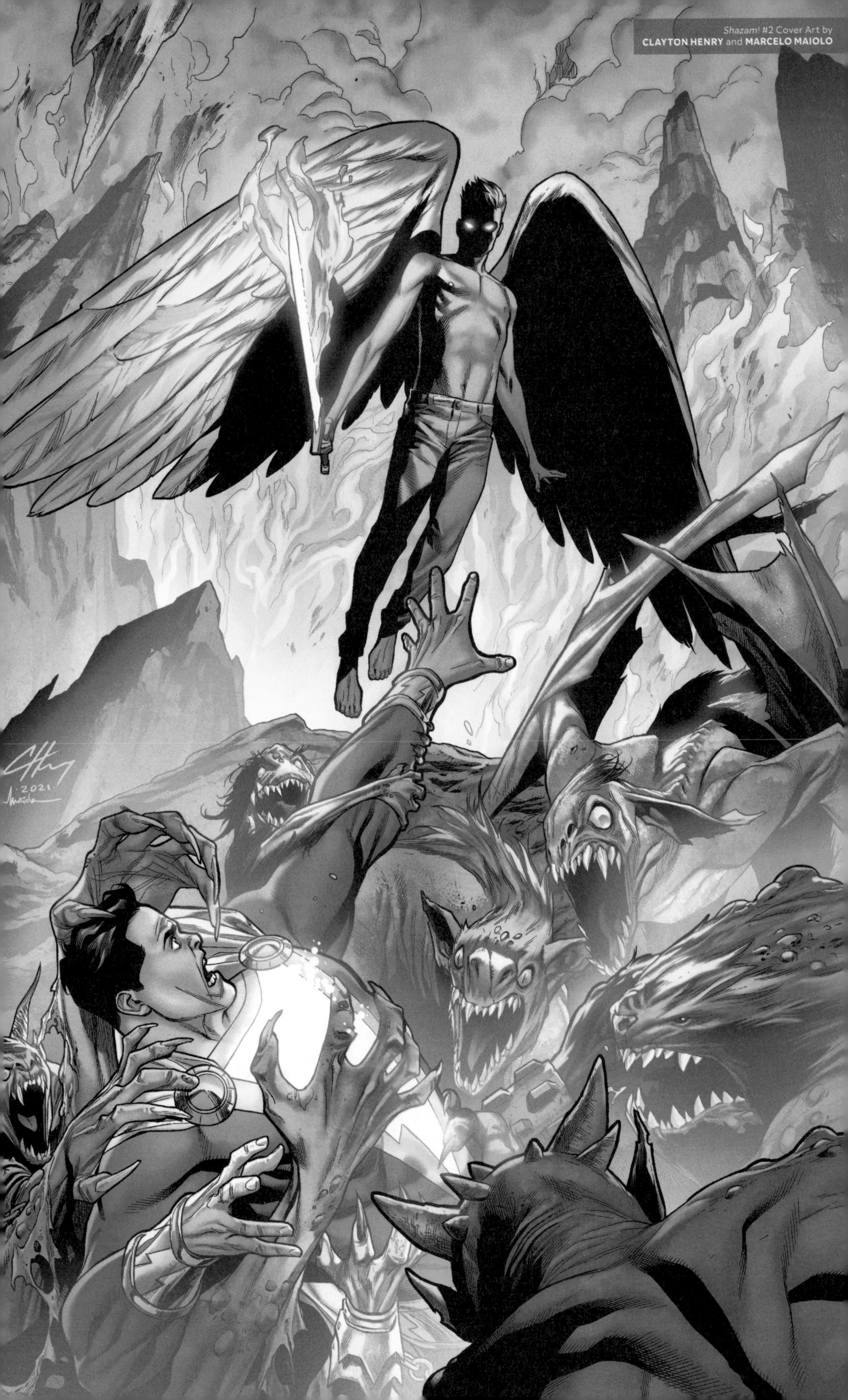

Shazam! #2 Cover Art by
CLAYTON HENRY and **MARCELO MAIOLO**

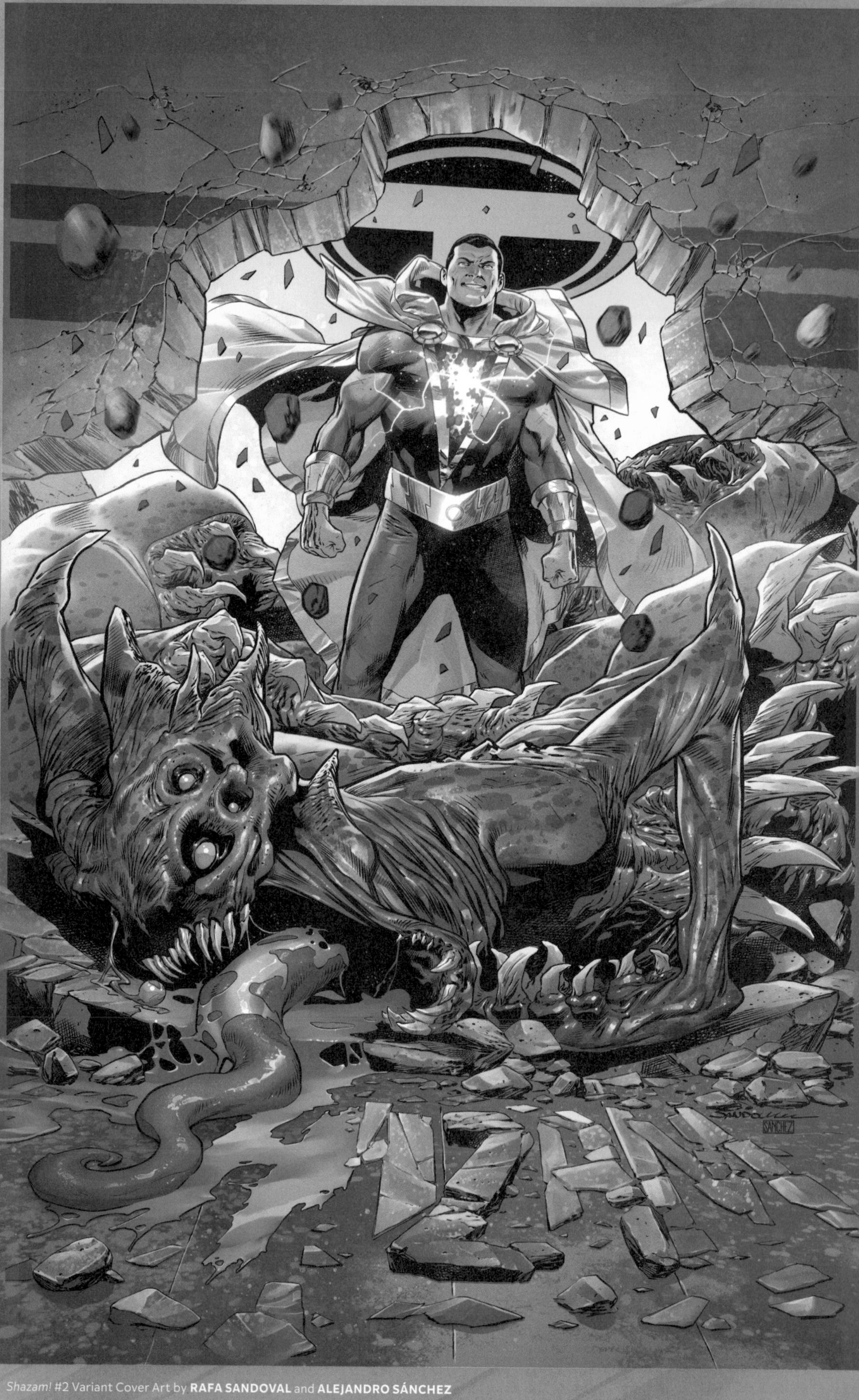
SANCHEZ

Shazam! #2 Variant Cover Art by **RAFA SANDOVAL** and **ALEJANDRO SÁNCHEZ**

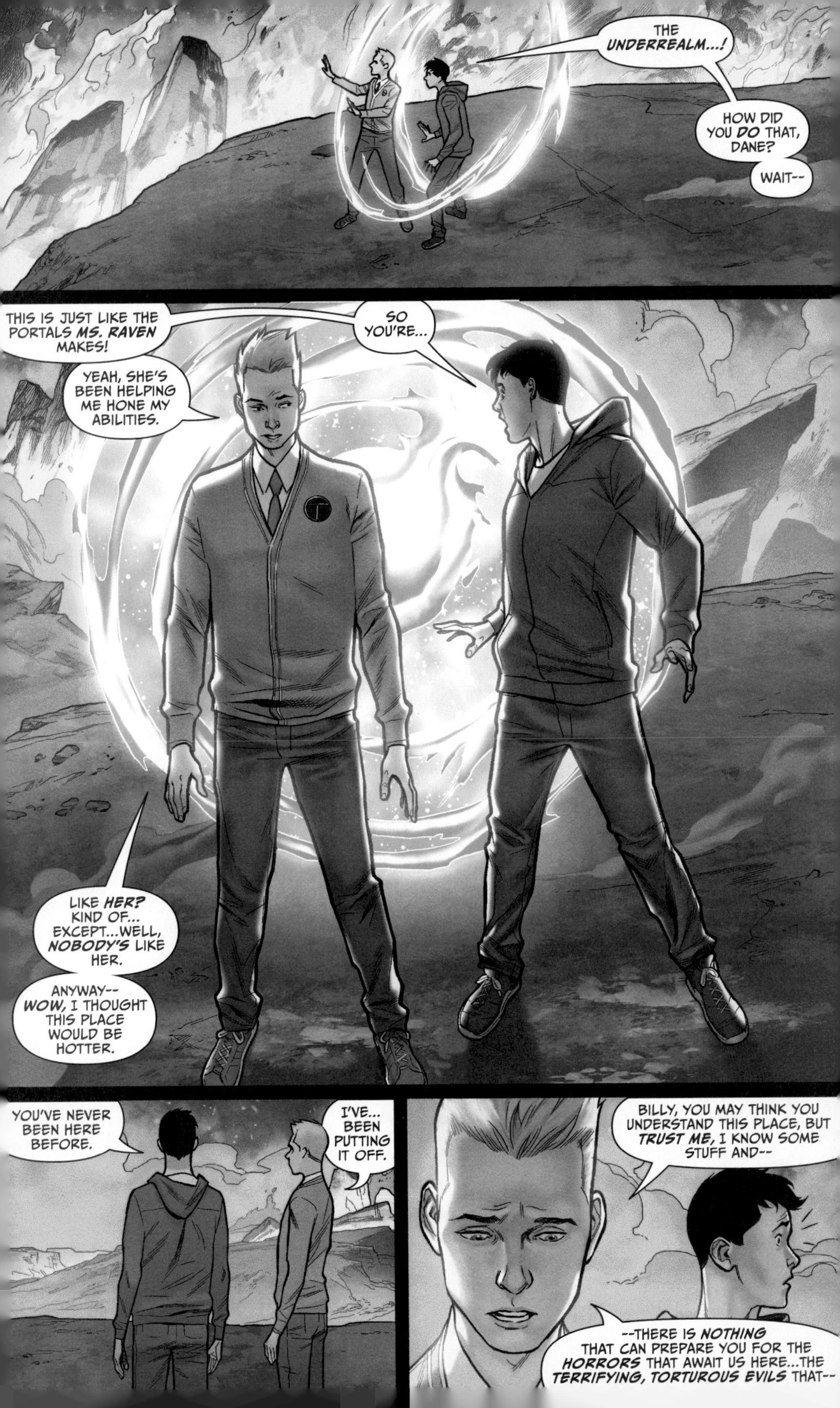
THE UNDERREALM...!
HOW DID YOU DO THAT, DANE?
WAIT--
THIS IS JUST LIKE THE PORTALS MS. RAVEN MAKES!
SO YOU'RE...
YEAH, SHE'S BEEN HELPING ME HONE MY ABILITIES.
LIKE HER? KIND OF... EXCEPT...WELL, NOBODY'S LIKE HER.
ANYWAY-- WOW, I THOUGHT THIS PLACE WOULD BE HOTTER.
YOU'VE NEVER BEEN HERE BEFORE.
I'VE... BEEN PUTTING IT OFF.
BILLY, YOU MAY THINK YOU UNDERSTAND THIS PLACE, BUT TRUST ME, I KNOW SOME STUFF AND--
--THERE IS NOTHING THAT CAN PREPARE YOU FOR THE HORRORS THAT AWAIT US HERE...THE TERRIFYING, TORTUROUS EVILS THAT--

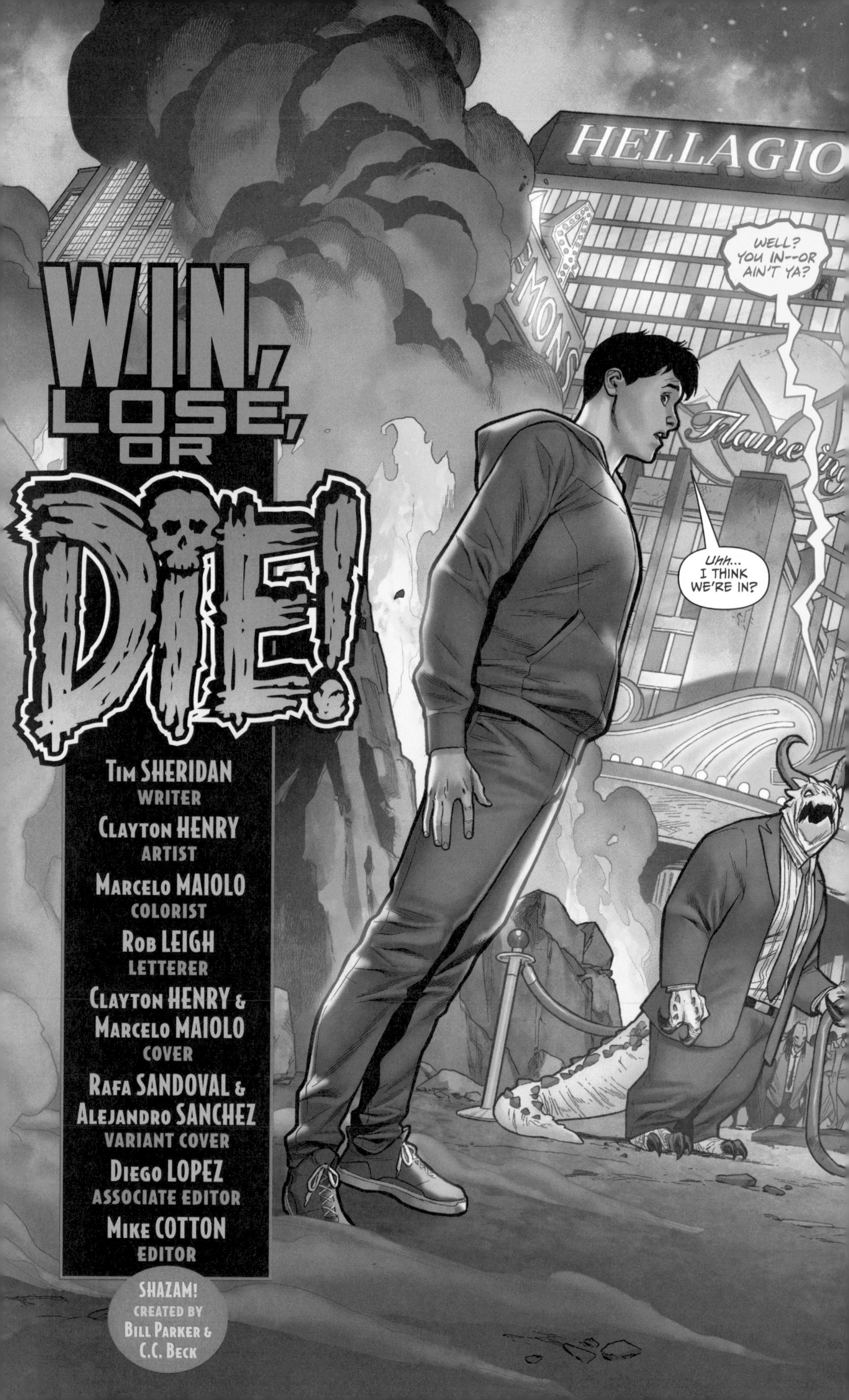
HELLAGIO
WELL? YOU IN--OR AIN'T YA?
Uhh... I THINK WE'RE IN?
WIN, LOSE, OR DIE!
TIM SHERIDAN WRITER
CLAYTON HENRY ARTIST
MARCELO MAIOLO COLORIST
ROB LEIGH LETTERER
CLAYTON HENRY & MARCELO MAIOLO COVER
RAFA SANDOVAL & ALEJANDRO SANCHEZ VARIANT COVER
DIEGO LOPEZ ASSOCIATE EDITOR
MIKE COTTON EDITOR
SHAZAM! CREATED BY BILL PARKER & C.C. BECK

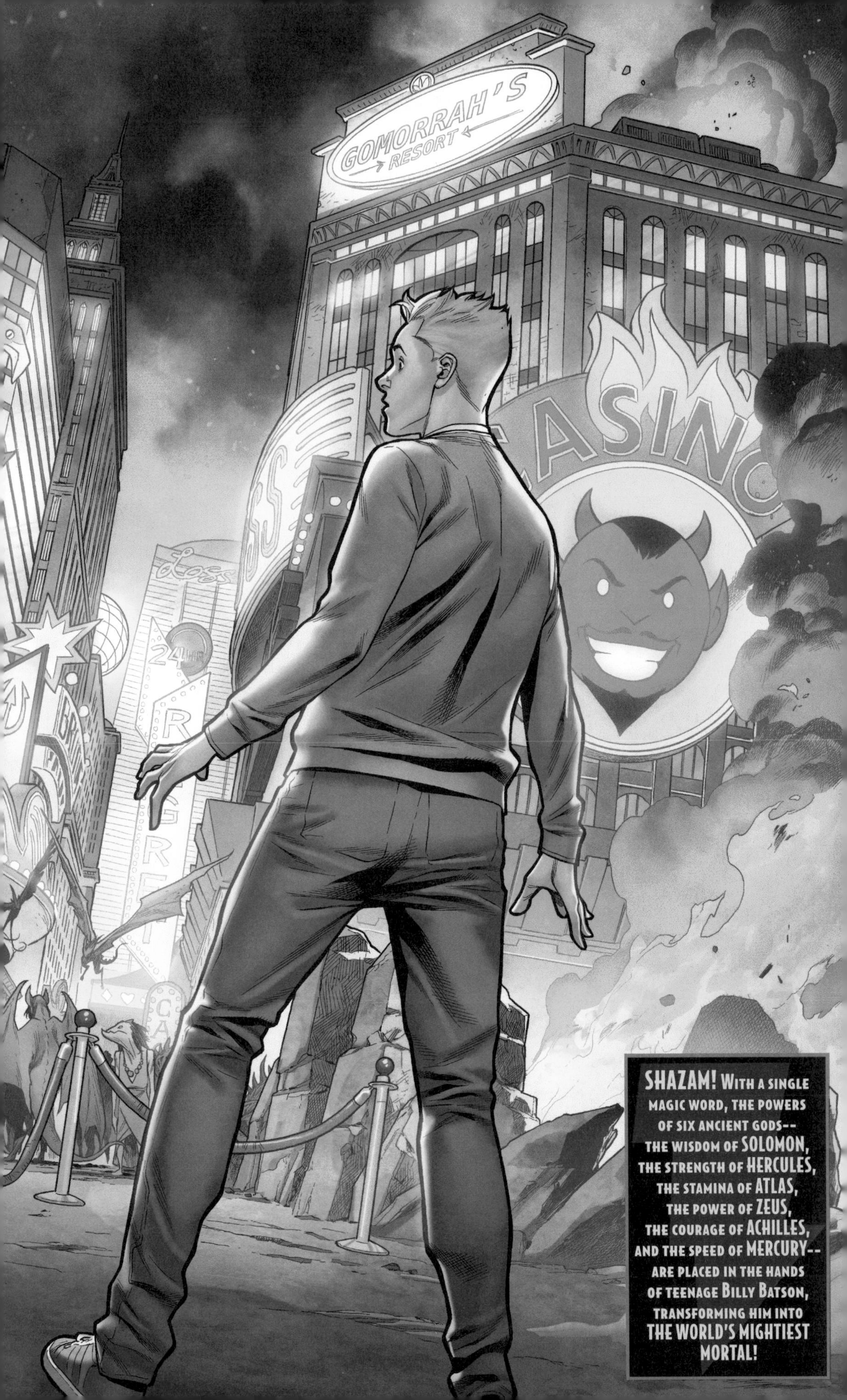
GOMORRAH'S
GOMORRAH RESORT
CASINO
24HR
SHAZAM! WITH A SINGLE MAGIC WORD, THE POWERS OF SIX ANCIENT GODS-- THE WISDOM OF SOLOMON, THE STRENGTH OF HERCULES, THE STAMINA OF ATLAS, THE POWER OF ZEUS, THE COURAGE OF ACHILLES, AND THE SPEED OF MERCURY-- ARE PLACED IN THE HANDS OF TEENAGE BILLY BATSON, TRANSFORMING HIM INTO THE WORLD'S MIGHTIEST MORTAL!

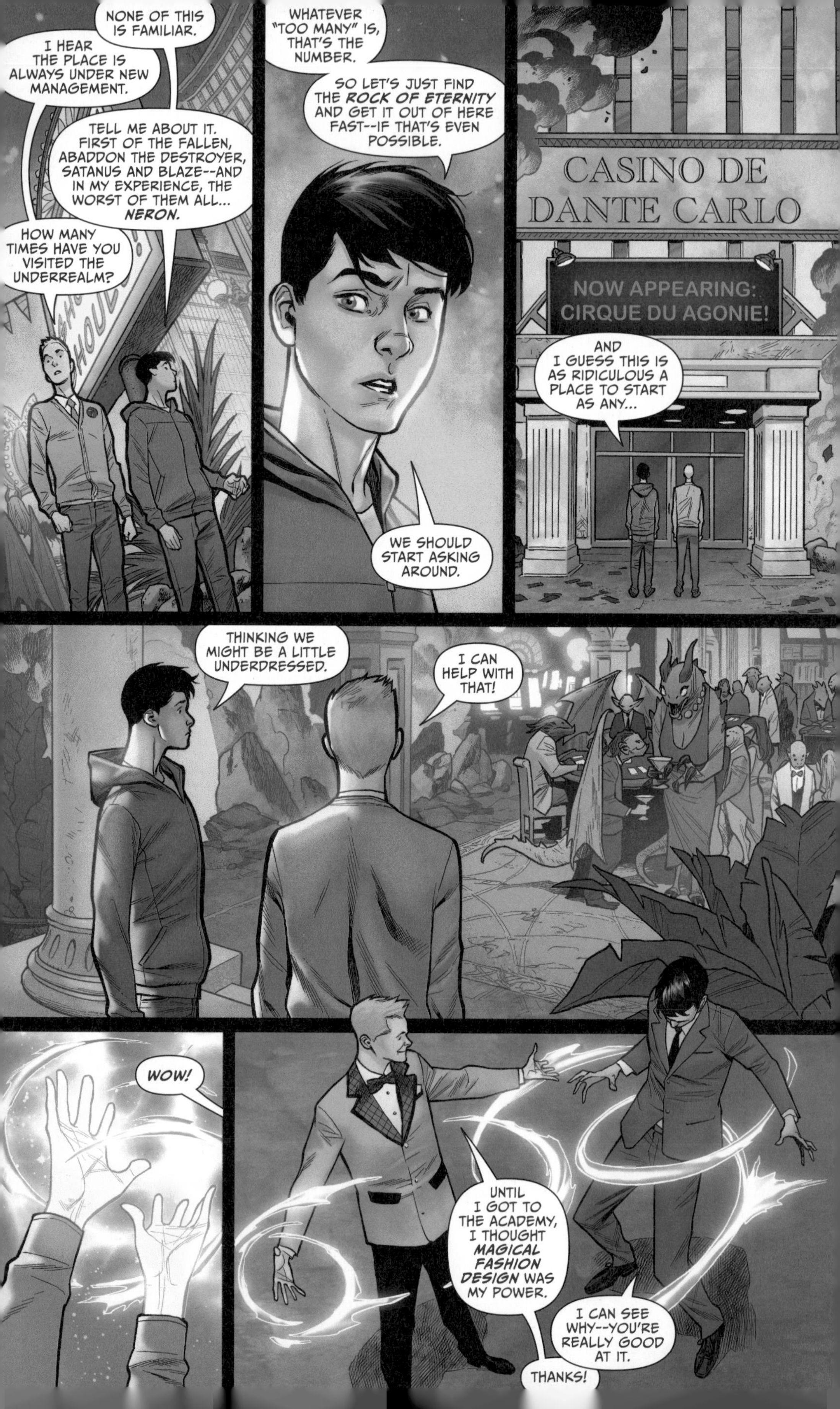
NONE OF THIS IS FAMILIAR.
I HEAR THE PLACE IS ALWAYS UNDER NEW MANAGEMENT.
TELL ME ABOUT IT. FIRST OF THE FALLEN, ABADDON THE DESTROYER, SATANUS AND BLAZE--AND IN MY EXPERIENCE, THE WORST OF THEM ALL... NERON.
HOW MANY TIMES HAVE YOU VISITED THE UNDERREALM?
WHATEVER "TOO MANY" IS, THAT'S THE NUMBER.
SO LET'S JUST FIND THE ROCK OF ETERNITY AND GET IT OUT OF HERE FAST--IF THAT'S EVEN POSSIBLE.
WE SHOULD START ASKING AROUND.
CASINO DE DANTE CARLO
NOW APPEARING: CIRQUE DU AGONIE!
AND I GUESS THIS IS AS RIDICULOUS A PLACE TO START AS ANY...
THINKING WE MIGHT BE A LITTLE UNDERDRESSED.
I CAN HELP WITH THAT!
WOW!
UNTIL I GOT TO THE ACADEMY, I THOUGHT MAGICAL FASHION DESIGN WAS MY POWER.
I CAN SEE WHY--YOU'RE REALLY GOOD AT IT.
THANKS!

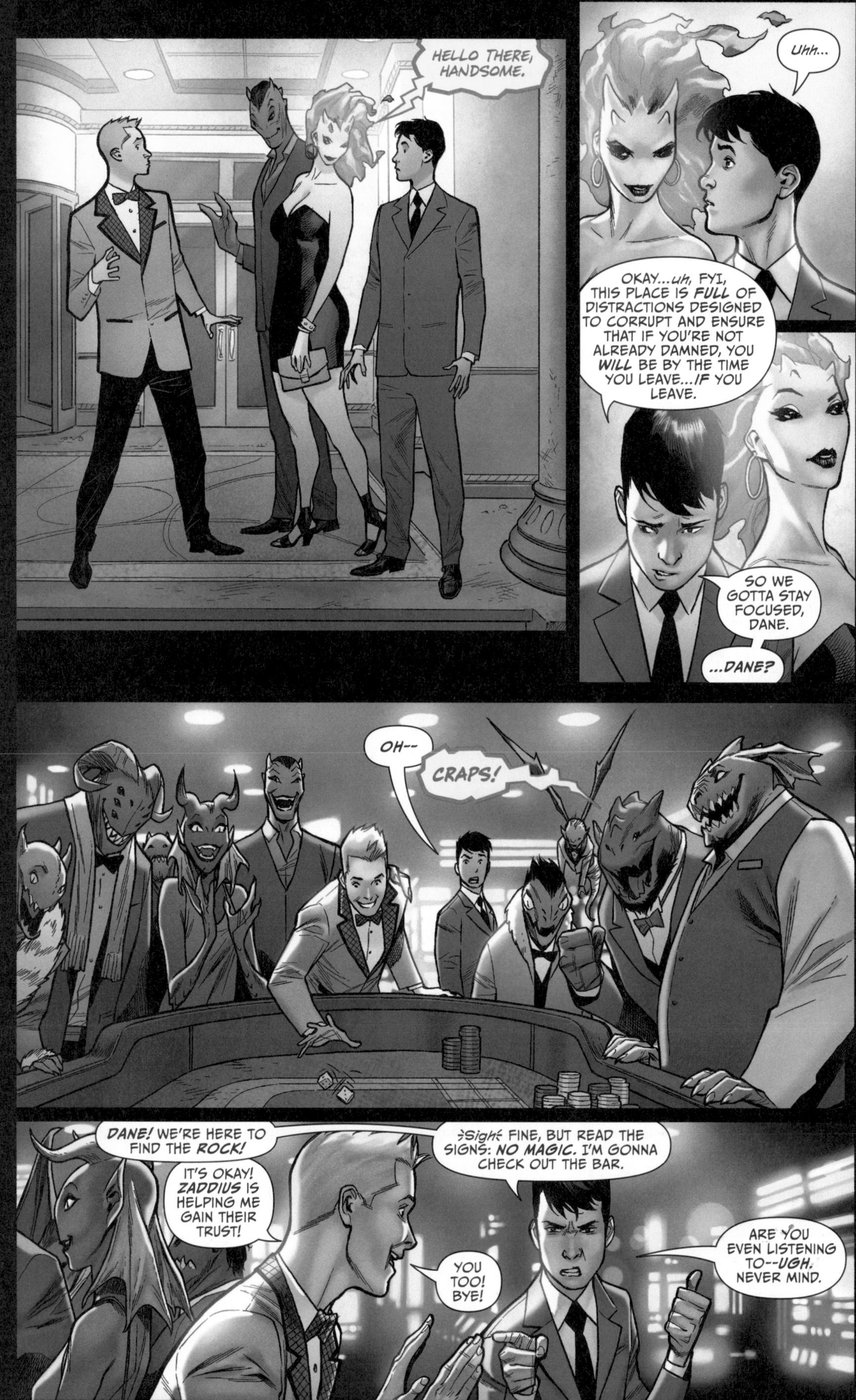
HELLO THERE, HANDSOME.
Uhh...
OKAY...uh, FYI, THIS PLACE IS FULL OF DISTRACTIONS DESIGNED TO CORRUPT AND ENSURE THAT IF YOU'RE NOT ALREADY DAMNED, YOU WILL BE BY THE TIME YOU LEAVE...IF YOU LEAVE.
SO WE GOTTA STAY FOCUSED, DANE.
...DANE?
OH--
CRAPS!
DANE! WE'RE HERE TO FIND THE ROCK!
IT'S OKAY! ZADDIUS IS HELPING ME GAIN THEIR TRUST!
YOU TOO! BYE!
Sigh FINE, BUT READ THE SIGNS: NO MAGIC. I'M GONNA CHECK OUT THE BAR.
ARE YOU EVEN LISTENING TO--UGH. NEVER MIND.

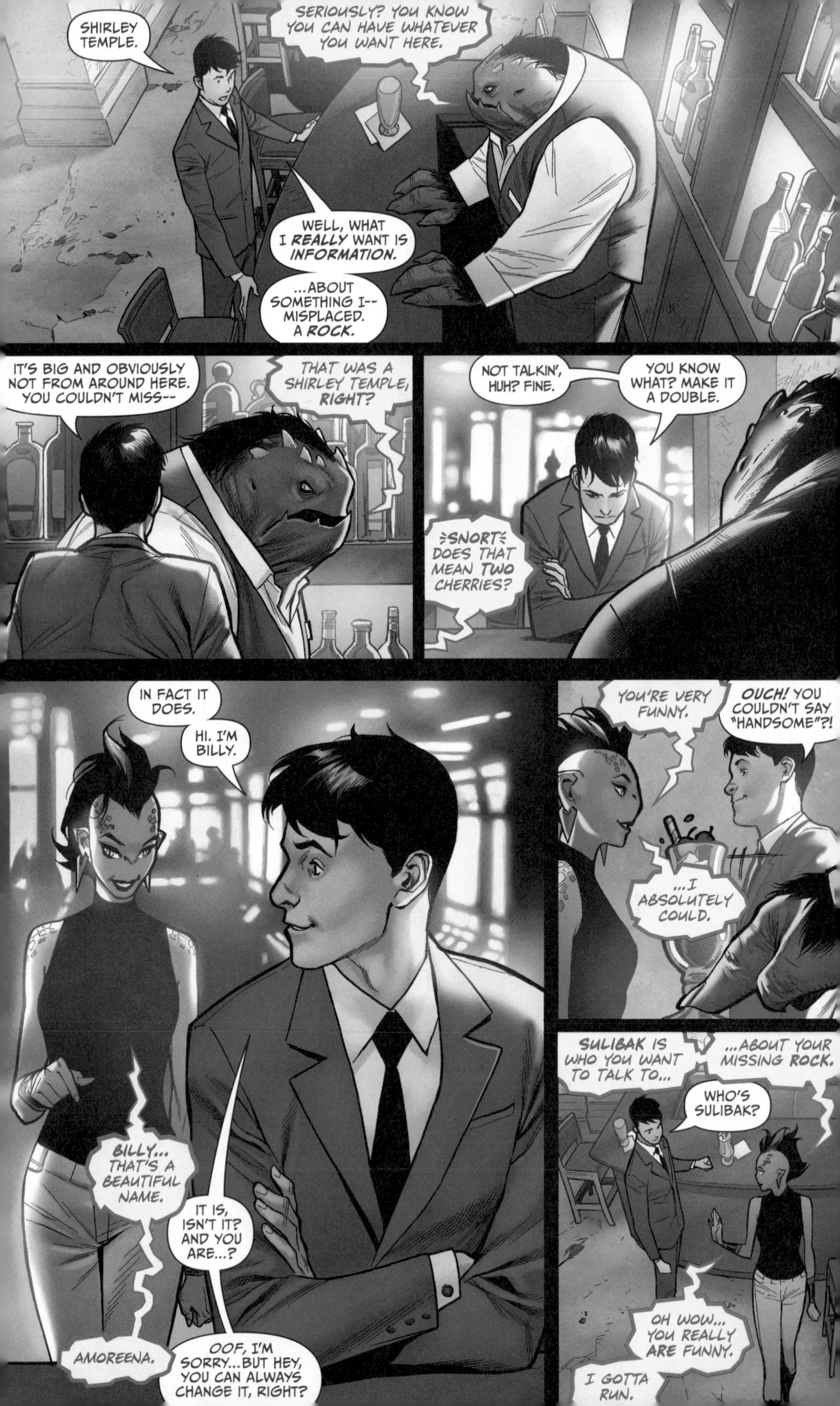

SHIRLEY TEMPLE.
SERIOUSLY? YOU KNOW YOU CAN HAVE WHATEVER YOU WANT HERE.
WELL, WHAT I **REALLY** WANT IS ***INFORMATION.***
...ABOUT SOMETHING I--MISPLACED. A ***ROCK.***
IT'S BIG AND OBVIOUSLY NOT FROM AROUND HERE. YOU COULDN'T MISS--
THAT WAS A SHIRLEY TEMPLE, ***RIGHT?***
NOT TALKIN', HUH? FINE.
YOU KNOW WHAT? MAKE IT A DOUBLE.
SNORT DOES THAT MEAN **TWO** CHERRIES?
IN FACT IT DOES.
HI. I'M BILLY.
BILLY... THAT'S A BEAUTIFUL NAME.
IT IS, ISN'T IT? AND YOU ARE...?
AMOREENA.
OOF, I'M SORRY...BUT HEY, YOU CAN ALWAYS CHANGE IT, RIGHT?
YOU'RE VERY FUNNY.
OUCH! YOU COULDN'T SAY "HANDSOME"?!
...I ABSOLUTELY COULD.
SULIBAK IS WHO YOU WANT TO TALK TO...
...ABOUT YOUR MISSING **ROCK.**
WHO'S SULIBAK?
OH WOW... YOU REALLY **ARE** FUNNY.
I GOTTA RUN.

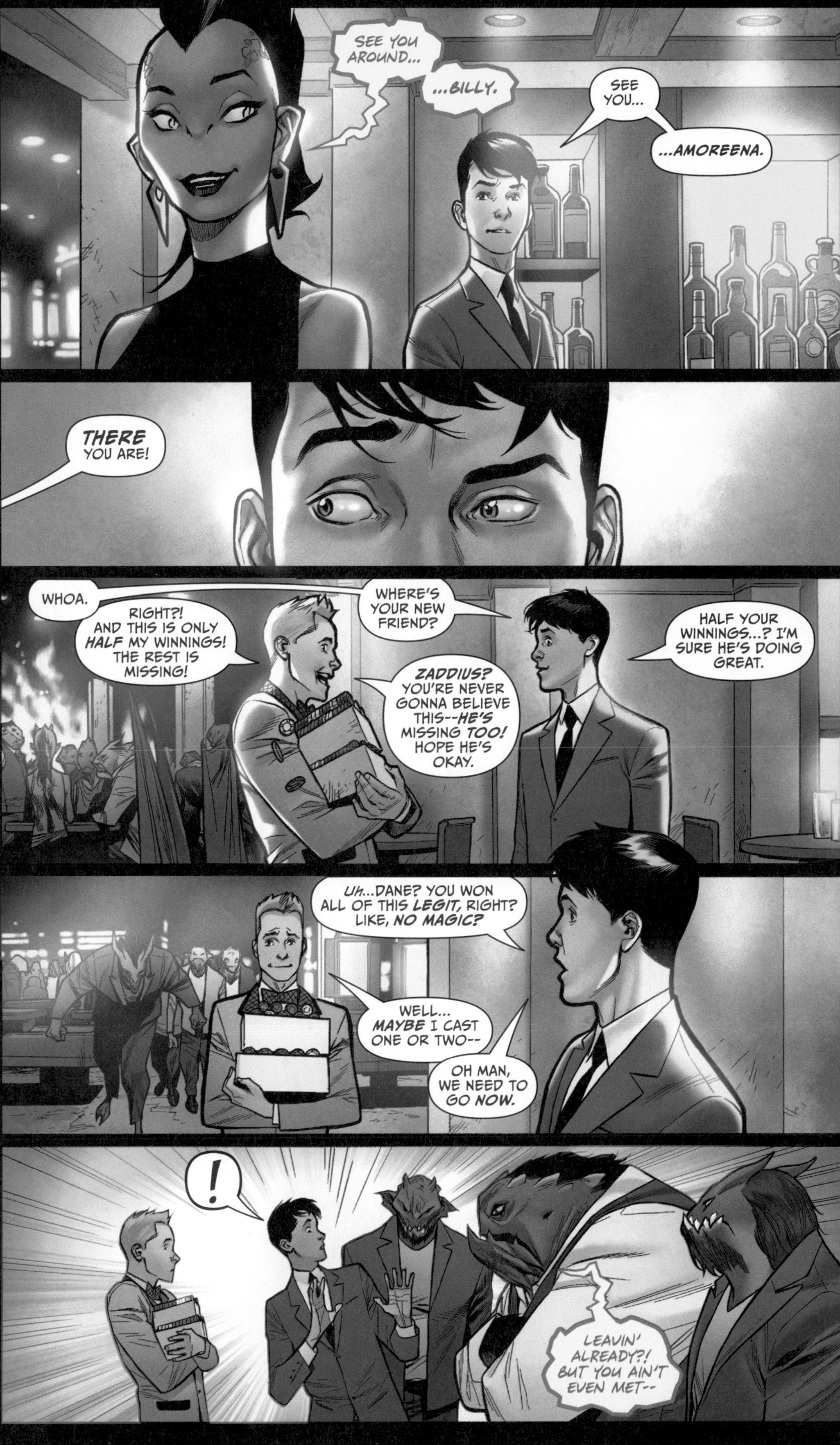

SEE YOU AROUND...
...BILLY.
SEE YOU...
...AMOREENA.
THERE YOU ARE!
WHOA.
RIGHT?! AND THIS IS ONLY HALF MY WINNINGS! THE REST IS MISSING!
WHERE'S YOUR NEW FRIEND?
ZADDIUS? YOU'RE NEVER GONNA BELIEVE THIS--HE'S MISSING TOO! HOPE HE'S OKAY.
HALF YOUR WINNINGS...? I'M SURE HE'S DOING GREAT.
Uh...DANE? YOU WON ALL OF THIS LEGIT, RIGHT? LIKE, NO MAGIC?
WELL... MAYBE I CAST ONE OR TWO--
OH MAN, WE NEED TO GO NOW.
!
LEAVIN' ALREADY?! BUT YOU AIN'T EVEN MET--

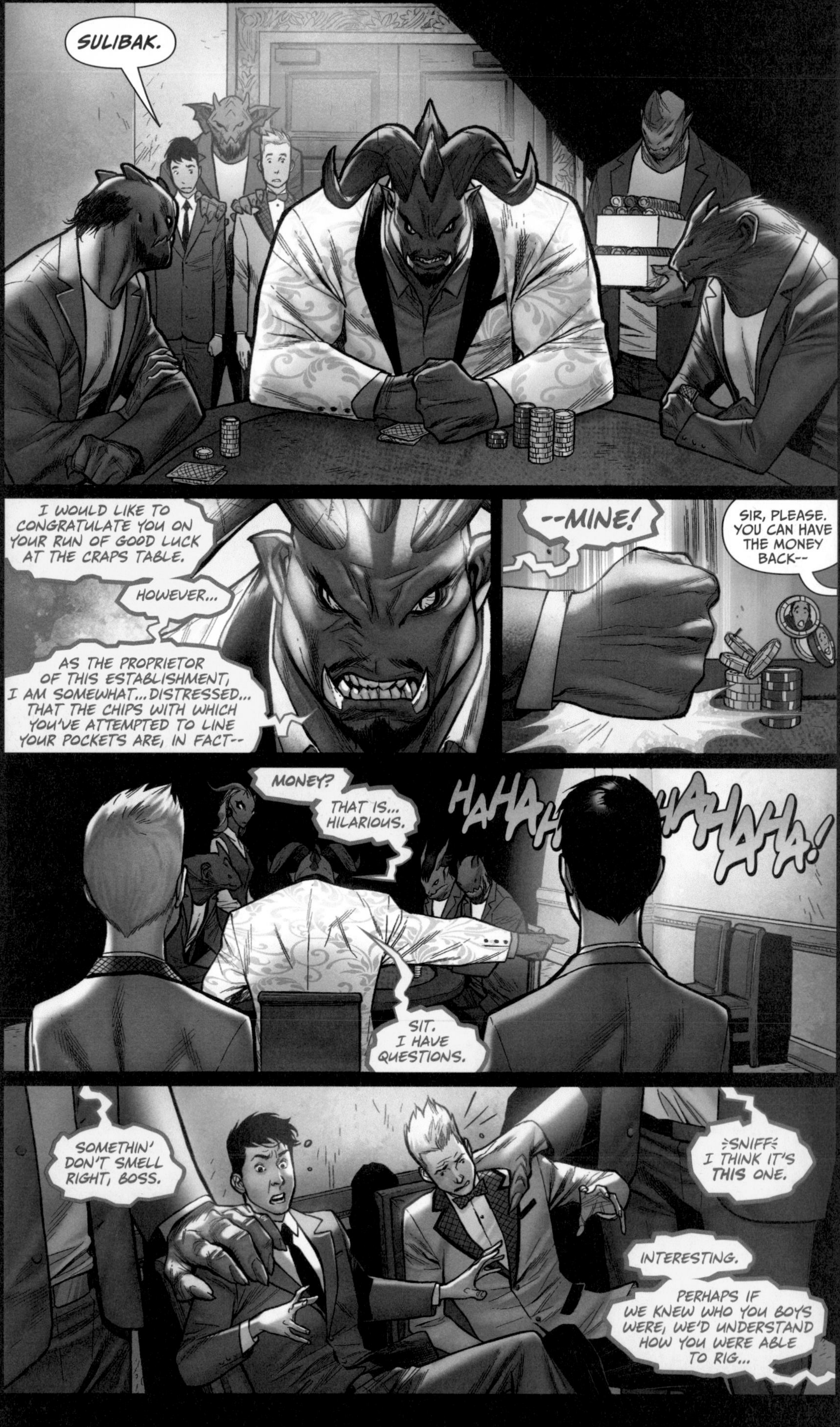

SULIBAK.
I WOULD LIKE TO CONGRATULATE YOU ON YOUR RUN OF GOOD LUCK AT THE CRAPS TABLE.
HOWEVER...
AS THE PROPRIETOR OF THIS ESTABLISHMENT, I AM SOMEWHAT...DISTRESSED... THAT THE CHIPS WITH WHICH YOU'VE ATTEMPTED TO LINE YOUR POCKETS ARE, IN FACT--
--MINE!
SIR, PLEASE. YOU CAN HAVE THE MONEY BACK--
MONEY?
THAT IS... HILARIOUS.
HAHAHAHAHAHAHA!
SIT. I HAVE QUESTIONS.
SOMETHIN' DON'T SMELL RIGHT, BOSS.
SNIFF I THINK IT'S THIS ONE.
INTERESTING.
PERHAPS IF WE KNEW WHO YOU BOYS WERE, WE'D UNDERSTAND HOW YOU WERE ABLE TO RIG...

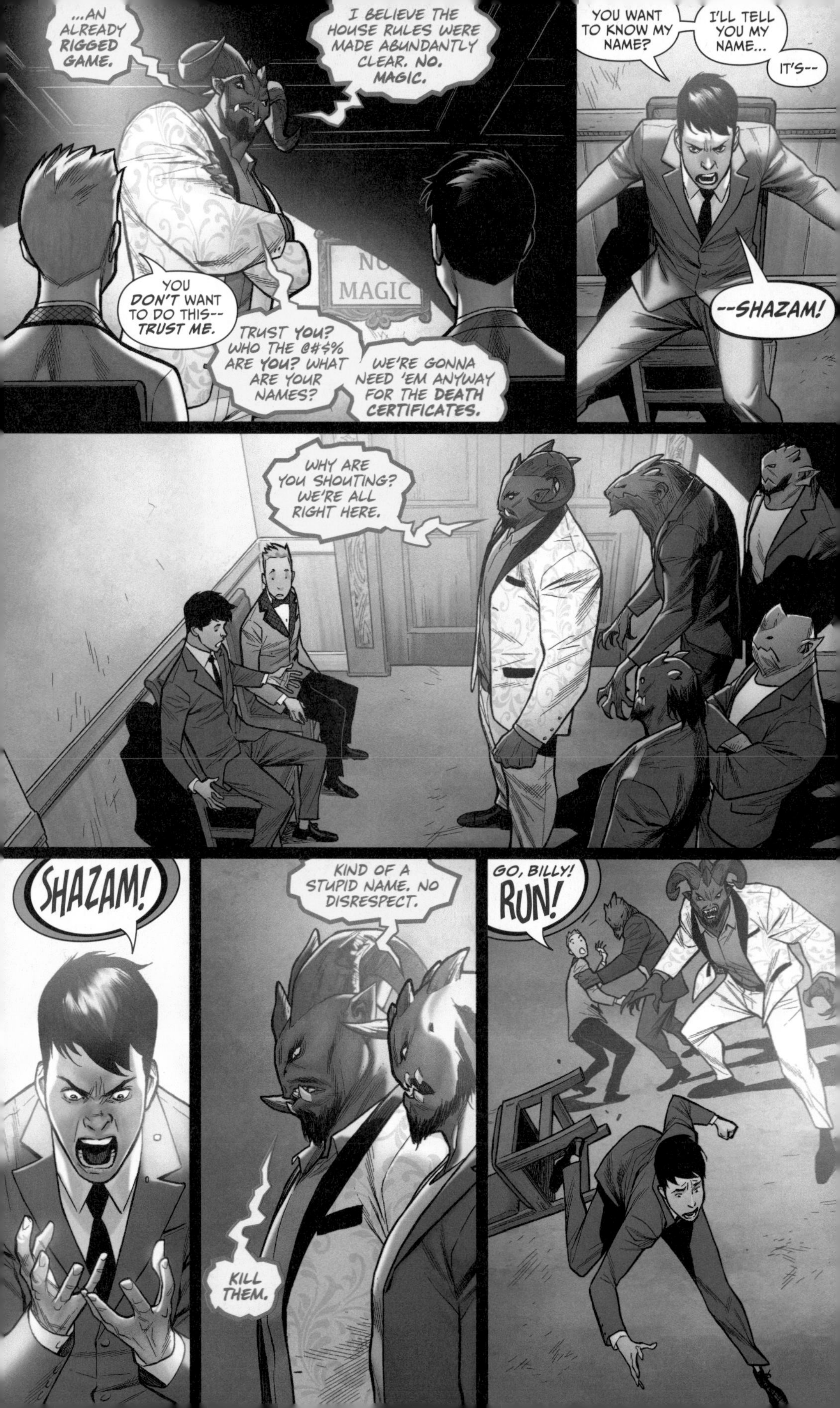
...AN ALREADY RIGGED GAME.
I BELIEVE THE HOUSE RULES WERE MADE ABUNDANTLY CLEAR. NO. MAGIC.
NO MAGIC
YOU DON'T WANT TO DO THIS-- TRUST ME.
TRUST YOU? WHO THE @#$% ARE YOU? WHAT ARE YOUR NAMES?
WE'RE GONNA NEED 'EM ANYWAY FOR THE DEATH CERTIFICATES.
YOU WANT TO KNOW MY NAME?
I'LL TELL YOU MY NAME...
IT'S--
--SHAZAM!
WHY ARE YOU SHOUTING? WE'RE ALL RIGHT HERE.
SHAZAM!
KIND OF A STUPID NAME. NO DISRESPECT.
KILL THEM.
GO, BILLY! RUN!

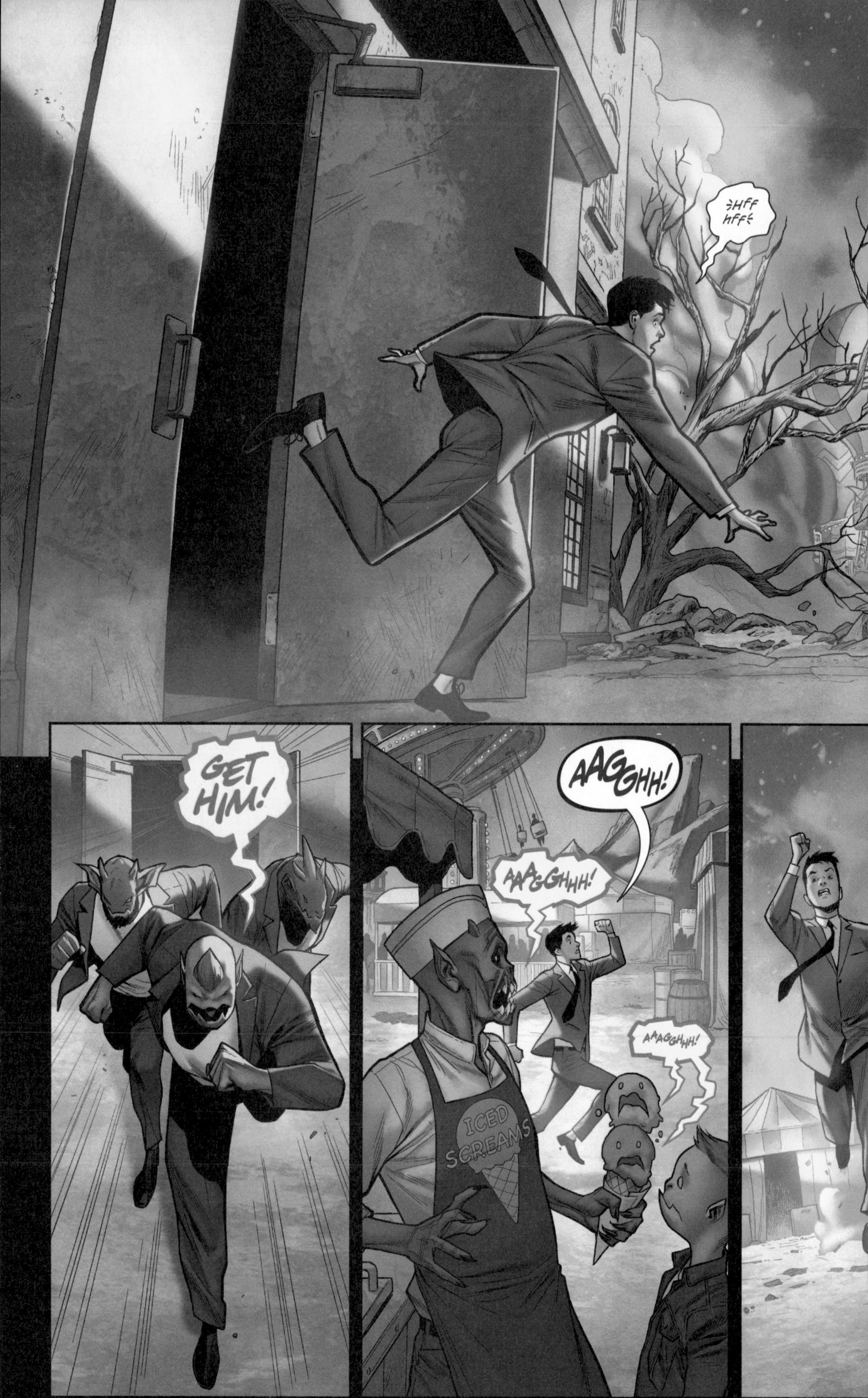
HFF HFF
GET HIM!
AAGGHH!
AAAGGHHH!
AAAGGHHH!
ICED SCREAMS

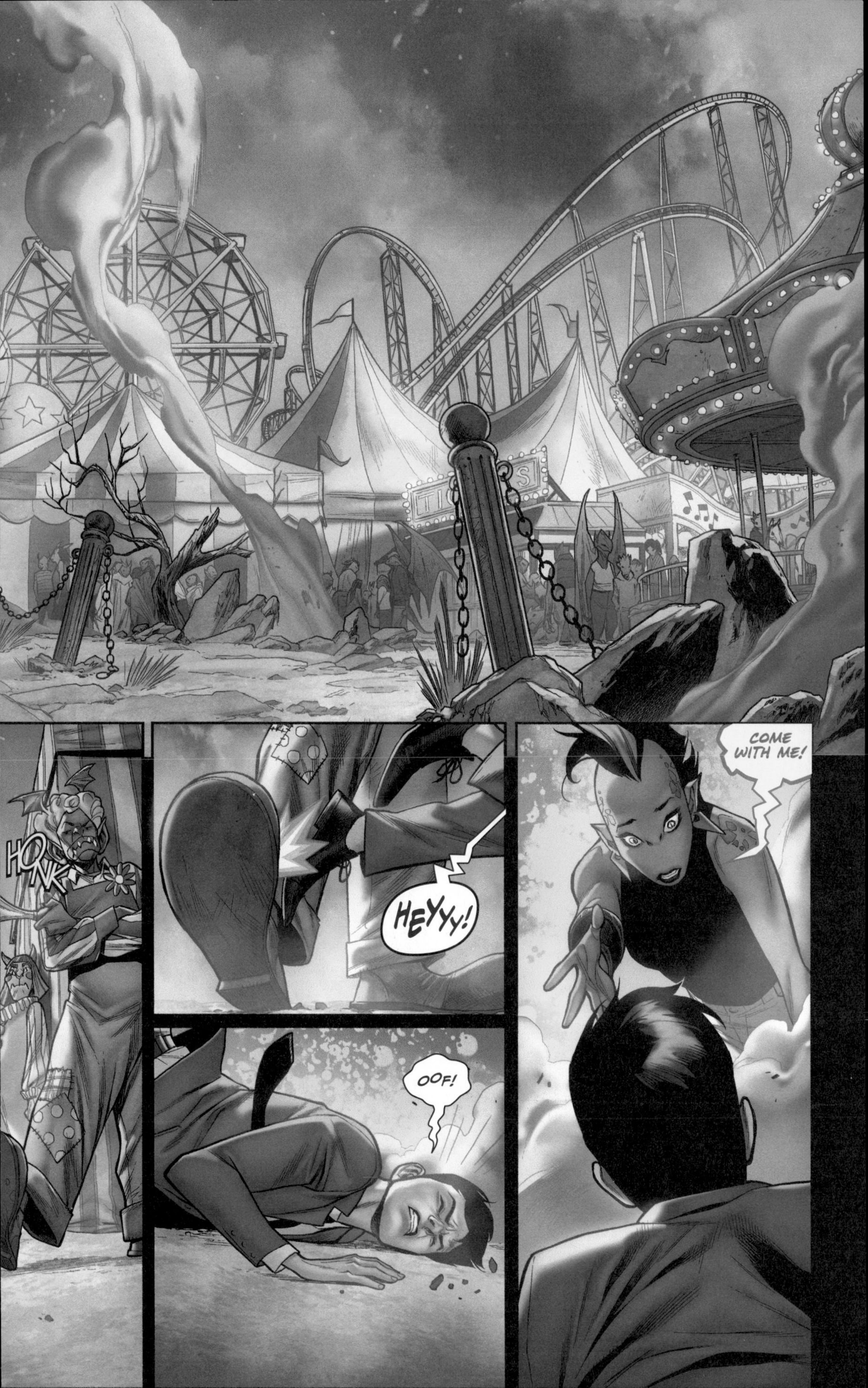
HONK
HEYYY!
OOF!
COME WITH ME!

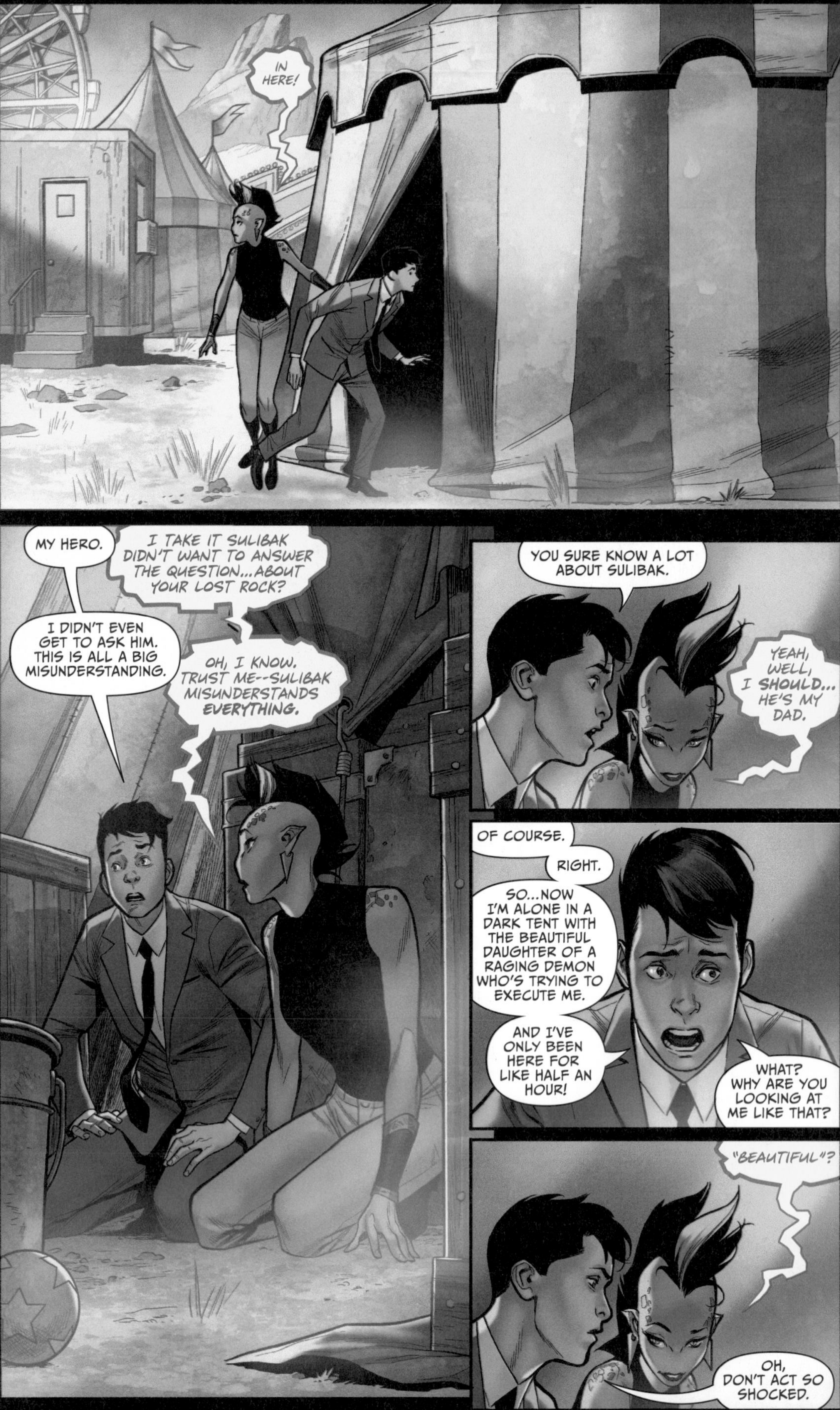
IN HERE!
MY HERO.
I TAKE IT SULIBAK DIDN'T WANT TO ANSWER THE QUESTION...ABOUT YOUR LOST ROCK?
I DIDN'T EVEN GET TO ASK HIM. THIS IS ALL A BIG MISUNDERSTANDING.
OH, I KNOW. TRUST ME--SULIBAK MISUNDERSTANDS EVERYTHING.
YOU SURE KNOW A LOT ABOUT SULIBAK.
YEAH, WELL, I SHOULD... HE'S MY DAD.
OF COURSE.
RIGHT.
SO...NOW I'M ALONE IN A DARK TENT WITH THE BEAUTIFUL DAUGHTER OF A RAGING DEMON WHO'S TRYING TO EXECUTE ME.
AND I'VE ONLY BEEN HERE FOR LIKE HALF AN HOUR!
WHAT? WHY ARE YOU LOOKING AT ME LIKE THAT?
"BEAUTIFUL"?
OH, DON'T ACT SO SHOCKED.

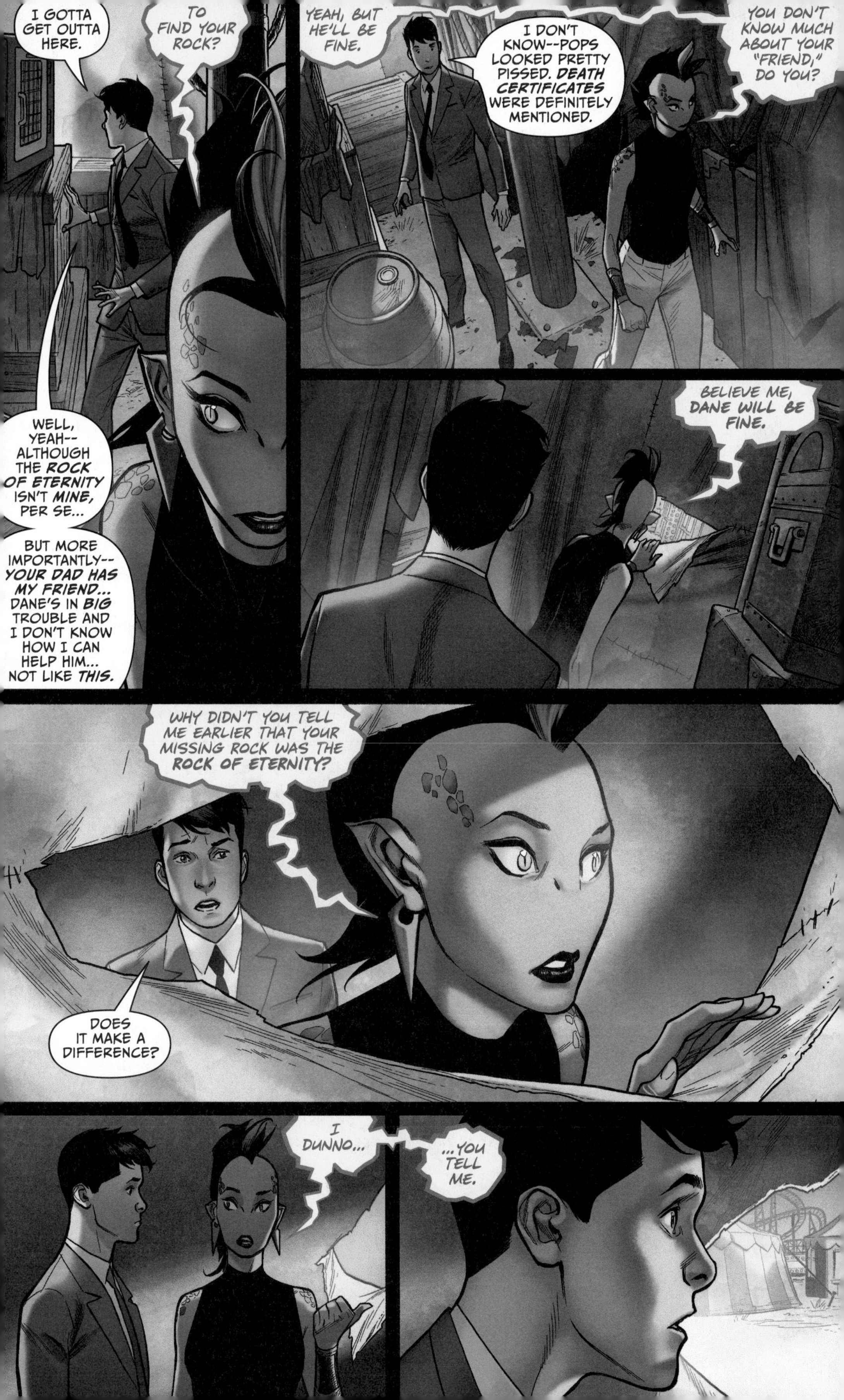
I GOTTA GET OUTTA HERE.
TO FIND YOUR ROCK?
WELL, YEAH-- ALTHOUGH THE ROCK OF ETERNITY ISN'T MINE, PER SE...
BUT MORE IMPORTANTLY-- YOUR DAD HAS MY FRIEND... DANE'S IN BIG TROUBLE AND I DON'T KNOW HOW I CAN HELP HIM... NOT LIKE THIS.
YEAH, BUT HE'LL BE FINE.
I DON'T KNOW--POPS LOOKED PRETTY PISSED. DEATH CERTIFICATES WERE DEFINITELY MENTIONED.
YOU DON'T KNOW MUCH ABOUT YOUR "FRIEND," DO YOU?
BELIEVE ME, DANE WILL BE FINE.
WHY DIDN'T YOU TELL ME EARLIER THAT YOUR MISSING ROCK WAS THE ROCK OF ETERNITY?
DOES IT MAKE A DIFFERENCE?
I DUNNO...
...YOU TELL ME.

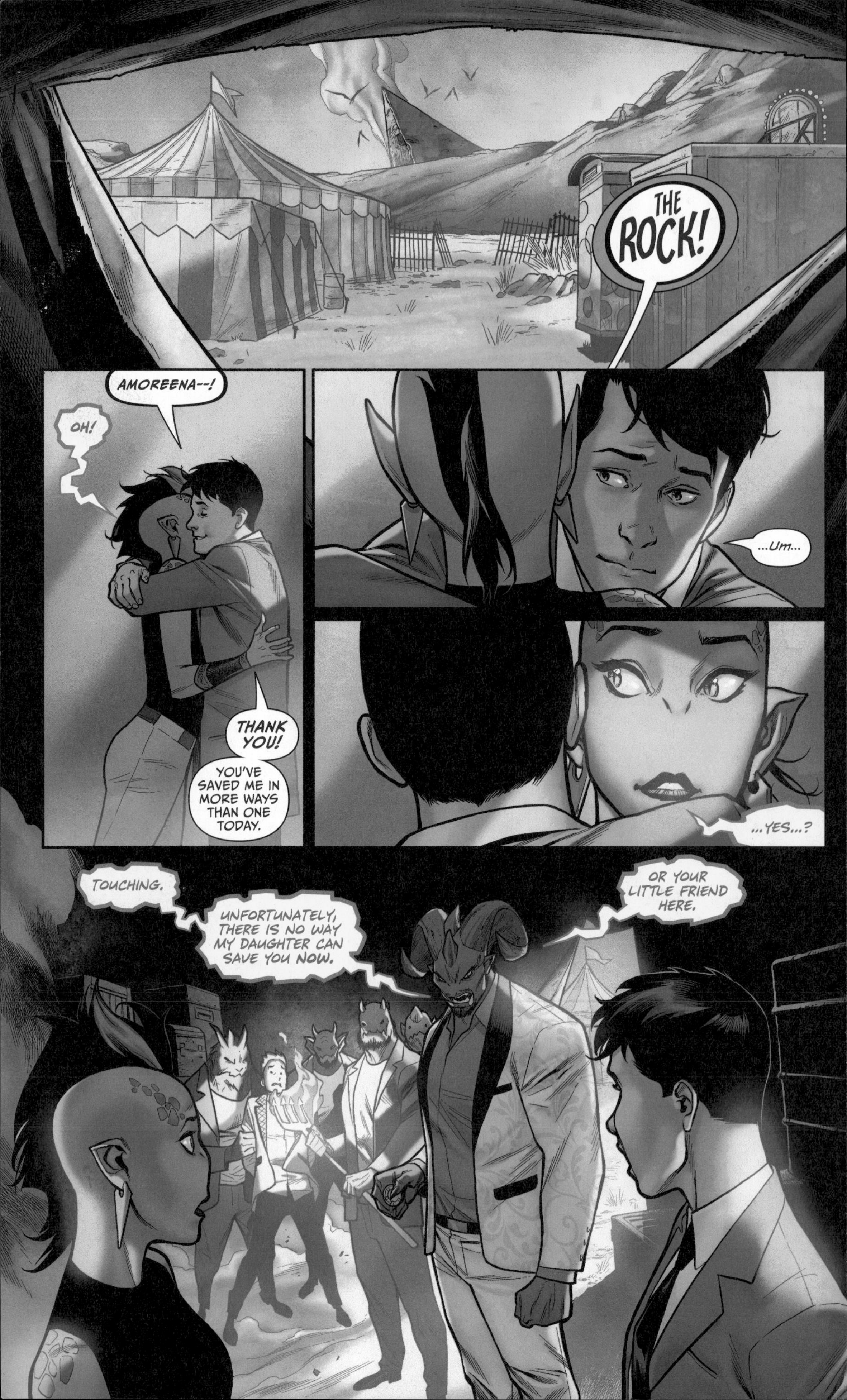
THE ROCK!
AMOREENA--!
OH!
THANK YOU!
YOU'VE SAVED ME IN MORE WAYS THAN ONE TODAY.
...Um...
...YES...?
TOUCHING.
UNFORTUNATELY, THERE IS NO WAY MY DAUGHTER CAN SAVE YOU NOW.
OR YOUR LITTLE FRIEND HERE.

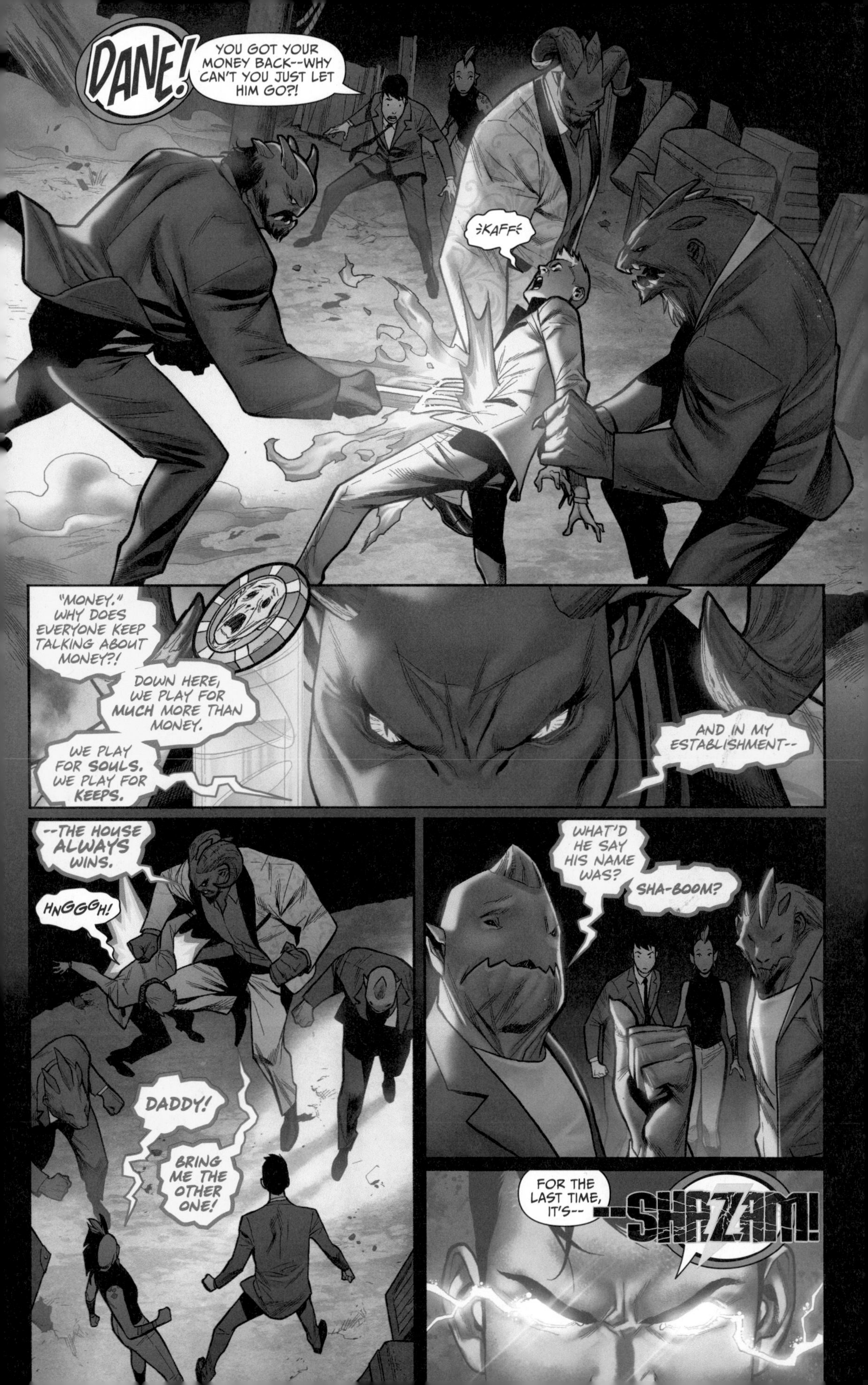
DANE!
YOU GOT YOUR MONEY BACK--WHY CAN'T YOU JUST LET HIM GO?!
KAFF
"MONEY." WHY DOES EVERYONE KEEP TALKING ABOUT MONEY?!
DOWN HERE, WE PLAY FOR MUCH MORE THAN MONEY.
WE PLAY FOR SOULS. WE PLAY FOR KEEPS.
AND IN MY ESTABLISHMENT--
--THE HOUSE ALWAYS WINS.
HNGGGH!
DADDY!
BRING ME THE OTHER ONE!
WHAT'D HE SAY HIS NAME WAS?
SHA-BOOM?
FOR THE LAST TIME, IT'S--
--SHAZAM!

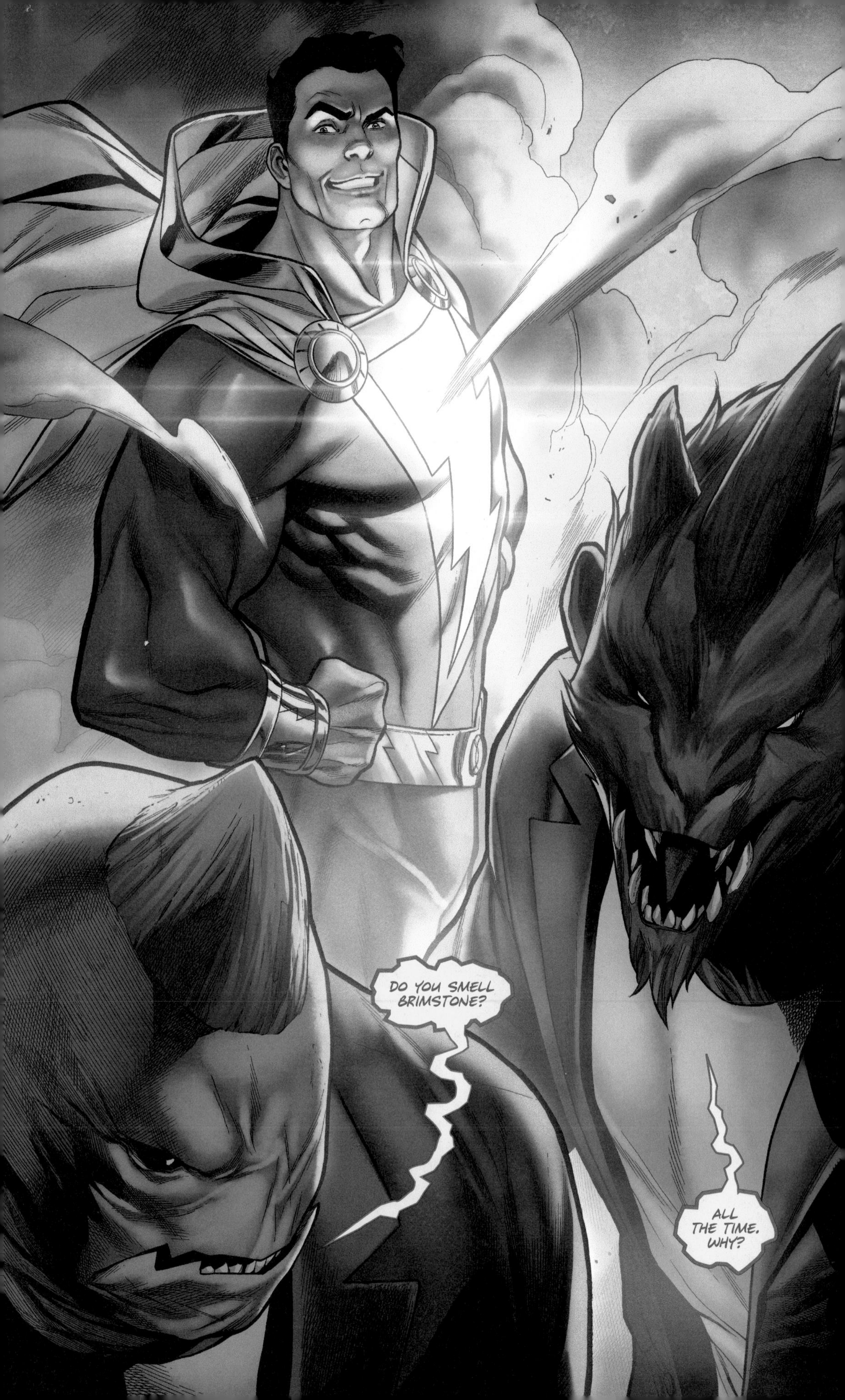
DO YOU SMELL BRIMSTONE?
ALL THE TIME. WHY?

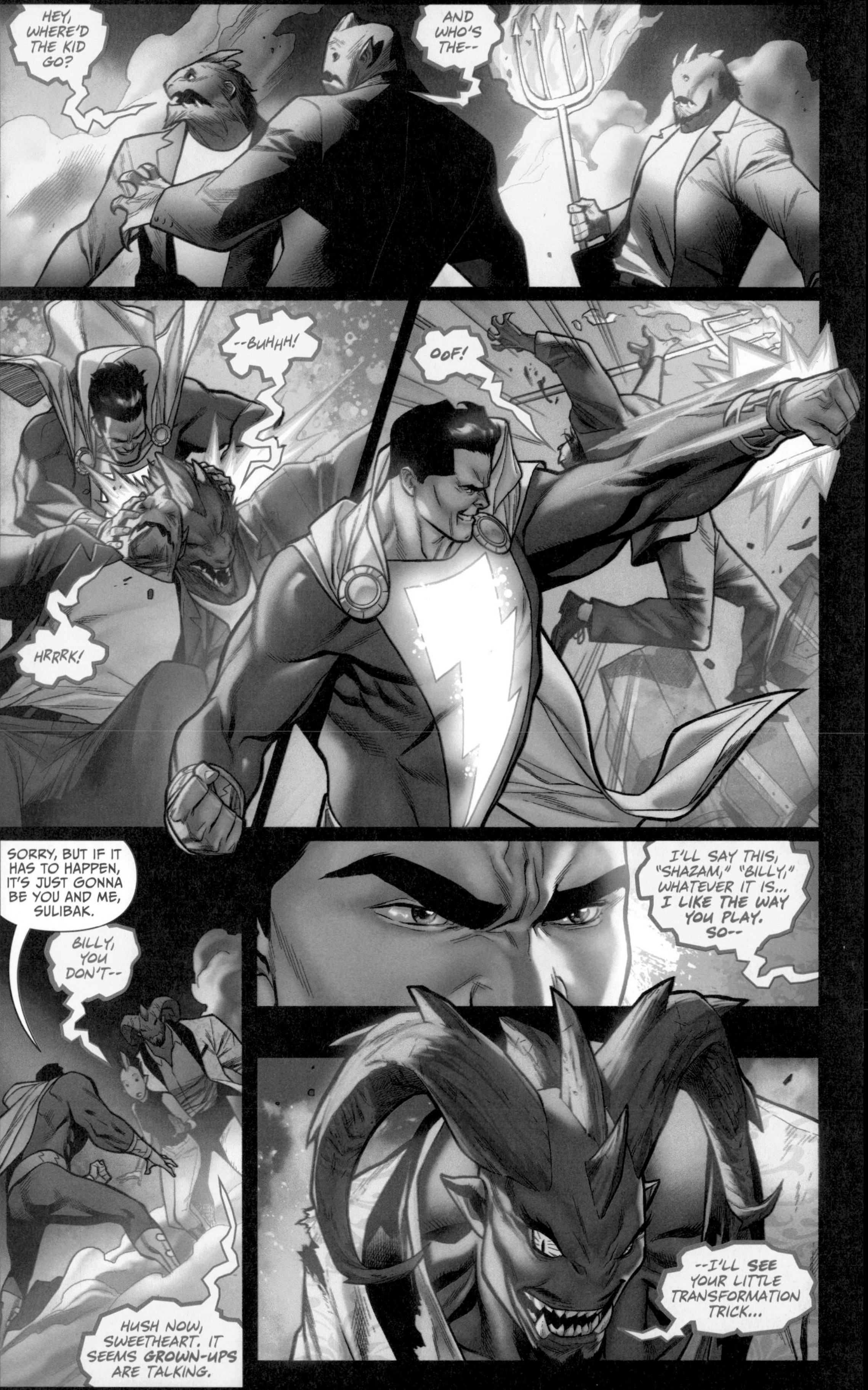

HEY, WHERE'D THE KID GO?
AND WHO'S THE--
--BUHHH!
OOF!
HRRRK!
SORRY, BUT IF IT HAS TO HAPPEN, IT'S JUST GONNA BE YOU AND ME, SULIBAK.
BILLY, YOU DON'T--
HUSH NOW, SWEETHEART. IT SEEMS GROWN-UPS ARE TALKING.
I'LL SAY THIS, "SHAZAM," "BILLY," WHATEVER IT IS... I LIKE THE WAY YOU PLAY. SO--
--I'LL SEE YOUR LITTLE TRANSFORMATION TRICK...

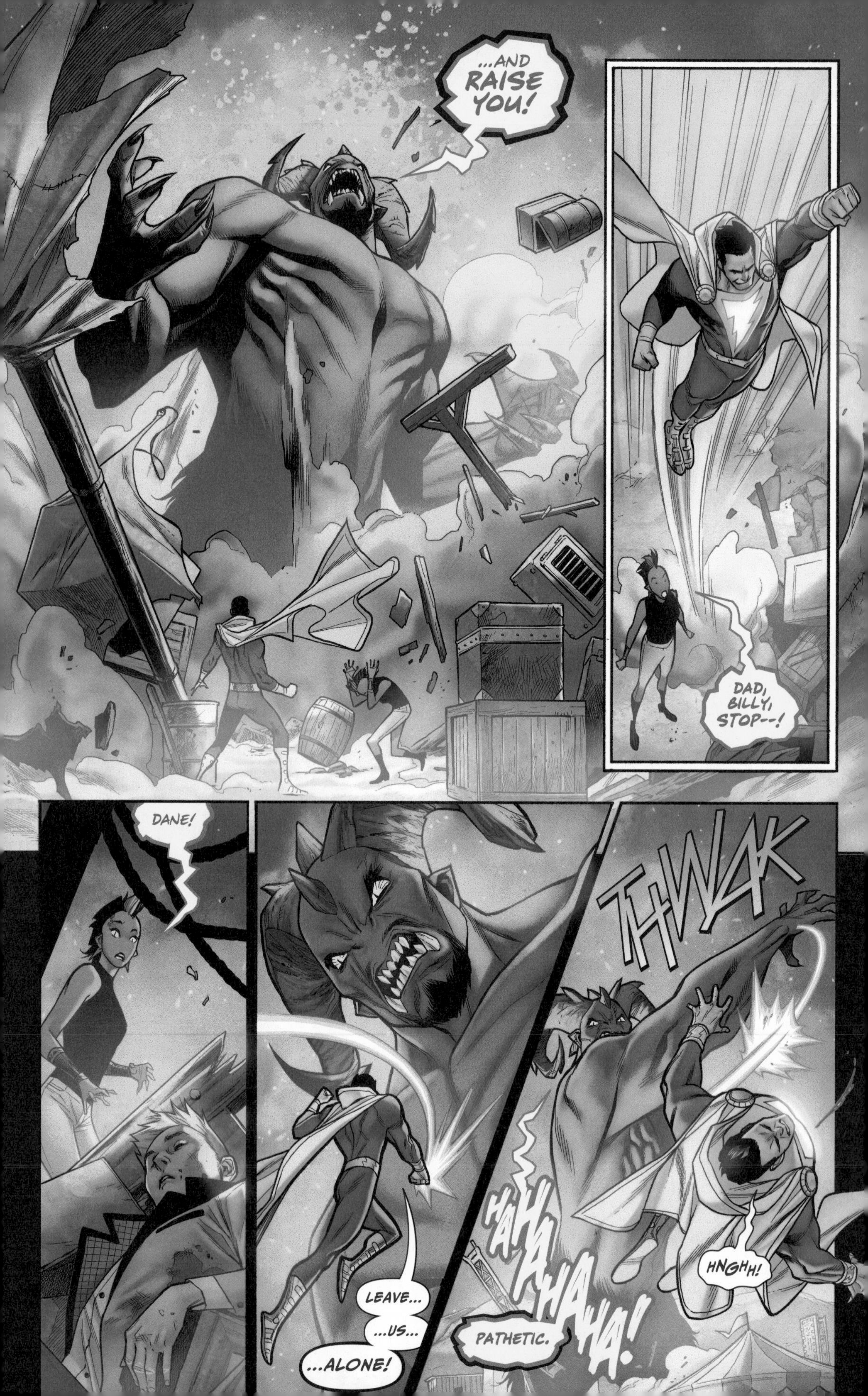
...AND RAISE YOU!
DAD, BILLY, STOP--!
DANE!
LEAVE...
...US...
...ALONE!
THWAK
HAHAHAHAHA!
PATHETIC.
HNGHH!

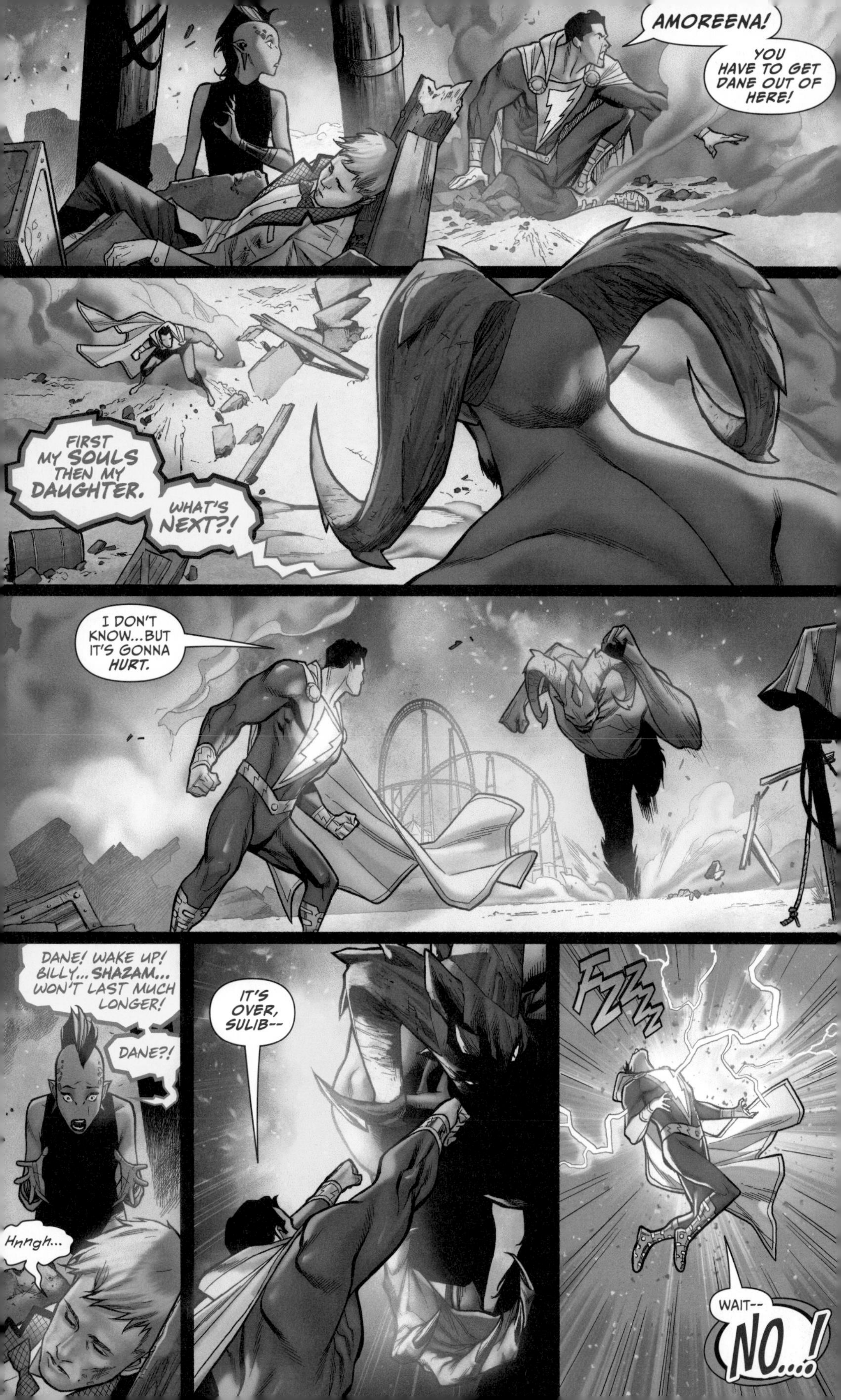
AMOREENA!
YOU HAVE TO GET DANE OUT OF HERE!
FIRST MY SOULS THEN MY DAUGHTER.
WHAT'S NEXT?!
I DON'T KNOW...BUT IT'S GONNA HURT.
DANE! WAKE UP! BILLY... SHAZAM... WON'T LAST MUCH LONGER!
DANE?!
Hnngh...
IT'S OVER, SULIB--
FZZZ
WAIT--
NO...!

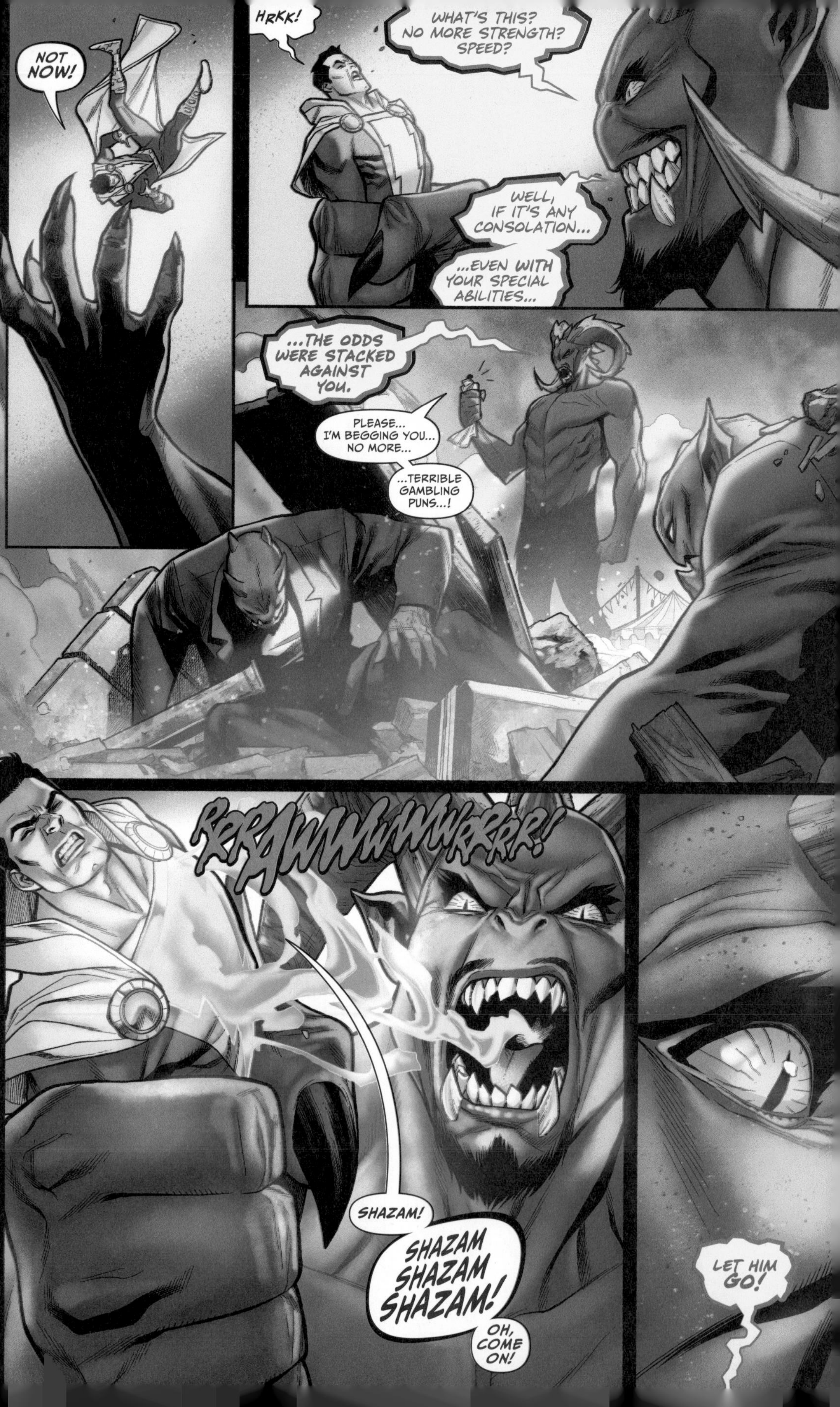
NOT NOW!
HRKK!
WHAT'S THIS? NO MORE STRENGTH? SPEED?
WELL, IF IT'S ANY CONSOLATION...
...EVEN WITH YOUR SPECIAL ABILITIES...
...THE ODDS WERE STACKED AGAINST YOU.
PLEASE... I'M BEGGING YOU... NO MORE...
...TERRIBLE GAMBLING PUNS...!
RRRAWWWWWRRRR!
SHAZAM!
SHAZAM SHAZAM SHAZAM!
OH, COME ON!
LET HIM GO!

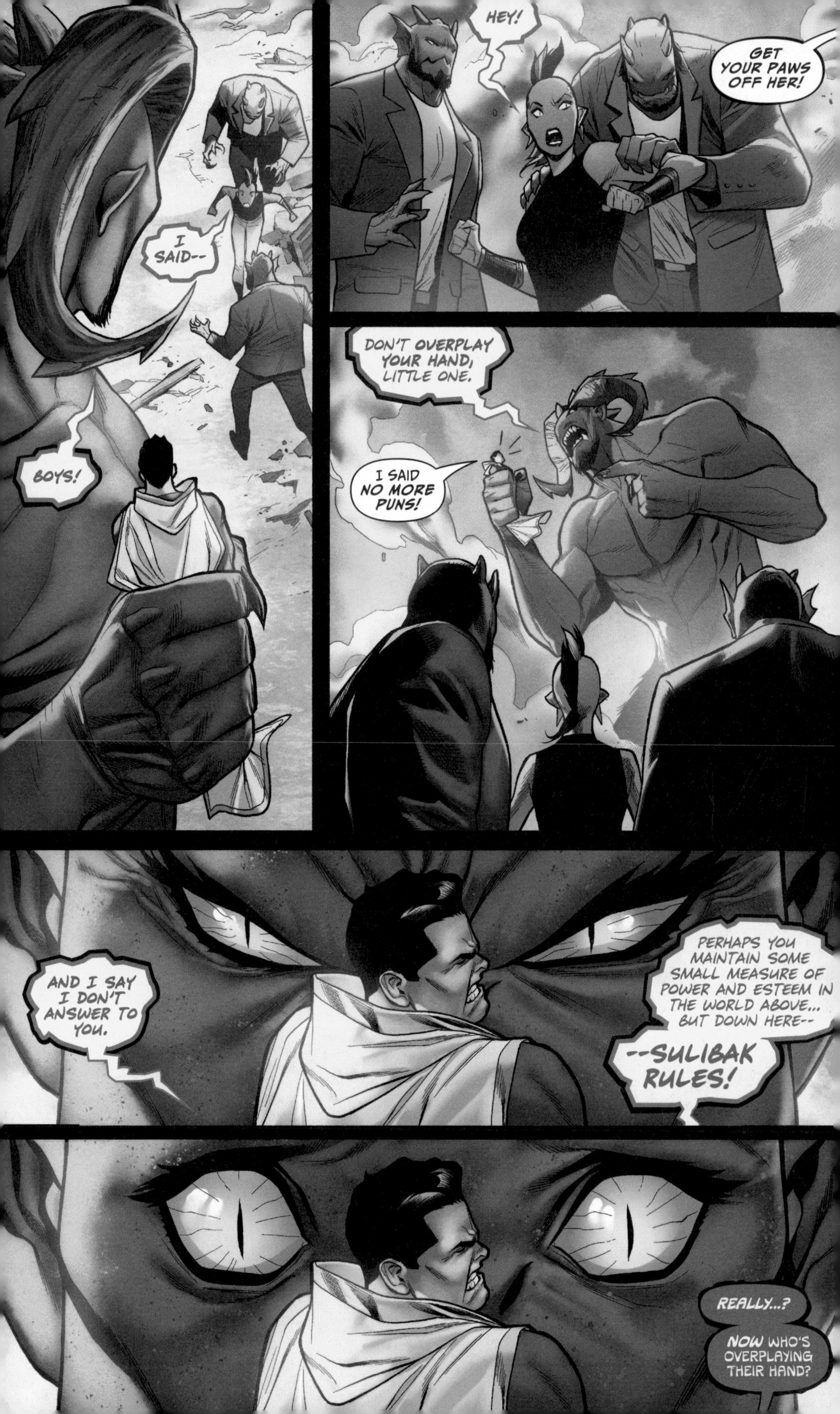

I SAID--
BOYS!
HEY!
GET YOUR PAWS OFF HER!
DON'T OVERPLAY YOUR HAND, LITTLE ONE.
I SAID NO MORE PUNS!
AND I SAY I DON'T ANSWER TO YOU.
PERHAPS YOU MAINTAIN SOME SMALL MEASURE OF POWER AND ESTEEM IN THE WORLD ABOVE... BUT DOWN HERE--
--SULIBAK RULES!
REALLY...?
NOW WHO'S OVERPLAYING THEIR HAND?

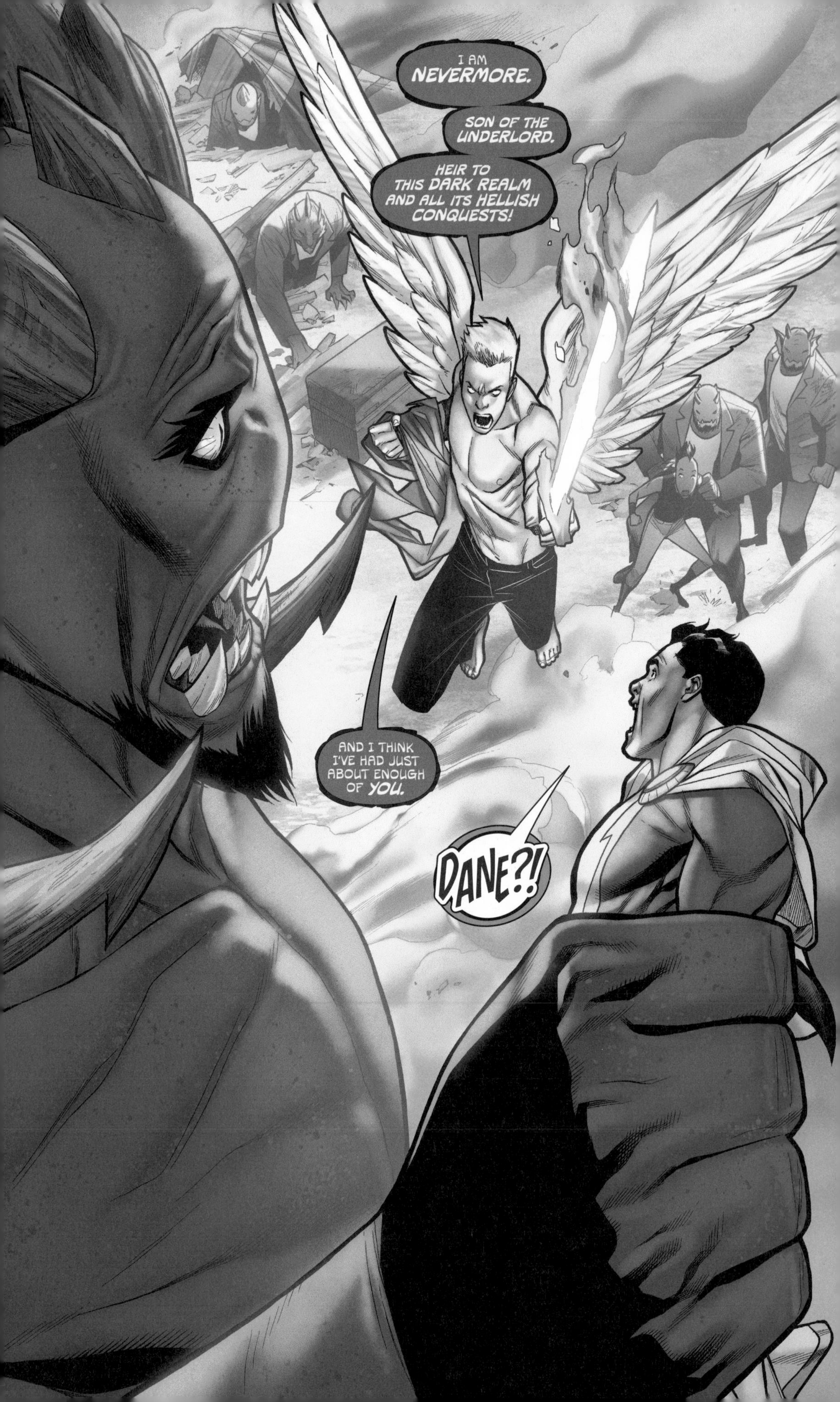
I AM NEVERMORE.
SON OF THE UNDERLORD.
HEIR TO THIS DARK REALM AND ALL ITS HELLISH CONQUESTS!
AND I THINK I'VE HAD JUST ABOUT ENOUGH OF YOU.
DANE?!

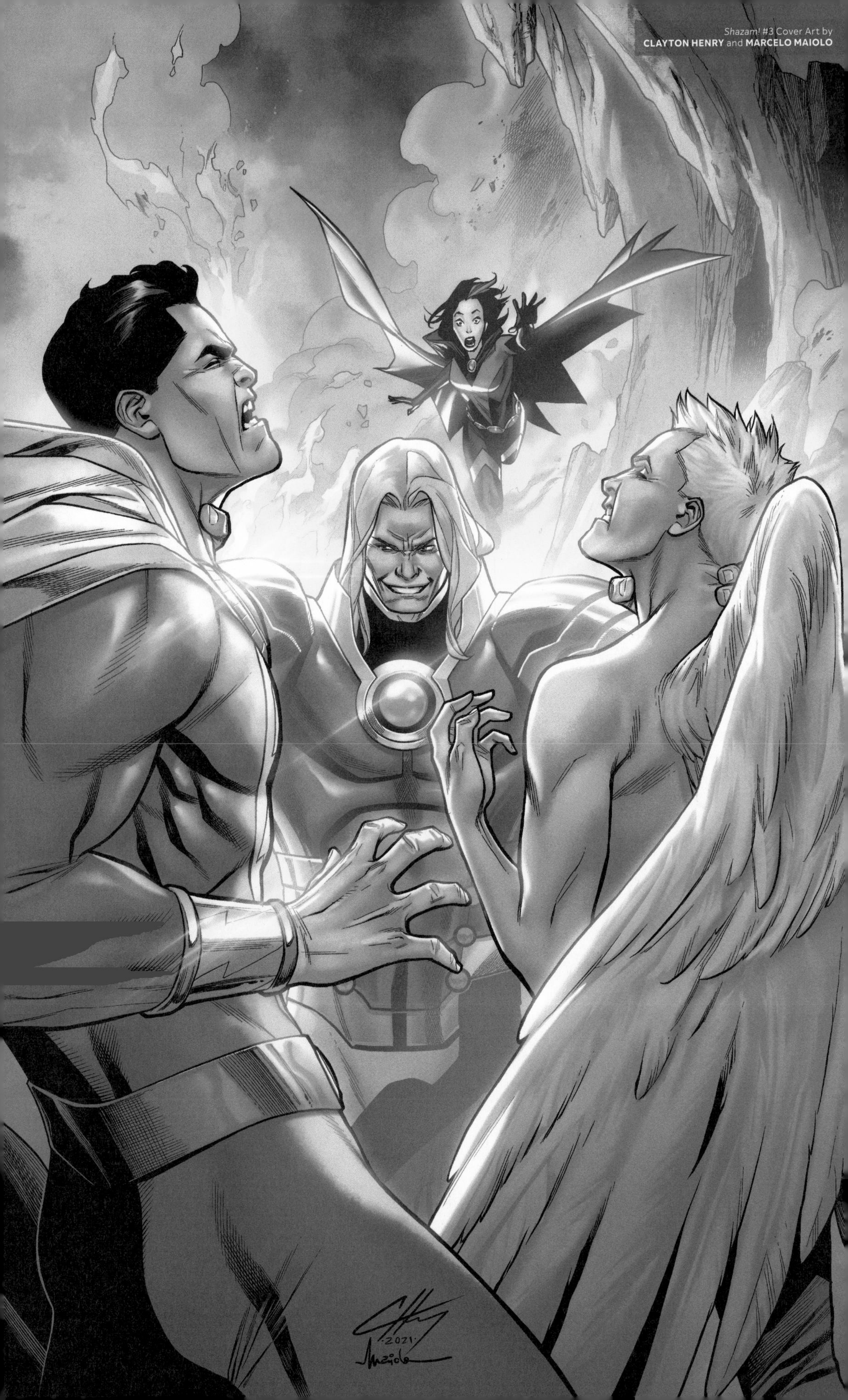

Shazam! #3 Cover Art by
CLAYTON HENRY and **MARCELO MAIOLO**

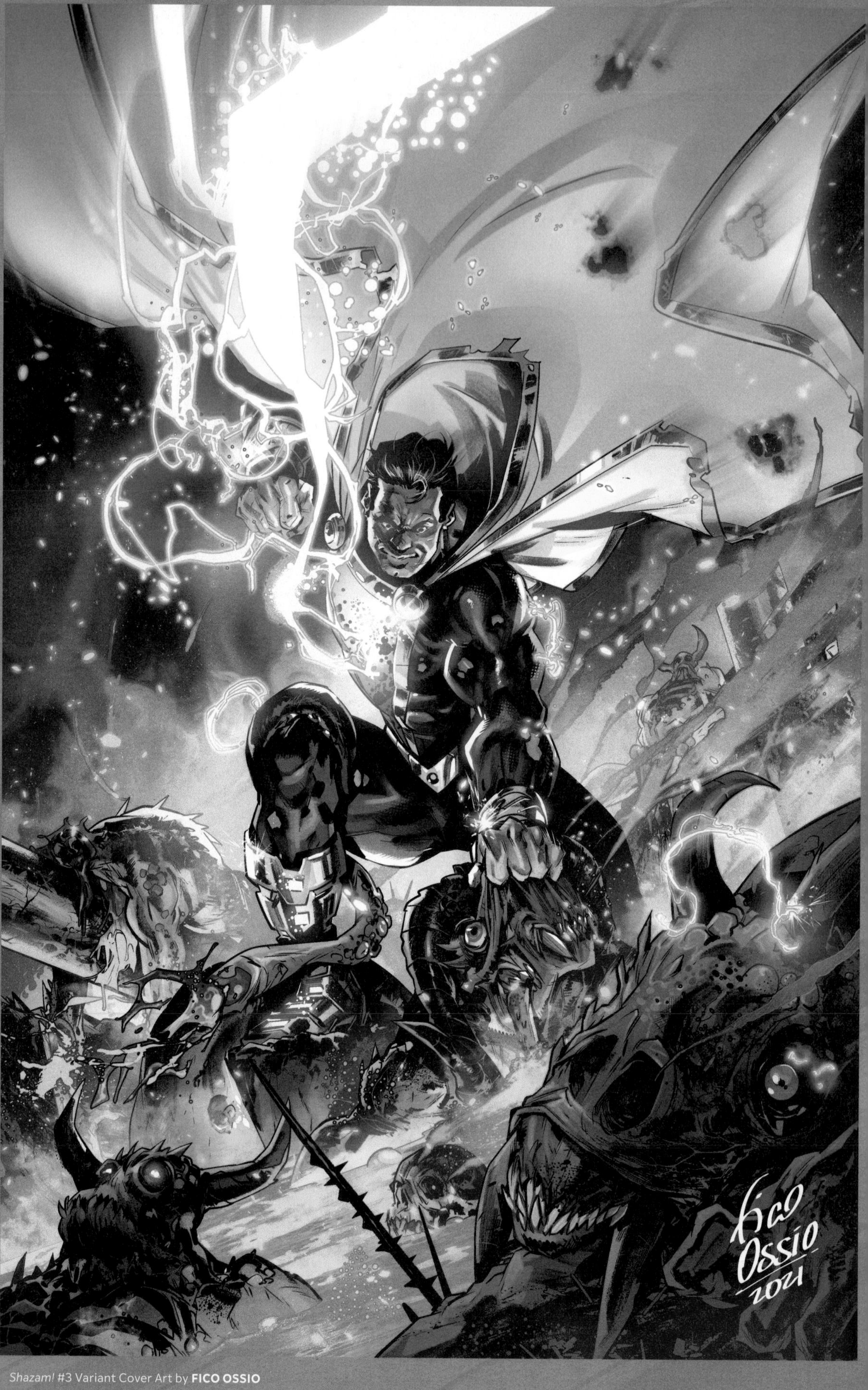

Shazam! #3 Variant Cover Art by **FICO OSSIO**

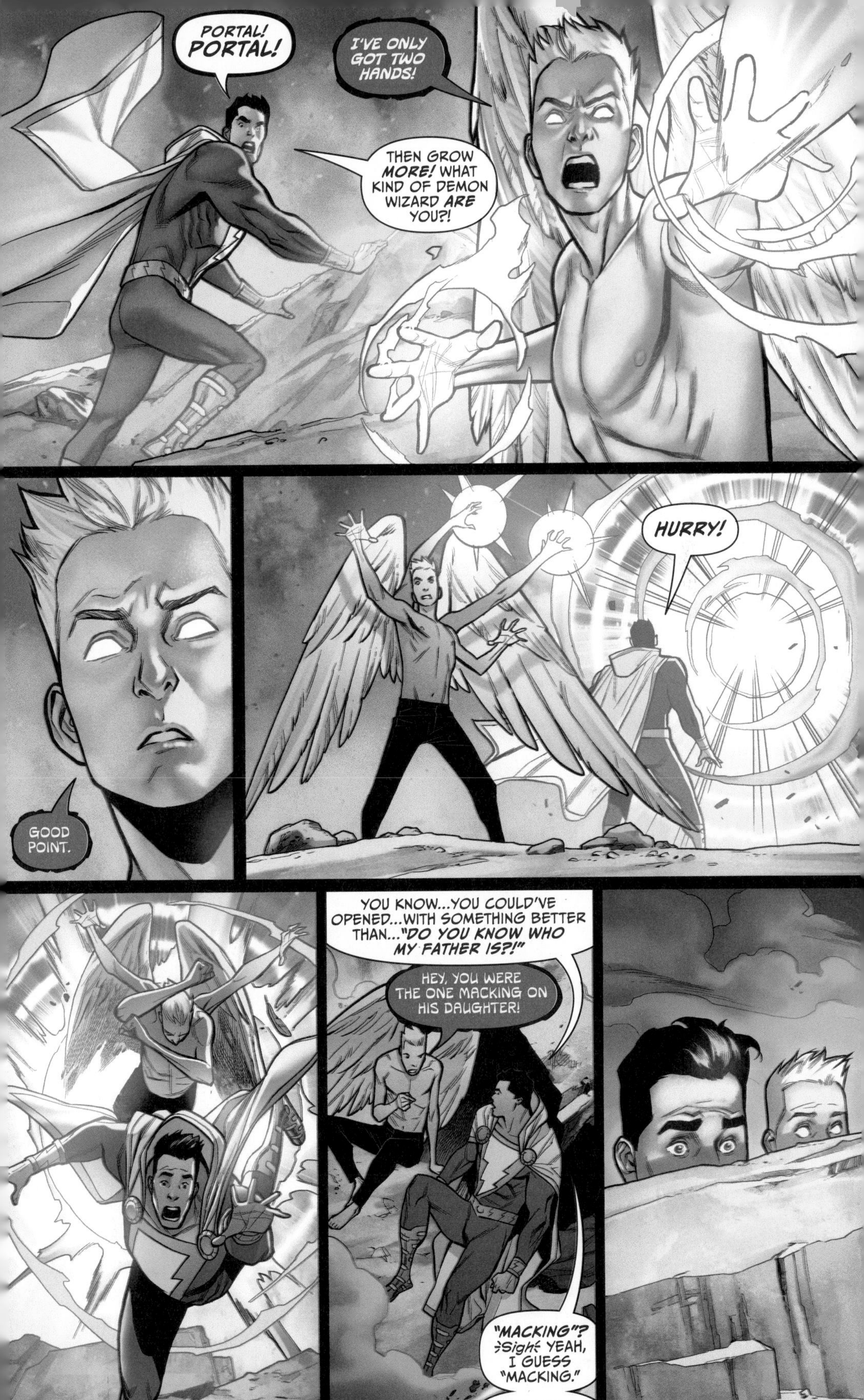

PORTAL! PORTAL!
I'VE ONLY GOT TWO HANDS!
THEN GROW MORE! WHAT KIND OF DEMON WIZARD ARE YOU?!
GOOD POINT.
HURRY!
YOU KNOW...YOU COULD'VE OPENED...WITH SOMETHING BETTER THAN..."DO YOU KNOW WHO MY FATHER IS?!"
HEY, YOU WERE THE ONE MACKING ON HIS DAUGHTER!
"MACKING"? Sigh YEAH, I GUESS "MACKING."
HOW LONG 'TIL THEY FIND US THIS TIME?

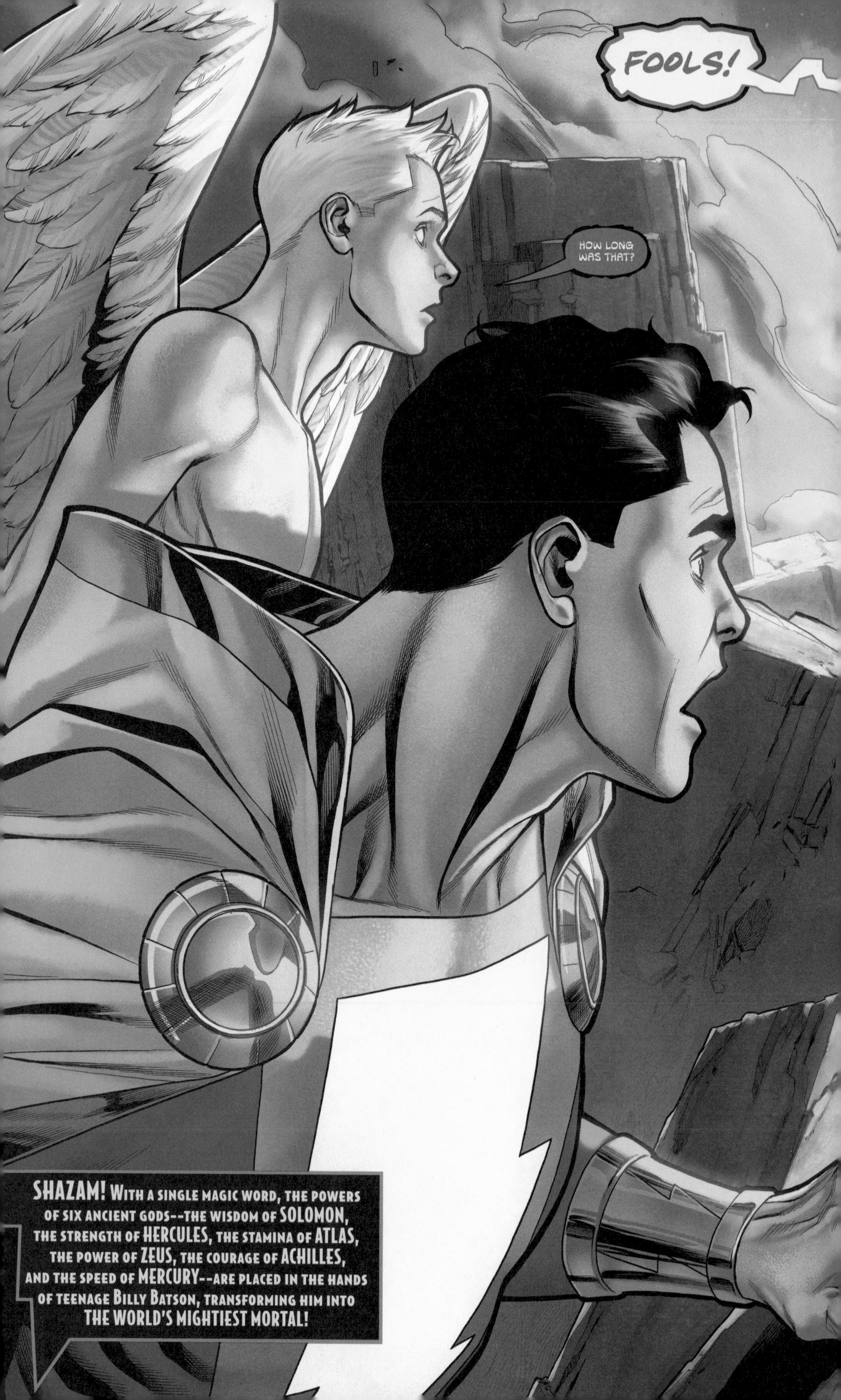
FOOLS!
HOW LONG WAS THAT?
SHAZAM! WITH A SINGLE MAGIC WORD, THE POWERS OF SIX ANCIENT GODS--THE WISDOM OF SOLOMON, THE STRENGTH OF HERCULES, THE STAMINA OF ATLAS, THE POWER OF ZEUS, THE COURAGE OF ACHILLES, AND THE SPEED OF MERCURY--ARE PLACED IN THE HANDS OF TEENAGE BILLY BATSON, TRANSFORMING HIM INTO THE WORLD'S MIGHTIEST MORTAL!

YOU CAN'T ESCAPE THE WRATH OF SULIBAK!
SONS OF PERDITION!
SHAZAM! CREATED BY BILL PARKER & C.C. BECK
TIM SHERIDAN WRITER
CLAYTON HENRY ARTIST
MARCELO MAIOLO COLORIST
ROB LEIGH LETTERER
HENRY & MAIOLO COVER
FICO OSSIO VARIANT COVER
DIEGO LOPEZ EDITOR
MIKE COTTON SENIOR EDITOR

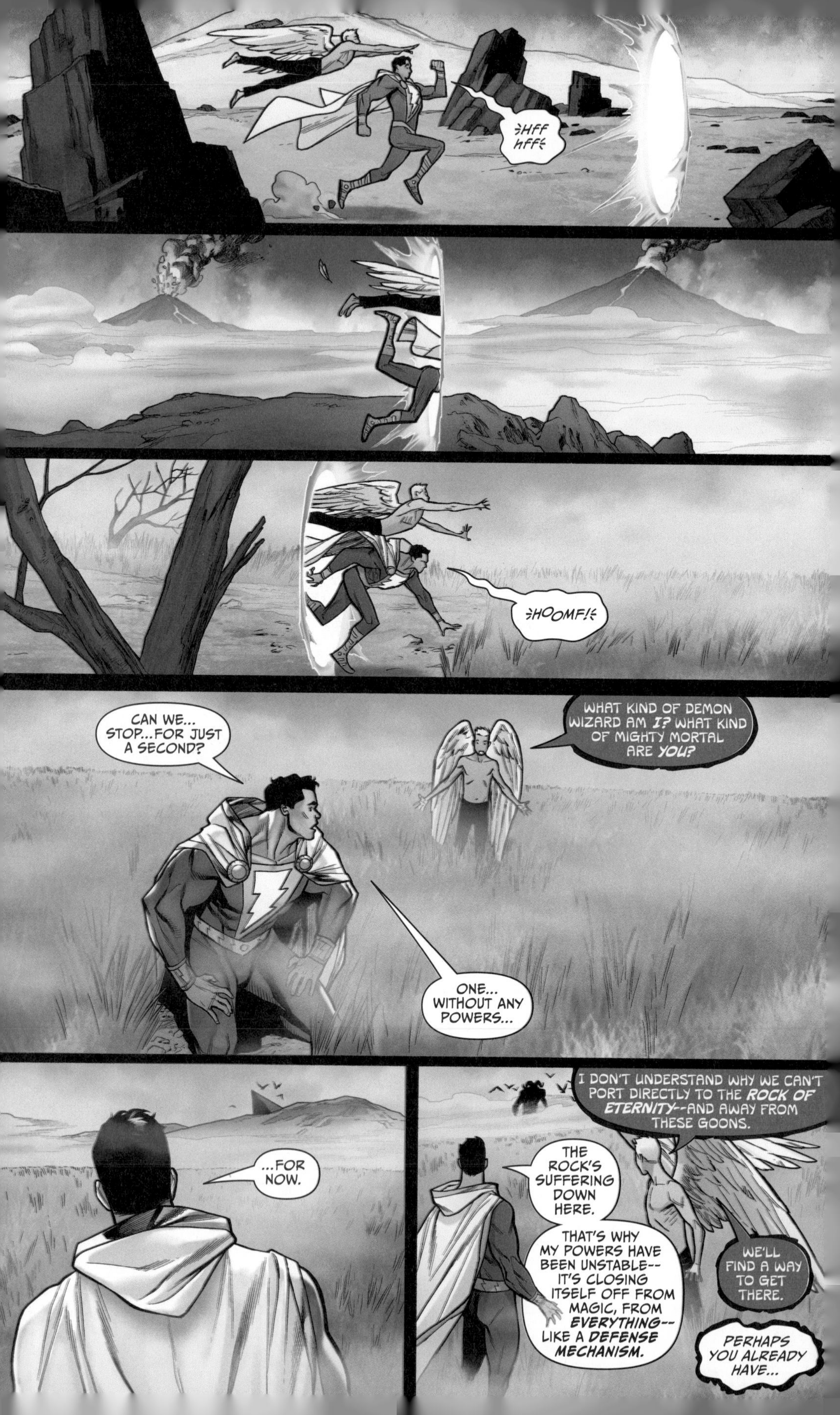
HFF HFF
HOOMF!
CAN WE... STOP...FOR JUST A SECOND?
WHAT KIND OF DEMON WIZARD AM I? WHAT KIND OF MIGHTY MORTAL ARE YOU?
ONE... WITHOUT ANY POWERS...
...FOR NOW.
I DON'T UNDERSTAND WHY WE CAN'T PORT DIRECTLY TO THE ROCK OF ETERNITY--AND AWAY FROM THESE GOONS.
THE ROCK'S SUFFERING DOWN HERE.
THAT'S WHY MY POWERS HAVE BEEN UNSTABLE-- IT'S CLOSING ITSELF OFF FROM MAGIC, FROM EVERYTHING-- LIKE A DEFENSE MECHANISM.
WE'LL FIND A WAY TO GET THERE.
PERHAPS YOU ALREADY HAVE...

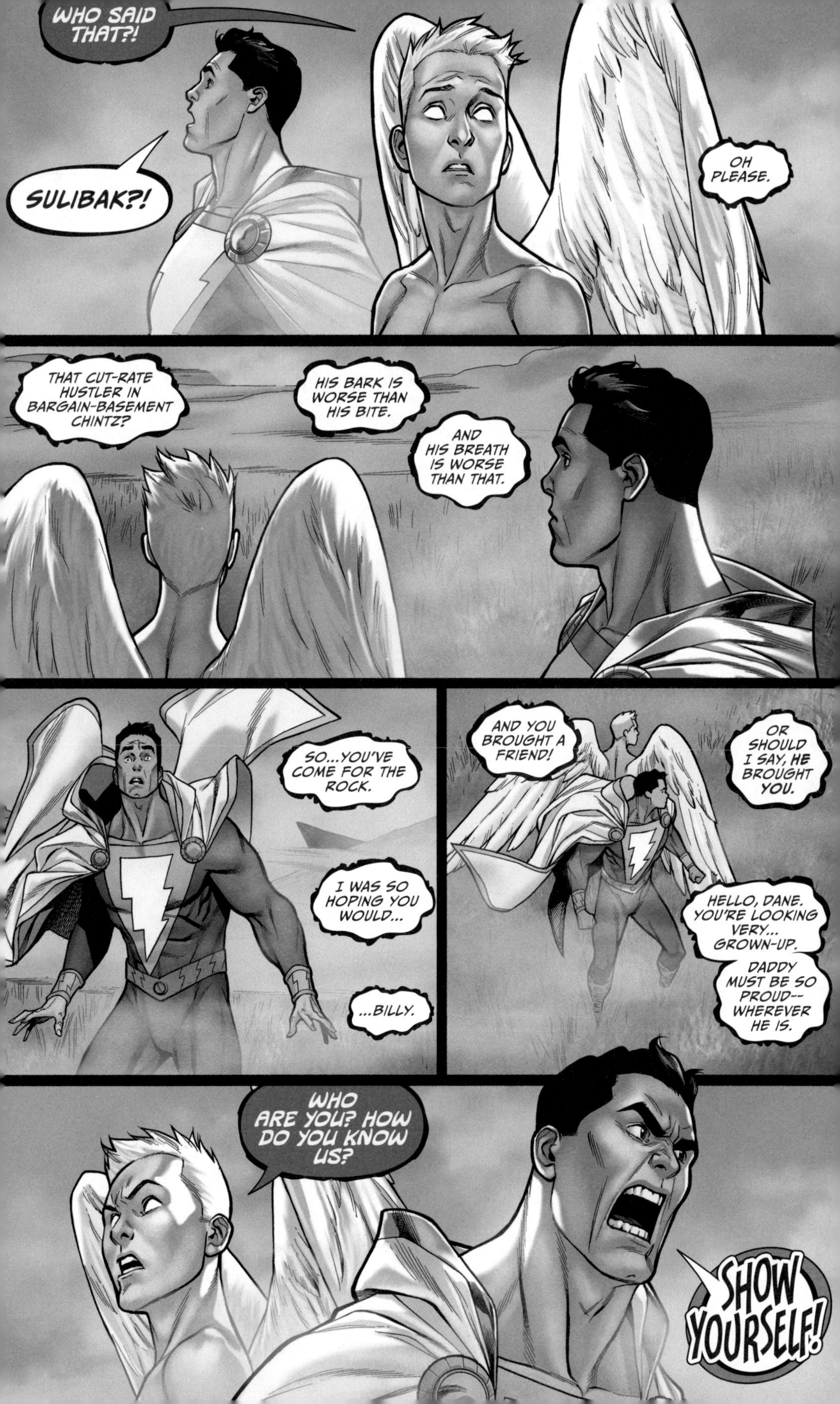

WHO SAID THAT?!
SULIBAK?!
OH PLEASE.
THAT CUT-RATE HUSTLER IN BARGAIN-BASEMENT CHINTZ?
HIS BARK IS WORSE THAN HIS BITE.
AND HIS BREATH IS WORSE THAN THAT.
SO...YOU'VE COME FOR THE ROCK.
I WAS SO HOPING YOU WOULD...
...BILLY.
AND YOU BROUGHT A FRIEND!
OR SHOULD I SAY, HE BROUGHT YOU.
HELLO, DANE. YOU'RE LOOKING VERY... GROWN-UP.
DADDY MUST BE SO PROUD--WHEREVER HE IS.
WHO ARE YOU? HOW DO YOU KNOW US?
SHOW YOURSELF!

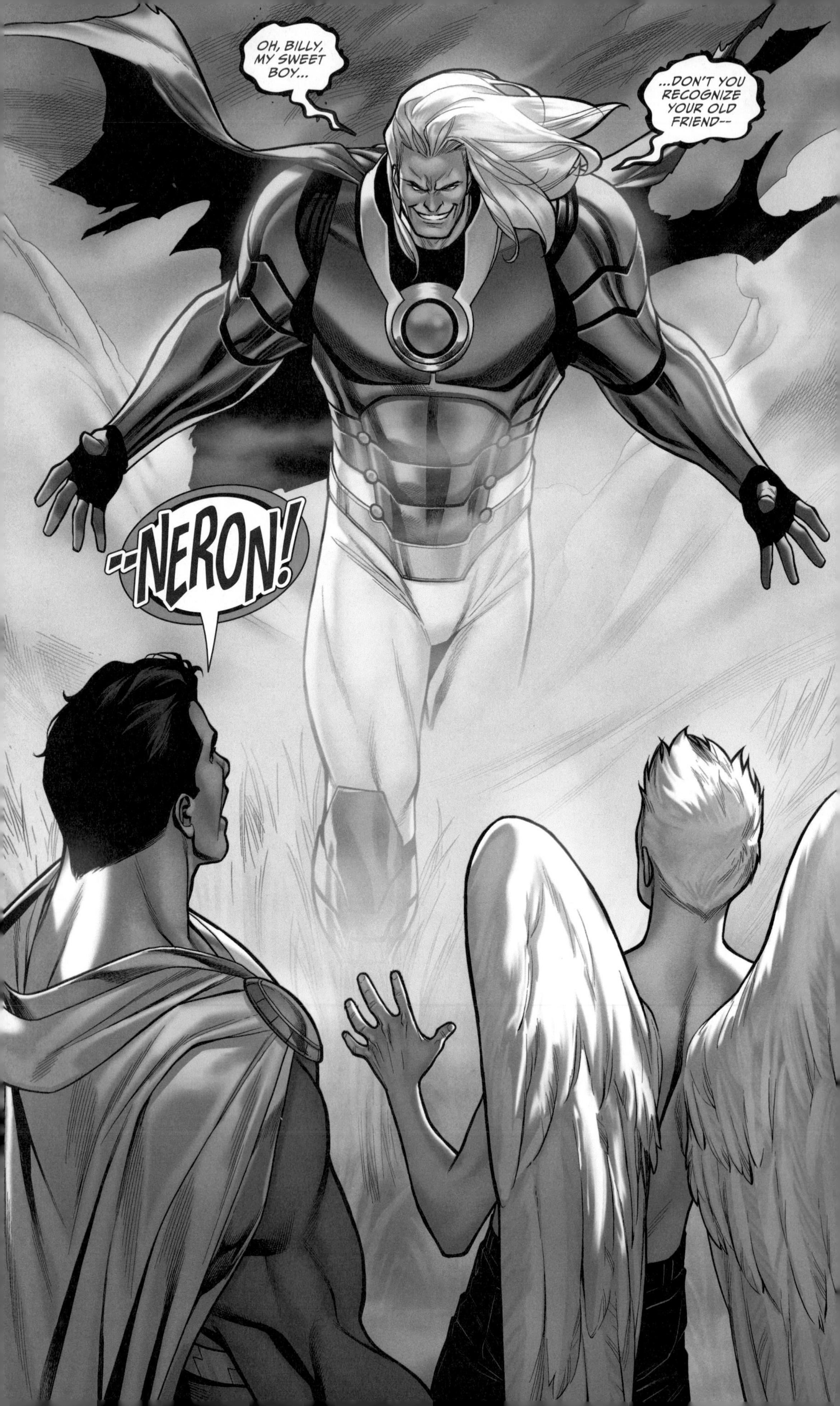
OH, BILLY, MY SWEET BOY...
...DON'T YOU RECOGNIZE YOUR OLD FRIEND--
--NERON!

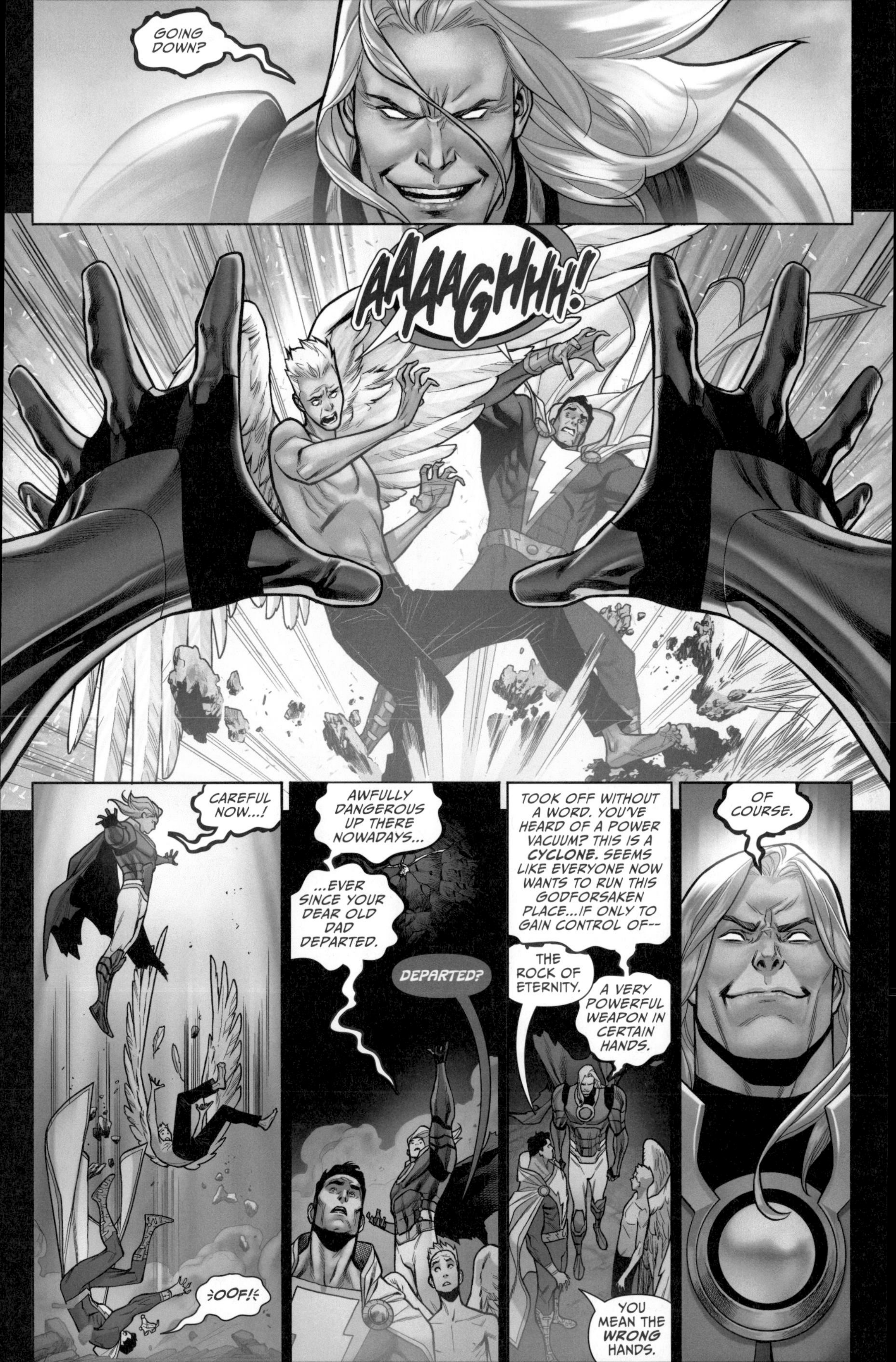
GOING DOWN?
AAAAGHHH!
CAREFUL NOW...!
OOF!
AWFULLY DANGEROUS UP THERE NOWADAYS...
...EVER SINCE YOUR DEAR OLD DAD DEPARTED.
DEPARTED?
TOOK OFF WITHOUT A WORD. YOU'VE HEARD OF A POWER VACUUM? THIS IS A CYCLONE. SEEMS LIKE EVERYONE NOW WANTS TO RUN THIS GODFORSAKEN PLACE...IF ONLY TO GAIN CONTROL OF--
THE ROCK OF ETERNITY.
A VERY POWERFUL WEAPON IN CERTAIN HANDS.
YOU MEAN THE WRONG HANDS.
OF COURSE.

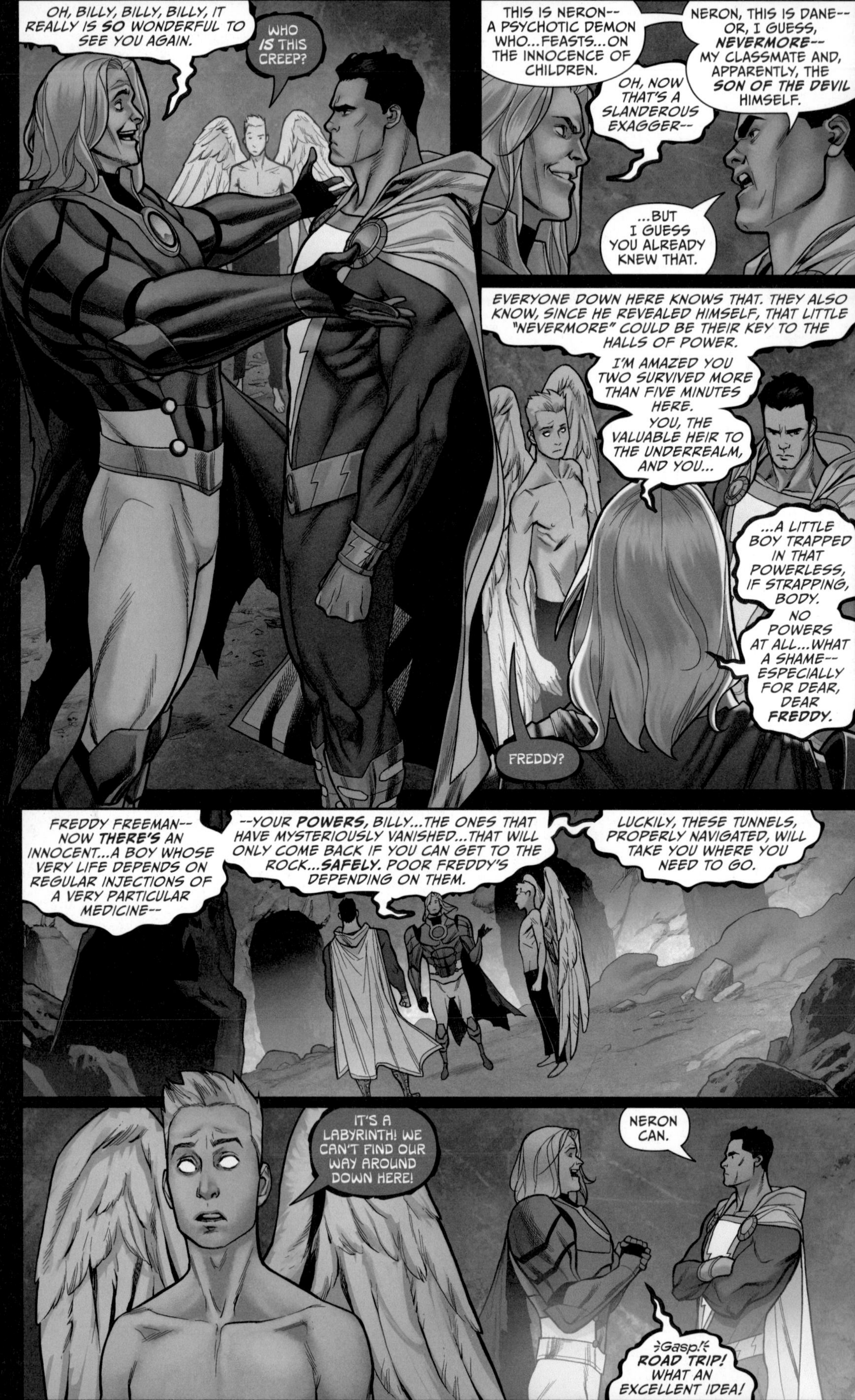

OH, BILLY, BILLY, BILLY, IT REALLY IS **SO** WONDERFUL TO SEE YOU AGAIN.
WHO **IS** THIS CREEP?
THIS IS NERON-- A PSYCHOTIC DEMON WHO...FEASTS...ON THE INNOCENCE OF CHILDREN.
NERON, THIS IS DANE-- OR, I GUESS, **NEVERMORE**-- MY CLASSMATE AND, APPARENTLY, THE **SON OF THE DEVIL** HIMSELF.
OH, NOW THAT'S A SLANDEROUS EXAGGER--
...BUT I GUESS YOU ALREADY KNEW THAT.
EVERYONE DOWN HERE KNOWS THAT. THEY ALSO KNOW, SINCE HE REVEALED HIMSELF, THAT LITTLE "NEVERMORE" COULD BE THEIR KEY TO THE HALLS OF POWER.
I'M AMAZED YOU TWO SURVIVED MORE THAN FIVE MINUTES HERE.
YOU, THE VALUABLE HEIR TO THE UNDERREALM, AND YOU...
...A LITTLE BOY TRAPPED IN THAT POWERLESS, IF STRAPPING, BODY.
NO POWERS AT ALL...WHAT A SHAME-- ESPECIALLY FOR DEAR, DEAR **FREDDY**.
FREDDY?
FREDDY FREEMAN-- NOW **THERE'S** AN INNOCENT...A BOY WHOSE VERY LIFE DEPENDS ON REGULAR INJECTIONS OF A VERY PARTICULAR MEDICINE--
--YOUR **POWERS**, BILLY...THE ONES THAT HAVE MYSTERIOUSLY VANISHED...THAT WILL ONLY COME BACK IF YOU CAN GET TO THE ROCK...**SAFELY**. POOR FREDDY'S DEPENDING ON THEM.
LUCKILY, THESE TUNNELS, PROPERLY NAVIGATED, WILL TAKE YOU WHERE YOU NEED TO GO.
IT'S A LABYRINTH! WE CAN'T FIND OUR WAY AROUND DOWN HERE!
NERON CAN.
Gasp! **ROAD TRIP!** WHAT AN EXCELLENT IDEA!

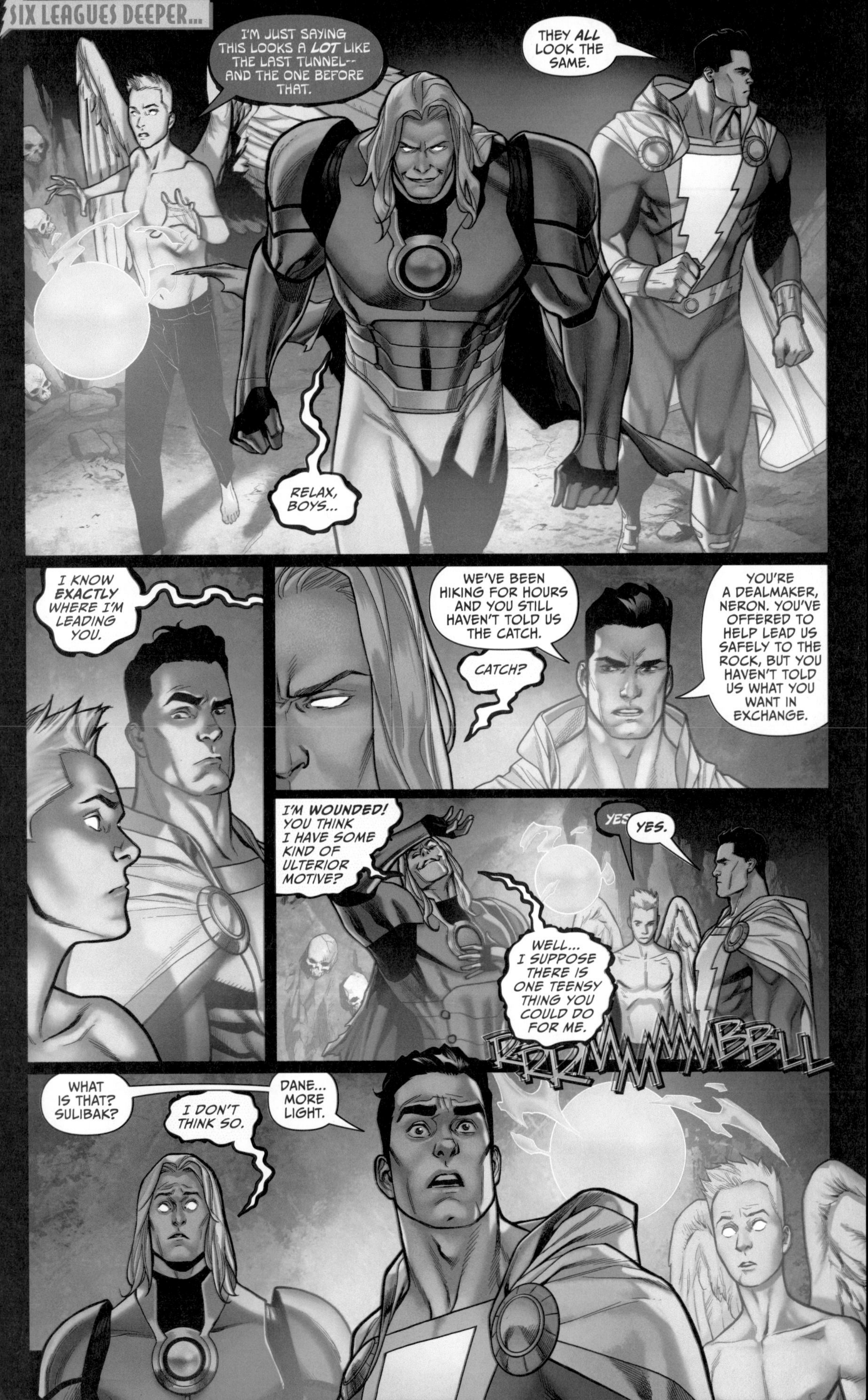
SIX LEAGUES DEEPER...
I'M JUST SAYING THIS LOOKS A LOT LIKE THE LAST TUNNEL-- AND THE ONE BEFORE THAT.
THEY ALL LOOK THE SAME.
RELAX, BOYS...
I KNOW EXACTLY WHERE I'M LEADING YOU.
WE'VE BEEN HIKING FOR HOURS AND YOU STILL HAVEN'T TOLD US THE CATCH.
CATCH?
YOU'RE A DEALMAKER, NERON. YOU'VE OFFERED TO HELP LEAD US SAFELY TO THE ROCK, BUT YOU HAVEN'T TOLD US WHAT YOU WANT IN EXCHANGE.
I'M WOUNDED! YOU THINK I HAVE SOME KIND OF ULTERIOR MOTIVE?
YES
YES.
WELL... I SUPPOSE THERE IS ONE TEENSY THING YOU COULD DO FOR ME.
RRRMMMMMBBLL
WHAT IS THAT? SULIBAK?
I DON'T THINK SO.
DANE... MORE LIGHT.

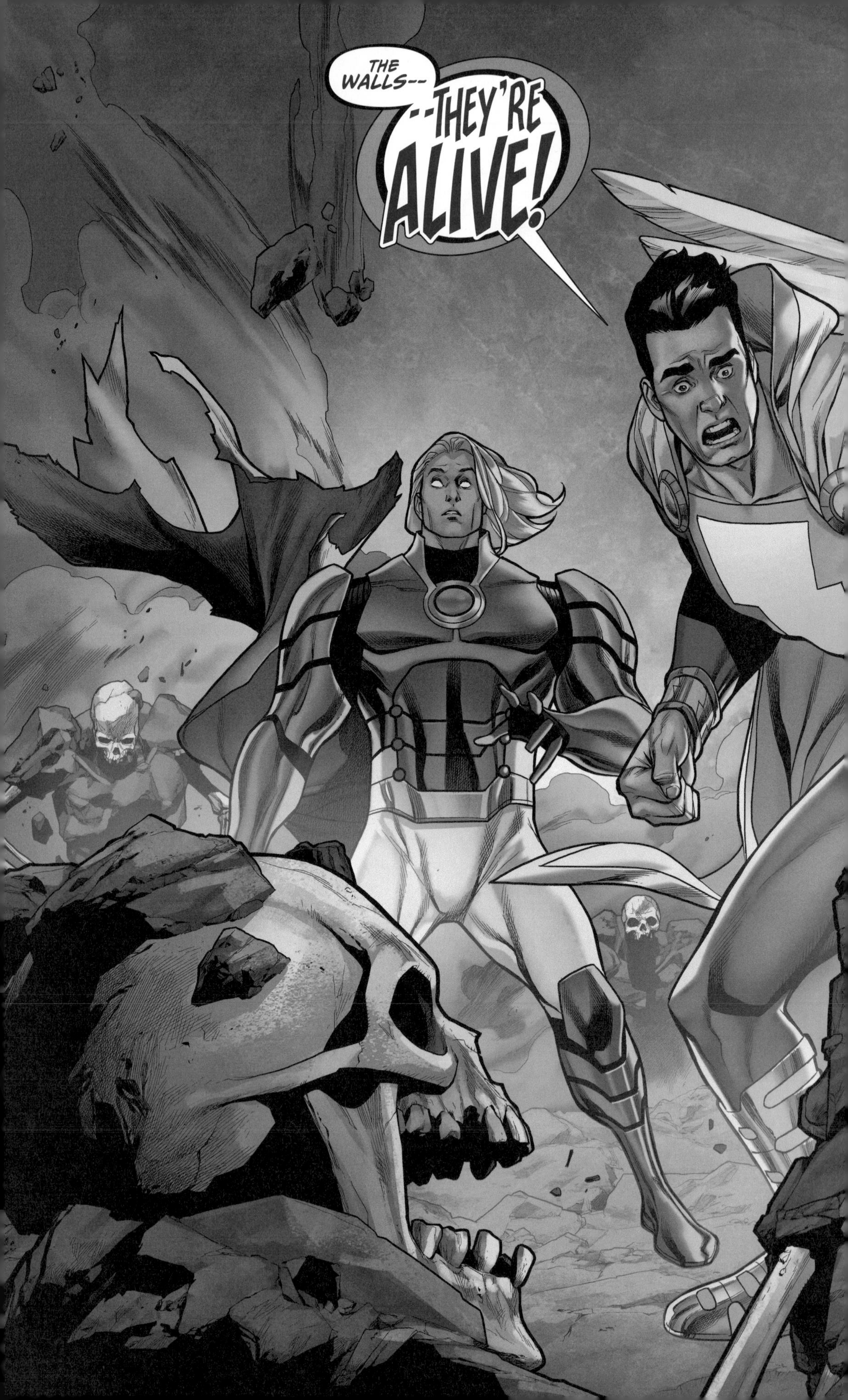
THE WALLS--
--THEY'RE ALIVE!

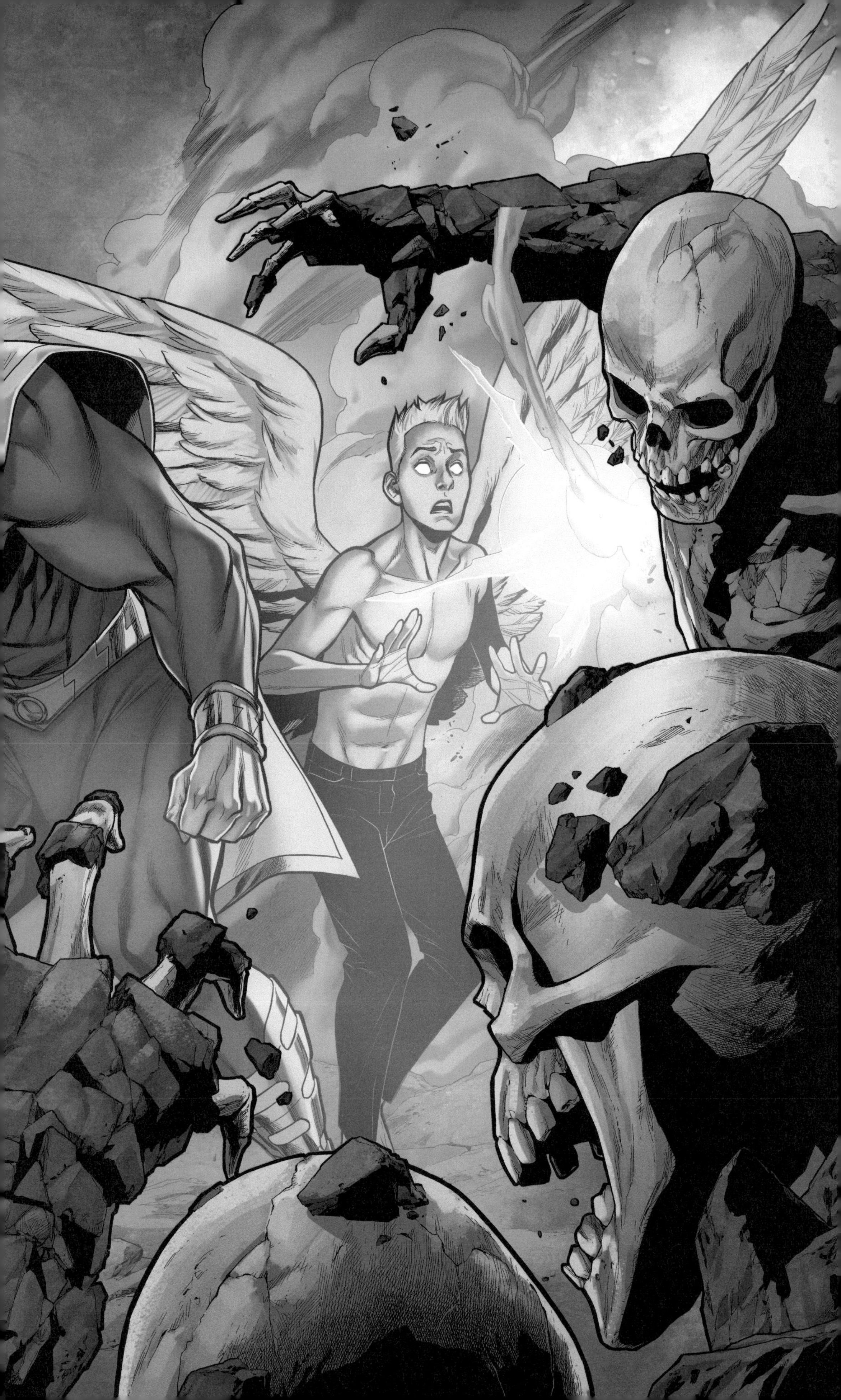

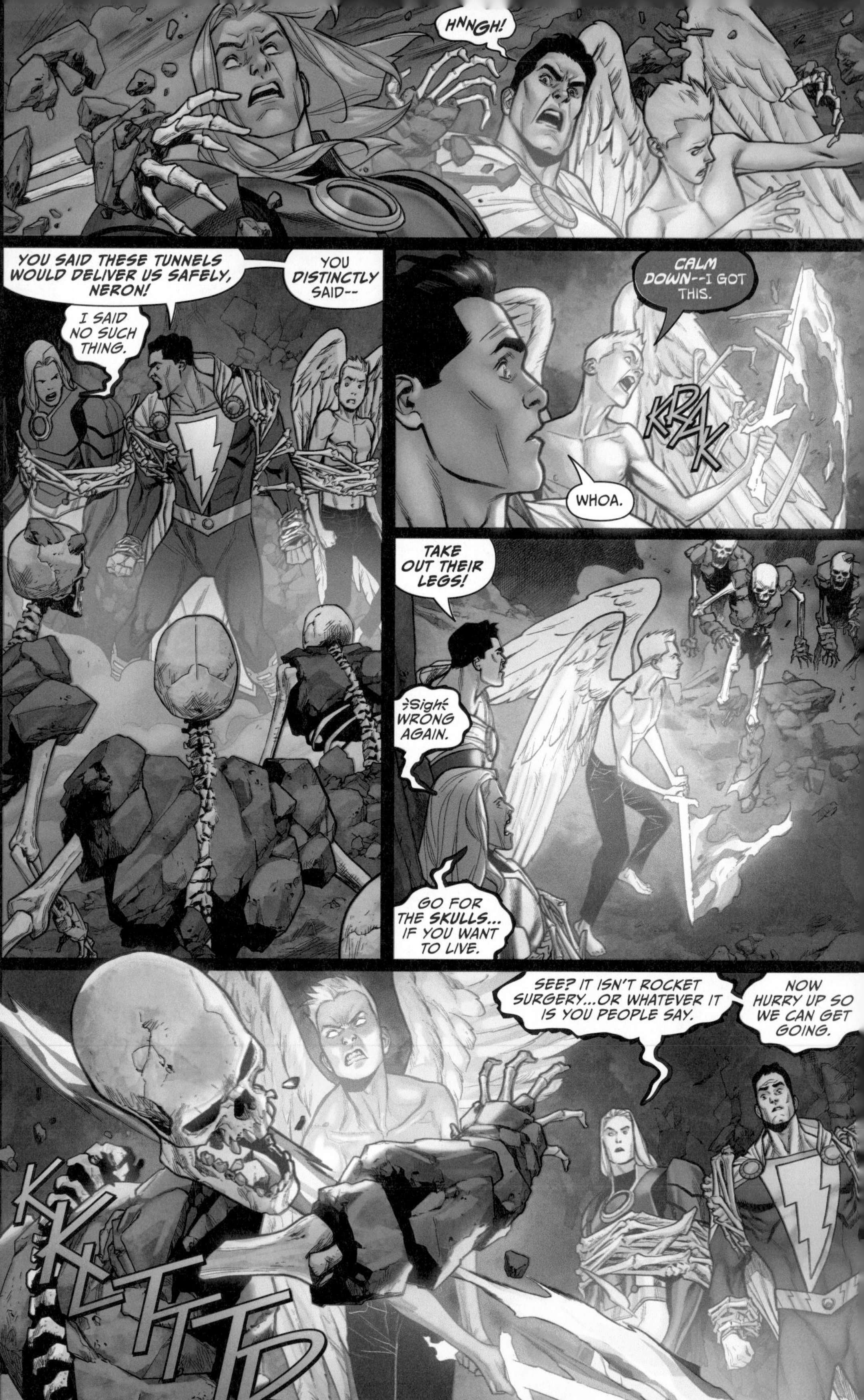
HNNGH!
YOU SAID THESE TUNNELS WOULD DELIVER US SAFELY, NERON!
YOU DISTINCTLY SAID--
I SAID NO SUCH THING.
CALM DOWN--I GOT THIS.
KRAK
WHOA.
TAKE OUT THEIR LEGS!
Sigh WRONG AGAIN.
GO FOR THE SKULLS... IF YOU WANT TO LIVE.
SEE? IT ISN'T ROCKET SURGERY...OR WHATEVER IT IS YOU PEOPLE SAY.
NOW HURRY UP SO WE CAN GET GOING.
KKLTTTR

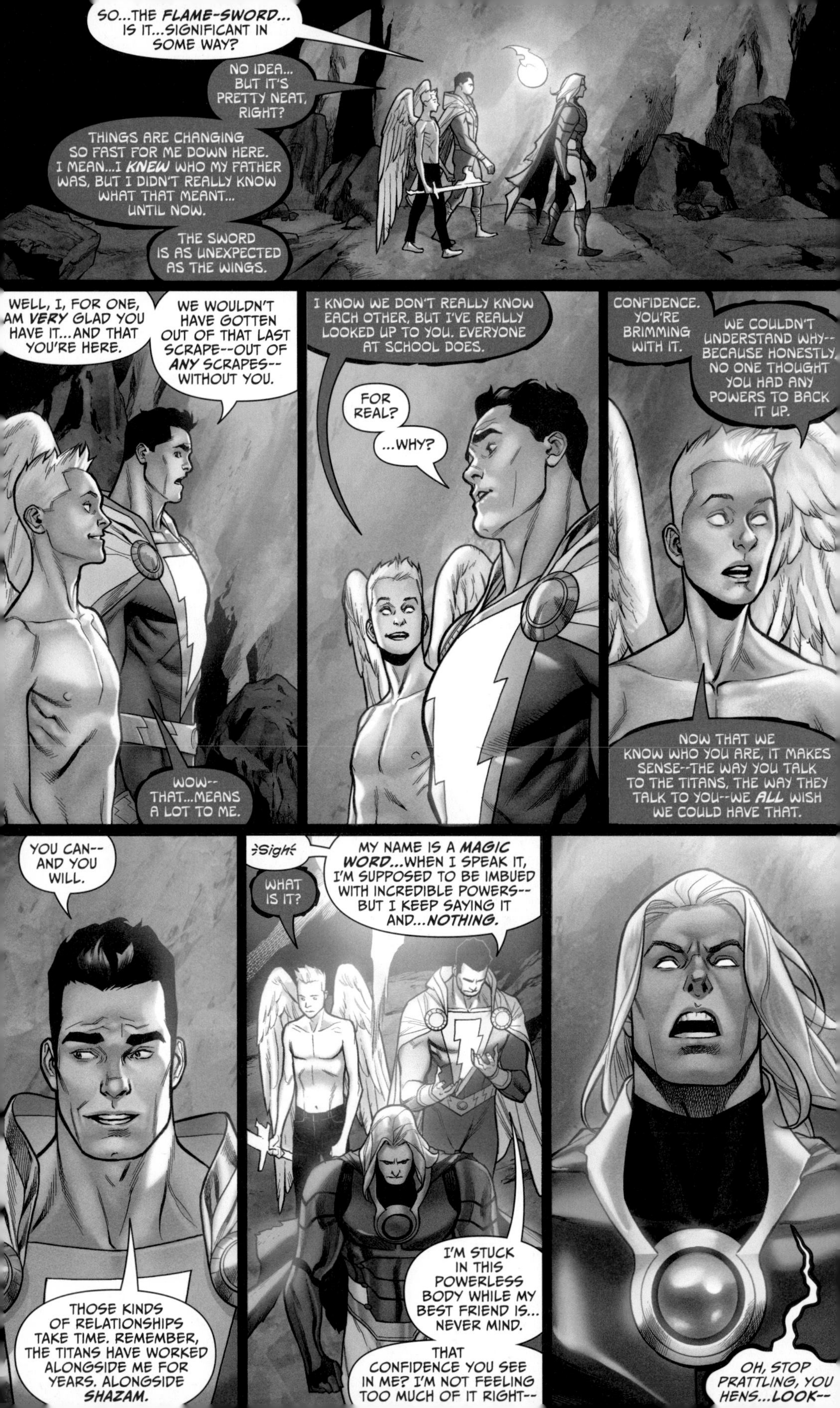
SO...THE FLAME-SWORD... IS IT...SIGNIFICANT IN SOME WAY?
NO IDEA... BUT IT'S PRETTY NEAT, RIGHT?
THINGS ARE CHANGING SO FAST FOR ME DOWN HERE. I MEAN...I KNEW WHO MY FATHER WAS, BUT I DIDN'T REALLY KNOW WHAT THAT MEANT... UNTIL NOW.
THE SWORD IS AS UNEXPECTED AS THE WINGS.
WELL, I, FOR ONE, AM VERY GLAD YOU HAVE IT...AND THAT YOU'RE HERE.
WE WOULDN'T HAVE GOTTEN OUT OF THAT LAST SCRAPE--OUT OF ANY SCRAPES--WITHOUT YOU.
WOW--THAT...MEANS A LOT TO ME.
I KNOW WE DON'T REALLY KNOW EACH OTHER, BUT I'VE REALLY LOOKED UP TO YOU. EVERYONE AT SCHOOL DOES.
FOR REAL?
...WHY?
CONFIDENCE. YOU'RE BRIMMING WITH IT.
WE COULDN'T UNDERSTAND WHY--BECAUSE HONESTLY, NO ONE THOUGHT YOU HAD ANY POWERS TO BACK IT UP.
NOW THAT WE KNOW WHO YOU ARE, IT MAKES SENSE--THE WAY YOU TALK TO THE TITANS, THE WAY THEY TALK TO YOU--WE ALL WISH WE COULD HAVE THAT.
YOU CAN--AND YOU WILL.
THOSE KINDS OF RELATIONSHIPS TAKE TIME. REMEMBER, THE TITANS HAVE WORKED ALONGSIDE ME FOR YEARS. ALONGSIDE SHAZAM.
Sigh
WHAT IS IT?
MY NAME IS A MAGIC WORD...WHEN I SPEAK IT, I'M SUPPOSED TO BE IMBUED WITH INCREDIBLE POWERS--BUT I KEEP SAYING IT AND...NOTHING.
I'M STUCK IN THIS POWERLESS BODY WHILE MY BEST FRIEND IS... NEVER MIND.
THAT CONFIDENCE YOU SEE IN ME? I'M NOT FEELING TOO MUCH OF IT RIGHT--
OH, STOP PRATTLING, YOU HENS...LOOK--

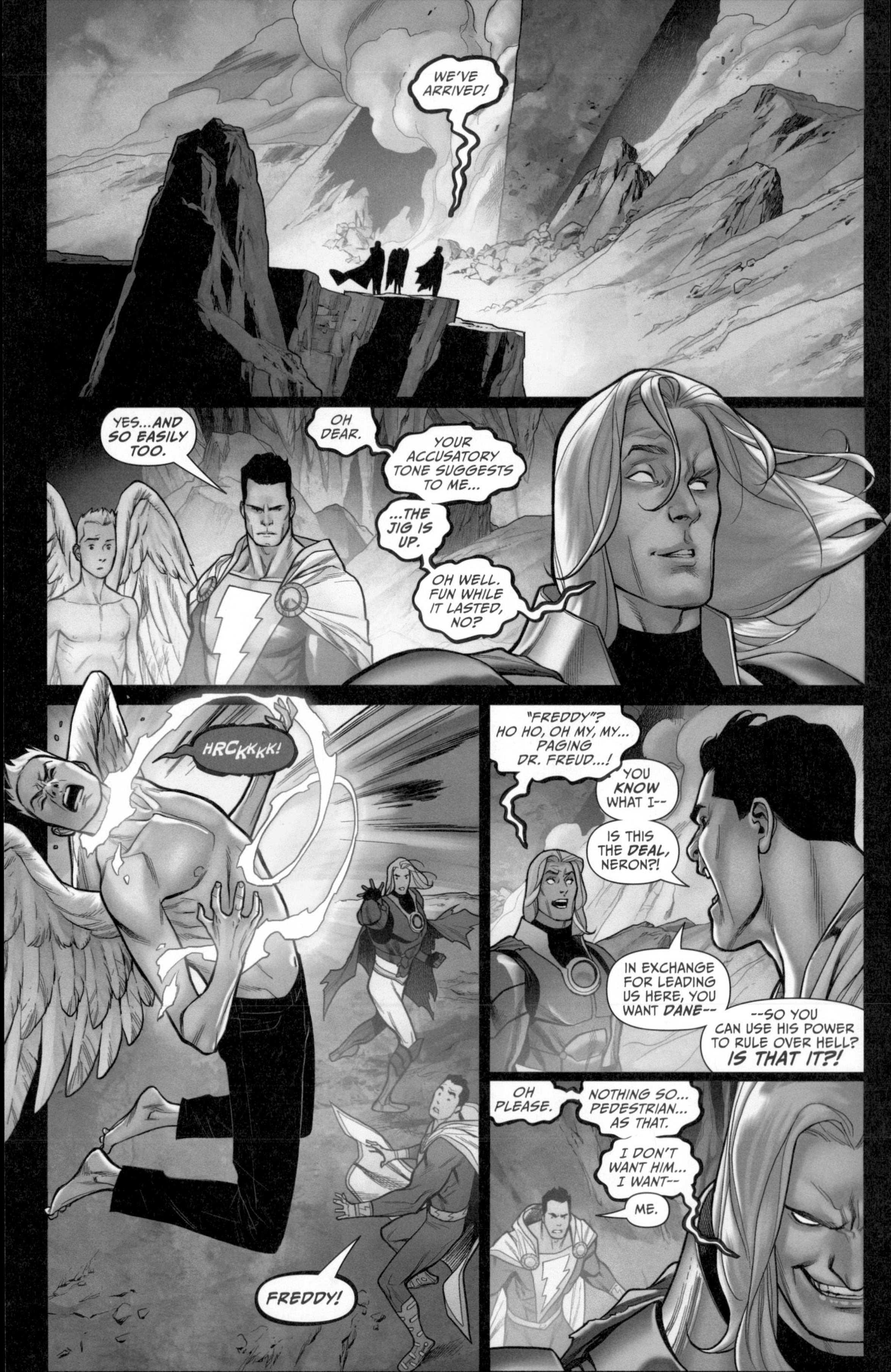

WE'VE ARRIVED!
YES...AND SO EASILY TOO.
OH DEAR.
YOUR ACCUSATORY TONE SUGGESTS TO ME...
...THE JIG IS UP.
OH WELL. FUN WHILE IT LASTED, NO?
HRCKKKK!
FREDDY!
"FREDDY"? HO HO, OH MY, MY... PAGING DR. FREUD...!
YOU KNOW WHAT I--
IS THIS THE DEAL, NERON?!
IN EXCHANGE FOR LEADING US HERE, YOU WANT DANE--
--SO YOU CAN USE HIS POWER TO RULE OVER HELL? IS THAT IT?!
OH PLEASE.
NOTHING SO... PEDESTRIAN... AS THAT.
I DON'T WANT HIM... I WANT--
ME.

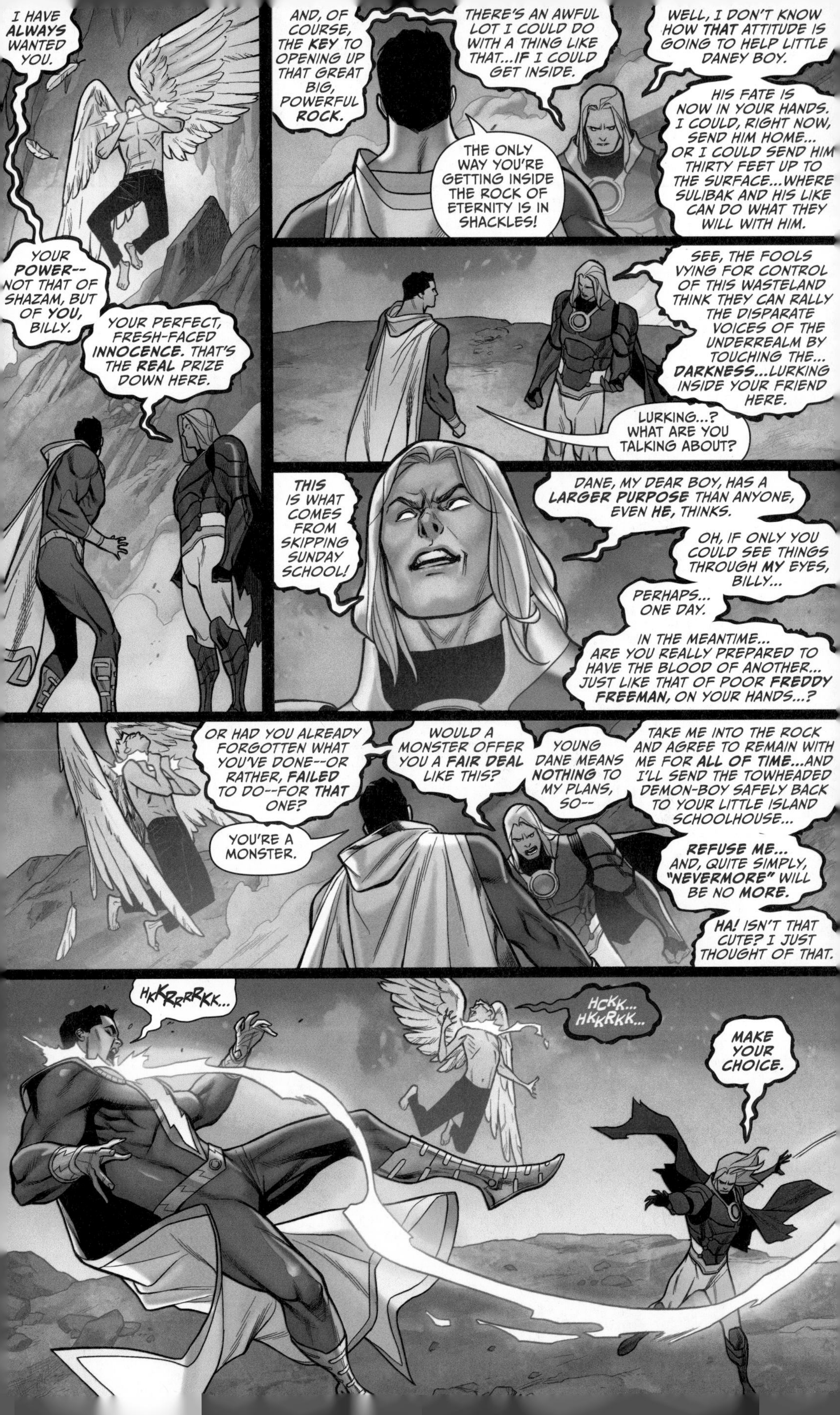

I HAVE **ALWAYS** WANTED YOU.
YOUR **POWER**-- NOT THAT OF SHAZAM, BUT OF **YOU**, BILLY.
YOUR PERFECT, FRESH-FACED **INNOCENCE**. THAT'S THE **REAL** PRIZE DOWN HERE.
AND, OF COURSE, THE **KEY** TO OPENING UP THAT GREAT BIG, POWERFUL **ROCK**.
THERE'S AN AWFUL LOT I COULD DO WITH A THING LIKE THAT...**IF** I COULD GET INSIDE.
THE ONLY WAY YOU'RE GETTING INSIDE THE ROCK OF ETERNITY IS IN SHACKLES!
WELL, I DON'T KNOW HOW **THAT** ATTITUDE IS GOING TO HELP LITTLE DANEY BOY.
HIS FATE IS NOW IN YOUR HANDS. I COULD, RIGHT NOW, SEND HIM HOME... OR I COULD SEND HIM THIRTY FEET UP TO THE SURFACE...WHERE SULIBAK AND HIS LIKE CAN DO WHAT THEY WILL WITH HIM.
SEE, THE FOOLS VYING FOR CONTROL OF THIS WASTELAND THINK THEY CAN RALLY THE DISPARATE VOICES OF THE UNDERREALM BY TOUCHING THE... **DARKNESS**...LURKING INSIDE YOUR FRIEND HERE.
LURKING...? WHAT ARE YOU TALKING ABOUT?
THIS IS WHAT COMES FROM SKIPPING SUNDAY SCHOOL!
DANE, MY DEAR BOY, HAS A **LARGER PURPOSE** THAN ANYONE, EVEN **HE**, THINKS.
OH, IF ONLY YOU COULD SEE THINGS THROUGH **MY** EYES, BILLY...
PERHAPS... ONE DAY.
IN THE MEANTIME... ARE YOU REALLY PREPARED TO HAVE THE BLOOD OF ANOTHER... JUST LIKE THAT OF POOR **FREDDY FREEMAN**, ON YOUR HANDS...?
OR HAD YOU ALREADY FORGOTTEN WHAT YOU'VE DONE--OR RATHER, **FAILED** TO DO--FOR **THAT** ONE?
YOU'RE A MONSTER.
WOULD A MONSTER OFFER YOU A **FAIR DEAL** LIKE THIS?
YOUNG DANE MEANS **NOTHING** TO MY PLANS, SO--
TAKE ME INTO THE ROCK AND AGREE TO REMAIN WITH ME FOR **ALL OF TIME**...AND I'LL SEND THE TOWHEADED DEMON-BOY SAFELY BACK TO YOUR LITTLE ISLAND SCHOOLHOUSE...
REFUSE ME... AND, QUITE SIMPLY, **"NEVERMORE"** WILL BE NO **MORE**.
HA! ISN'T THAT CUTE? I JUST THOUGHT OF THAT.
HKKRRRRKK...
HCKK... HKKRKK...
MAKE YOUR CHOICE.

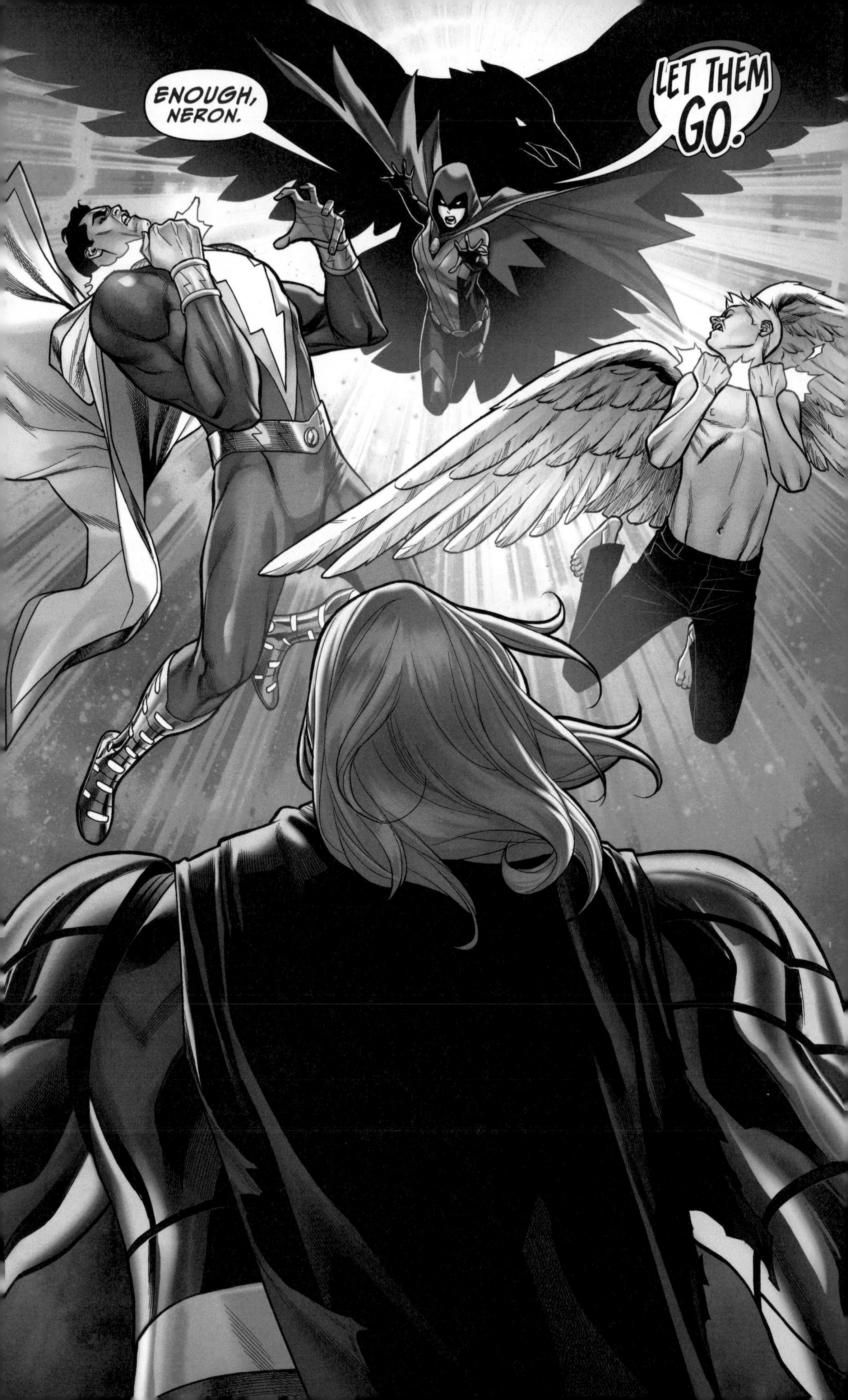
ENOUGH, NERON.
LET THEM GO.

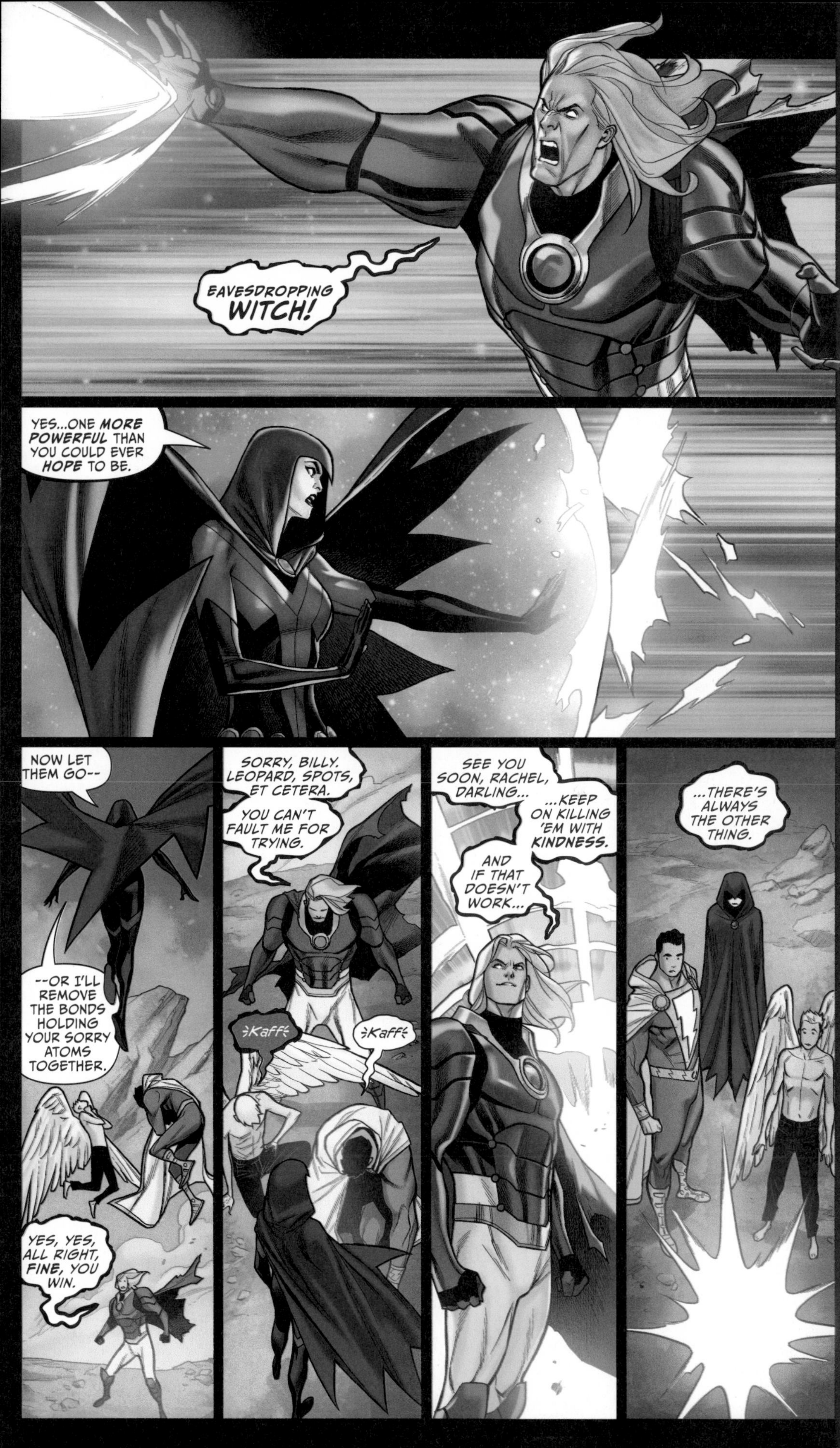
EAVESDROPPING WITCH!
YES...ONE MORE POWERFUL THAN YOU COULD EVER HOPE TO BE.
NOW LET THEM GO--
--OR I'LL REMOVE THE BONDS HOLDING YOUR SORRY ATOMS TOGETHER.
YES, YES, ALL RIGHT, FINE, YOU WIN.
SORRY, BILLY. LEOPARD, SPOTS, ET CETERA.
YOU CAN'T FAULT ME FOR TRYING.
KAFF
KAFF
SEE YOU SOON, RACHEL, DARLING...
...KEEP ON KILLING 'EM WITH KINDNESS.
AND IF THAT DOESN'T WORK...
...THERE'S ALWAYS THE OTHER THING.

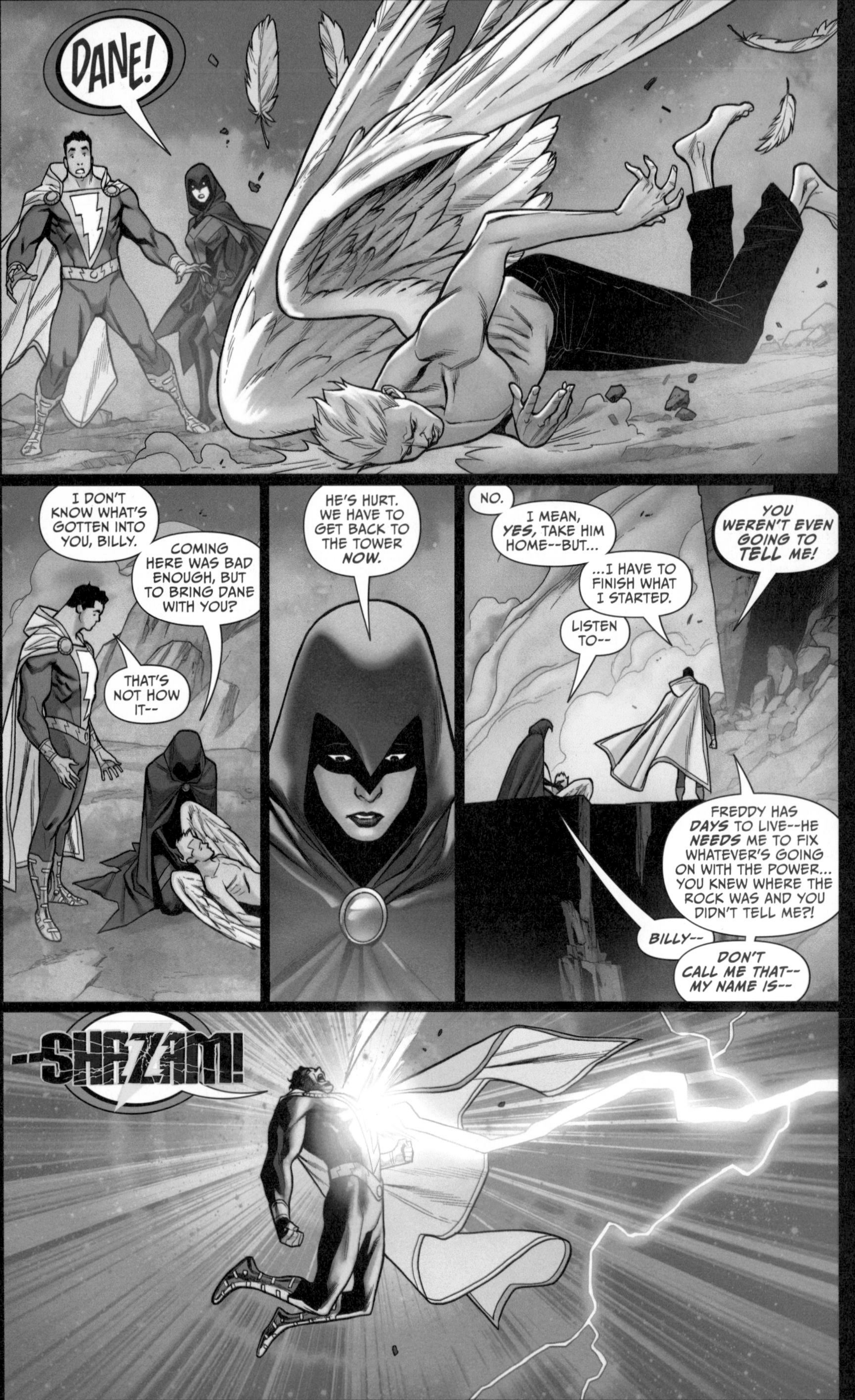
DANE!
I DON'T KNOW WHAT'S GOTTEN INTO YOU, BILLY.
COMING HERE WAS BAD ENOUGH, BUT TO BRING DANE WITH YOU?
THAT'S NOT HOW IT--
HE'S HURT. WE HAVE TO GET BACK TO THE TOWER NOW.
NO.
I MEAN, YES, TAKE HIM HOME--BUT...
...I HAVE TO FINISH WHAT I STARTED.
LISTEN TO--
YOU WEREN'T EVEN GOING TO TELL ME!
FREDDY HAS DAYS TO LIVE--HE NEEDS ME TO FIX WHATEVER'S GOING ON WITH THE POWER... YOU KNEW WHERE THE ROCK WAS AND YOU DIDN'T TELL ME?!
BILLY--
DON'T CALL ME THAT-- MY NAME IS--
-SHAZAM!

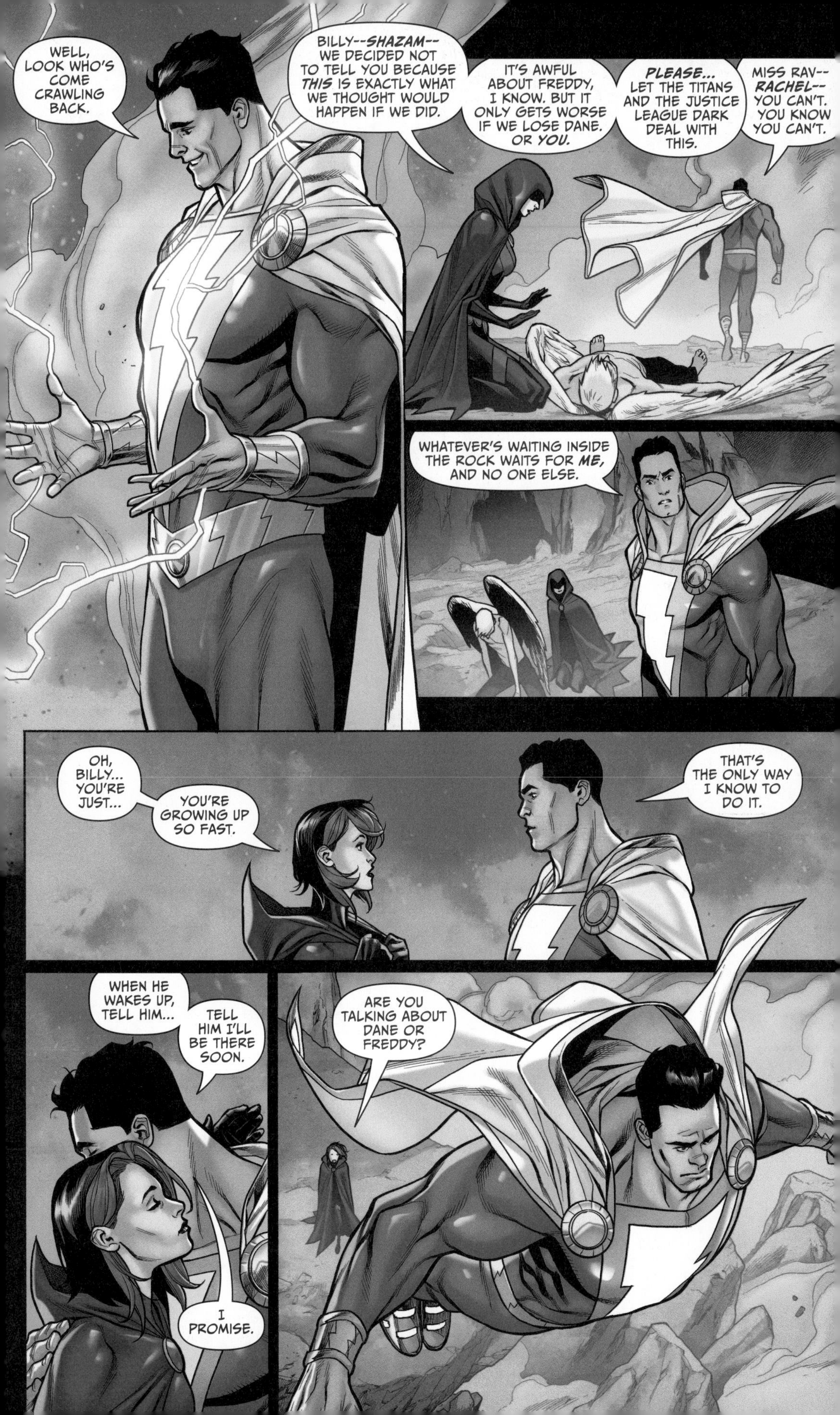

WELL, LOOK WHO'S COME CRAWLING BACK.
BILLY--SHAZAM--WE DECIDED NOT TO TELL YOU BECAUSE THIS IS EXACTLY WHAT WE THOUGHT WOULD HAPPEN IF WE DID.
IT'S AWFUL ABOUT FREDDY, I KNOW. BUT IT ONLY GETS WORSE IF WE LOSE DANE. OR YOU.
PLEASE... LET THE TITANS AND THE JUSTICE LEAGUE DARK DEAL WITH THIS.
MISS RAV--RACHEL--YOU CAN'T. YOU KNOW YOU CAN'T.
WHATEVER'S WAITING INSIDE THE ROCK WAITS FOR ME, AND NO ONE ELSE.
OH, BILLY... YOU'RE JUST...
YOU'RE GROWING UP SO FAST.
THAT'S THE ONLY WAY I KNOW TO DO IT.
WHEN HE WAKES UP, TELL HIM...
TELL HIM I'LL BE THERE SOON.
I PROMISE.
ARE YOU TALKING ABOUT DANE OR FREDDY?

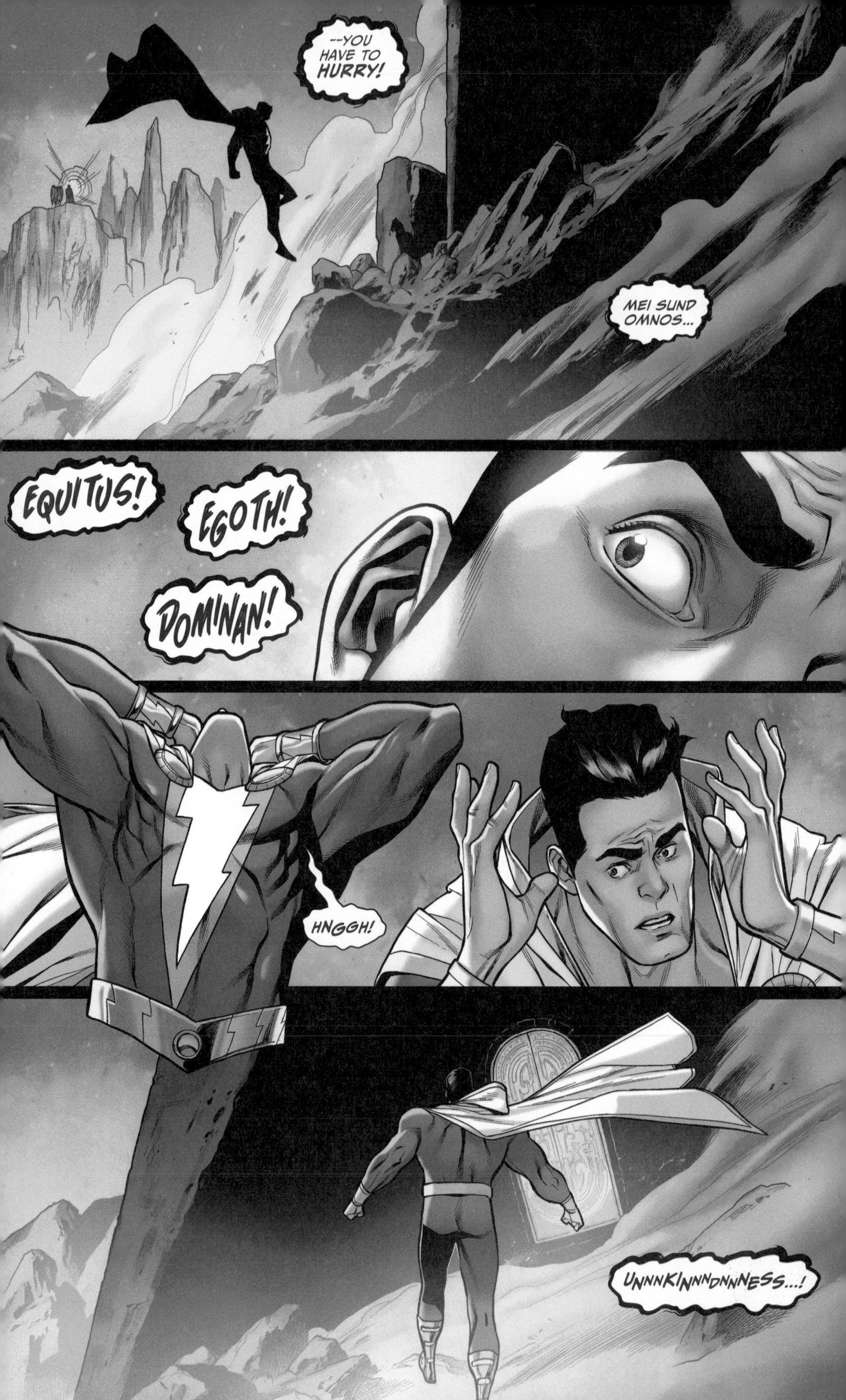
--YOU HAVE TO HURRY!
MEI SUND OMNOS...
EQUITUS!
EGOTH!
DOMINAN!
HNGGH!
UNNNKINNNDNNNESS...!

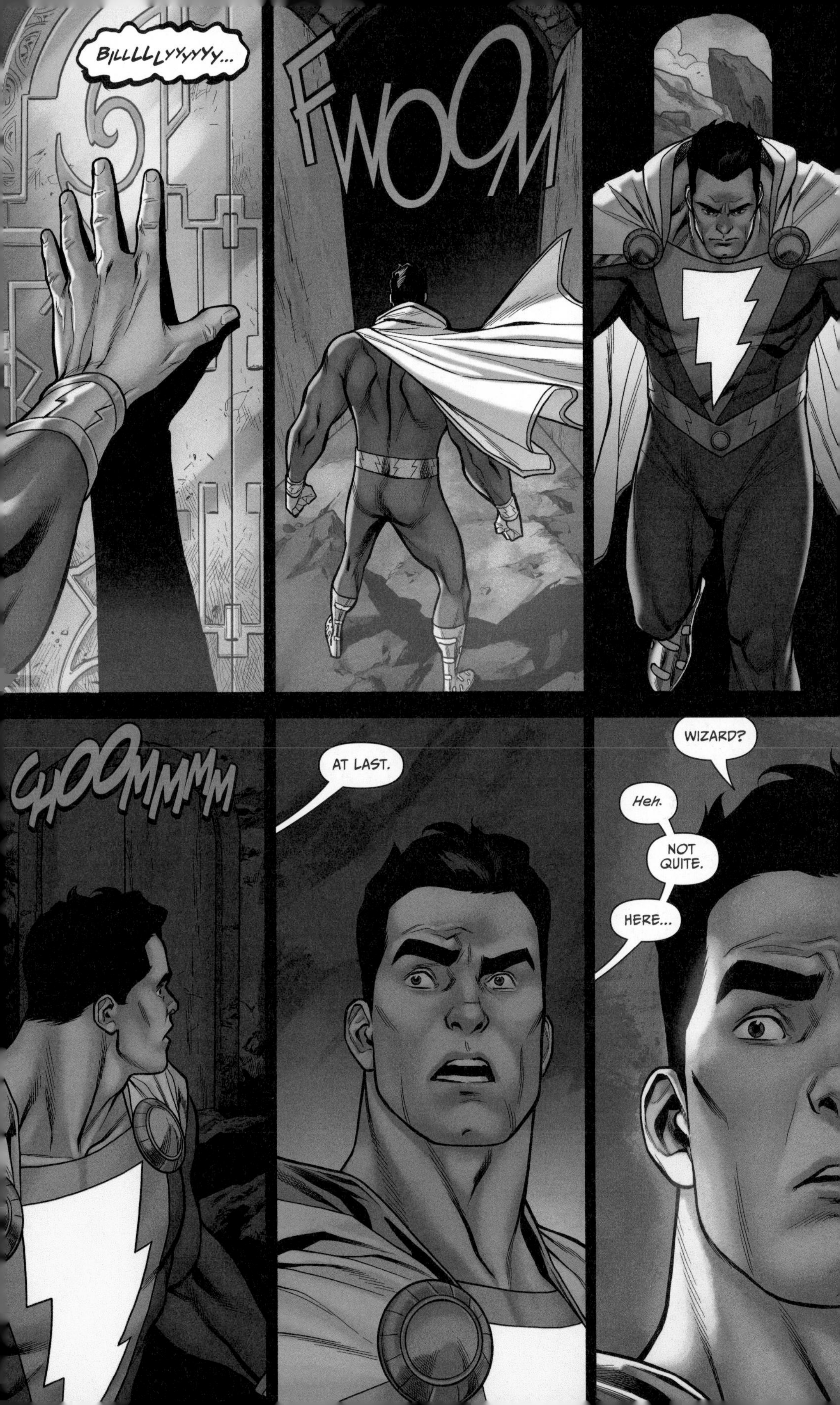
BILLLLLYYYYYY...
FWOOM
CHOOMMMM
AT LAST.
WIZARD?
Heh.
NOT QUITE.
HERE...

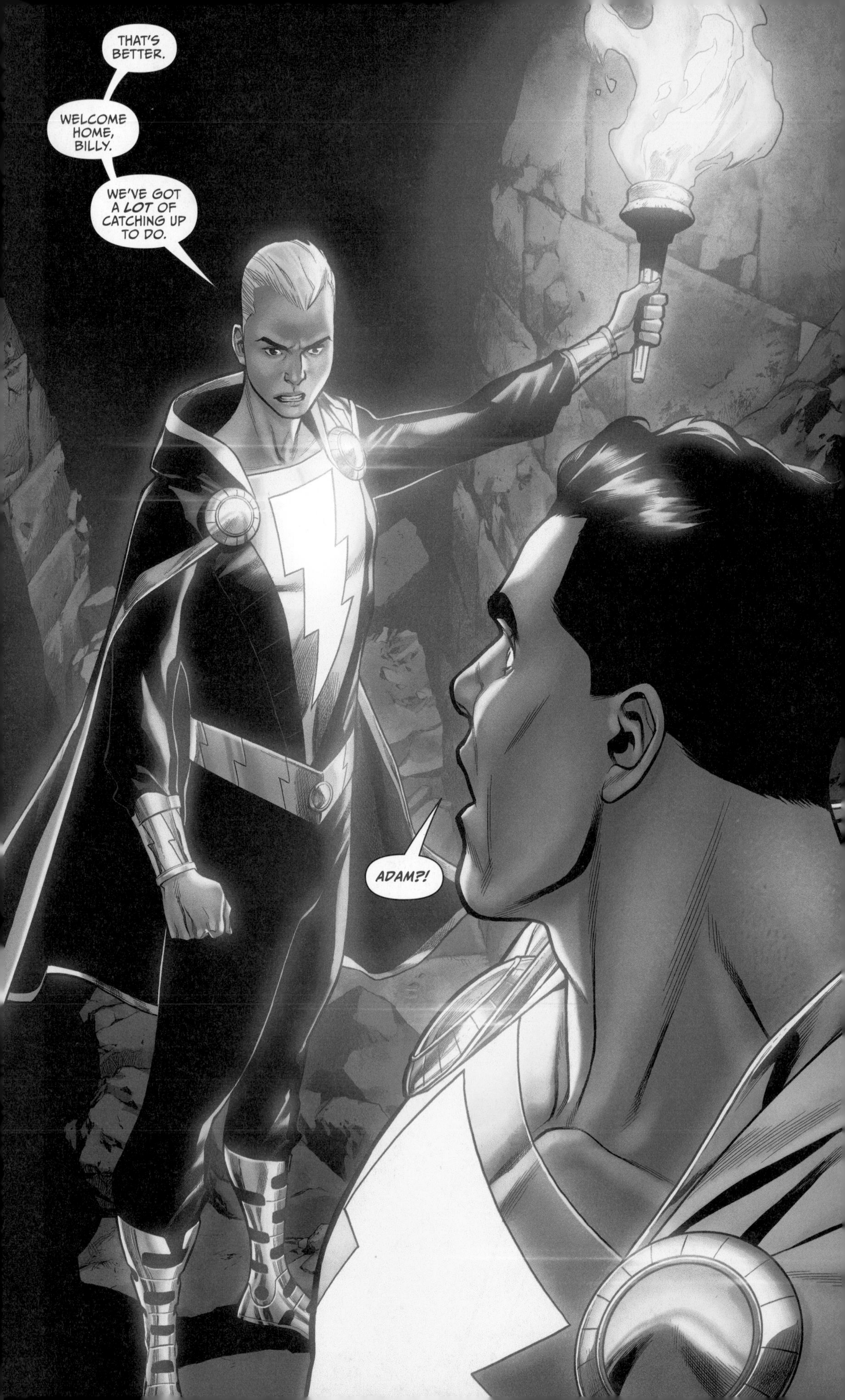

THAT'S BETTER.
WELCOME HOME, BILLY.
WE'VE GOT A LOT OF CATCHING UP TO DO.
ADAM?!

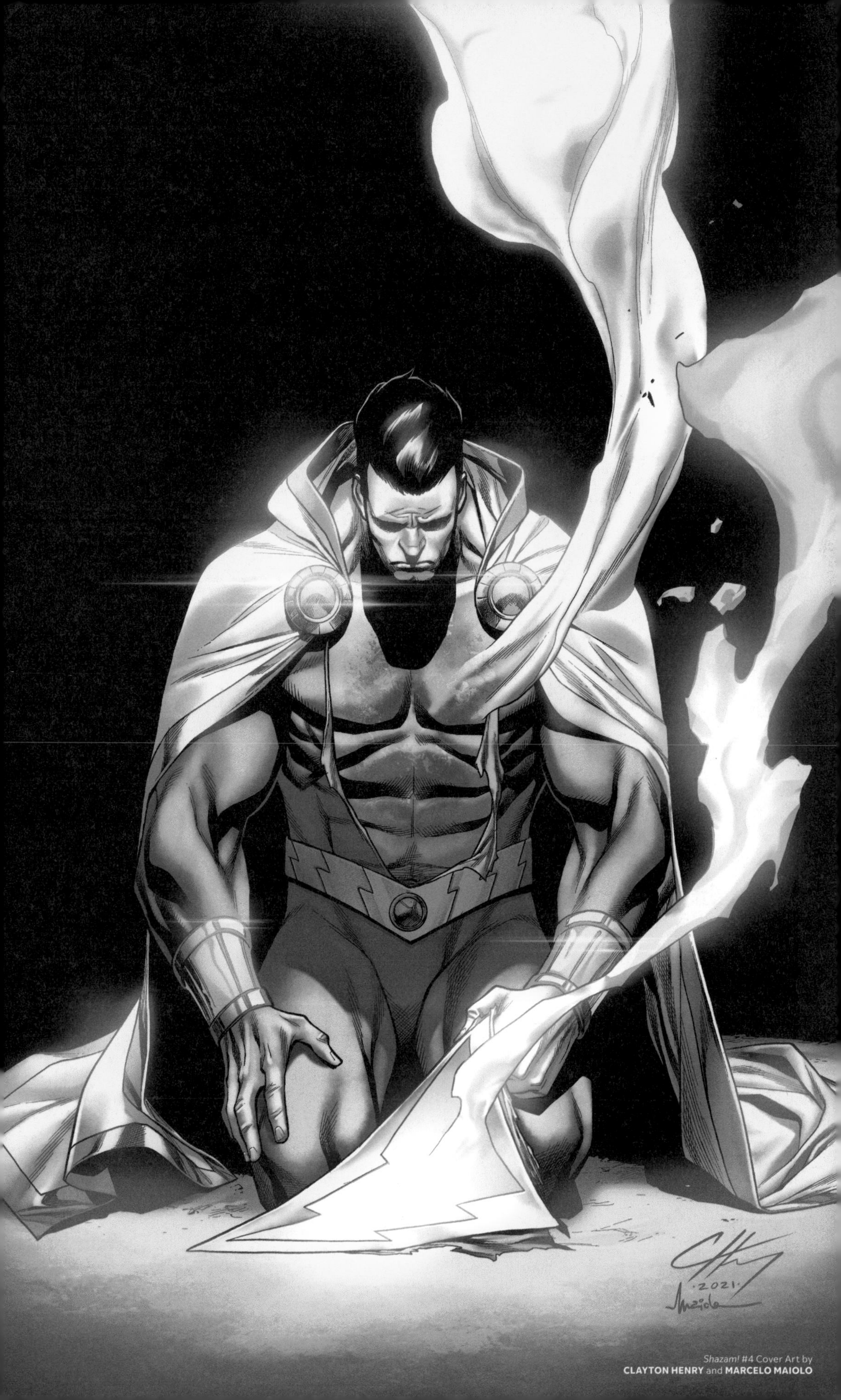

·2021·

Shazam! #4 Cover Art by
CLAYTON HENRY and **MARCELO MAIOLO**

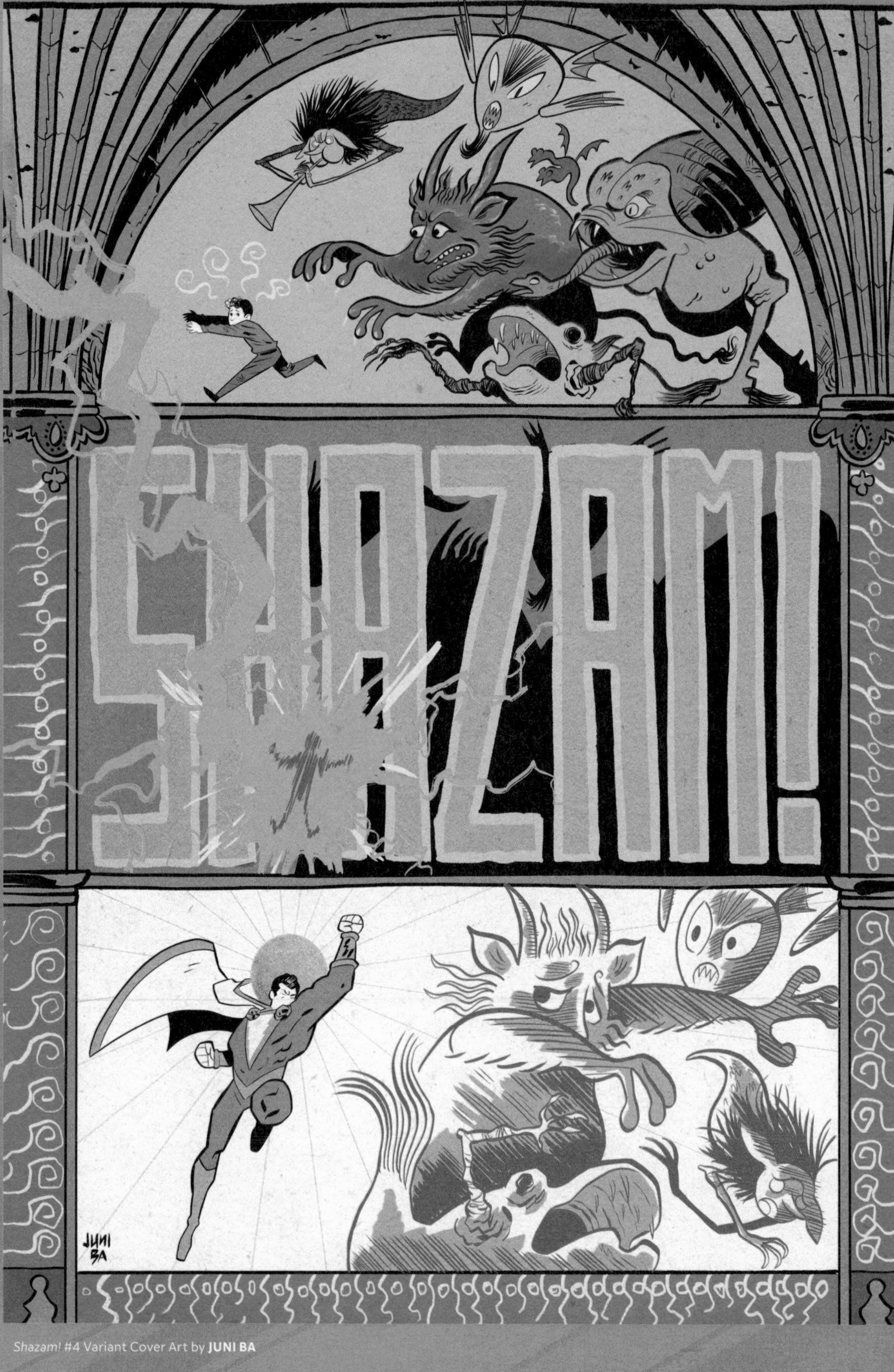
SHAZAM!
JUNI BA

Shazam! #4 Variant Cover Art by **JUNI BA**

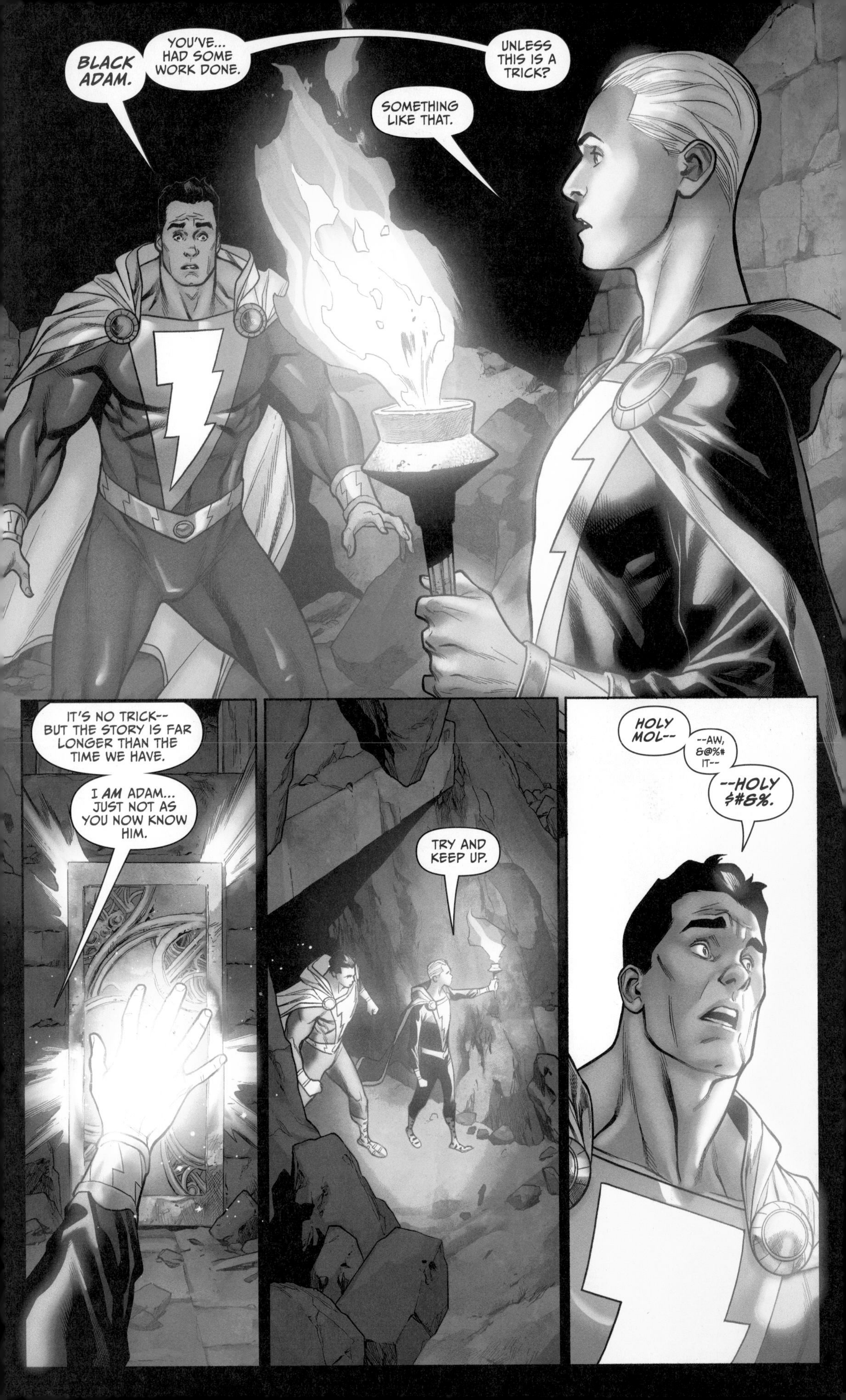
BLACK ADAM.
YOU'VE... HAD SOME WORK DONE.
UNLESS THIS IS A TRICK?
SOMETHING LIKE THAT.
IT'S NO TRICK-- BUT THE STORY IS FAR LONGER THAN THE TIME WE HAVE.
I AM ADAM... JUST NOT AS YOU NOW KNOW HIM.
TRY AND KEEP UP.
HOLY MOL--
--AW, &@%# IT--
--HOLY $#&%.

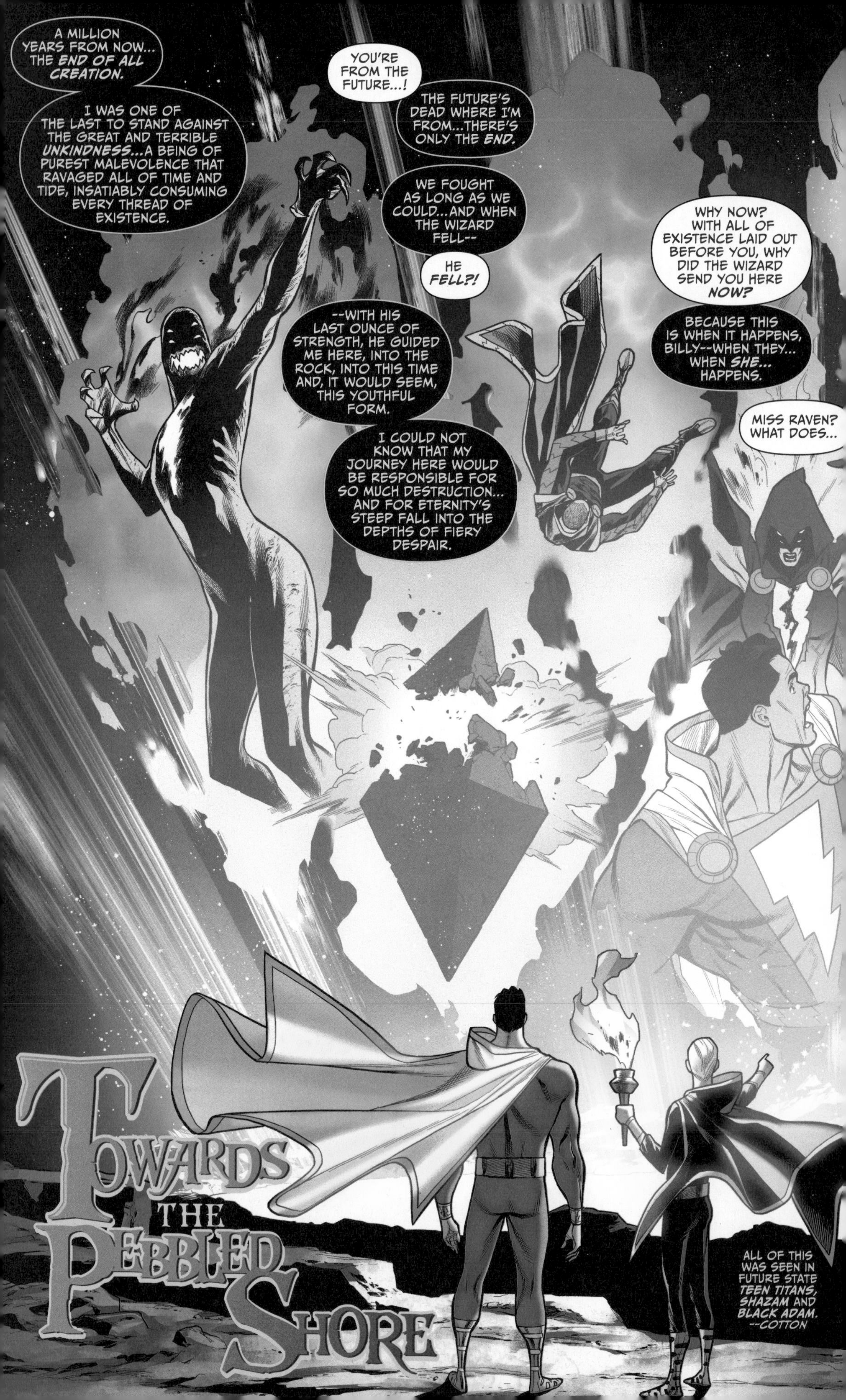
A MILLION YEARS FROM NOW... THE END OF ALL CREATION.
I WAS ONE OF THE LAST TO STAND AGAINST THE GREAT AND TERRIBLE UNKINDNESS...A BEING OF PUREST MALEVOLENCE THAT RAVAGED ALL OF TIME AND TIDE, INSATIABLY CONSUMING EVERY THREAD OF EXISTENCE.
YOU'RE FROM THE FUTURE...!
THE FUTURE'S DEAD WHERE I'M FROM...THERE'S ONLY THE END.
WE FOUGHT AS LONG AS WE COULD...AND WHEN THE WIZARD FELL--
HE FELL?!
--WITH HIS LAST OUNCE OF STRENGTH, HE GUIDED ME HERE, INTO THE ROCK, INTO THIS TIME AND, IT WOULD SEEM, THIS YOUTHFUL FORM.
I COULD NOT KNOW THAT MY JOURNEY HERE WOULD BE RESPONSIBLE FOR SO MUCH DESTRUCTION... AND FOR ETERNITY'S STEEP FALL INTO THE DEPTHS OF FIERY DESPAIR.
WHY NOW? WITH ALL OF EXISTENCE LAID OUT BEFORE YOU, WHY DID THE WIZARD SEND YOU HERE NOW?
BECAUSE THIS IS WHEN IT HAPPENS, BILLY--WHEN THEY... WHEN SHE... HAPPENS.
MISS RAVEN? WHAT DOES...
TOWARDS THE PEBBLED SHORE
ALL OF THIS WAS SEEN IN FUTURE STATE TEEN TITANS, SHAZAM AND BLACK ADAM. --COTTON

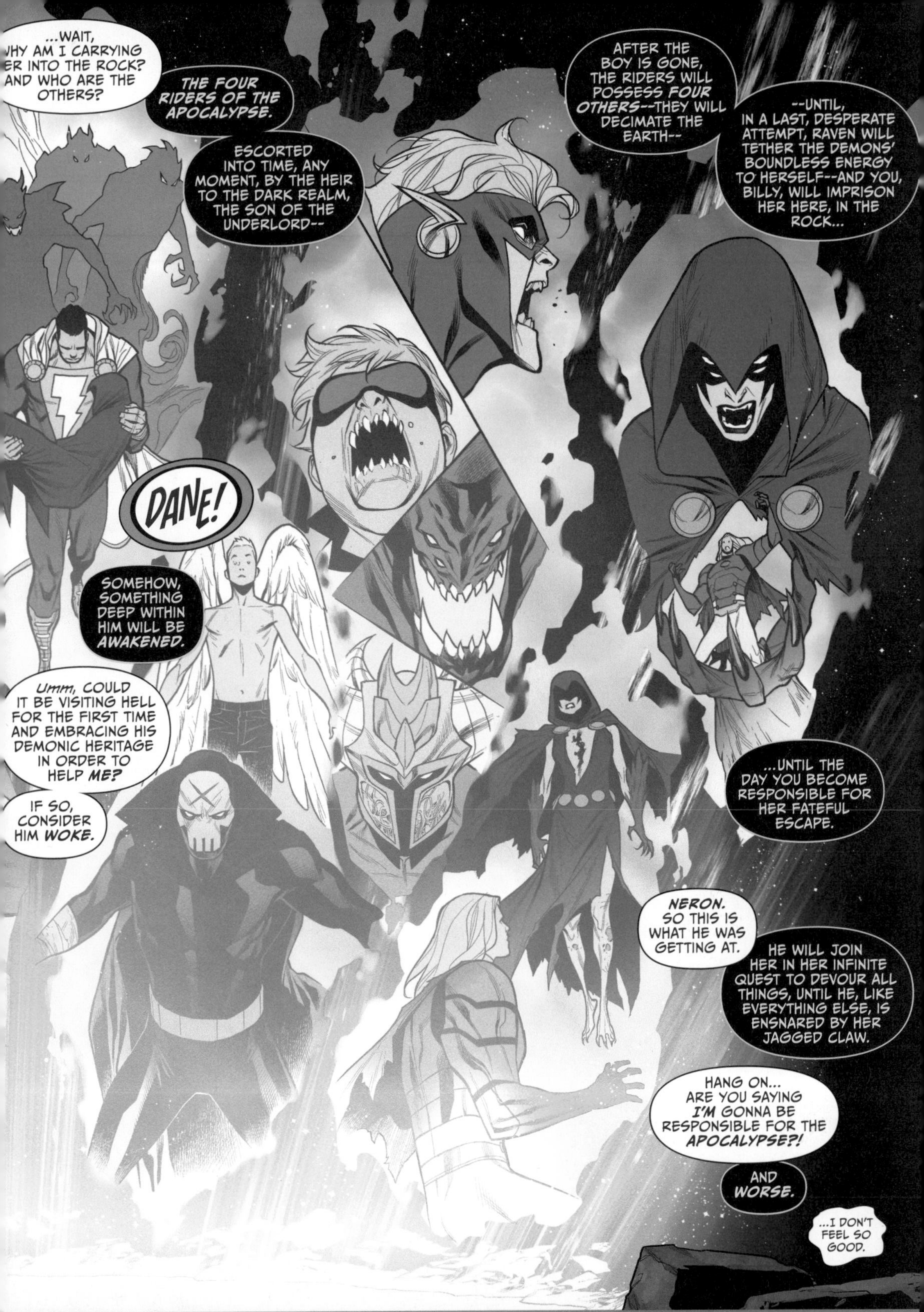

...WAIT, HY AM I CARRYING ER INTO THE ROCK? AND WHO ARE THE OTHERS?
THE FOUR RIDERS OF THE APOCALYPSE.
ESCORTED INTO TIME, ANY MOMENT, BY THE HEIR TO THE DARK REALM, THE SON OF THE UNDERLORD--
AFTER THE BOY IS GONE, THE RIDERS WILL POSSESS FOUR OTHERS--THEY WILL DECIMATE THE EARTH--
--UNTIL, IN A LAST, DESPERATE ATTEMPT, RAVEN WILL TETHER THE DEMONS' BOUNDLESS ENERGY TO HERSELF--AND YOU, BILLY, WILL IMPRISON HER HERE, IN THE ROCK...
DANE!
SOMEHOW, SOMETHING DEEP WITHIN HIM WILL BE AWAKENED.
Umm, COULD IT BE VISITING HELL FOR THE FIRST TIME AND EMBRACING HIS DEMONIC HERITAGE IN ORDER TO HELP ME?
IF SO, CONSIDER HIM WOKE.
...UNTIL THE DAY YOU BECOME RESPONSIBLE FOR HER FATEFUL ESCAPE.
NERON. SO THIS IS WHAT HE WAS GETTING AT.
HE WILL JOIN HER IN HER INFINITE QUEST TO DEVOUR ALL THINGS, UNTIL HE, LIKE EVERYTHING ELSE, IS ENSNARED BY HER JAGGED CLAW.
HANG ON... ARE YOU SAYING I'M GONNA BE RESPONSIBLE FOR THE APOCALYPSE?!
AND WORSE.
...I DON'T FEEL SO GOOD.

TIM SHERIDAN	CLAYTON HENRY	MARCELO MAIOLO	ROB LEIGH	HENRY & MAIOLO	JUNI BA	DIEGO LOPEZ	MIKE COTTON
WRITER	ARTIST	COLORIST	LETTERER	COVER	VARIANT COVER	EDITOR	SENIOR EDITOR

SHAZAM! WITH A SINGLE MAGIC WORD, THE POWERS OF SIX ANCIENT GODS--THE WISDOM OF SOLOMON, THE STRENGTH OF HERCULES, THE STAMINA OF ATLAS, THE POWER OF ZEUS, THE COURAGE OF ACHILLES, AND THE SPEED OF MERCURY--ARE PLACED IN THE HANDS OF TEENAGE BILLY BATSON, TRANSFORMING HIM INTO THE WORLD'S MIGHTIEST MORTAL!

SHAZAM! CREATED BY BILL PARKER & C.C. BECK

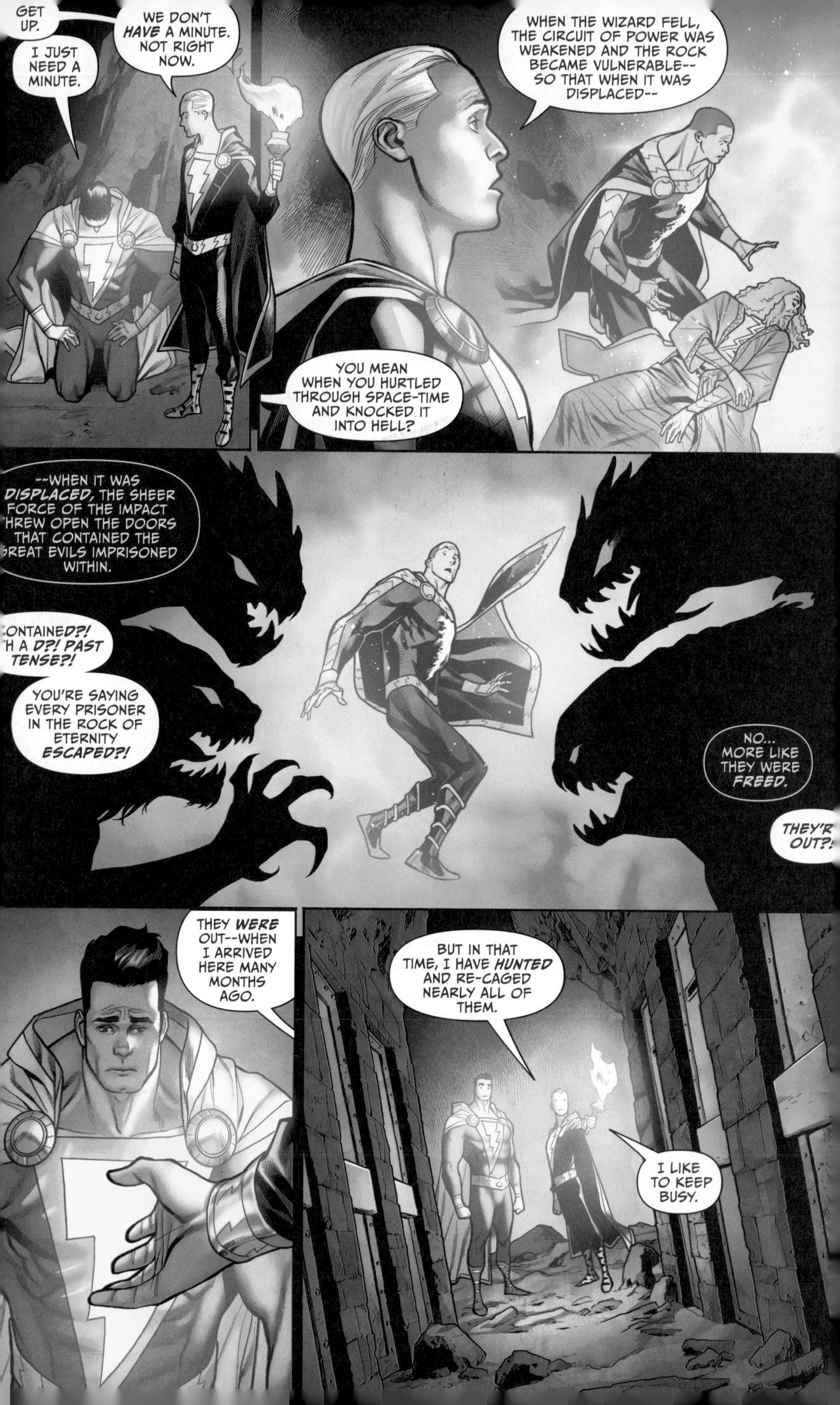
GET UP.
I JUST NEED A MINUTE.
WE DON'T HAVE A MINUTE. NOT RIGHT NOW.
WHEN THE WIZARD FELL, THE CIRCUIT OF POWER WAS WEAKENED AND THE ROCK BECAME VULNERABLE-- SO THAT WHEN IT WAS DISPLACED--
YOU MEAN WHEN YOU HURTLED THROUGH SPACE-TIME AND KNOCKED IT INTO HELL?
--WHEN IT WAS DISPLACED, THE SHEER FORCE OF THE IMPACT THREW OPEN THE DOORS THAT CONTAINED THE GREAT EVILS IMPRISONED WITHIN.
CONTAINED?! TH A D?! PAST TENSE?!
YOU'RE SAYING EVERY PRISONER IN THE ROCK OF ETERNITY ESCAPED?!
NO... MORE LIKE THEY WERE FREED.
THEY'R OUT?!
THEY WERE OUT--WHEN I ARRIVED HERE MANY MONTHS AGO.
BUT IN THAT TIME, I HAVE HUNTED AND RE-CAGED NEARLY ALL OF THEM.
I LIKE TO KEEP BUSY.

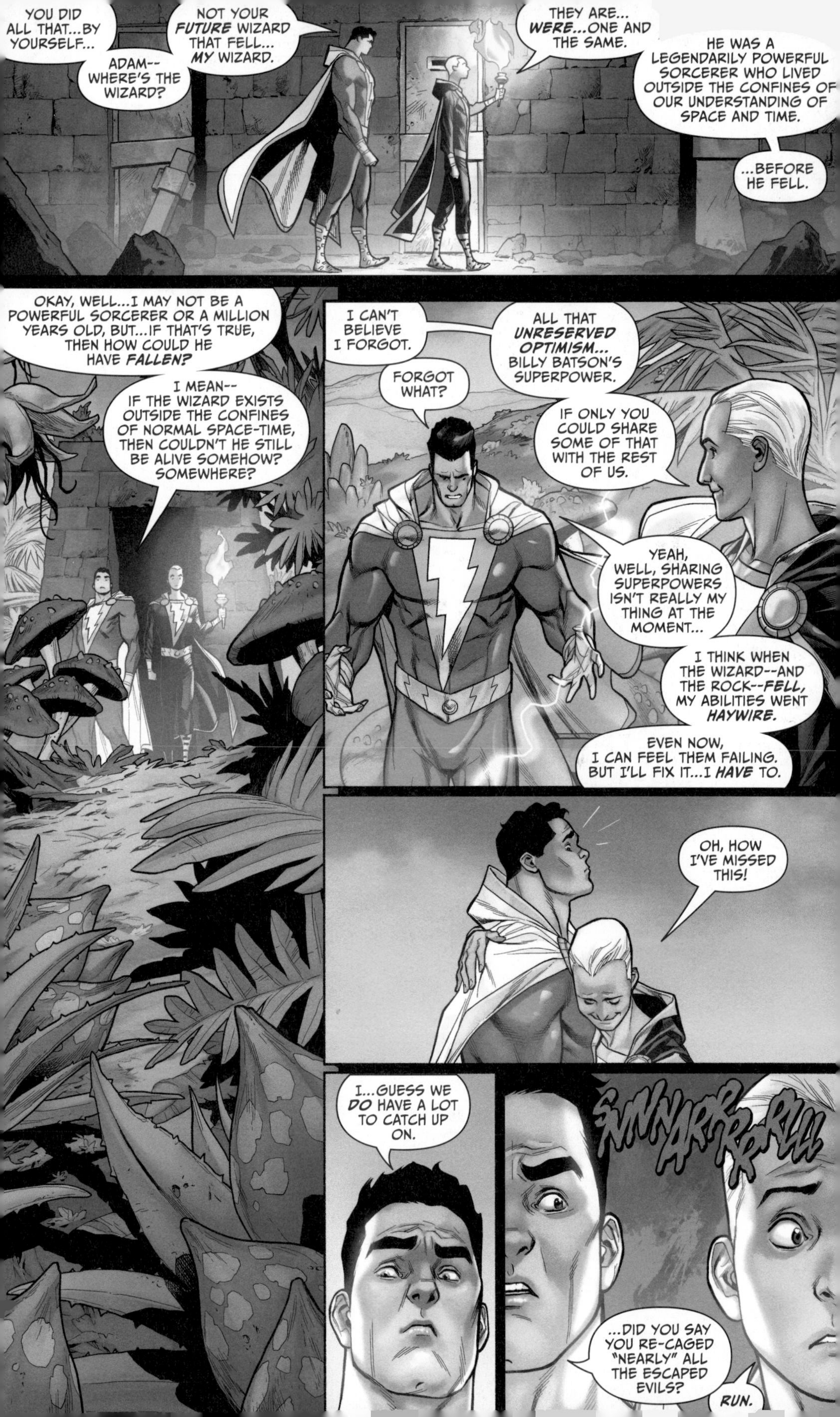
YOU DID ALL THAT...BY YOURSELF...
ADAM-- WHERE'S THE WIZARD?
NOT YOUR FUTURE WIZARD THAT FELL... MY WIZARD.
THEY ARE... WERE...ONE AND THE SAME.
HE WAS A LEGENDARILY POWERFUL SORCERER WHO LIVED OUTSIDE THE CONFINES OF OUR UNDERSTANDING OF SPACE AND TIME.
...BEFORE HE FELL.
OKAY, WELL...I MAY NOT BE A POWERFUL SORCERER OR A MILLION YEARS OLD, BUT...IF THAT'S TRUE, THEN HOW COULD HE HAVE FALLEN?
I MEAN-- IF THE WIZARD EXISTS OUTSIDE THE CONFINES OF NORMAL SPACE-TIME, THEN COULDN'T HE STILL BE ALIVE SOMEHOW? SOMEWHERE?
I CAN'T BELIEVE I FORGOT.
FORGOT WHAT?
ALL THAT UNRESERVED OPTIMISM... BILLY BATSON'S SUPERPOWER.
IF ONLY YOU COULD SHARE SOME OF THAT WITH THE REST OF US.
YEAH, WELL, SHARING SUPERPOWERS ISN'T REALLY MY THING AT THE MOMENT...
I THINK WHEN THE WIZARD--AND THE ROCK--FELL, MY ABILITIES WENT HAYWIRE.
EVEN NOW, I CAN FEEL THEM FAILING. BUT I'LL FIX IT...I HAVE TO.
OH, HOW I'VE MISSED THIS!
I...GUESS WE DO HAVE A LOT TO CATCH UP ON.
SUNNARRRRLLL
...DID YOU SAY YOU RE-CAGED "NEARLY" ALL THE ESCAPED EVILS?
RUN.

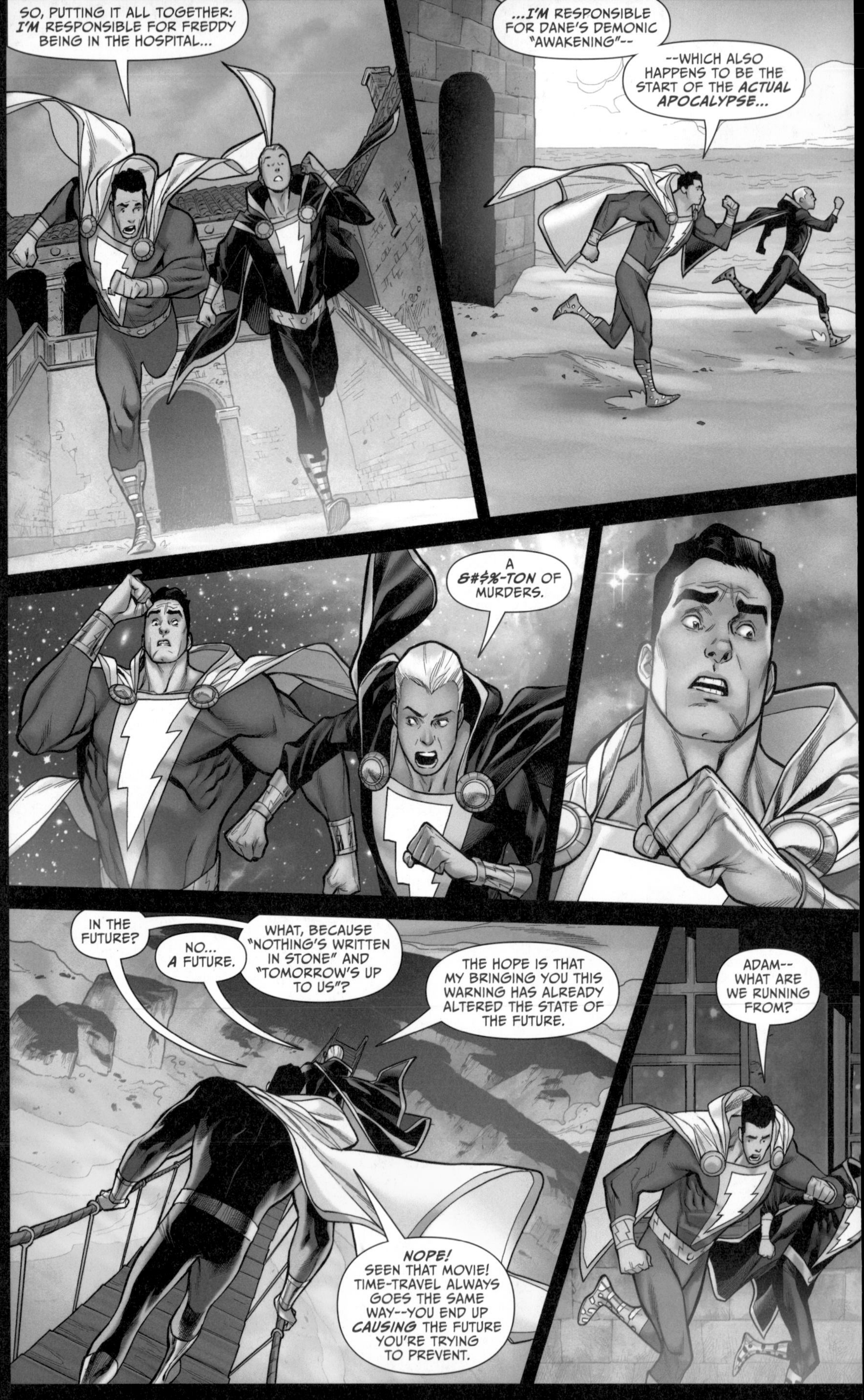
SO, PUTTING IT ALL TOGETHER: *I'M* RESPONSIBLE FOR FREDDY BEING IN THE HOSPITAL...
...*I'M* RESPONSIBLE FOR DANE'S DEMONIC "AWAKENING"--
--WHICH ALSO HAPPENS TO BE THE START OF THE *ACTUAL APOCALYPSE*...
A *&#$%-TON* OF MURDERS.
IN THE FUTURE?
NO... *A* FUTURE.
WHAT, BECAUSE "NOTHING'S WRITTEN IN STONE" AND "TOMORROW'S UP TO US"?
THE HOPE IS THAT MY BRINGING YOU THIS WARNING HAS ALREADY ALTERED THE STATE OF THE FUTURE.
NOPE! SEEN THAT MOVIE! TIME-TRAVEL ALWAYS GOES THE SAME WAY--YOU END UP *CAUSING* THE FUTURE YOU'RE TRYING TO PREVENT.
ADAM--WHAT ARE WE RUNNING FROM?

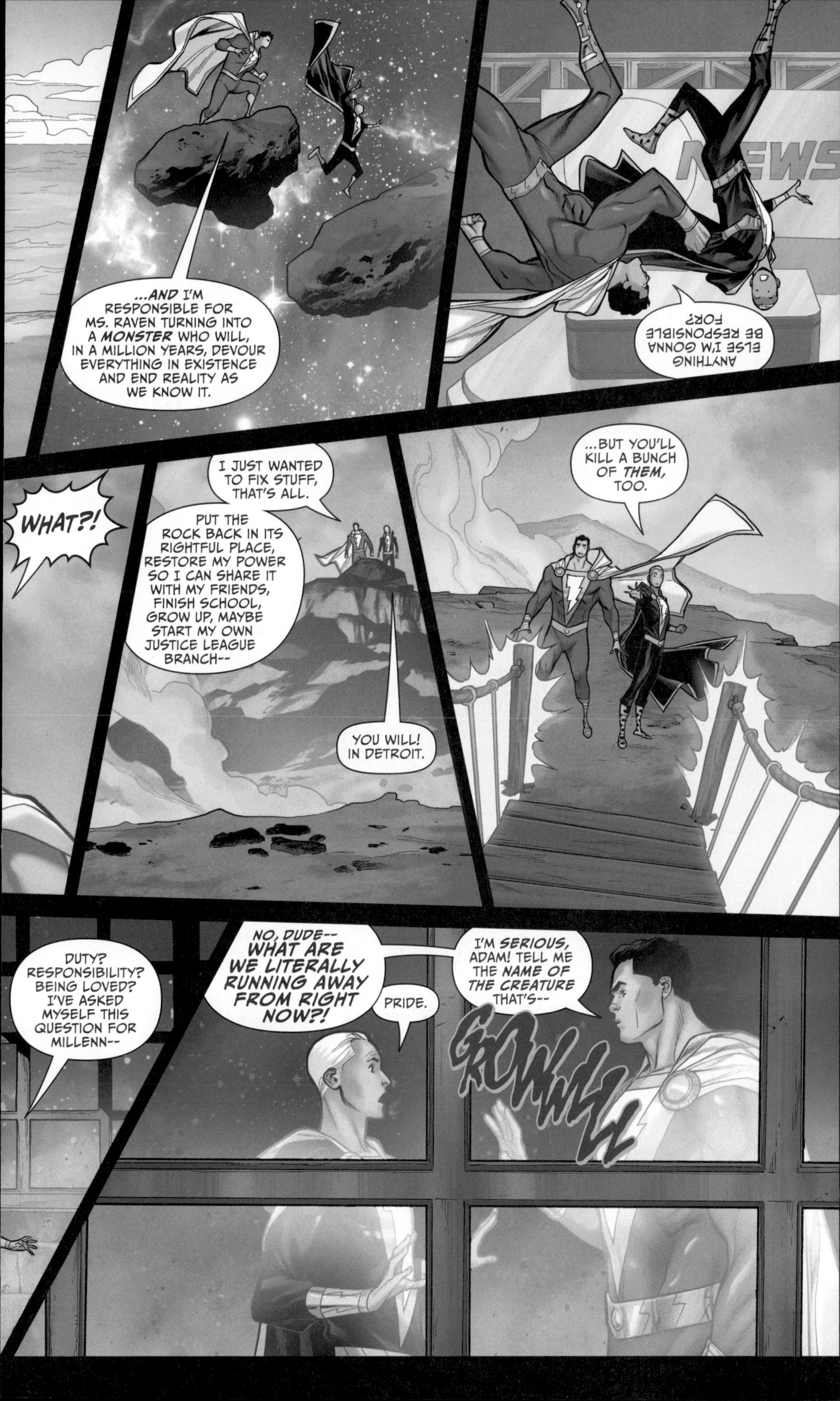

...AND I'M RESPONSIBLE FOR MS. RAVEN TURNING INTO A MONSTER WHO WILL, IN A MILLION YEARS, DEVOUR EVERYTHING IN EXISTENCE AND END REALITY AS WE KNOW IT.
ANYTHING ELSE I'M GONNA BE RESPONSIBLE FOR?
WHAT?!
I JUST WANTED TO FIX STUFF, THAT'S ALL.
PUT THE ROCK BACK IN ITS RIGHTFUL PLACE, RESTORE MY POWER SO I CAN SHARE IT WITH MY FRIENDS, FINISH SCHOOL, GROW UP, MAYBE START MY OWN JUSTICE LEAGUE BRANCH--
YOU WILL! IN DETROIT.
...BUT YOU'LL KILL A BUNCH OF THEM, TOO.
DUTY? RESPONSIBILITY? BEING LOVED? I'VE ASKED MYSELF THIS QUESTION FOR MILLENN--
NO, DUDE-- WHAT ARE WE LITERALLY RUNNING AWAY FROM RIGHT NOW?!
PRIDE.
I'M SERIOUS, ADAM! TELL ME THE NAME OF THE CREATURE THAT'S--

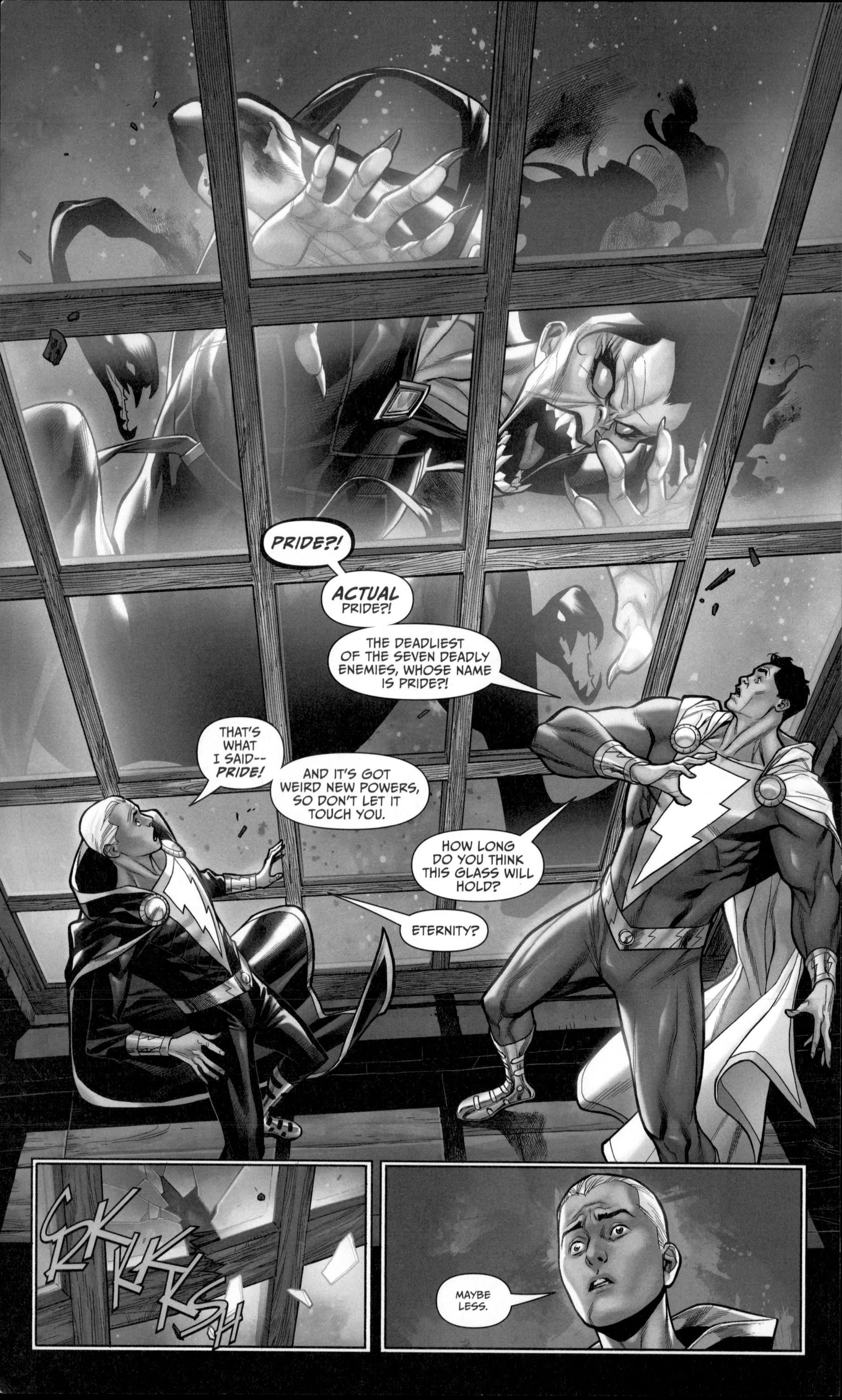
PRIDE?!
ACTUAL PRIDE?!
THE DEADLIEST OF THE SEVEN DEADLY ENEMIES, WHOSE NAME IS PRIDE?!
THAT'S WHAT I SAID-- PRIDE!
AND IT'S GOT WEIRD NEW POWERS, SO DON'T LET IT TOUCH YOU.
HOW LONG DO YOU THINK THIS GLASS WILL HOLD?
ETERNITY?
CRKKKKKSH
MAYBE LESS.

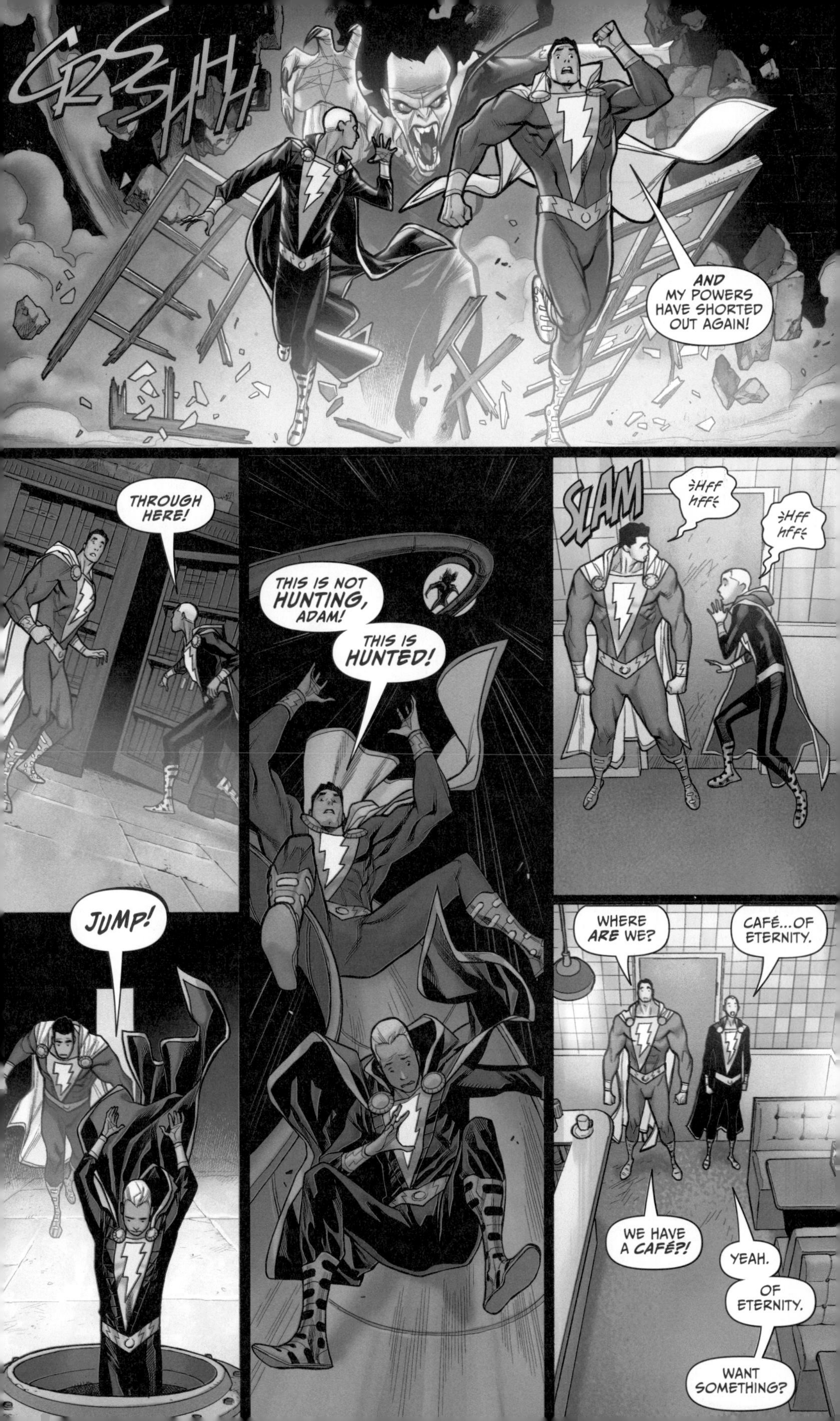
GRSHHH
AND MY POWERS HAVE SHORTED OUT AGAIN!
THROUGH HERE!
JUMP!
THIS IS NOT HUNTING, ADAM!
THIS IS HUNTED!
SLAM
HFF HFF
HFF HFF
WHERE ARE WE?
CAFÉ...OF ETERNITY.
WE HAVE A CAFÉ?!
YEAH.
OF ETERNITY.
WANT SOMETHING?

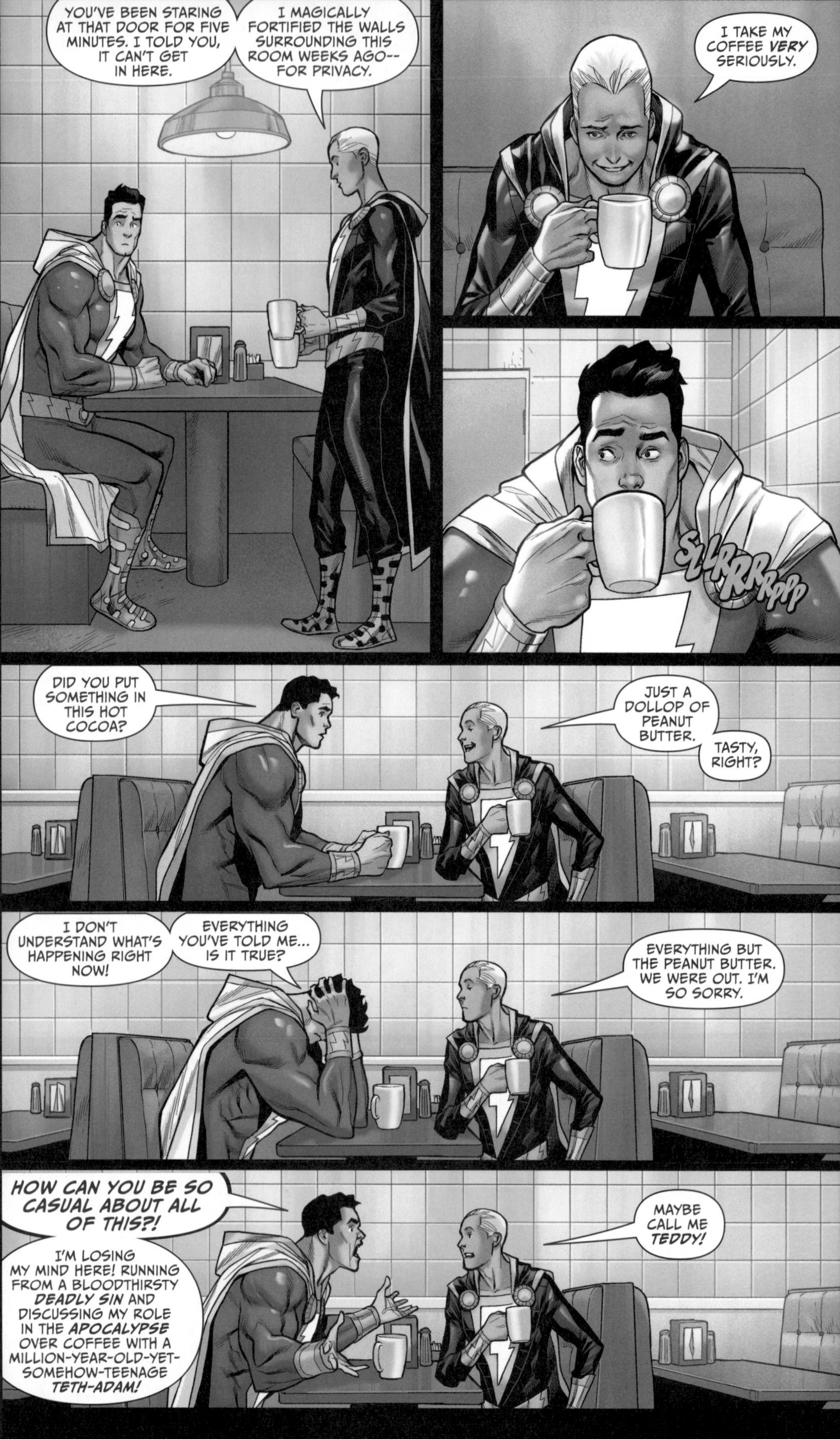
YOU'VE BEEN STARING AT THAT DOOR FOR FIVE MINUTES. I TOLD YOU, IT CAN'T GET IN HERE.
I MAGICALLY FORTIFIED THE WALLS SURROUNDING THIS ROOM WEEKS AGO-- FOR PRIVACY.
I TAKE MY COFFEE VERY SERIOUSLY.
SLLRRRRPPP
DID YOU PUT SOMETHING IN THIS HOT COCOA?
JUST A DOLLOP OF PEANUT BUTTER.
TASTY, RIGHT?
I DON'T UNDERSTAND WHAT'S HAPPENING RIGHT NOW!
EVERYTHING YOU'VE TOLD ME... IS IT TRUE?
EVERYTHING BUT THE PEANUT BUTTER. WE WERE OUT. I'M SO SORRY.
HOW CAN YOU BE SO CASUAL ABOUT ALL OF THIS?!
I'M LOSING MY MIND HERE! RUNNING FROM A BLOODTHIRSTY DEADLY SIN AND DISCUSSING MY ROLE IN THE APOCALYPSE OVER COFFEE WITH A MILLION-YEAR-OLD-YET-SOMEHOW-TEENAGE TETH-ADAM!
MAYBE CALL ME TEDDY!

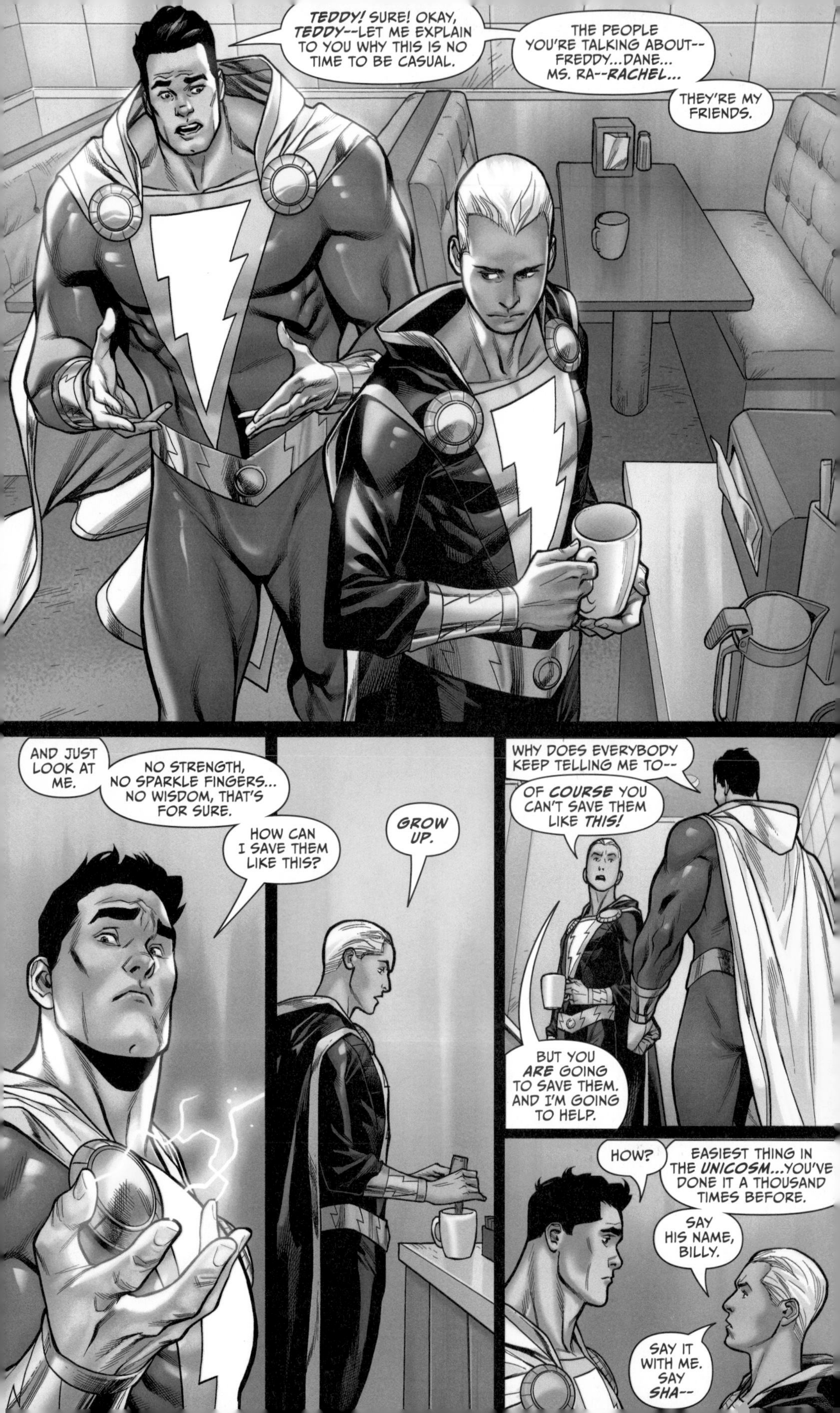
TEDDY! SURE! OKAY, TEDDY--LET ME EXPLAIN TO YOU WHY THIS IS NO TIME TO BE CASUAL.
THE PEOPLE YOU'RE TALKING ABOUT-- FREDDY...DANE... MS. RA--RACHEL...
THEY'RE MY FRIENDS.
AND JUST LOOK AT ME.
NO STRENGTH, NO SPARKLE FINGERS... NO WISDOM, THAT'S FOR SURE.
HOW CAN I SAVE THEM LIKE THIS?
GROW UP.
WHY DOES EVERYBODY KEEP TELLING ME TO--
OF COURSE YOU CAN'T SAVE THEM LIKE THIS!
BUT YOU ARE GOING TO SAVE THEM. AND I'M GOING TO HELP.
HOW?
EASIEST THING IN THE UNICOSM...YOU'VE DONE IT A THOUSAND TIMES BEFORE.
SAY HIS NAME, BILLY.
SAY IT WITH ME. SAY SHA--

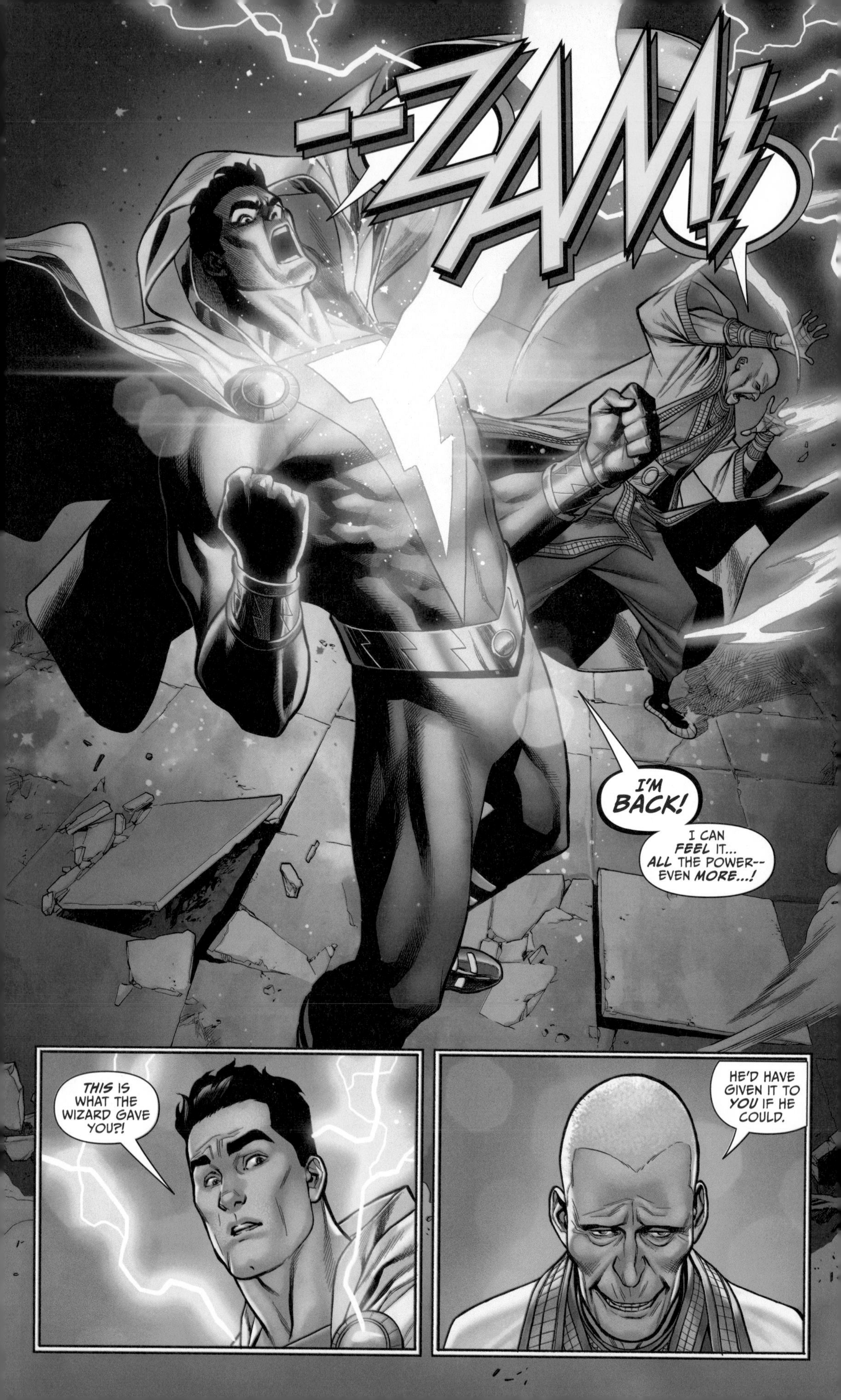
--ZAM!
I'M BACK!
I CAN FEEL IT... ALL THE POWER-- EVEN MORE...!
THIS IS WHAT THE WIZARD GAVE YOU?!
HE'D HAVE GIVEN IT TO YOU IF HE COULD.

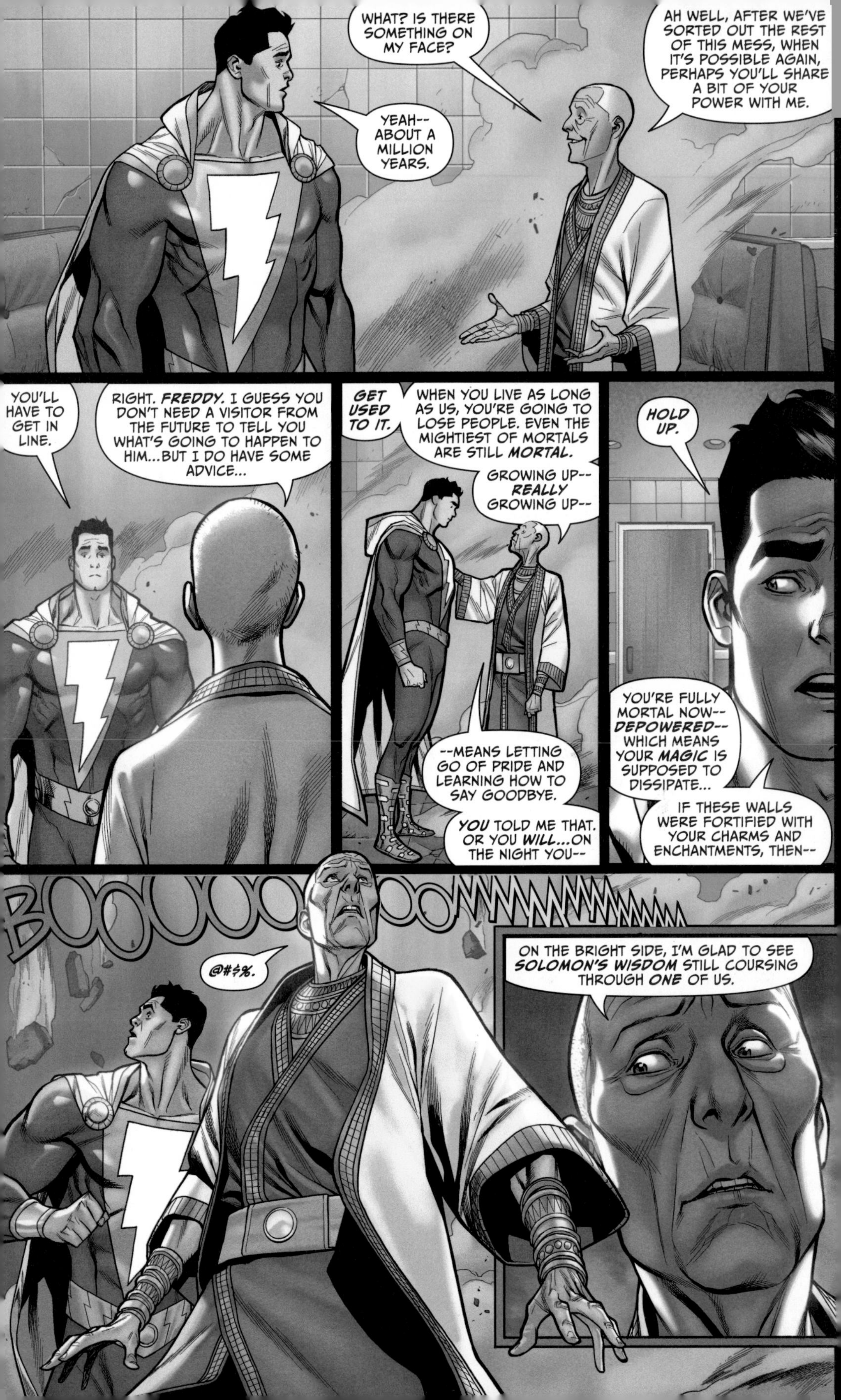
WHAT? IS THERE SOMETHING ON MY FACE?
YEAH-- ABOUT A MILLION YEARS.
AH WELL, AFTER WE'VE SORTED OUT THE REST OF THIS MESS, WHEN IT'S POSSIBLE AGAIN, PERHAPS YOU'LL SHARE A BIT OF YOUR POWER WITH ME.
YOU'LL HAVE TO GET IN LINE.
RIGHT. *FREDDY.* I GUESS YOU DON'T NEED A VISITOR FROM THE FUTURE TO TELL YOU WHAT'S GOING TO HAPPEN TO HIM...BUT I DO HAVE SOME ADVICE...
GET USED TO IT.
WHEN YOU LIVE AS LONG AS US, YOU'RE GOING TO LOSE PEOPLE. EVEN THE MIGHTIEST OF MORTALS ARE STILL *MORTAL.*
GROWING UP-- *REALLY* GROWING UP--
--MEANS LETTING GO OF PRIDE AND LEARNING HOW TO SAY GOODBYE.
YOU TOLD ME THAT. OR YOU *WILL...*ON THE NIGHT YOU--
HOLD UP.
YOU'RE FULLY MORTAL NOW-- *DEPOWERED--* WHICH MEANS YOUR *MAGIC* IS SUPPOSED TO DISSIPATE...
IF THESE WALLS WERE FORTIFIED WITH YOUR CHARMS AND ENCHANTMENTS, THEN--
BOOOOOOOOMMMMMMMM
@#$%.
ON THE BRIGHT SIDE, I'M GLAD TO SEE *SOLOMON'S WISDOM* STILL COURSING THROUGH *ONE* OF US.

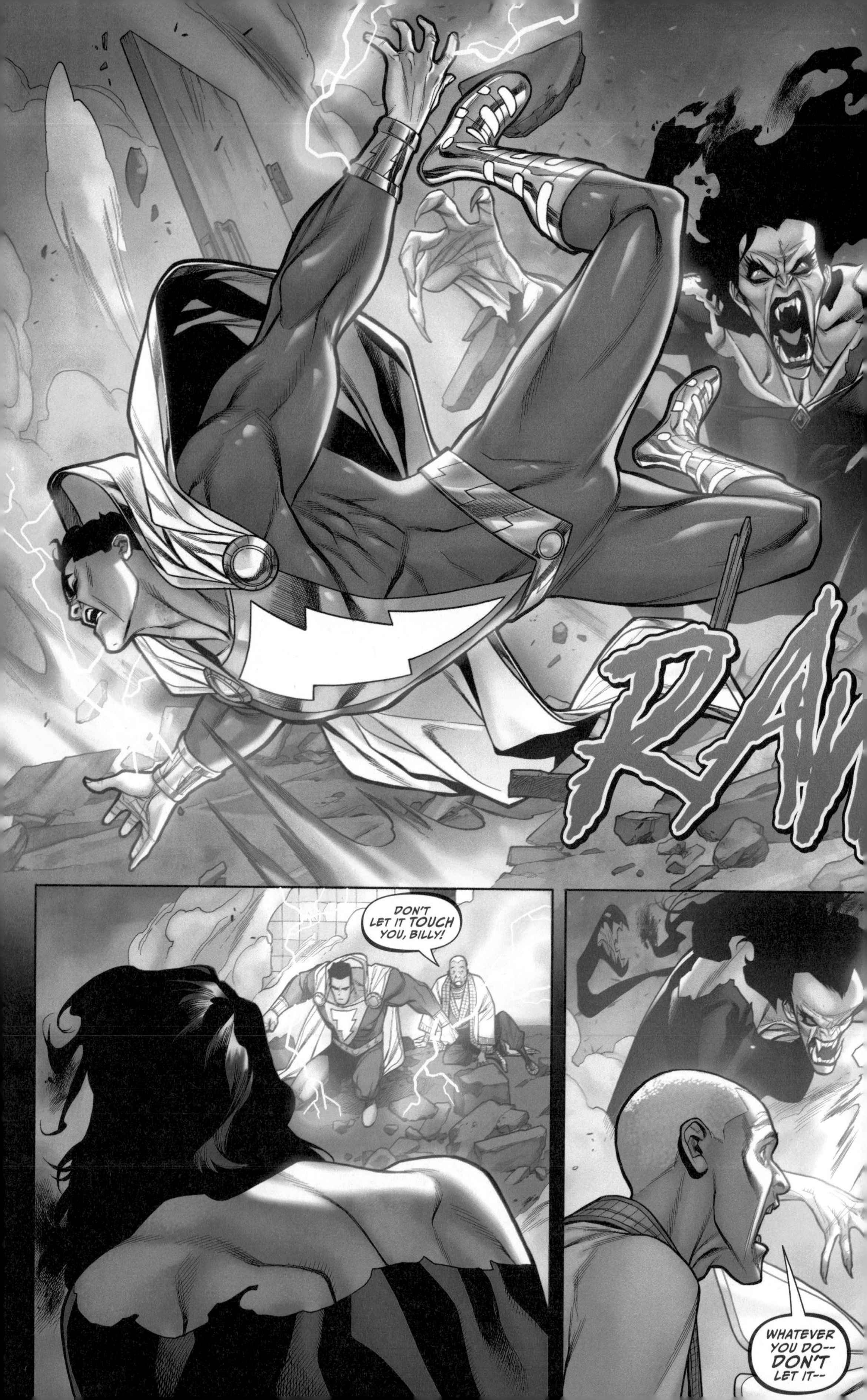

RAW
DON'T LET IT TOUCH YOU, BILLY!
WHATEVER YOU DO-- DON'T LET IT--

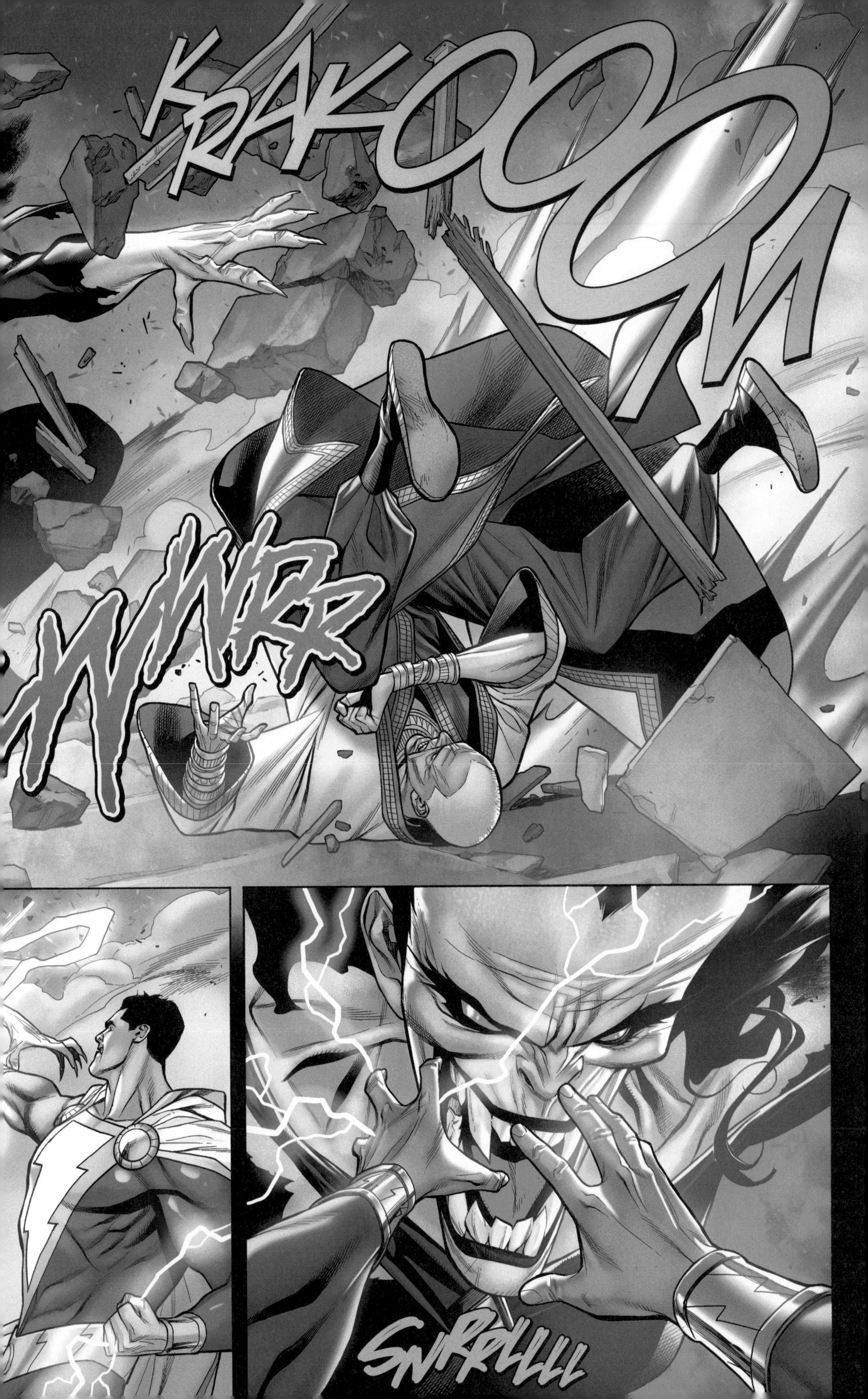
KRAKOOOOM
WNRR
SNRRLLLL

WH--WHAT...?

WHY DO I LOOK LIKE--

I... I GUESS... I TOOK A BIGGER HIT THAN I THOUGHT.

NAH, YOU WERE ALWAYS THIS BUSTED.

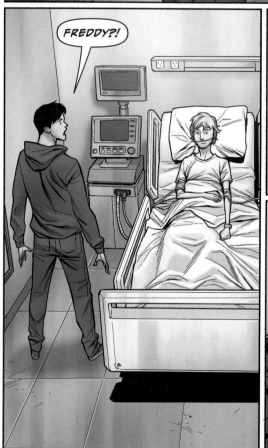

FREDDY?!

LOOK WHO FINALLY SHOWED UP.

RIGHT... YES...

I WAS GONNA COME EARLIER--ASK MARY--BUT I HAD TO TRY AND...

...DO...

...SOMETHING... FIRST?

WAIT, HOW DID I EVEN *GET* HERE?

≳Kaff≴ YOU'RE NOT TRYING... TO LEAVE...ALREADY-- ARE YA, BILL?

NO, THAT'S NOT... I MEAN, *JUST NOW* I WAS... SOMEWHERE...

I WAS...

WHY CAN'T I REMEMBER?!

WELL, YOU'RE HERE NOW.

YOU CAME TO HELP ME, RIGHT?

LIKE YOU ALWAYS DO.

ALL I'VE EVER WANTED IS TO HELP YOU FIGHT THIS, FREDDY.

MY...*OUR*... POWER MADE THAT POSSIBLE.

AND BELIEVE ME, I'VE *TRIED.* BUT I THINK EVEN THE *STAMINA OF ATLAS* HAS LIMITATIONS.

SOMETHING'S HAPPENED. THE POWER IS *UNSTABLE, UNPREDICTABLE.* IT TURNS ITSELF ON AND OFF WITHOUT WARNING. IT'S *WILD* AND *DANGEROUS.* AND THAT MEANS--

--I CAN'T SHARE IT ANYMORE.

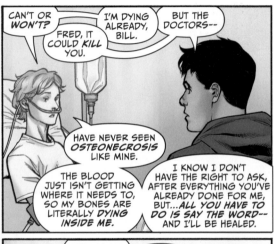

CAN'T OR *WON'T?*

FRED, IT COULD *KILL* YOU.

I'M DYING ALREADY, BILL.

BUT THE DOCTORS--

HAVE NEVER SEEN *OSTEONECROSIS* LIKE MINE.

THE BLOOD JUST ISN'T GETTING WHERE IT NEEDS TO, SO MY BONES ARE LITERALLY *DYING INSIDE* ME.

I KNOW I DON'T HAVE THE RIGHT TO ASK, AFTER EVERYTHING YOU'VE ALREADY DONE FOR ME, BUT...*ALL YOU HAVE TO DO IS SAY THE WORD--* AND I'LL BE HEALED.

JUST SAY IT, BILL.

JUST ONE TIME, RIGHT NOW-- FOR ME.

THE POWER TRAVELS IN A *LIGHTNING BOLT*--HOW COULD YOU EVEN WITHSTAND--

JUST @#$!$% SAY IT!

YOU-- YOU'RE NOT FREDDY.

YOU *TOUCHED ME* AND NOW SOMEHOW...

THIS IS ALL *FAKE!* WE'RE STILL IN THE ROCK, AREN'T WE?!

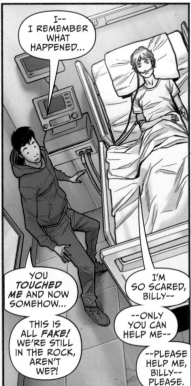

I-- I REMEMBER WHAT HAPPENED...

I'M SO SCARED, BILLY--

--ONLY YOU CAN HELP ME--

--PLEASE HELP ME, BILLY-- PLEASE.

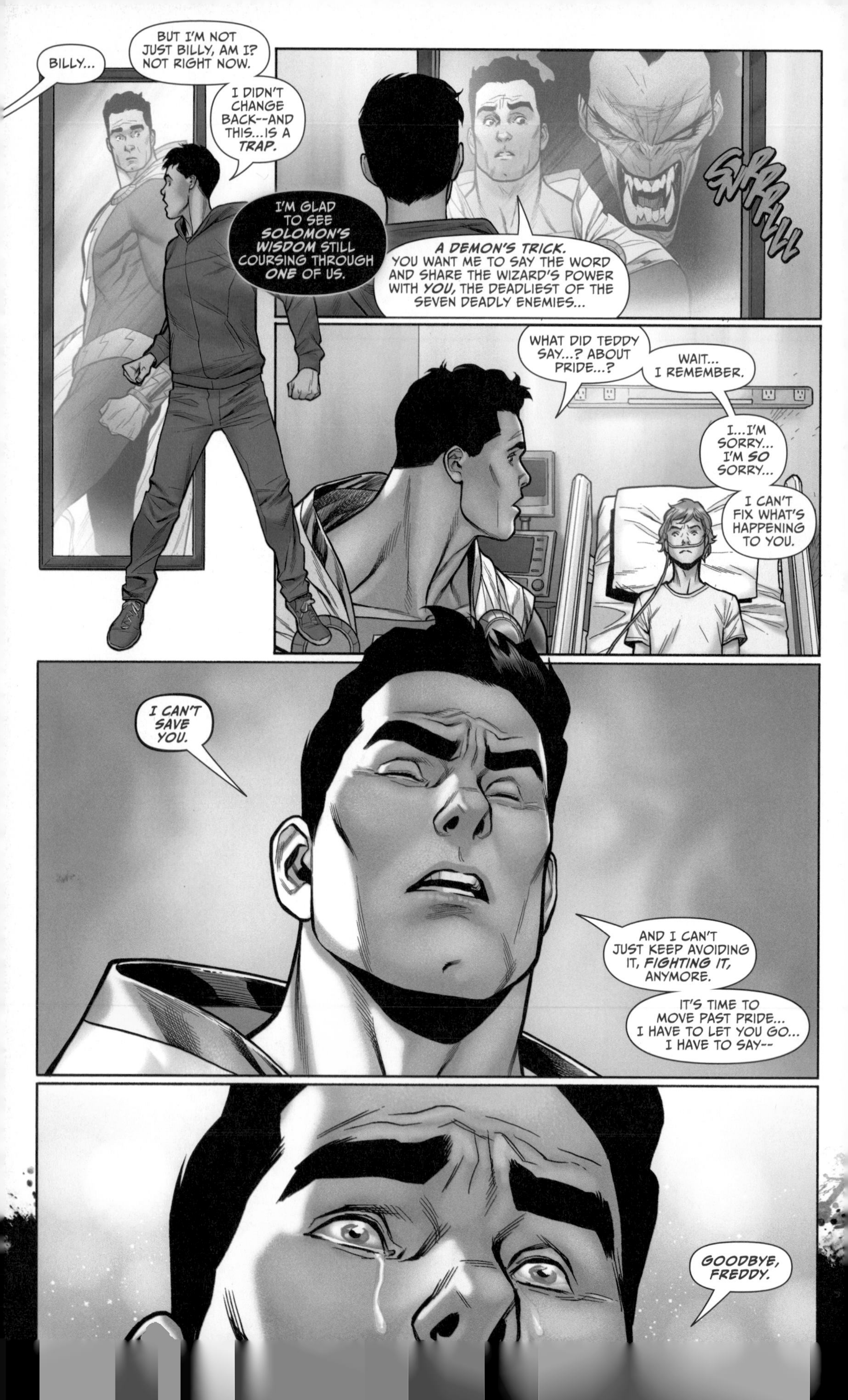
BILLY...
BUT I'M NOT JUST BILLY, AM I? NOT RIGHT NOW.
I DIDN'T CHANGE BACK--AND THIS...IS A *TRAP.*
I'M GLAD TO SEE *SOLOMON'S WISDOM* STILL COURSING THROUGH *ONE* OF US.
A DEMON'S TRICK. YOU WANT ME TO SAY THE WORD AND SHARE THE WIZARD'S POWER WITH *YOU,* THE DEADLIEST OF THE SEVEN DEADLY ENEMIES...
SNARRLLL
WHAT DID TEDDY SAY...? ABOUT PRIDE...?
WAIT... I REMEMBER.
I...I'M SORRY... I'M *SO* SORRY...
I CAN'T FIX WHAT'S HAPPENING TO YOU.
I CAN'T SAVE YOU.
AND I CAN'T JUST KEEP AVOIDING IT, *FIGHTING IT,* ANYMORE.
IT'S TIME TO MOVE PAST PRIDE... I HAVE TO LET YOU GO... I HAVE TO SAY--
GOODBYE, FREDDY.

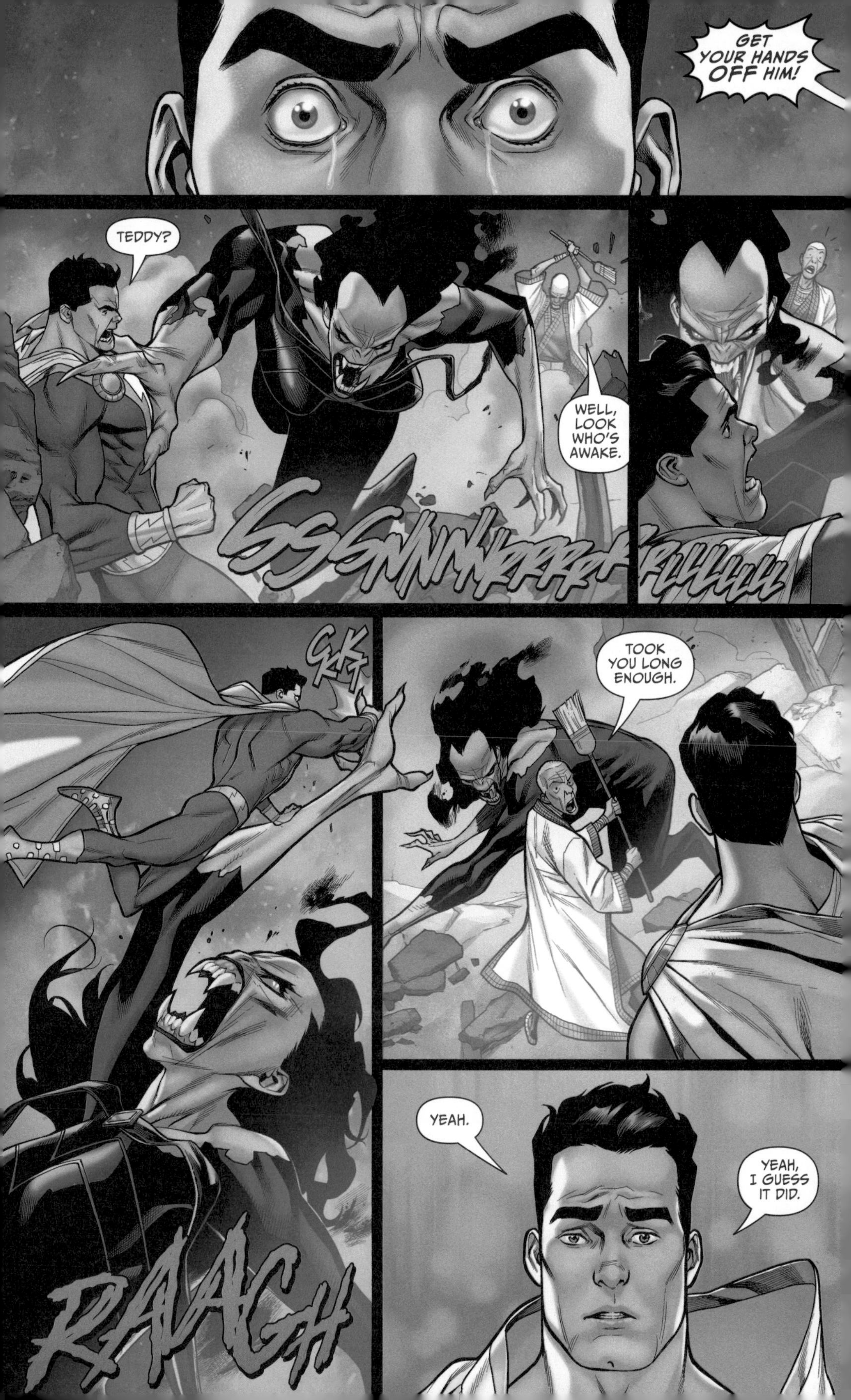
GET YOUR HANDS OFF HIM!
TEDDY?
WELL, LOOK WHO'S AWAKE.
SSSNNNKRRRKKLLLLLL
GKKT
RAAGH
TOOK YOU LONG ENOUGH.
YEAH.
YEAH, I GUESS IT DID.

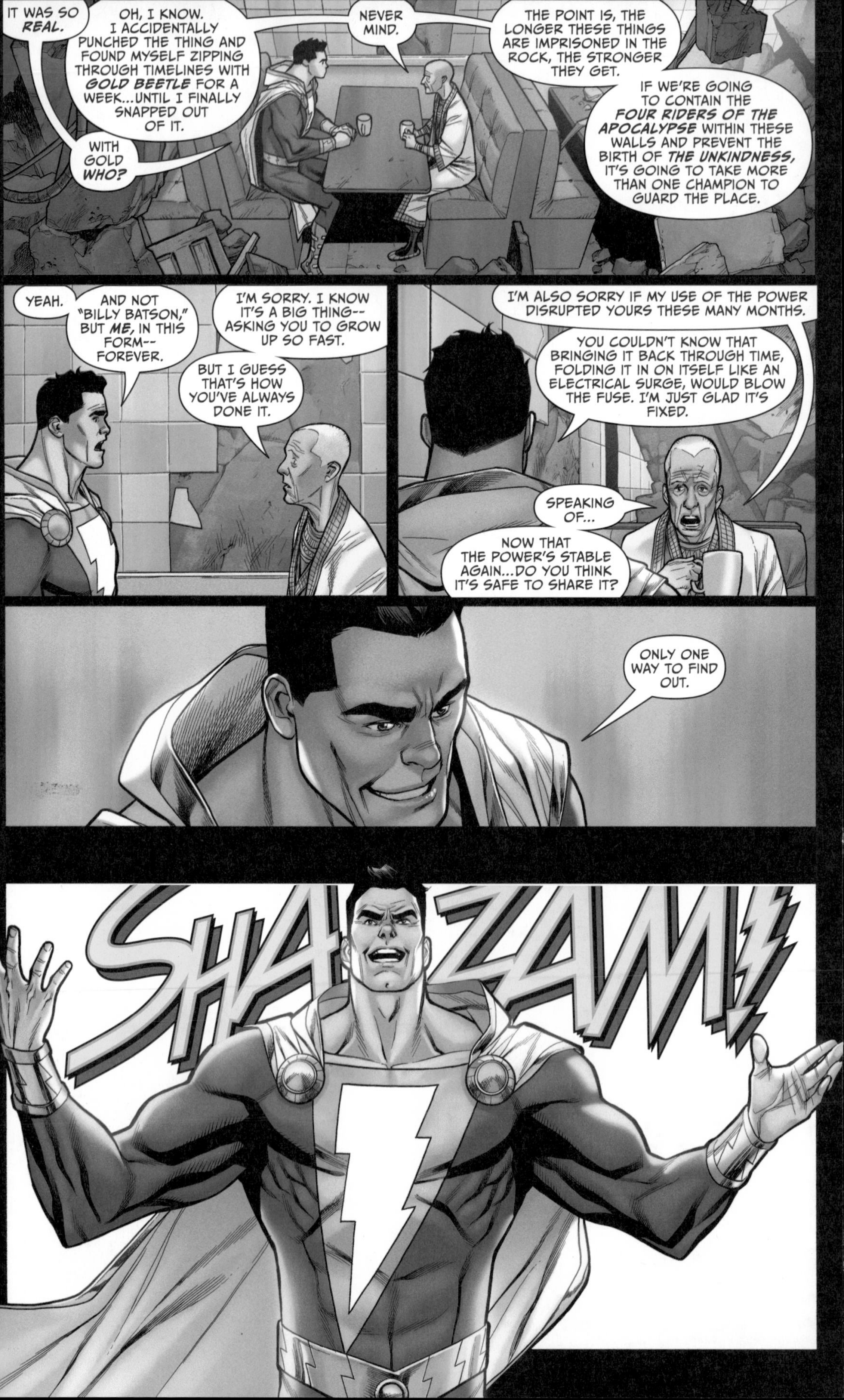
IT WAS SO REAL.
OH, I KNOW. I ACCIDENTALLY PUNCHED THE THING AND FOUND MYSELF ZIPPING THROUGH TIMELINES WITH GOLD BEETLE FOR A WEEK...UNTIL I FINALLY SNAPPED OUT OF IT.
WITH GOLD WHO?
NEVER MIND.
THE POINT IS, THE LONGER THESE THINGS ARE IMPRISONED IN THE ROCK, THE STRONGER THEY GET.
IF WE'RE GOING TO CONTAIN THE FOUR RIDERS OF THE APOCALYPSE WITHIN THESE WALLS AND PREVENT THE BIRTH OF THE UNKINDNESS, IT'S GOING TO TAKE MORE THAN ONE CHAMPION TO GUARD THE PLACE.
YEAH.
AND NOT "BILLY BATSON," BUT ME, IN THIS FORM--FOREVER.
I'M SORRY. I KNOW IT'S A BIG THING--ASKING YOU TO GROW UP SO FAST.
BUT I GUESS THAT'S HOW YOU'VE ALWAYS DONE IT.
I'M ALSO SORRY IF MY USE OF THE POWER DISRUPTED YOURS THESE MANY MONTHS.
YOU COULDN'T KNOW THAT BRINGING IT BACK THROUGH TIME, FOLDING IT IN ON ITSELF LIKE AN ELECTRICAL SURGE, WOULD BLOW THE FUSE. I'M JUST GLAD IT'S FIXED.
SPEAKING OF...
NOW THAT THE POWER'S STABLE AGAIN...DO YOU THINK IT'S SAFE TO SHARE IT?
ONLY ONE WAY TO FIND OUT.
SHAZAM!

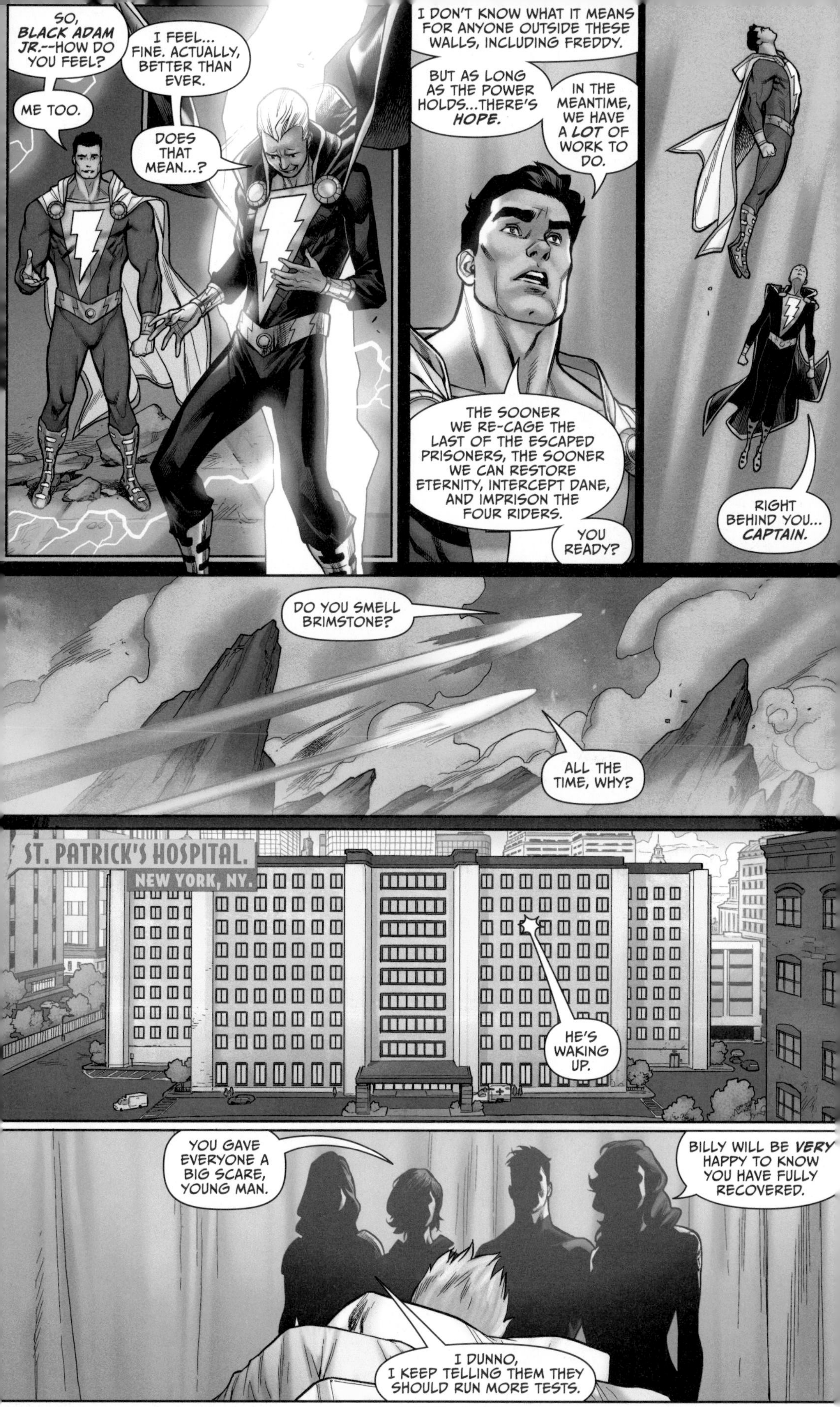

SO, BLACK ADAM JR.--HOW DO YOU FEEL?
I FEEL... FINE. ACTUALLY, BETTER THAN EVER.
ME TOO.
DOES THAT MEAN...?
I DON'T KNOW WHAT IT MEANS FOR ANYONE OUTSIDE THESE WALLS, INCLUDING FREDDY.
BUT AS LONG AS THE POWER HOLDS...THERE'S HOPE.
IN THE MEANTIME, WE HAVE A LOT OF WORK TO DO.
THE SOONER WE RE-CAGE THE LAST OF THE ESCAPED PRISONERS, THE SOONER WE CAN RESTORE ETERNITY, INTERCEPT DANE, AND IMPRISON THE FOUR RIDERS.
YOU READY?
RIGHT BEHIND YOU... CAPTAIN.
DO YOU SMELL BRIMSTONE?
ALL THE TIME, WHY?
ST. PATRICK'S HOSPITAL.
NEW YORK, NY.
HE'S WAKING UP.
YOU GAVE EVERYONE A BIG SCARE, YOUNG MAN.
BILLY WILL BE VERY HAPPY TO KNOW YOU HAVE FULLY RECOVERED.
I DUNNO, I KEEP TELLING THEM THEY SHOULD RUN MORE TESTS.

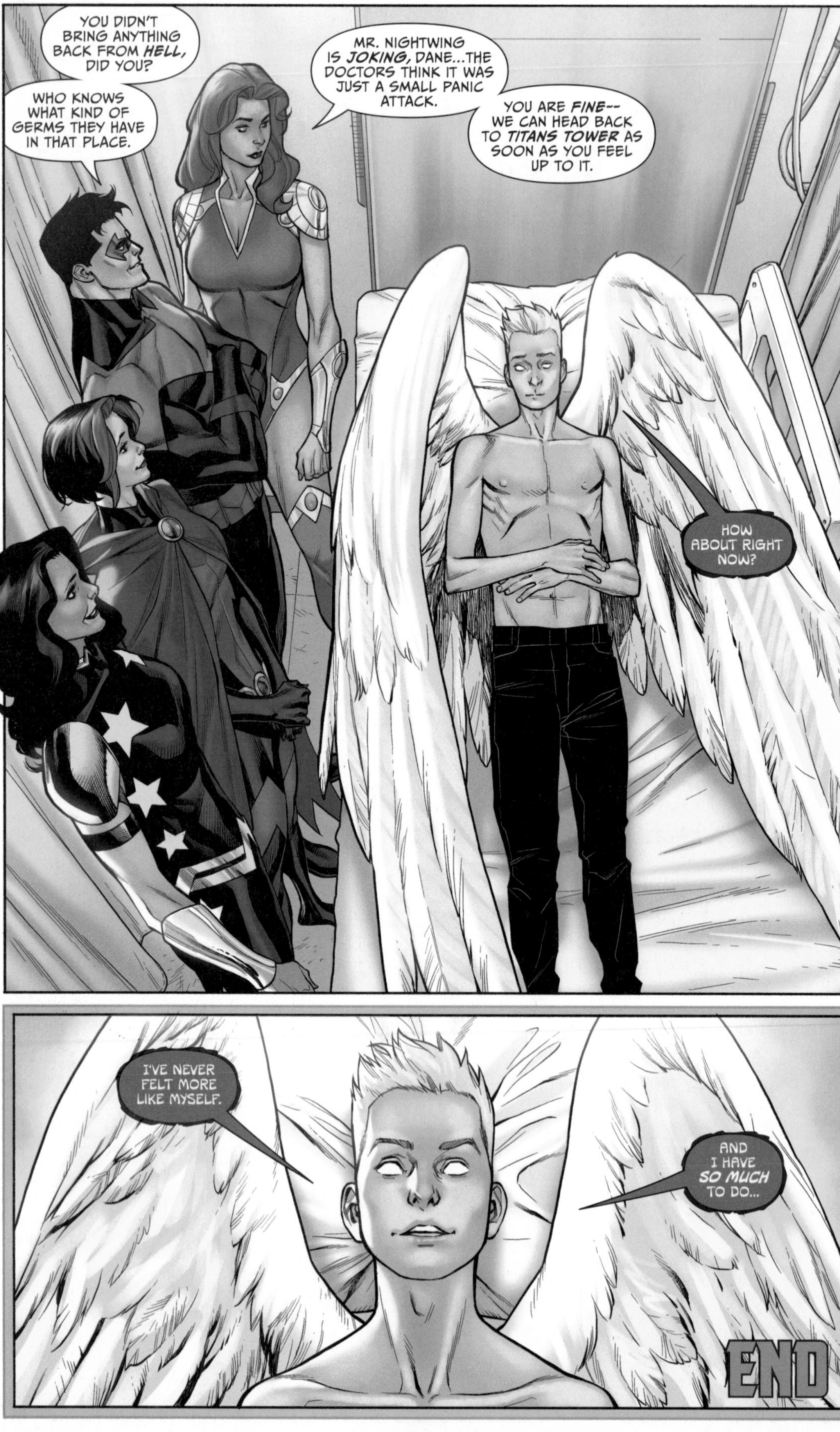

YOU DIDN'T BRING ANYTHING BACK FROM HELL, DID YOU?
WHO KNOWS WHAT KIND OF GERMS THEY HAVE IN THAT PLACE.
MR. NIGHTWING IS JOKING, DANE...THE DOCTORS THINK IT WAS JUST A SMALL PANIC ATTACK.
YOU ARE FINE-- WE CAN HEAD BACK TO TITANS TOWER AS SOON AS YOU FEEL UP TO IT.
HOW ABOUT RIGHT NOW?
I'VE NEVER FELT MORE LIKE MYSELF.
AND I HAVE SO MUCH TO DO...
END

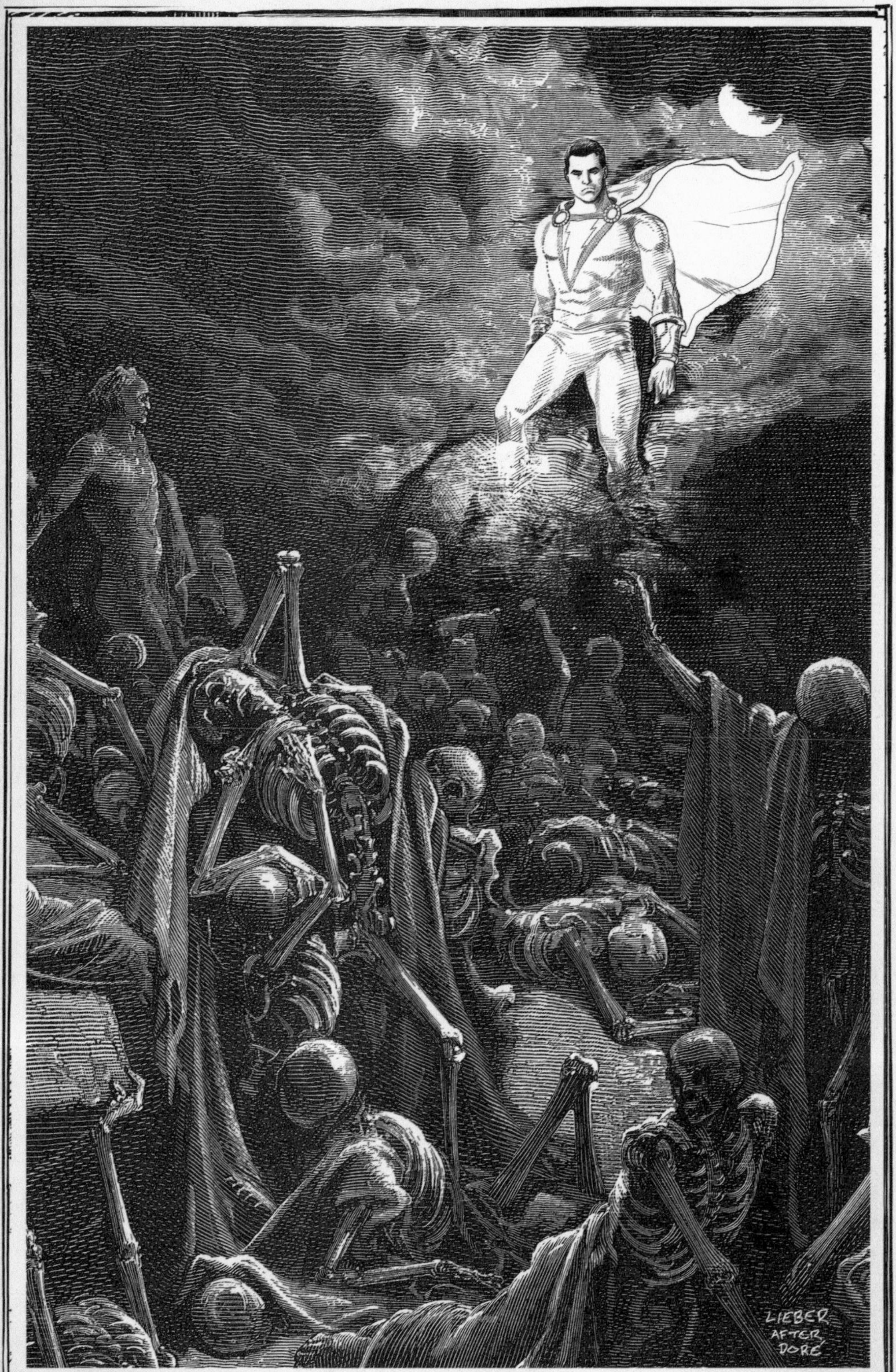
LIEBER
AFTER
DORÉ

Shazam! #1 Variant Cover Art by **STEVE LIEBER**

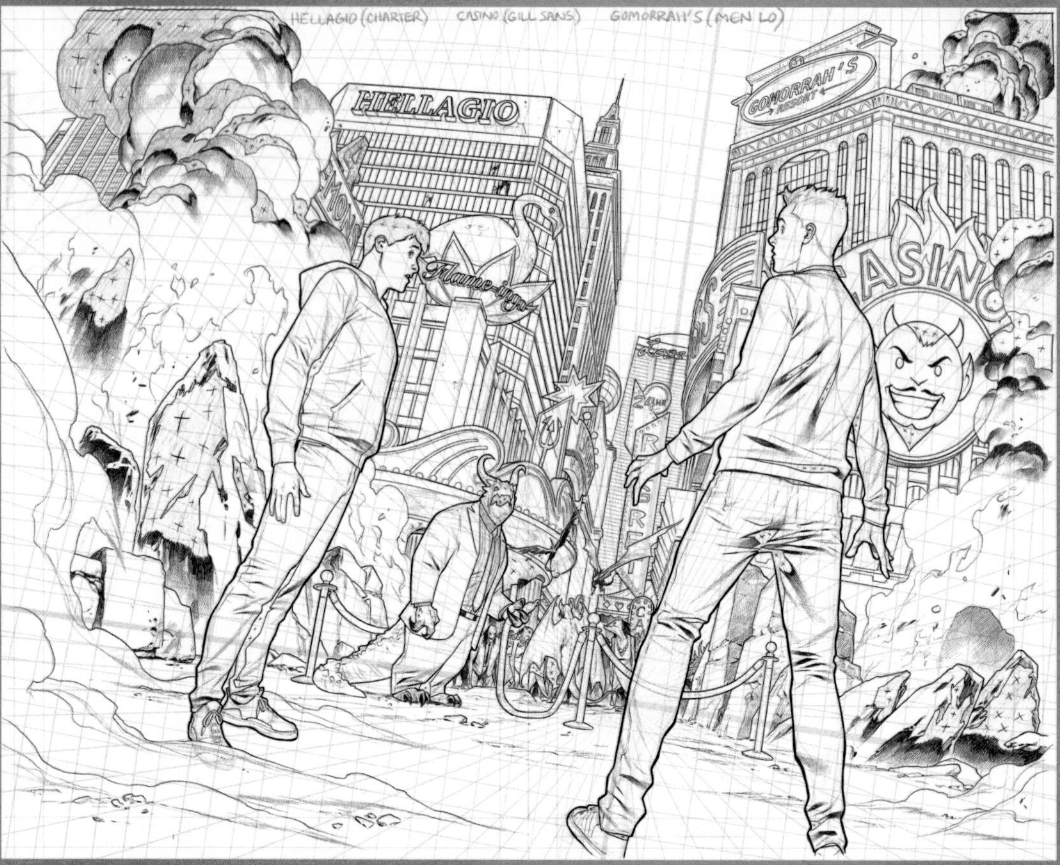
HELLAGIO (CHARTER) CASINO (GILL SANS) GOMORRAH'S (MEN LO)
HELLAGIO
GOMORRAH'S
RESORT
Flame-ingo
CASINO
24HR

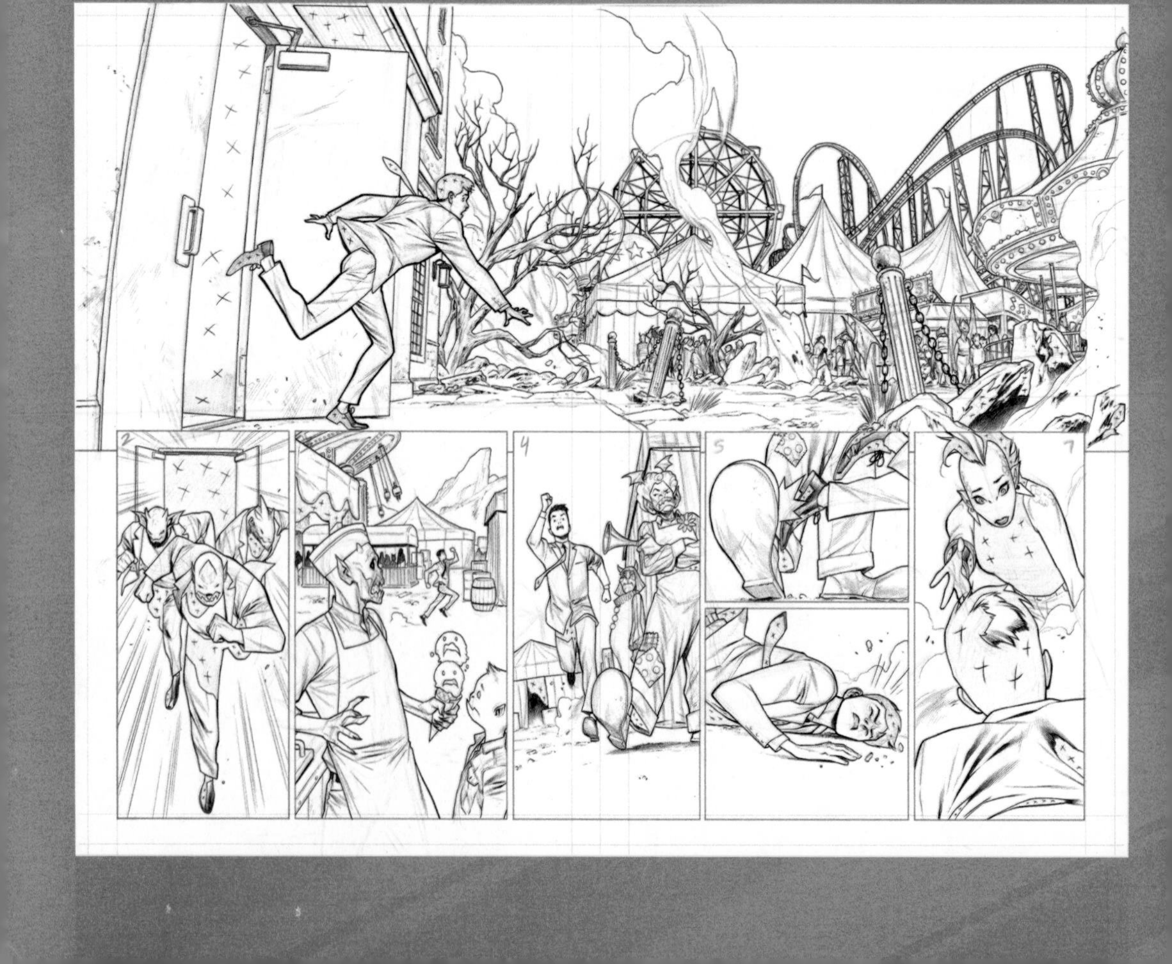

Art and Designs by
CLAYTON HENRY

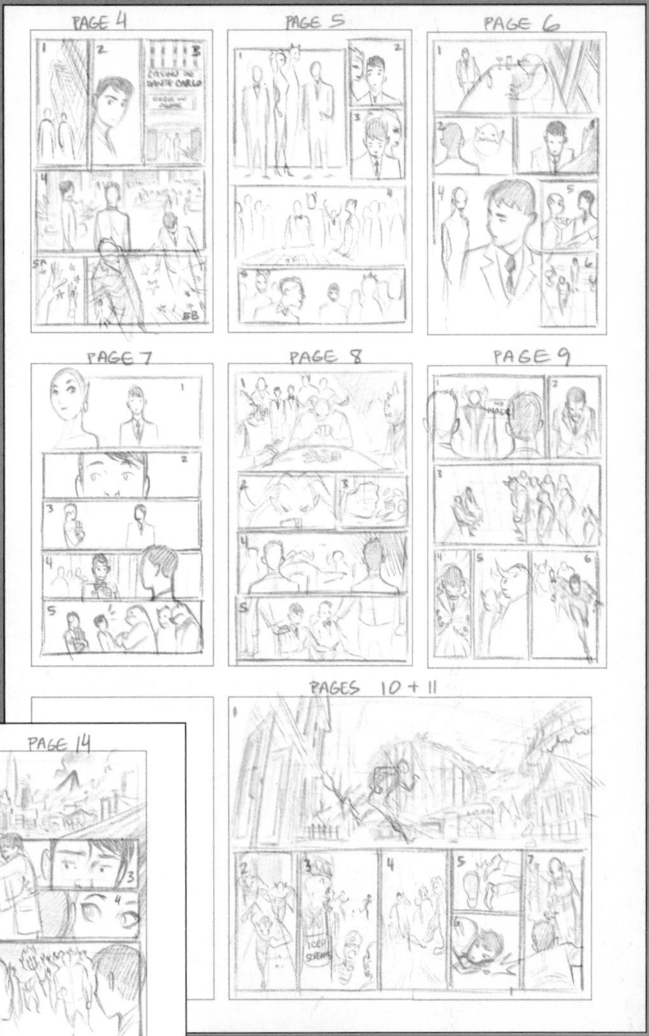
PAGE 4
PAGE 5
PAGE 6
PAGE 7
PAGE 8
PAGE 9
PAGES 10 + 11

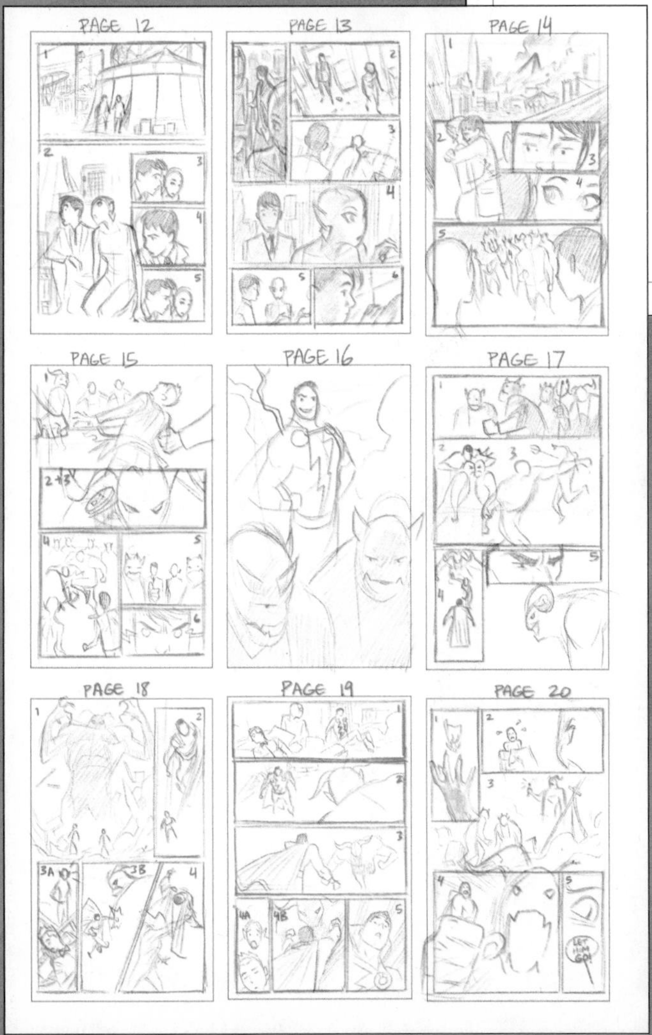
PAGE 12
PAGE 13
PAGE 14
PAGE 15
PAGE 16
PAGE 17
PAGE 18
PAGE 19
PAGE 20

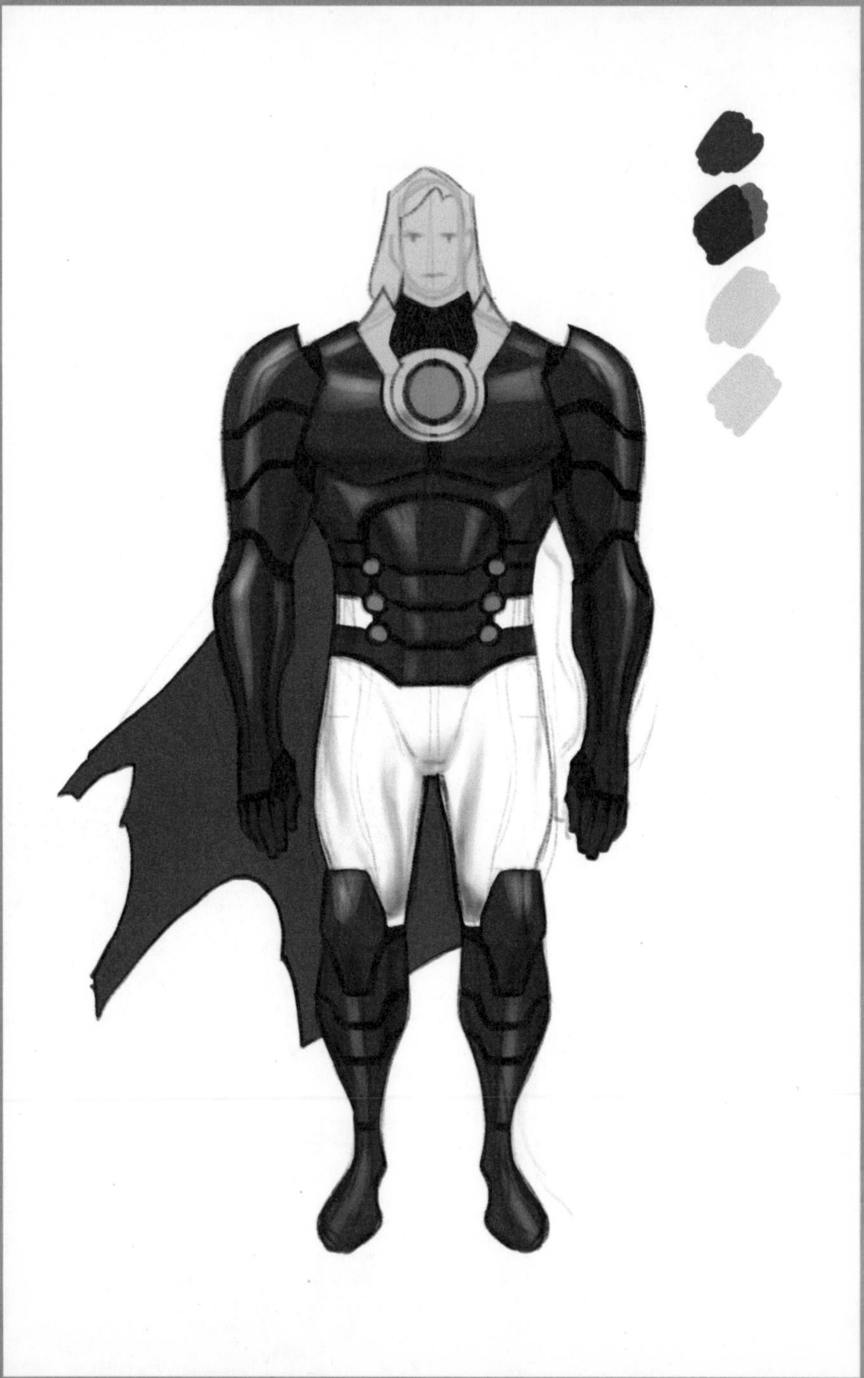